NATO AND THE EUROPEAN UNION

The great accessions and unions of kingdoms do likewise stir up wars; for when a state grows to an overpower, it is like a great flood, that will be sure to overflow.

Francis Bacon, *Essays*

NATO and the European Union
New World, New Europe, New Threats

Edited by

HALL GARDNER
The American University of Paris, France

LONDON AND NEW YORK

First published 2004 by Ashgate Publishing

Published 2017 by Routledge
2 Park Square, Milton Park, Abingdon, Oxfordshire OX14 4RN
711 Third Avenue, New York, NY 10017, USA

First issued in paperback 2017

Routledge is an imprint of the Taylor & Francis Group, an informa business

Copyright © Hall Gardner 2004

Hall Gardner has asserted his right under the Copyright, Designs and Patents Act, 1988, to be identified as the editor of this work.

All rights reserved. No part of this book may be reprinted or reproduced or utilised in any form or by any electronic, mechanical, or other means, now known or hereafter invented, including photocopying and recording, or in any information storage or retrieval system, without permission in writing from the publishers.

Notice:
Product or corporate names may be trademarks or registered trademarks, and are used only for identification and explanation without intent to infringe.

British Library Cataloguing in Publication Data
NATO and the European Union : new world, new Europe, new
　　threats
　　1.North Atlantic Treaty Organization 2.European Union 3. War
　　on Terrorism, 2001- 4.Security, International 5. Terrorism
　　6.United States - Foreign relations - 1989- 7. European
　　Union countries - Foreign relations 8. Russia (Federation) -
　　Foreign relations
　　I. Gardner, Hall
　　327.7'30090511

Library of Congress Cataloging-in-Publication Data
NATO and the European Union : new world, new Europe, new threats / edited by Hall Gardner.
　　p. cm.
　　Includes bibliographical references and index.
　　ISBN 0-7546-3801-4
　　1. European Union countries--Foreign relations. 2. National security--European Union countries. 3. European Union. 4. North Atlantic Treaty Organization. 5. War on Terrorism, 2001 - I. Gardner, Hall.

JZ1570.A9N38 2004
355'.031'091821--dc22

2004046135

ISBN 13: 978-1-138-25881-5 (pbk)
ISBN 13: 978-0-7546-3801-8 (hbk)

Contents

List of Contributors — vii
Preface — x

Introduction: Alliances, "War on Terrorism" and Weapons of Mass Destruction — 1
Hall Gardner

PART I: THE STRATEGIC IMPACT OF SEPTEMBER 11

Chapter 1: Asymmetrical Conflict: A Critical Assessment — 31
Marwan Bishara

Chapter 2: From "Balance" to "Imbalance" of Terror — 49
Hall Gardner

PART II: THE FUTURE OF NATO

Chapter 3: Thinking About and Beyond NATO — 79
Simon Serfaty

Chapter 4: NATO's 2002 Enlargement: US-Allied Views on European Security — 91
Marco Rimanelli

Chapter 5: Looking Down the Road: NATO-EU Relations in the Age of Intelligence and the "Age of Access" — 107
Alexis Debat

Chapter 6: The EU and NATO Enlargement: A Russian View — 115
Nadia Alexandrova Arbatova

Chapter 7: A MAP for Russia — 122
Ira Straus

PART III: NATO, THE EU AND THE "WAR ON TERRORISM"

Chapter 8: Toward New Euro-Atlantic Euro-Mediterranean
Security Communities 149
Hall Gardner

Chapter 9: Dealing with Terrorism: The EU and NATO 171
Karsten D. Voigt

Chapter 10: German Perceptions on the "War Against Terrorism"
in a Historical Perspective 181
Norbert Baas

Chapter 11: Six Dimensions of the Growing Transatlantic Divide:
Are the US and Europe Definitively Driving Themselves Apart? 198
Marcel Van Herpen

PART IV: "WAR ON TERRORISM": REGIONAL AND GLOBAL RAMIFICATIONS

Chapter 12: Central Asia and the West After September 11 219
Robert M. Cutler

Chapter 13: Russia and the US in the New Balance of Power in
Central Asia 232
Anton Koslov

Chapter 14: Kashmir and a New Cold War 242
Sten Widmalm

Chapter 15: Iran and the New Threats in the Persian Gulf and
Middle East Since 9/11 252
Steven Ekovich

Chapter 16: Preclusive War with Iraq: Regional and Global
Ramifications 278
Hall Gardner

Index *317*

List of Contributors

Nadia Alexandrova Arbatova is Head of the Department on European Political Studies at the Institute for World Political Economy and International Relations (IMEMO), Russian Academy of Sciences and Director of the Center on International Relations, Institute of Europe, Russian Academy of Science.

Norbert Baas is Ambassador, Special Envoy of the German Foreign Office for Russia, Central Asia and the Caucasus.

Marwan Bishara is a writer and editorialist, a researcher at the École des Hautes Études en Sciences Sociales (EHESS), Paris, a lecturer at The American University of Paris, and author of *Palestine/Israel: Peace or Apartheid Prospects for Resolving the Conflict* (London: Zed Books, 2001).

Robert M. Cutler is Research Fellow, Institute of European and Russian Studies, Carleton University, Canada. Educated at MIT and the University of Michigan, he has specialized in interdisciplinary international affairs of Europe and Eurasia, publishing and consulting widely for over twenty years.

Alexis Debat, former advisor to the French Minister of Defense on Transatlantic Affairs, is a visiting professor at Middlebury College, a Senior Consultant to ABC News in New York, and Washington Bureau Chief of *Politique Internationale*. Dr. Debat is at work on the largest manuscript ever written on the history of the Central Intelligence Agency, to be published next year in Europe and the United States.

Steven Ekovich earned his Ph.D. at the University of California, Irvine. He currently teaches at The American University of Paris and the Institut d'Études Politiques de Paris. He previously taught at several other French *grandes écoles* and has been a tutor at the French foreign ministry. He was the first American to graduate from the French war college (Institut des Hautes Études de Défense Nationale).

Hall Gardner is Professor and Chair, Department of International Affairs, The American University of Paris, France. His publications include *Dangerous Crossroads: Europe, Russia and the Future of NATO* (Westport, CT: Praeger, 1997); *Surviving the Millennium: American Global Strategy, the Collapse of the Soviet Empire, and the Question of Peace* (Westport, CT: Praeger, 1994). He is editor of, and contributor to, *Central and Southeastern Europe in Transition: Perspectives on Success and Failure* (Westport, CT: Praeger, 2000) and co-editor of, and contributor to, *The New Transatlantic Agenda: Facing the Challenges of Global Governance* (Aldershot: Ashgate, September 2001). His publication, "Aligning for the Future" appeared in the *Harvard International Review* (Winter, 2003).

Anton Koslov is an Assistant Professor in the International Affairs Department at the American University of Paris. He is a consultant to the OECD in Paris, and Director of the Interdisciplinary Center for the Study of Corruption.

Marco Rimanelli is Professor of U.S.-European Affairs & International Security at Saint Leo University-Florida. He was twice Scholar-in-Residence at the U.S. State Department and other agencies on NATO Enlargement, Iraq (1999-2001) and U.S.-Soviet/Russian nuclear arms control (1991-1992).

Simon Serfaty is the director of the Europe Program at the Center for Strategic and International Studies (CSIS) in Washington, DC, and Eminent Scholar and professor of U.S. foreign policy with the Graduate Programs in International Studies at Old Dominion University in Norfolk, Virginia. Prior to these positions, Dr. Serfaty was affiliated with the Johns Hopkins University for more than twenty years as professor, director of its Center on European Studies in Bologna, Italy, as well as executive director of the Johns Hopkins Foreign Policy Institute. Dr. Serfaty is the author, coauthor, and editor of numerous publications. His most recent books include *The European Finality Debate and its National Dimensions* (editor, 2003), *La France vue par les États-Unis: réflexions sur la francophobie à Washington* (2002), *Memories of Europe's Future: Farewell to Yesteryear* (1999), and *Stay the Course: European Unity and Atlantic Solidarity* (1997).

List of Contributors

Ira Straus is U.S. Coordinator of the Committee on Eastern Europe and Russia in NATO, an independent international association formed in 1992 as the first public organization in the West to promote discussion on NATO expansion and dedicated to exploration of the full range of options on NATO's enlargement and transformation. He has taught courses on international relations and on NATO-EU issues in Western universities and as Fulbright professor at the Moscow State Institute of International Relations.

Marcel Van Herpen is director of the Cicero Foundation, a pro-EU think tank (www.cicerofoundation.org).

Karsten D. Voigt is Coordinator for German-American Cooperation at the Foreign Office of the Federal Republic of Germany, Berlin.

Sten Widmalm is the author of *Kashmir in Comparative Perspective— Democracy and Violent Separatism in India* (Curzon/Routledge, 2002). He is currently working as Assistant Professor, and as the Director of the Master's Programme in Development Studies at the Department of Government of Uppsala University.

Preface

Numerous books and articles written prior to the 11 September 2001 attacks on the World Trade Center and Pentagon often raised the question as to why the threat of terrorism appeared to obtain so much public and governmental attention as compared to other, seemingly more pressing, problems and risks to human life. As the death toll due to automobile accidents, urban murders, cancer, heart disease, AIDS and other diseases, among other phenomena, have appeared to be statistically more significant than acts of anti-state "terrorism," and as both the number of attacks and consequent deaths appeared to be diminishing in magnitude prior to 11 September 2001, it was argued that governmental resources should be better applied elsewhere—in an era of increasingly limited resources.[1]

One could furthermore make the case that officially supported "state terrorism" during the 20th century (whether it be acts of state terrorism by the Communist party of the Soviet Union, the National Socialists of Nazi Germany or the Khmer Rouge of Cambodia, among many other examples) has, in both historical and contemporary perspectives, instigated far greater crimes affecting the rights and lives of millions, than have acts of anti-state terrorism, sponsored by either individuals or partisan groups. The burning of the Reichstag, for example, which was really more of an act of sabotage than of terrorism, was used by Adolph Hitler as a pretext to galvanize a far more dangerous National Socialist political movement, and engage in other acts of "state terrorism." As was the case for the Soviet Union or Nazi Germany, totalitarian states actually thrive on indiscriminate terror as their very essence.[2]

Here, it should be pointed out that the contemporary post-1945 use of the term "terrorism" has, in effect, inverted its original meaning. The modern usage of the word "terrorist" often refers to *guerrilleros*—a term that originated from the Spanish bands who resisted Napoleon's conquest of Spain[3]—or groups who violently oppose a particular state or states, and which may or may not possess backing from legitimate authorities. (Here, contemporary "terrorist" organizations may or may not possess squads of armed combatants.) The roots of the term "terrorism," however, actually originates from the use of terror by those who seized state power in France and largely signifies a "system" or "regime of terror," or those who supported the "reign of terror" from March 1793 to July 1794.[4] In other words, the term that first referred specifically to "terrorism" by state authorities, or "state-supported terrorism," has evolved to signify the use of largely indiscriminate violence against the state or civilian population for political purposes, to simplify the definition.

It is consequently this historical inversion of the meaning of the word "terrorism" and of the role of the "terrorist" that is at the very root of the dilemma as to how to best deal with the phenomenon. This double-faceted nature of "terrorism" and "state-terrorism" must be thoroughly investigated if it is at all possible to truly eradicate all forms of "terrorism," as well as weapons of terror, such as weapons of mass destruction (WMD), as political-military instruments of violence. The danger raised here is then is any expansion of the "war on terrorism" risks falling into the trap set by the terrorists themselves, that is, to take violent and ill-considered actions that appear to prove the veracity of their propaganda. It could mean acting in ways that mimic the indiscriminate acts of the terrorists themselves, and risk venturing into conflicts and wars that were not initially foreseen or expected particularly if policies and actions are not agreed to through a concerted and truly "multilateral" agreement among the major powers and regional actors most concerned.

The response to anti-state terrorism could possibly be a declaration of war that violates traditional post-Westphalia conceptions of territorial state sovereignty—that "terrorizes" the elites in command but also the civilian population as well. States may accordingly use extreme means to contain insurgencies, such as assassination, torture, "death squads" and summary execution, indiscriminate bombings, "ethnic cleansing," rape *en masse*, genocide, detention camps, or other forms of violence. Once the cycle of terror and counter-terror installs itself, it may prove difficult to pull back, and set limits on the potential over-reactions of the state in regard to freedom of press, speech, rights of individuals and minority groups. The domestic response of states to any act of violence by armed partisan groups may thus be that of "terrorizing the terrorists." State terror thus seeks to vanquish anti-state terror, but with no clear end in sight.

In this context, "terrorism" is really one tactic or form of "strategic leveraging"[5] out of a whole range of possible political-military options utilized by both state and partisan non-state or anti-state actors intended to achieve domestic and/or international ends, depending upon their capabilities and intentions. In many ways, terrorism is just one tool out of many possible options that is often used for *political-psychological* effects by both anti-state or pro-state groups or actors who are fighting for a self-propagated cause, and who often seek recognition for that cause, assuming they do not desire to keep their involvement secret. Terror comes out of a barrel of a gun no matter who is aiming it, and often seeks to impose a system of government *from above* (state terrorism) or *from outside* (anti-state terrorism).

Following the horrors of September 11 and the war with Iraq, what should be the appropriate policy options for the United States, European Union, Russia and other states to follow in regard to the continuing war/fight against "terrorism"? Specifically, can the governments of the NATO and EU countries, which have largely appeared to be incapable of stamping out crime, drug smuggling, child labor, prostitution, or illegal immigration, ultimately succeed in the struggle against "terrorism" and against the other significant "new" threats, including Weapons of Mass Destruction developed by what should preferably be called "parvenu," rather than "rogue," states?

Are the American and European democracies truly capable of taking effective concerted measures against *potential* as well as *actual*, threats? What is the best way to proceed? Are military means the only path? What of diplomatic compromise, trade, aid, international investments as means to separate "terrorists" from their supporters? What kind of reforms will be needed to get countries and international regimes to interact in the most effective manner possible? Should all actions (military or diplomatic) taken be multilateral, involving the European Union and Russia and/or China—in truly concerted action with the United States? Or should they be unilateral, with the United States leading, and then coercing *or* co-opting states to join in a "coalition of the willing"? Or should any actions taken be more truly international, involving firm UN mandates? Or will the reality turn out to be far more anarchical—states to pick and choose their responses depending upon national interests and circumstances, in other words, *à la carte*?

The "new threats" must be understood and assessed in the broadest possible range of their strategic, military, political, economic, social and ideological and media contexts so as determine how to best respond. Yet official US policy is now engaged in the "war on terrorism"; official European Union policy supports the "fight against terrorism." The difference between "war" and "fight" reveals a significant difference in the US and EU approaches to dealing with the crisis, and illustrates the difficulty in achieving a concerted policy. The essential basis of the US-EU dispute lies in the fact that the phrase "war on terrorism" appears to imply that "terrorism" represents a form of political entity that can somehow be eliminated; yet acts of "terrorism" can only be eliminated if both states and political groups miraculously renounce all forms of indiscriminate violence as viable political-military options—an unlikely possibility.

Failure to agree on common terms indicates a deeper inability to develop a common US-EU policy, a fact that became even more evident in regard to the "war with Iraq." What were the key threats posed by the Iraqi regime? Was it development of Weapons of Mass Destruction? Was it Iraqi support for international terrorism? Was it the repression of the Iraqi people i.e. state terrorism? The fact that the US and EU (France and Germany) could not meet eye to eye in resolving this crisis together may make it more difficult to reach common positions in regard to similar threats posed by other states and anti-state actors—unless *both* sides can learn from their errors in regard to Iraq.

NATO and the European Union: New World, New Europe, New Threats accordingly examines the global political-military ramifications of September 11 and the Iraq crisis as seen through the eyes of the major powers; it focuses on US and NATO policy as it interacts with the European Union and with Russia, and looks toward a way to reconcile US, EU policies in the aftermath of the Iraqi crisis.

The contributors to the book represent a mix of policy makers, policy analysts, and academics; the intent is to thus to create dialogue between different groups that are not always brought together into the same house to speak. The book was compiled in the aftermath of September 11, and in the midst of the war in Afghanistan (when the hope to achieve a new global concert was high) but also in anticipation of a direct military intervention in Iraq. It was thus written at the time when NATO and European consensus building, as well as a common foreign policy for the EU, increasingly appeared to be unraveling in response to US threats to utilize force against Iraq with or without UN approval; it was then completed just after the second Persian Gulf war in 2003.

Part I, *The Strategic Impact of September 11*, the Introduction and Chapters 1 and 2, critically analyze the strategic implications of the "new" threats posed by the strikes on the World Trade Center and Pentagon and the total failure of Cold War conceptions of deterrence. In the Introduction, **Hall Gardner** analyzes the post-September 11 syndrome and analyses the political and strategic issues raised by both "anti-state terrorism" and "state-supported terrorism." In the opening chapter, **Marwan Bishara** makes the provocative argument that the "war-on-terrorism" is a war without borders, with dangerous repercussions for the legitimacy of the post-1945 nation-state system as a whole, in which the very forces of "globalization" are in the process of undermining the state sovereignty. Bishara's provocative thesis questions the very possibility of global governorship by states of the "north" in that *asymmetrical conflict* seeks to exploit all forms of military, political, social and psychological weaknesses of advanced northern societies. His chapter thus serves as an appropriate warning as to the very ability of NATO and the EU to "manage" the post-September 11 crisis. **Hall Gardner** argues that the Cold War "balance of terror" has degenerated into a post-Cold War "imbalance." In critiquing the views of Albert Wohlstetter, a forerunner of neo-conservatism, Gardner argues that the Cold War strategy of *deterrence* should be replaced by a new strategy of *multilateral dissuasion*, involving engaged irenic diplomacy and multilateral security and defense commitments—as the most appropriate means to deal with the "new threats."

Part II, *The Future of NATO* Chapters 3–7, look at the changing structure and politics of NATO as the primary defense and security organization intended to provide strategic deterrence. These chapters delineate the key issues and problems that have arisen from the largely uncoordinated NATO and EU "double enlargement" and from the new NATO-EU-Russian relationship. **Simon Serfaty** argues that although the rumors of an impending death of the transatlantic partnership are hardly new, the *déjà entendu* of past discord should not invite complacency. If they are to survive as relevant organizations, both NATO and the EU must radically reform to meet the new challenges. **Marco Rimanelli** then explicates in great detail the NATO-European policy disputes inherent in the decision to enlarge NATO in successive waves. He warns, from an American perspective, that all Allies must quickly "muscle up" their forces along side those of the United States, while the latter must truly balance both its national interests as well as transatlantic security. **Alexis Debat** examines the fundamental changes taking place between American and European military capabilities and intelligence in the "age of access" and discusses their effects upon NATO and the EU. Against the pessimists, he argues that the EU can develop complementary military and technological capabilities to NATO; criticisms of Europe's "weak" defense budgets do not exactly address the real questions that underwrite the future of European security and its relationship to NATO in confrontation with the new threats. **Nadia Alexandrova Arbatova** argues that NATO and EU enlargement are not complementary processes as generally argued in the west, for example, but represent two very different, if not contradictory, processes from the Russian perspective; she argues for closer Russian-EU links, as opposed to closer NATO-Russian ties. **Ira Straus** then examines what can be expected of the new NATO-Russian relationship. While downplaying the role of the EU, he argues against the views that Russia cannot be included in NATO without destroying the latter. Basing his views on American efforts to transform former opponents into Allies through a progressive geo-historical evolution, Straus then outlines ways to implement a policy of greater US-Russian geostrategic engagement as well as through a new Membership Action Plan (MAP) for Russian to enter NATO.

Part III, *NATO, the EU, and the "War on Terrorism"* Chapters 8–11 scrutinize the applied aspects of the "war on terrorism" and the nature of the "new threats" as seen through American and European eyes. **Hall Gardner** argues that a long term and effective war on "terrorism" following the September 11 "attacks" on the World Trade Center and the Pentagon will require a much closer and long term U.S.-NATO-EU relationship with Russia than has previously been considered; otherwise the new-found entente with Russia, if not NATO itself, could well disintegrate. Recognizing that the forces of globalization may well tear asunder states throughout the developing world, he argues for greater regional integration and the fostering of regional "security communities" or "confederations" coordinated by a new *Transatlantic Political-Economic and Strategic Council*, as a means to deal with the political tensions generated by both state and anti-state "terrorism." **Karsten D. Voigt** argues that contrary to the fears of some in Europe, US military actions in regard to the war in Afghanistan have not destabilized the Islamic world, and that America's policy does include elements of humanitarian aid, even going so far as the "nation-building" previously so frowned upon, especially by American neo-conservatives. On the other hand, the Europeans are making a much greater contribution, in military terms as well, than many American commentators are willing to admit. The policies are more complementary than generally realized. **Norbert Baas**, in profoundly examining the critical issues raised by both "anti-state" and "state-supported" terrorism as it pertains to German history and contemporary Europe, asks the crucial question: Where are the borderlines between the war against terrorism (Al-Qaida, destruction of the terrorist network) and a more general and new strategic orientation against the dangers of states building up weapons of mass destruction (the "axis of evil")? In arguing against American neo-conservatives, he explains why German opposition to the US/UK intervention in Iraq was not due to "moralism, idealism, or pacifism." **Marcel Van Herpen** then explores the differences between Europe and the US on how to fight the new international 'hyperterrorism' and discusses the apparently growing divergence between the US and Europe in terms of a gap in perceptions, capabilities, attitudes, values, religions and strategies.

Part IV, *"War on Terrorism": Regional and Global Ramifications* Chapters 12–16, focuses on the regional and global ramifications of the crisis, in an effort to put an end to the underlying geostrategic, political-economic, socio-cultural and normative disputes that have helped to stimulate terrorism and the proliferation of WMD. **Robert M. Cutler** looks at the crisis in Central Asia from the perspective of the regional powers, and examines Sino-Russian influence in the region. He furthermore speculates as to the future nature of the global system and argues provocatively that the "unipolarity-versus-multipolarity tensions now characterizing international affairs will be replaced by a bipolarity such as emerged in the 1890s (Triple Entente versus the Triple Alliance) and led to the First World War." **Anton Koslov** analyzes the US-Russian inter-relationship in regard to that seemingly distant region that suddenly came so close to the average American on 11 September 2001, and examines the factors that led the US to at least tacitly support the Taliban until 1998. He argues that a joint US-Russian role in central Asia can help create a new system of collective security for the region. **Sten Widmalm** looks at South Asia and analyses the dangerous nuclear face off between India and Pakistan. He predicts a new division of the world, in which the border of the blocs runs straight through Kashmir. **Steven Ekovich** examines the failure of the US "double containment" policy in regard to Iran and Iraq, with an emphasis on actual and potential Iranian "threats." He critically examines US-EU policy options in regard to the nature of Islamic Republic's support for terrorism, its efforts to build nuclear weapons and other WMD. He examines Iran's geo-economics of oil and poppies, as well as the legitimacy crisis now confronting the Islamic regime, and then questions the prospects for "democratic" change. **Hall Gardner** examines the geo-strategy of "sequencing" and "even handedness" in regard to the US decision to intervene in Iraq and its efforts to achieve a peace settlement between Israel and the Palestinian Authority, as well as between India and Pakistan, among other disputes, such as that with North Korea. It is argued that the US risks geostrategic and political-economic overextension, and could be confronted with the formation of new countervailing alliances, if a more concerted multilateral strategy cannot soon be implemented in dealing with a seemingly expanding number of disputes and conflicts.

Many, but not all, of these chapters, originated in the conference *New World, New Europe, New Threats: NATO and the European Union in the New Millennium* held at the French Senate, quite accidentally, on 7 December 2001, exactly sixty years after that "day in infamy," a conference sponsored by the American University of Paris and the North Atlantic Treaty Organization. The editor would like to thank Anthony Triolo and Rita Solanke, for their assistance in editing, not to overlook Julian Lindley-French, for his help organizing the conference, and Mickey Newman, without whom the whole project would have never been initiated. And always, the Gardner family for putting up with yet another project that is seemingly forever in the process of being "almost completed."

Notes

1. See for example, comments by Walter Laqueur, *The Age of Terrorism* (Boston: Little, Brown and Co, 1987). In the 1980s, a total of 571 Americans died in 1,701 attacks recorded overseas, while even less, a total of 87, were killed in the 1990s in a total of 1,372 attacks aimed against US targets abroad. US State Department figures, which do not record deaths attributed to "state terrorism," observed that the absolute number of international terrorist attacks in 2001 declined to 346, down from 426 in 2000, although a total of 3,547 persons were killed in international terrorist attacks in 2001 with ninety percent of the fatalities (roughly 3000) occurring in the September 11 attacks. In 2000, 409 persons died in anti-state terrorist attacks. On the other hand, the Bureau of Democracy, Human Rights, and Labor of the US State Department does discuss both state and anti-state "terrorism," but under the rubric of "human rights" in its yearly country reports: http://www.state.gov/g/drl/ hr/.

    Secret "terrorist" organizations are, of course, not new. The *sicarrii* of the time of the Zealot struggle in Palestine (66-73 BC) engaged in unconventional ways of murdering political opponents, as did the Assassins of the Ismaili sect of Hassan Ibn al-Sabbah in the 11th century—the "Old Man in the Mountain," who killed Conrad of Montferrat, the crusader King of Jersuslem, among others, mythologized by Marco Polo writing long after al-Sabbah's death. The contemporary media have often compared Ossama Bin Laden to Hassan al-Sabbah. Yet a more appropriate comparison to al-Sabbah is the Iranian Shi'ite leader Ayatollah Khoemeni, coupled with his fanatical *Hezbollah* or *Islamic Jihad*, which was responsible for the suicide truck bombing of both the US Embassy and the US Marine barracks in Beirut in 1983, among other actions. Both Khoemeni and Hassan Sabbah originated from the same region of Persia/Iran. It is perhaps also not surprising that Saddam Hussein, with his Baath socialist pan-Arab ideology, comes from the same region, Tikrit, as did the Kurdish leader of the Arab jihad against the Christian crusaders, Saladin.
2. Hannah Arendt, *The Origins of Totalitarianism* (Harvest Books, 1973), p. 6 and Chapter 13, "Ideology and Terror."
3. Karl Marx described the Spanish guerrillas in this way: "The French were obliged to be constantly armed against an enemy who, continually flying, always reappeared, and was everywhere without being actually seen, the mountains serving as so many curtains." 'It was,' says the Abbé de Pradt, 'neither battles nor engagements which exhausted the French forces, but the incessant molestations of an invisible enemy, who, if pursued, became lost among the people, out of which he reappeared immediately afterward with renewed strength. The lion in the fable tormented to death by a gnat gives a true picture of the French army.'" Karl Marx, *Revolutionary Spain* http://www.marxists.org/archive/marx/works/1854/revolutionary-spain/ch05.htm.
4. Walter Laqueur, *The Age of Terrorism*, 11.
5. On strategic leveraging, see Hall Gardner, *Surviving the Millennium: American Global Strategy, the Collapse of the Soviet empire and the Question of Peace* (Praeger: Westport, CT, 1994).

Introduction

Alliances, "War on Terrorism" and Weapons of Mass Destruction

Hall Gardner

The destructive power of the 11 September 2001 attacks on the World Trade Center and Pentagon, the two prime symbols of American economy and power, plus the failed attempt to strike the White House (or another prime target) by a fourth passenger jet, generated the media image of unthinkable madness, the outrageous blasphemy involved in attacking highly revered symbols, and the willingness to engage in self-sacrifice, in addition to the killing of roughly three thousand innocent individuals of differing nationalities and religions.

The outrageous nature of the attacks, instigated by a nomadic, seemingly invisible, if not "virtual," enemy, went far beyond previous acts of anti-state terrorism in their destructive impact—as acts of anti-state terrorism have evolved from their late 19th century into their more violent 20th century manifestations.[1] The attacks then forced attention to the "pan-Islamic" cause and began to impel state leaderships to choose camps—in the meanwhile provoking controversy, dissent, and division. In effect, such outrageous attacks were intended to prove determination to achieve their political cause at whatever price and to gain international recognition for that struggle. Although it is really impossible to tell for sure due to degree of disinformation and misinformation, as well as censorship, the September 11 attack *appears* to be the consequence of an unholy alliance between self-proclaimed "pan-Islamic" insurgent movements or "cells" (most prominently, Osama Bin Laden's Al-Qaeda) and a number of other unknown or undisclosed support groups. Conspiracy theories abound.

In the weeks following the September 11 attacks, it was also not clear who was responsible for the mailing of anthrax germs to the US congress, CIA headquarters and news media that likewise took place in late 2001–02. The source of anthrax is also in dispute: evidence has pointed to laboratories in the United States. Coupled with the anthrax scare, an embittered ex-Persian Gulf War veteran, dubbed the "Beltway sniper," went on a killing spree in 2002 in the Washington, DC area.

All these events merely added to the confused and uncertain atmosphere of "terror" that these groups, their sympathizers, and their copycats hoped to evoke. The September 11 attacks, plus the anthrax scare and the Beltway sniper, thus appeared to reinforce the warning, first articulated by Alexander Hamilton in *The Federalist No. 23*, that "The authorities essential to the care of the common defense are these – to raise armies – to build and equip fleets – to prescribe rules for the government of both – to direct their operations – to provide for their support. *These powers ought to exist without limitation: Because it is impossible to foresee or define the extent and variety of national exigencies, or the corresponding extent and variety of means which may be necessary to satisfy them.* The circumstances that endanger the safety of the nation are infinite; and for this reason no constitutional shackle can wisely be imposed on the power to which the care of it is committed ..."[2]

Confronted with a number of circumstances that did "endanger" the nation, the Bush administration consequently engaged in a number of internal and external security measures after the events of September 11. In regard to internal security, the Bush administration passed the Homeland Security Act, which was to assist "terrorism preparedness," as well as the USA Patriot Act, which has given the Federal government largely unprecedented intrusive powers into the lives of American citizens.[3]

The US almost immediately raised defense spending by roughly $40 billion, an amount larger than the entire defense budget of any single EU country. By the year 2003, the Bush administration demanded $74.7 billion in *supplemental* defense spending, in effect expanding the "war on terrorism" to the war against the regime of Saddam Hussein.[4] The question now, as originally evoked by Alexander Hamilton, is to what extent can the US continue to engage against all possible contingencies and prepare against all possible dangers—without risking potential political-military-economic overextension and the potential loss of its perceived domestic and international legitimacy—if not its basic freedoms.

On the international side, the war against Al-Qaeda and the Taliban in Afghanistan was supported as an action of "self defense" in that the September 11 attacks were judged to be a threat to international peace and security under Chapter 7, Article 51 of the UN Charter under UN Security Resolution 1368 pressed for by France on 12 September 2001. Washington was consequently able to gain UN, NATO and EU support for its actions in Afghanistan despite some questions as to whether Washington possessed substantiated evidence to link Al-Qaeda and the Taliban to the September 11 attacks. There were also questions raised as to whether the US should have more closely abided by UN procedures and international law before engaging in the use of force.[5]

NATO consequently invoked, for the first time in its history, Article V of the North Atlantic Treaty, meaning that an attack against one ally represented an attack against all, as "collective defense." The NATO allies, plus most western and eastern European states, including Russia, wholeheartedly supported, at least in political terms, the first phase of the "war on terrorism" which resulted in the defeat of the Taliban leadership of Afghanistan, and the subsequent hunt for Bin Laden and other Al-Qaeda members. The war in Afghanistan was taken in support of the Northern Alliance, whose leader, General Massoud, had been mortally injured two days before the 11 September 2001 attacks by Al-Qaeda members posing as journalists. In effect, the September 11 attacks (although they may have been planned at least since 1996) can be regarded as kind of "pre-emptive" strike—in the sense that they were timed when Northern Alliance leader General Massoud had been trying to obtain financial and military support from the US and EU for his anti-Taliban cause—prior to his assassination.

The Bush Administration was accordingly able to obtain solid UN and international support for its war against Al-Qaeda and the Taliban; by contrast, it was unable to convince the majority of permanent and non-permanent UN Security Council (UNSC) members of the necessity for a so-called "preemptive" attack against Iraq. The UN Security Council had unanimously supported the complete disarmament of Iraq in accord with UN Resolution 1441 in November 2002; but not all UNSC members supported "regime change" or considered such military action as truly "defensive." The permanent UNSC members France, Russia, and China all opposed US action against Iraq. On the UNSC, only the UK supported the US position, and both the US and UK obtained support from Spain, Italy, Poland and most other eastern European countries. With Germany being one of the non-permanent UNSC members, the Franco-German refusal, in particular, to back "regime change" in Iraq led to a bitter and acrimonious inter-Allied dispute. (See Karsten D. Voigt, Chapter 9, Norbert Bass, Chapter 10.) The French then became the brunt of Washington's ire for taking the lead in the opposition—and despite France's previous support for UNSC Resolution 1368 in support of the war in Afghanistan.

In opting to act without a clear UN mandate, Washington's decision to intervene in Iraq without immediate and certain provocation that could be justified by self-defense, not only raised the key question as to whether such military powers ought to "exist without limitation" and without constitutional checks, as argued by Hamilton, but also whether such actions should possibly be limited by means of multilateral "checks and balances" of international regimes and countervailing powers or regional groupings. Here, French, Russian and Chinese calls for a more "multipolar" world order to counter US hegemony as a "hyperpower" in the words of former French Foreign Minister Hubert Vedrine (an issue raised prior to US intervention in Iraq) led Washington, at least in part, to take a more assertive approach in attempting to break up EU cohesion and unity.

History will judge as to whether the preclusive intervention in Iraq will prove "positive" or "negative" in regard to achieving regional and world peace. US Senator Robert Byrd represented one few voices of opposition in the US Senate who had forewarned of the war's consequences for US-European relations.[6] Former NATO Supreme Commander Wesley Clark had called the war "inevitable" but "like elective surgery."[7] Certainly, much as the French and German Cassandras forewarned, the aftermath has shown that it will be extremely difficult to pick up the pieces; Washington has been drawn into a quagmire, if not quicksand, from which it will prove difficult to extricate itself.

NATO and the European Union

During the Cold War, the United States had largely been able to build a consensus within NATO, despite the 1956 Suez crisis in which France and Britain intervened against Egypt in support of Israel, and despite some significant dissent within NATO as to how to deal with the Soviet "threat" and the deployment of nuclear weaponry in Germany in the 1950s and 1980s. NATO, however, never really acted "out of area": Soviet interventions in eastern Europe met with no direct confrontation.

By contrast, in the post-Cold War era, NATO consensus has been generally more difficult to sustain. This is largely due to the fact that NATO has increasingly moved "out of area" since the Bosnian conflict and toward non-defensive non-Article V "enforcement" actions. The strategic choice to engage in non-defensive actions raised questions as to NATO's original purpose as a "collective defense" organization and opened often-acrimonious debate both within NATO and the UN Security Council (UNSC). While the legitimacy of the UNSC to decide questions involving the use of force has been disputed, and despite the fact that the UNSC and UN as a whole is in dire need of reform in order to better reflect the political economic relations of the post-Cold War international community, the fact of the matter is that the North Atlantic Treaty (NAT) itself stipulates that NATO must bring the question of non-defensive non-Article V enforcement actions before the UN Security Council.[8]

NATO actions in Bosnia took place side-by-side the UN under the "dual key" principle; but NATO actions (dubbed "war by committee") in the war "over" Kosovo, however, took place without a clear UNSC mandate. US actions in Afghanistan were supported by both the UN (under Article 51 of the UN Charter) and NATO (under Article V of the NAT); NATO itself was only peripherally involved in direct intervention in Afghanistan but became involved in peacekeeping in 2003, as it has in Bosnia and Kosovo. US actions against the Iraqi regime, however, were largely taken outside both the UN and NATO frameworks, except for NATO's "collective defense" of Turkey. (See Hall Gardner, Chapter 8.)

Prior to September 11, the newly unified Europe had attempted to assert greater self-confidence through the formation of a Common European Foreign and Security Policy (CEFSP), but it has thus far been unable to get its act together. From the American perspective, the Europeans have not yet provided sufficient military reinforcement for effectively intervening against the "new threats" (the EuroForce, developed for peacekeeping operations, has thus far been regarded by American military advisers as a "hollow shell"). The EU was largely unable to develop a common policy in regard to the crises in Bosnia and Kosovo in its own backyard, and bickered with US policy in both cases; the EU possessed only limited special force capabilities that could be effective in Afghanistan; and it faced severe divisions in to how to deal with Iraq. (See Simon Serfaty, Chapter 3; Marco Rimanelli, Chapter 4. On the changing nature of European defense capabilities, see Alexis Debat, Chapter 5.)

US and European differences in post-Cold War threat perceptions became even more pronounced once it became clear that the second phase of the "war on terrorism" would focus not just on the activities of specific terrorist groups, but would target states other than Afghanistan (such as Iraq, Iran or Syria) that possessed or that planned to develop weapons of mass destruction (WMD), or that supported terrorist groups. While the United States girded up for a long term "war on terrorism," the Europeans tended to underplay the virulence of the American response seeing it as a "fight" not a "war." (See Marcel Van Herpen, Chapter 11.) The US has tended to argue that new terrorism is novel in both *intent* and *capabilities* and thus *qualitatively* different; Europeans, however, tend to argue that the new terrorism may be different in terms of *capabilities*, but it has not changed fundamentally in *intent*.

As the United States intensified its threats to intervene against Iraq, mutual imprecations echoed across the Atlantic. Americans accused the continental Europeans of "pacifism" and "anti-Americanism." Europeans counter-accused US policy as being arrogant, over assertive and of attempting to sustain its hegemonic predominance. In effect, the two sides based their policies not only upon conflicting interests (such as rights to develop Iraqi oil reserves), but also upon conflicting values and principles. Thus, at a deeper level, American two party democratic liberalism, with its predominant federal government and military-industrial (and university) complex, has tended to clash with the essentially social democratic approach of continental Europe, with its more inter-governmental and confederal make-up that emphasizes the need for consensus building and compromise among the differing state-nations and multi-party factions.

As indicated above, the US approach to the UN also differed. Despite the fact that the US helped build the post-1945 international legal regimes and superstructure, the United States has tended to use the UN as a vehicle for its policy, but only when needed; the Europeans, on the other hand, have argued that the UN, as imperfect as it is, represents the sole legitimizing body and basis for international law for actions governing enforcement and military intervention. From the perspective of American neo-conservatives, the UN possesses less legitimacy in regard to the use of force than does NATO and those states that have obtained their legitimacy by becoming "constitutional democracies," in particular, the United States. (As they can be depicted "national universalists" fired by a "crusading spirit" in the terms of classical realist theorist, Hans Morgenthau, neo-conservatives argue that the United States is "exceptional," if not *above* international law, as it represents a country that must assert "leadership."[9])

Washington's conception of international legal culture has thus differed with that of the Europeans: the United States has tended to take a looser interpretation of international law than have post-Cold War European policy makers, whose post-Cold War approach has generally been stricter—although the concepts of "humanitarian intervention" and "right to intervene" (*droit d'ingerence*) have begun to challenge the traditional post-Westphalia concepts of state sovereignty of both Americans and Europeans, yet without clearly defining the precise conditions in which states can *legally* violate traditional notions of sovereignty.

Europeans argued that "preclusive" war in Iraq without a clear UNSC mandate would not be legitimate and could open the door to unilateral interventions elsewhere. They questioned where was the precise balance between the old international norms in which the state was completely sovereign within its territory and the newly developing international normative system which seems to be moving from the right of "humanitarian" intervention to that of "preclusive" intervention.

The key questions were: "Why take action here rather than elsewhere? Who makes the decision to intervene, and based on what legitimate authority?"[10] The Europeans furthermore argued that preclusive military action would not necessarily help to resolve the dilemma of how to deal with other countries that had developed, or were in the process of developing, WMD. Such intervention could send a signal that other states could attempt to build up their own WMD as a deterrent against the US and then engage in unilateral interventions whenever and wherever they saw the rise of potential threats.

The Europeans countered that regime change in Iraq by forceful military intervention would result in greater, and not less, political-economic instability and terrorism, particularly if such intervention was not strongly supported by indigenous Iraqi groups. US efforts to impose democracy *from above* would involve long term peacekeeping and could possibly backfire. The European critique was based on the fact that US post-Cold War efforts to build "democratic" states have largely proved ineffective or inconclusive in Panama, Haiti, Bosnia, Kosovo, and Afghanistan. It was argued that military intervention in Iraq would not be welcomed as "liberation" but as "occupation"—and could further destabilize Arab/Islamic countries in the region.

Although some Europeans analysts may have exaggerated the difficulties it would take to defeat Iraq, they believed that strong multilateral diplomatic pressure (combined with US military pressures) on Saddam Hussein to significantly reduce his military capabilities and eliminate WMD would have ultimately helped reduce tensions throughout the entire region without a forced change of regime. Stronger weapons inspections could have involved the deployment of French, German, if not Russian troops, to back up UN inspectors with real muscle (and simultaneously guarantee Iraqi security)—an option not taken. Saddam Hussein may have also proposed that 2,000 US weapons inspectors could also participate, including the FBI, as part of a failed back channel effort to avert war, a proposal that included cooperation in fighting terrorism and "full support for any U.S. plan" in the Arab-Israeli peace process, as well free elections in two years.[11]

The Americans, however, argued that even an improved sanctions regime would not work as long as Saddam Hussein remained in power he would continue to play "cat and mouse" with UN inspectors and would eventually strengthen his military capabilities and repressive government. Instead, Washington envisioned the formation of entirely new regional relationships to be spearheaded by a "democratic-federal" Iraq and that would ultimately lead to political reforms in Syria, Iran, as well as Saudi

Arabia. Regime change in Iraq would be most immediately followed by a "two-state" resolution to the Israeli-Palestinian conflict under the Road Map for Peace once the Iraqi "threat" had been vanquished; UK Prime Minister Tony Blair called it a question of "even-handedness."

Without giving the belated French and German (and Russian) proposals for more muscular inspections a chance, the United States and UK, having engaged in a massive military build-up, opted for military intervention, basing their actions loosely on UN Resolution 1441, as well as bilateral agreements signed between the US and Iraq after the 1991 Persian Gulf War. In effect, the US argued that the costs of eliminating the regime of Saddam Hussein as soon as possible would be less than eliminating it later, but this argument largely depended upon precisely what kind of regime would take its place, the difficulties in kick-starting a collapsed economy (and how long the US-UK would need to "occupy" the country). The long-term costs also depended upon the nature of the new political games to be played by both states and insurgent (or "terrorist") groups within Iraq and in the region following the conflict.

In short, the transatlantic dispute over Iraq represented a foreign policy fiasco that accentuated the differences in threat perceptions, political-economic interests, and global leadership styles between the United States, France and Germany—as well as Russia and China. In terms of the EU, the consequences of all this may well be a significant short-term set back for the CEFSP; it could also result in a reconsideration of the relationship between the "core" European states of France and Germany and the states in eastern Europe, and lead major core states to assert their interests over the lesser states, if possible, within the EU framework.

On the other hand, the Iraq affair may provide an evolutionary shock effect or what has been called "convergent evolution"[12] toward a CEFSP. Despite US efforts to play the UK, Spain, and eastern European states (particularly Poland) against France and Germany, the EU expanded its membership to 25. Most importantly, the EU appears to be moving closer together through the establishment of a presidency and a single foreign minister, who would be appointed by EU leaders and who would maintain a seat on the European Commission, and who would conduct CEFSP, based unanimity. Not-so-ironically, US pressures on London may have shaken the basis of the US-UK special relationship, pushing London closer to Paris and Berlin. Even the UK may ultimately join the Euro in the next five years, despite having ruled out such a possibility in 2003.

Yet even as the EU forms a new overarching political framework, the US will begin to take the EU seriously only once it can develop more complementary military capabilities with those of the US itself. Here, the

US has expected NATO countries to develop a NATO Response Force that is intended to complement and not compete with, the EU's proposed Rapid Reaction Force, which will focus on peacekeeping duties of the Petersberg tasks. (See Simon Serfaty, Chapter 3; Marco Rimanelli, Chapter 4; Karsten D. Voigt, Chapter 9.)

In many ways, the EU will soon be forced out of its comfortable nest on Venus (as depicted in the stereotyped views of neo-conservative Robert Kagan) as the US begins to downsize away from more expensive, and less strategically positioned bases in Germany, and step toward Poland, Romania and Bulgaria, as well as toward Georgia, Azerbaijan and Djibouti, as well as states in Africa, which are closer to the "new threats." The overall strategic-political-economic implications of "downsizing," however, have not been assessed. In its ostensible attempt to "reward" coalition allies and "punish" those who did not support US policy in Iraq (plans to reduce bases and troops in Germany have been considered at least since the Clinton administration), this decision could have major and negative repercussions on Allied relations, in that it ignores the role of troop deployments for political purposes of *deterrence* and *reassurance, not to overlook sustaining trade and investment.*

As some 70,000 US forces are to be downsized in Germany, as well as in Turkey, NATO itself may take a back seat in most military operations except for those involving peacekeeping missions—the increasing importance of which should not be downplayed. As opposed to its original mission as a "collective defense" organization, NATO has increasingly become a "conflict prevention" and "peacekeeping" organization. At the same time, however, NATO should not lose its residual collective defense capability in the not to-be-entirely dismissed scenario that Russia could degenerate into a *revanchist* power, particularly if the US and the EU are not ultimately able to sustain Moscow in a new concerted relationship for whatever reason. Here, the importance of a reformed NATO, which engages in overlapping security cooperation with Russia and a strengthened European Union, and other partners, and which keeps a residual collective defense capability, should not be underestimated—as has been implied by the satirical "NATO is Dead! Long Live NATO!" theme played by neo-conservative critics.[13]

A Largely Incomplete Diplomatic Revolution

The 11 September 2001 attacks initially provoked a profound—and thus far incomplete—diplomatic revolution and shift in American alliances that involved a fundamental reassessment of the intentions, interests and military capabilities of both former Cold War friends and foes—with potentially dangerous consequences that, in Francis Bacon's words could lead to imperial "overflow."[14]

After September 11, Russia was regarded in a new light, as a potential ally as opposed to a foe. Most significantly, between December 2001-May 2002, the United States agreed to bring Russia into a closer relationship with NATO, so that the now nineteen members of the North Atlantic Council could meet directly with Russia, in the "19 plus 1" format. Russia does not possess the right to veto, but it can make its opinion and interests more directly known. (See Ira Straus, Chapter 7.) At the same time, however, Moscow has retained close military ties to China and, as the prospects of unilateral US military intervention in Iraq loomed closer, Moscow opposed US policy and looked toward an entente with France and Germany, partly in hopes of entering into a "new" form of membership with the European Union, in the assumption that NATO will not open its doors to full cooperation. (See Nadia Arbatova, Chapter 6.)

The newfound post-September 11 American-Russian entente, at least initially before the Iraq crisis, raised the suspicions of both the Europeans and Chinese. France and Germany tended to see the traditional US-UK special relationship, combined with the new NATO-Russian accord (NATO's "19 plus 1" formula of May 2002), as a form of "double containment" of an expanding and united Europe. Prior to the Iraq conflict, the Franco-German duo tended to see the American effort to play the "Russian card" as a potential means to place a check on the new Europe itself—in that the US could appeal to Moscow, if the EU did not support American initiatives. As war with Iraq loomed on the horizon, however, France and Germany began to play the Russian "card" against US policy.

From Beijing's perspective, China has traditionally regarded closer US-Russian relations as a step toward "encirclement," linked also to the US alliance with Japan and US defensive support for Taiwan. Since September 11, China has consequently appeared to flip-flop in response to the new US-Russian ties. While not wanting to alienate the United States, Beijing tended to lean more positively toward Russia and the European Union. The Chinese tended to regard the war with Iraq as inevitable, but also opposed American "unilateralism" and "hegemony." Despite US efforts to wean China and Russia away from an alliance with France and Germany, the latter forged a bloc to oppose the war with Iraq. Following the war, it is still unclear which direction these states will turn. Certainly in May-June 2003, the US took steps to make amends, with every state that opposed US policy, but disagreements and bitterness remained on both sides. (Turkish commentators thought President Bush had tried to make amends with everyone but Ankara!)

The American entente with Russia has also meant a tilt toward Russian interests in Central Asia, even prior to September 11. In effect, the new US-Russian entente (assuming it can be sustained long after the Iraq war) tended to further pit the oil-producing rivals Saudi Arabia and Russia against each other, at least before their rapprochement in 2003, as the two have battled for control and influence over central Asia since Soviet collapse and withdrawal from Afghanistan. (See Anton Koslov, Chapter 13.) In fact, it is legitimate to speculate as to whether Al-Qaeda would have ever arisen in the first place, if the US had been willing to forge a deal with Mikhail Gorbachev involving a continuing Russian political role in Afghanistan and resulting in a settlement supervised by both the US and USSR as opposed to a total Soviet withdrawal. (See Ira Straus, Chapter 7.)

Highly Lopsided Polycentrism

Post-Cold War geopolitical relationships had already begun a major geotectonic shift following Soviet collapse, European unification, and the rise of China as a regional power with increasingly global interests. Given the highly uneven spread of dual-use technology and economic capabilities, as well as regional differentiation accentuated by the transnational economic forces of "globalization," the ability of lesser states to obtain Weapons of Mass Destruction (WMD), combined with the numerous threats posed by partisan groups with pan-religious, pan-national, ethno-nationalist or secessionist ideologies, have tended to exacerbate many tensions and conflicts that evidently existed in the past, but which have so suddenly, after 11 September, boiled with new vehemence to the surface.

The end of the Cold War has resulted in a continuing unraveling of the essentially bipolar global structure. The new world dis-equilibrium has resulted in the formation of a *highly lopsided or highly uneven polycentric* global order that appears to favor the United States at present. Soviet collapse, not so accidentally following German unification, opened up a new *shatterbelt* that extends from Finland and the Baltic states and to ex-Yugoslavia and from there to the Caucasus and deep into central Asia with Afghanistan at the belly button, and which then connects with the Middle East/ Persian Gulf, and has begun to interlink with tensions in Africa.

This new *shatterbelt* (that does not fit so neatly with Samuel Huntington's conception of a fault line of potentially clashing civilizations) accordingly links Turkey and traces of former Ottoman influence in the Caucasus and Central Asia with the Middle East/Persian Gulf (Iraq) and then with the Eurasian rimland, India, Pakistan and Afghanistan, as well as with the resource-rich, yet impoverished, regions of Africa. Concurrently, the fact that Moscow has fallen from "superpower status" (from a global *triphibious* land, sea, and air power to an essentially land-locked state) has indirectly permitted the rise of a more independent China, as it now seeks to move from the status of a *continental*, to a *triphibious*, power. The rise of China has, in addition to previous fears of the Soviet "threat," led Japan to gradually expand its insular naval capabilities—not to overlook the fact China's rivalry with India likewise influenced the latter's decision to go nuclear, along with its rivalry with Pakistan.

The collapse of Soviet power and Moscow's global outreach has consequently opened the doors to conflicts that either had been more or less limited or "double contained" during the Cold War years, or else to new conflicts or contests for power, many of which had been fuelled by the "superpowers" during the Cold war, and which could find new sources of fuel in the post-Cold War disequilibrium from among the rival claims of states, anti-state organizations, as well as partisan movements who possess ideologies at odds with the predominant liberal democratic "ethos" and who possess goals that, more often than not, conflict with US, European and/or Russian global interests. Many of these states or partisan groups have threatened to wield new and varied forms of strategic leveraging involving threats to engage in a number of *guéguerres*, or regional wars of attrition, in what has been dubbed *asymmetrical* warfare.

In effect, the collapse of the bipolar world order (and of the Soviet Union) itself has largely left the United States as the lone policeman on the block, making it difficult to forge a concerted multilateral policy against the threats of "terrorism," state-supported "terrorism," secessionist movements, and the rise of *parvenu* states capable of building WMD. The risk raised here is that the colossal sums the United States has spent on both the "war on terrorism" and the war with Iraq, combined with necessary post-conflict peacekeeping, police enforcement and counter-insurgency, could ultimately prove to be its Achilles heel.[15] In essence, fighting from a far much weaker financial base, Al-Qaeda (joined directly or indirectly by other groups or states) may hope to stretch out American capabilities in such a way as to "win" through wars of attrition.

The largely uncoordinated "double enlargement" of NATO and European Union into ex-Soviet territories (see Chapters 3–7); NATO intervention in the Balkans and Kosovo, and US-UK intervention in Iraq, have been coupled with a series of crises involving China and Taiwan, nuclear tensions involving India and Pakistan, as well as Iran and North Korea. Other issues that could stretch political will and resources include the political manipulation of Islam from Morocco to the Philippines and from Uzbekistan to Nigeria (from where the US expects to import some 25 percent of its oil in the near future), continuing acts of terror and counter-terror between Israelis and Palestinians, narco-terrorism in Columbia, Afghanistan (where poppy production has augmented substantially after US intervention against the Taliban). These conflicts coupled with extreme political-economic instability, state collapse and secessionist movements in many regions, not to overlook what has been called "World War III in Africa"—all threaten to overextend American and European military capabilities and political will.

Following the crises over Bosnia, Kosovo and Iraq, the US and its allies will likewise need to forge more concerted policies—if the *guéguerres* of today are not to degenerate into major power clashes of tomorrow. The UN will also need to undergo significant structural reforms if it is to survive as a viable guide for the world community. The complexity of issues and clashing interests have thus far led the insular powers of the United States and United Kingdom (with their potentially unraveling "special relationship") to assess the "new threats" very differently than the continental powers of France and Germany. In this respect, the geo-strategic disputes between the United States and the Franco-German "core" as to how to deal with Russia, China, rising *parvenu* states and partisan actors can, to a significant degree, be compared and contrasted with the interwar disputes between England and France, followed by the disintegration of the League of Nations—before World War II.[16] One can also compare and contrast the goals of pan-Islamic terrorists of today with those of the "pan-Serb" Black Hand before World War I, for example, or those of the Croatian *Ustache* before World War II, among other groups. (See Norbert Baas, Chapter 10.)

Weapons of Terror

With Nazi Germany acquiring nuclear weapons as the initial catalyst,[17] nuclear weapons were first developed in the Manhattan program by the US and UK. Once the nuclear genie was out of the bottle, it was only a matter of four years for the Soviet Union to acquire nuclear weapons in 1949; by the 1960s, the so-called "balance of terror" was established. The post-Cold War global system, however, is now in *imbalance*—if not totally out of equilibrium. (See Hall Gardner, Chapter 2.)

Such a situation has consequently created a wider range of potential threats and new dilemmas for nuclear and conventional deterrence than were present during the Cold War—in a new geopolitical system of highly lopsided or highly uneven power capabilities. After being acquired by the US, UK, and USSR, nuclear weapons and their delivery capabilities spread to France (which developed its nuclear deterrent primarily in opposition to the USSR, but also to keep the US "honest" in its promises to defend Europe). China acquired such capabilities vis-à-vis the US and Soviet nuclear threats, as well as to assert it own regional interests. India believed it necessary to possess the ultimate weapon to protect itself against China. Pakistan believed it needed the weapon to counter that of India; Israel (which has not yet publicly declared its possession of such weaponry) claimed to need it against any combination of Arab/Islamic states; Iraq stated that it needed the ultimate weapon against Iran and Israel; Iran against Iraq and Israel; North Korea against the United States, if not Japan, which has the technological capabilities to develop nuclear weapons if it so wishes. (On Iranian and Israeli nuclear capabilities, see Steven Ekovich, Chapter 15.) Other states, however, including Sweden, Argentina, Brazil, as well as South Africa, all started nuclear programs, but then decided against the nuclear option. In one of the first examples of post-Cold War *multilateral dissuasion*, Ukraine agreed to eliminate its nuclear weapons in exchange for UN Security Council security guarantees.

Rather than bringing a "peace dividend," Soviet collapse not only lowered the effectiveness of state restrictions to prevent the possible spread of dual use technology and WMD, but it also freed states and partisan movements to operate more independently of Soviet (and to a certain extent, American) controls by utilizing aspects of strategic and economic leveraging to obtain new military capabilities. Post-Cold War legislation passed by US Senators Sam Nunn and Richard Lugar has been intended to help Moscow destroy its nuclear weaponry, as have EU cooperative threat reduction activities in Russia, so as to prevent that weaponry from falling into the hands of parvenu states and terrorist groups. Yet many engineers from developing countries have been trained in US or European universities and can also put two and two together.[18] The fact that neither UN nor US weapons inspectors have, at the time of this writing, found WMD in Iraq has led to speculation that such weaponry could have been sold to third parties—assuming it was not destroyed and that Iraq truly did possess such capabilities, as claimed by the Bush Administration.[19]

Questions of Legitimacy and "Double Standards"

In many ways, the rise of total warfare in modern times (really since the American Civil War and World War I, German aerial attacks on Guernica in the Spanish Civil War, combined with the unleashing of the ultimate weapon of terror—"black rain"—in Hiroshima and Nagasaki at the end of World War II in response to surprise pre-emptive air strikes at Pearl Harbor) has worked to disintegrate the ethical distinction between civilian and military targets.[20] As nuclear and missile capabilities improved, nuclear strategists made a distinction between counter-force (military) and counter-value (population) targets—as if the "circular error probability" of nuclear blasts would not indiscriminately hit both the military and the general population. Concurrently, the brutal efforts of the advanced "civilized" countries to put down national independence movements and acts of "terrorism" in Vietnam, Algeria, Afghanistan, among others, has raised the question of "double standards."[21]

On a deeper level, much as the American Civil War (and its consequences) challenged the notion of "states rights" (the right of southern—and northern border states—to possess slaves), the new post-Cold War wave of US overseas expansion, following the Spanish American War, as well as the extension of US hegemony overseas after World War II, has begun to challenge on a global scale (albeit unilaterally and selectively) the rights of "state sovereignty": i.e., the rights of state leaderships to engage in crimes against humanity, ethnic cleansing, genocide, as well as the right of states to develop WMD.[22] These issues led to the US policies in support of *humanitarian intervention* and of *pre-emption* under the Clinton Administration. *Pre-emption* in regard to WMD was then formalized into doctrine by the Bush Jr. Administration. (See Hall Gardner, Chapter 2.)

While mid-19th and 20th century warfare concentrated on developing more and more powerful and explosive weaponry capable of mass destruction, the late 20th and early 21st centuries have largely been taken over by the "revolution in military affairs." The increasing accuracy and stealth capabilities of the new weaponry at least theoretically makes it possible for military strategists to discriminate more clearly as to which targets they seek to strike with a minimum of accidental strikes upon the civilian population or what has euphemistically been called "collateral damage."[23] The mantra repeated in the 1991 Persian Gulf War was that US cruise missile strikes would be "surgical," as satellites would guide weaponry. (Laser, wire or satellite guided only about 10 percent of weaponry used in the Gulf War, however; the figure was up to 60 percent in Afghanistan.) Yet precisely as American military capabilities have generally become more accurate, the weapons of potential opponents have become more powerful and much more "dirty" (as have the fighting styles)—in compensation for the fact that those opponents cannot come close to matching American technological competence and military-industrial-financial resources. (See Marwan Bishara, Chapter 1.)

As the accuracy of high technology warfare has become more precise (and as circular error probability has declined), the chances of indiscriminate strikes have been greatly reduced. At the same time, however, military strikes against "dual use" military/civilian capabilities can adversely affect civilian populations, as can the use of ostensibly "non-violent" economic sanctions and other "non-violent" pressures and threats. The distinction between *indiscriminate* and *discriminate* actions thus becomes blurred as populations become caught in the crossfire. This fact leaves a "gray area" for opponents to make conflicting claims, as each side blames the other for the responsibility in harming innocent civilian populations. Pan-Islamic propaganda, for example, pointed to the effects of the 1990-91 Persian Gulf war and the UN economic sanctions imposed upon the Iraqi people as the cause of extremely high infant mortality rates, birth defects, and malnutrition (chorine for water purification was banned, for example, as it could used in chemical warfare). By contrast, the United States blamed Iraqi social-economic problems upon the regime of Saddam Hussein and argued that areas under UN supervision in Iraqi Kurdistan, for example, did not exhibit the same problems.

The spread of ever more powerful weaponry and new technological means to deliver those destructive capabilities has furthermore been accompanied by another phenomenon: The willingness to engage in martyrdom as well as in indiscriminate violence and mass murder, rationalized as a "legitimate" self defense. In his 1996 Declaration of War, Bin Laden stated, "Terrorizing you, while you are carrying arms on our land, is a legitimate and morally demanded duty." Then on 21 October 2001, he made the infamous statement, "if killing the ones that kill our sons is terrorism, then let history witness that we are terrorists." Al-Qaeda's innovation in the realm of tactics is to go beyond traditional guerrilla actions of "hit and run" to tactics of "hit"—but not "run."

The fact that states throughout the Cold War and after have continued to engage in indiscriminate attacks or engage paramilitaries against their domestic political opponents has, in turn, helped to breed a new generation of anti-state "terrorists" with differing goals but who make no distinction between combatants, political decision-makers, and non-combatants. What is important is the political symbolism and the media coverage that advertises the movement in the effort to gain adherents.

Attacks on tourists, for example, appear designed to disrupt local economies that may depend on globalization in an attempt impel social tensions and conflict. Moreover, both state leaderships and terrorists alike may also be willing to use civilian populations as human shields and/or hostages. State forces may attack urban areas; terrorists may fight from within heavily populated areas. Ironically, US high tech weaponry, precisely because it lessens "collateral damage," may enhance low-tech resistance, particularly if the insurgency moves to urban areas.

It is really in these murky gray areas of propagandistic half-truths and accusations of "double standards" that the rhetorical and media aspects of the "new threats" have begun to emanate. As a means to rationalize their own acts of terror and for purposes of propaganda, both *parvenu* states and anti-state actors begin to play, on the one hand, with questions of legitimacy and borderline legality, and, on the other, with double standards in which major powers appear to act above and beyond international law—or else appear shape law to suit their own interests. In this regard, the "war on terrorism" can be used as a pretext for opposing necessary political reforms and challenges to corrupt or dictatorial authority, resulting in the fact that a significant number of ethno-national and secessionist movements have been branded as "terrorist."[24]

The UN Security Council and Weapons of Mass Destruction (WMD)

Much as partisan movements challenge official authority, *parvenu* states that attempt to develop WMD have likewise begun to challenge the legitimacy of the "legal" possession of the "ultimate weapon" by the five "predominant" states. The fact that the UN Security Council, since the 1967 Nuclear Non-Proliferation Treaty, legitimized its own possession of nuclear weapons as a nuclear *pentarchy* appears to represent an arbitrary dividing line in the view of nuclear "have-nots" and nuclear *parvenus*, such a India and Pakistan, as well as North Korea. The fact that neither the major powers, nor the UN Security Council, have granted strong security guarantees to the above states, which may feel insecure due to regional threats, in exchange for giving up the quest to obtain nuclear weaponry or WMD has led these states to develop these systems on their own volition and cost.

American neo-conservatives argue that both the American and European need to accept the reality of "double standards";[25] yet accusations of "double standards" play a key role in the rise of new threats—as well as in the propaganda of "terrorist" movements, who tend to see their cause as "just" and the other side as engaging in acts of "state terrorism" and of supporting "nuclear terror." Moreover, the fact that the illegal possession of WMD by key allies of the major powers appears to be tolerated, if not given overt or covert support, once again raises questions of double standards, particularly if some states are asked to disarm, but not others. Such double standards make the possibility of regional "nuclear free zones" more difficult to achieve, and work against the option of overlapping multilateral security guarantees by UNSC members. Here, the probable possession of nuclear weapons by Israel as a "deterrent" vis-à-vis the Arab/Islamic states and the possibility that Japan with its high tech capabilities can rapidly develop such weapons vis-à-vis North Korea (or China), represent at least two cases in point.

The post-Cold War collapse of the US-Soviet "balance of terror" has consequently led to efforts to circumvent the forces of US deterrence through sneak attack—or what the Pentagon has called "asymmetrical" warfare, or an "imbalance of terror." Chemical and biological weaponry, for example, represent the "poor man's atomic weapon," particularly if coupled with missile capabilities—or other means of delivery. What may thus be considered "novel" is the fact that non-state actors, as well as lesser states, can now acquire WMD; lesser states and the so-called "post-modern terrorist" can actually assemble and threaten the use of tremendous destructive powers, through dirty bombs or chemical or biological warfare.

Preclusive Intervention? Or Engaged Diplomacy, Sanctions And More Muscular Weapons Inspections?

Al-Qaeda attacks on the World Trade Center and Pentagon have unleashed a number of anti-systemic social, political and economic forces that have begun to divide major allies and could result in US overextension—if the US attempts to pursue militarily all its actual opponents, and in the process, creates new antagonisms. Here, it will prove crucial for EU and other allied states to fill in the gaps where the US cannot act, in a form of complementarity or *symbiosis*.

From the outset, the Bush administration's formulation of a "war on terrorism," represented a misnomer that raised European skepticism. The term possessed perilous repercussions that could result in a war without limits, as the list of actual and potential "terrorist" and "state terrorist" threats is endless. Precisely who one considers a "terrorist" often depends upon one's political bias; moreover, one countries' "rogue state" may be another's "ally" or "client" and vice versa.[26] This is not to overlook the fact that many of these groups identify the United States itself as a "terrorist" state (despite the latter's post-Cold War efforts to limit "collateral damage" in its military operations) and because the United States itself continues to support regimes accused buy other states of engaging in terrorism, or else ignores such accusations.

Not only is the "war on terrorism" dangerously misleading, but the Bush administration additionally and unskillfully linked three very different states (Iraq, Iran and North Korea) in its conception of the "axis of evil" in January 2002. In addition to the false analogy to World War II and its simplistic Manichean and millenarian biblical overtones, this depiction appears to imply that these three states have joined in a common alliance. The use of Biblical language furthermore reinforces the millenarian views of religiously oriented "terrorist" organizations; concurrently, it makes it difficult to adopt the appropriate policy to each differing situation.

The American tendency to "demonize" its opponents furthermore over simplifies issues by focusing on individual leaders (Slobodan Milosevic, Saddam Hussein, Ossama Bin Laden, Kim Jong-Il, etc.) rather than examining the deeper and more complex and more intractable political and social causes—so that policy can be more easily explained to the public and pushed through Congress.[27] Most problematic, the geopolitics of media *demonization* tends to foreclose the very possibility of working out compromise—as negotiated deals would tend to legitimize the power of very leadership that has been repeatedly called the epitome of "evil."

In many ways, the neo-liberal tendencies of the administration of President Clinton (in regard to Slobodan Milosevic as a supporter of ethnic cleansing as a form of "state terrorism" in Kosovo, after the Bosnian war in 1995) and the neo-conservative tendencies of the administration of George Bush Jr. (in regard to Saddam Hussein as a producer of WMD and supporter of "state terrorism") have ironically tended to rule out engaged diplomatic options *a priori*, as their primary focus has been on engaging in regime change, rather than seeking to change the intentions and actions of the existing regime—though bargaining, negotiation, and compromise on perceived "vital" interests.

At the same time, however, the Bush administration finally opted for "regime change" in Iraq, it has, behind the scenes, attempted to defuse nuclear tensions between India and Pakistan, as well as North and South Korea, with China as a facilitator, finally following in the Clinton administrations footsteps, at least in regard to that dispute. The irony may be that after the United States engages militarily in Iraq, it may end up "appeasing" North Korea (assuming it does not go to war). It could possibly appease India over Pakistan, but it has not yet sought to engage in direct diplomacy designed to reconcile the two nuclear powers of the subcontinent, but seeks to work behind the scenes. From these examples, the Bush administration may be attempting to differentiate its policies to a greater extent than its millenarian "axis of evil" statements indicate.

On the one hand, those who advocate that all disputes and conflicts should be handled by diplomacy may be wrong in arguing against *any* recourse to the threat to use force; on the other, they may be right in insisting that all means of negotiation, international inspection, and bargaining must be pursued before the *threat* to use force moves into the actual act—actions which are essentially in accord with both "classical realist" and "just war" theories. In classical terms, realist strategy has argued that, *if necessary*, force should be *threatened* until the point in which both sides find the dispute "ripe for resolution." The *threat* to use force may in fact catalyze negotiations, unless *both* sides are prepared to go to war. (It takes two sides to go to war. One side can either "appease" the other, or else "capitulate.")

If two sides (or more) do opt for war, engagement could reach a "mutually hurting stalemate" in which sides finally opt for peace; at the same time, however, a mutually hurting stalemate may still result in perpetual violence and a war of attrition if opponents cannot be shown alternatives to conflict. Here is the importance of multilateral approach to conflict resolution. Negotiations, by themselves, may not necessarily lead to peace; they may actually represent ploys for gaining public support for going to war or else for avoiding a "necessary" war; negotiations can also provide pretext for rebuilding forces behind the promises of disengagement, cease fire, or pretended disarmament. On the other hand, such compromises can be possibly found in multilateral power-sharing frameworks, or else in regional agreements backed by multilateral security guarantees, in that the involvement by third parties may bring new resources and new inventive thinking that provides conflicting sides positive options that did not appear to exist in a bilateral context. While the question as to which interests are truly "vital" will generally be at the center of decisions to go to war, compromises over so-called "vital interests" can be made more possible with external guarantees, but only if the major actors see such compromise in their long-term interests.

This position assumes that particular conflicts may be potentially "ripe for resolution" and that partisan groups will, in fact, be willing to engage in secret or open dialogue and accept political compromise, involving territorial compensation, economic assistance, political-economic power sharing arrangements. Efforts to negotiate peace have largely proved successful in the cases of South Africa and Northern Ireland, for example, despite the evident difficulties; at the same time, efforts to achieve a negotiated settlement have thus far failed in the case of Indo-Pakistani or Israeli-Palestinian conflict.

Efforts to negotiate assumes that external diplomatic intervention (that may or may not require military intervention or require interpositionary peacekeeping forces) can ultimately help bring a resolution of the conflict, if the two sides can be pressed *from outside* into compliance through a concerted strategy of *multilateral dissuasion*. And finally, it assumes the possibility that disputes that have not yet reached a stage of conflict involving acts of partisan warfare or "terrorism" may be "ripe for prevention"—if the potential for conflict is envisioned early enough.[28]

Dialogue with "Terrorism"

Dealing diplomatically (with a mix of force and diplomacy) with "terrorists" or else with a regime that engages in "state terrorism" accordingly means choosing when to negotiate, and when to actually compromise (or appease) so as to reach a "compromise deal" if possible— if it is believed the other side will reciprocate. While the eradication of some groups may be feasible, history has shown that "terrorists" have a habit of finding new supporters depending upon the geopolitical circumstances. As Marwan Bishara points out in Chapter 1, Clausewitzian "war as the continuation of diplomacy by other means" has rarely succeeded in actualizing its political ends in *asymmetrical* colonial and neo-colonial conflicts. This implies that, in some circumstances, it may be necessary to engage in a secret or open dialogue and negotiations with those individuals and movements who have previously been dubbed "terrorists" or "state terrorists."

One prime example involving dialogue with "terrorism" (other than South Africa and African National Congress, and Northern Ireland and the Irish Republican Army) is, of course, the efforts to achieve peace between Israel and the Palestine Liberation Organization, made even more difficult after the 1996 assassination (by an Israeli extremist) of Israeli Prime Minister Yitzhak Rabin, after he had been pressed by President Clinton to shake hands with Yassir Arafat. Yet dialogue with anti-state terrorists has occurred in other regions as well that have more directly affected NATO and the EU. Albanian Kosovar leader Hashim Thaci, whose nationalist Kosova Liberation Army (the KLA/UCK) had been identified by the State Department as a terrorist organization in 1998, prior to the war "over" Kosovo, was then brought into the Kosovo government after the Kosovo war.[29] During the war "over" Kosovo, NATO, on the one hand, sided with Albanian Kosovars against the Serbian "ethnic cleansing"—what can be called state-supported "terrorism." Once NATO opted for military intervention against Serbian "ethnic cleansing," however, NATO then supported Kosovar "autonomy" once the war was over—as opposed to "independence" as demanded by the KLA/UCK. The fundamental geopolitical questions confronting Kosovo/Kosova itself have thus not been resolved: To sustain the region under an international mandate? To bring it into a new confederal arrangement with Serbia and Montenegro? To partition it? To permit it to become independent? (An international conference on the Balkans may be help answer these vital questions.)

On the other hand, NATO attempted to play "honest broker" in the conflict between the Macedonian state and Albanian secessionists, in part to prevent conflict between Greece and Turkey. The US and NATO have consequently been reluctant to label Albanian groups in Kosova or Macedonia as "terrorists." Rather, Albanian groups are now called "armed combatants." In Macedonian conflict, NATO deployed inter-positionary peacemaking forces in an effort to prevent both sides from escalating the conflict, and to disarm Albanian rebels. In late August 2001, after a six-month insurrection by Albanian rebels, some 3,500 NATO troops joined over 1,000 others already in Macedonia, initially for a limited period of time. NATO's mandate was then extended twice. Then in December 2002, after a historic EU-NATO deal setting the stage for such an accord, it was decided that the EU would take over peacekeeping from NATO in Macedonia late March 2003 (at a cost of $6 million for six months).

As was the case of Macedonia, which involved efforts by Macedonian paramilitaries to "terrorize" Albanians and force their expulsion in addition to meeting Albanian resistance, has shown, the effort to achieve a negotiated solution as an "honest broker" is not without its difficulties. NATO initially set an unreasonably short mandate that was extended; at the same time, the US has been consistently reluctant to engage its forces in long term "peacekeeping." Washington has seen its primary mission as "war fighting;" it also fears being overextended in too many peacekeeping activities. The EU, however, itself does not want to accept an essentially two-tiered alliance in the US initiates the "war-fighting" (without permitting "power" sharing) and in which the EU picks up the "garbage" by doing the "peacekeeping."

In the aftermath of the Cold War, the United States and the Europeans have taken conflicting positions in regard to Bosnia, Kosovo, and Iraq. In these cases, the United States has played Teddy Roosevelt's "big stick," the EU and UN have tended to speak softly; but the two sides did not really coordinate their roles. The US refused to accept UN-EU negotiated compromise with Slobodan Milosevic in 1993 in regard to the Bosnian crisis, regarding the Vance-Owen efforts as acts of "appeasement" but simultaneously refusing to deploy US troops as peacekeepers. The US then refused the possibility of a diplomatic settlement in regard to Kosovo, by opting for direct military intervention after the failed 1998 Rambouillet summit (in which "Annex B" stipulated NATO control over Serbia proper). The option of deploying NATO-Russian peacekeepers was not pursued.[30]

The pattern repeated itself, but this time in regard to UN-brokered diplomacy and war with Iraq—in which there had been intense differences in policy between those who proposed "preclusive intervention" versus those who argued for sustained containment combined with vigilant inspections. The US decision to engage in "humanitarian intervention" in Kosovo without clear and overt UN Security Council approval appears to have provided the precedent for US-UK military intervention in Iraq. The bitter UN debate over Iraq then broke up hopes for a truly concerted policy. Multilateralism thus failed to prevent war in the contexts of both Kosovo and Iraq, and to a certain extent, Bosnia.

New Alliance Formations? Or Overlapping Multilateral Security Guarantees?

There is another murky and uncertain aspect to the rise of new threats that has not obtained as much attention in the post-Cold War as it did during the Cold War. On the one hand, nuclear *parvenu* states can acquire significant military capacity through their own intrinsic resources; but, on the other, what if more powerful states ultimately seek to align more fully with such *parvenu* powers—and/or secretly support major terrorist organizations?

In isolation, such states and groups are increasingly difficult to manage and contain; but if granted military backing and security supports through alliances with even more powerful actors, the situation could be made even more threatening. The US consequently risks being undermined in political-economic terms by: 1) a new polycentric geo-economic world, with a "two front" economic war with the EU and Asia;[31] 2) multiple threats of terrorism, asymmetrical warfare, wars of attrition, combined with threats of states wielding WMD that could overextend US military engagements followed by peacekeeping interventions as the army appears more overstretched than naval or air forces. (Here, peacekeeping needs to be more integrated into actual military strategy; the new high tech wars may be "won" rapidly, but the conflicts may not necessarily be resolved in political terms and have thus generally required long-term peacekeeping, if not acts of counter-insurgency, a new form of *short war illusion*.)

The primary and fundamental reason for forging a sustained concerted relationship between the US, Europeans, Russia, and ultimately China, is consequently to preclude any of the major powers from forming strong alliances with *parvenu* states; it is also to preclude these powers from forming alliances among themselves against the United States, or other militarized powers. The real risk in the not-so-long term then is that the perceived "unilateralist" policies and alliances of the US could, in the not-so-distant future, lead Russia, China, Ukraine (and possibly even Japan and the Europeans) to seek countervailing military capabilities and/or form rival alliances—or else determine to support the military capabilities of third parties. Instead of seeking overlapping multilateral or international security accords, states could forge new bilateral and/or countervailing alliances that could then seek to support different and conflicting "parvenu" states as they attempt to obtain WMD, and support terrorism.

There is consequently a need for a long term *concerted* US-EU-Russian (and Chinese) policy from the very outset in order to work together: 1) to contain or eliminate (by either peaceful or forceful measures) threats from so-called "rogue" states who are seeking to acquire significant military capabilities; 2) to forestall the formation of potentially rival or conflicting alliance groupings. (See Robert M. Cutler, Chapter 12; Sten Widmalm, Chapter 14; Hall Gardner, Chapter 16.)

Although the threat of potentially rival or conflicting alliance groupings may appear to be exaggerated worst-case scenarios,[32] it is better to consider such behind the scenes and potential "threats" carefully and to develop long term political-military and diplomatic strategies to thwart such options before they become actualized. The deep divisions between the US and Europeans certainly weaken the prospects of a concerted and truly multilateral policy formation that provides overlapping security guarantees for both states and partisan groups that require protection. This fact indicates the continuing need to make significant reforms in NATO and EU defense planning—as well as the need to make a complete re-assessment of US global strategy as it confronts the "new threats" posed by "terrorism," state-supported "terrorism," the spread of WMD, and shifting alliance formations.

The fundamental dilemma will thus be to try to continue work in a concerted fashion to eradicate mutually perceived "terrorist networks" but, at the same time, to play "honest broker" among conflicting sides where issues of which side is "right" and which is "wrong" are not entirely clear, and where compromises in regard to "vital interests" appear plausible and when mediation between conflicting parties should be pursued. A more realistic and "co-optive" approach to dealing with the threat of terrorism and rise of states capable of developing WMD must be devised. Such a policy could utilize a mix of military intervention, containment, secret or open bargaining, and appeasement depending upon the situation and a case-by-case assessment and in accord with a strategy of *multilateral dissuasion*.

The US has taken on a Herculean task. Reconstructing Iraq, working to resolve the conflicts between Israel and Palestine and between India and Pakistan, not to overlook the necessity to quell tensions with

North Korea, through diplomatic recognition and overlapping multilateral security guarantees, should help set the stage for a general political-diplomatic settlement to the crisis. Yet, following preclusive military intervention in Iraq, it appears that concerted US-European-Russian policies will be more, rather than less, difficult to formulate and implement.

Notes

1. 19th century "terrorists" sustained a romantic self-sacrificing, yet moralistic, approach to violence, at least prior to the failure of the 1848 revolutions to change society. The failure of these revolutions to succeed then led to considerations of more drastic, but still limited, actions, until a more general change in social attitudes toward violence came about with concepts of total war and the advent of World War I. See Noel O'Sullivan "Terrorism, Ideology and Democracy" in *Terrorism, Ideology and Revolution*, ed. Noel Sullivan (Sussex: Wheatsheaf Books, 1986), 14–16. See also Norbert Baas, Chapter 10, this book.
2. Hamilton dampened the implications of his statement adding that the means ought to be proportioned to the end, and thus that the persons "from whose agency the attainment of any end is expected ought to possess the means by which it is to be attained."
3. On the domestic and legal implications of the "war on terrorism" on liberal societies, see Laura K. Donahue, "Fear Itself: Counter-terrorism, Individual Rights, and US Foreign Relations Post 9-11" in *Terrorism and Counter-terrorism* ed. Russell D. Howard and Reid L. Sawyer (Gilford: McGraw Hill, 2003).
4. The fiscal 2003 supplemental spending package includes $62.6 billion for operations in Iraq; $8.2 billion for international assistance programs with $2.48 billion for the Iraq Relief and Reconstruction Fund; $4.3 billion for homeland security initiatives; $3 billion for aviation assistance; and $136 million for the legislative branch. The total US Department of Defense budget in 2003 was $358.2 billion, with the new Department of Homeland Security costing $28.2 billion in 2003, not including costs of other agencies involved in security and defense.
5. Gilbert Achcar, *Clash of Barbarisms* (New York: Monthly Review Press, 2002).
6. As Senator Byrd put it: "This Administration has split traditional alliances, possibly crippling, for all time, international order-keeping entities like the United Nations and NATO. [It] has called into question the traditional worldwide perception of the United States as well-intentioned, peacekeeper. [It] has turned the patient art of diplomacy into threats, labeling, and name calling of the sort that reflects quite poorly on the intelligence and sensitivity of our leaders, and which will have consequences for years to come. We may have massive military might, but we cannot fight a global war on terrorism alone… We need the cooperation and friendship of our time-honored allies as well as the newer found friends whom we can attract with our wealth. Our awesome military machine will do us little good if we suffer another devastating attack on our homeland, which severely damages our economy. Our military manpower is already stretched thin and we will need the augmenting support of those nations who can supply troop strength, not just sign letters cheering us on." Senator Byrd, *Senate Remarks: We Stand Passively Mute*, 12 February 2003. http://byrd.senate.gov/byrd_newsroom/byrd_news_feb/news_2003_ february/news_2003_february_9.html.
7. Gen. Wesley Clark described the looming Iraq war as "inevitable" but "like elective surgery" during an interview on Meet the Press Sunday. "This will put us in a colonial position in the Middle East – a huge change for the United States," Wesley Clark: "Iraq

War 'Like Elective Surgery'" NewsMax Staff Monday, Feb. 17, 2003 http://www.newsmax.com/ archives/ articles/2003/2/16/153140. shtml.
8 Hall Gardner, "NATO and the UN," in *A History of NATO*, ed. Gustav Schmidt (Houndmill, Palgrave, 2001).
9 See Hans Morgenthau, *Politics Among Nations: The Struggle for Power and Peace* (New York: Alfred A. Knopf, 1971). On US *exceptionalism*, see Robert Kagan and William Kristol, eds., *Present Dangers* (San Francisco: Encounter Books: 2000). See also Project for a New American Century www.newamericancentury.org.
10 Speech by Dominique de Villepin, "Law, Force, Justice," IISS 27 March 2003 http://www.iiss.org/conferencepage.php?confID=56.
11 James Risen, "Iraq offered U.S. a Deal as the War Loomed," *International Herald Tribune*, 7 November 2003, 1.
12 Costanza Musu, "European Foreign Policy: A Collective Policy or a Policy of Converging Parallels" *European Foreign Affairs Review* 8:35-49, 2003, 49.
13 Charles Krauthammer, "NATO Is Dead, Long Live NATO," *Washington Post* 24 March 2002.
14 See also Hall Gardner, "Aligning for the Future," *Harvard International Review* (Winter 2003). What Francis Bacon called imperial "overflow" may result in new geopolitical conflicts and new imperial commitments that may exacerbate the costs of empire, and subsequent domestic political movements opposed to those policies.
15 The possibility of "overstretch" is a theme of Paul Kennedy: "the US is comprised of slightly less than 5 percent of the world's population; yet it imbibes 27 percent of the world's annual oil production, creates and consumes nearly 30 percent of its Gross World Product and spends a full 40 percent of ALL the world's defense expenditures. The Pentagon's budget is nowadays roughly equal to the defense expenditures of the next nine or ten highest defense-spending nations." See Paul Kennedy, "How America is Viewed by Others - And Does It Matter?," *New Perspectives Quarterly*, 25 February 2002.http://www.digitalnpq.org/global_services/global%20viewpoint/02-25-02.html. A multilateral approach to global defense and security questions involving both "power" and "responsibility" sharing, however, could help off-set the prospects of decline.
16 See Hall Gardner, "NATO, Russia, and Eastern European Security: Beyond the Interwar Analogy" in *NATO Looks East*, ed. Piotr Dutkiewicz and Robert J. Jackson (Westport, CT: Praeger, 1998).
17 This was true despite the fact that Germany's crash nuclear program did not bring the expected results. Jacques Richardson, *War, Science and Terrorism* (London: Frank Cass, 2002).
18 Tom Clancy and Russell Seitz, "Five Minutes Past Midnight," *The National Interest* No. 26 Winter 1991/92.
19 See John Prados, "Iraq: A Necessary War?" Bulletin of Atomic Scientists Vol 59, No. 3, May/June 2003. http://www.thebulletin.org/issues/2003/mj03/mj03 prados. html.
20 Paul Tibbets, who dropped the A-bomb on Hiroshima, killing more than 100,000 people, put the issue quite bluntly: "I don't like to use the word but, you see, in war there is no morality. None. And that goes for women and children... You hate to see them [civilian populations] as collateral damage, *but the weapon is non-selective. It has no discrimination.* That's the way I look at it." (Italics mine.) Michael Kelly "A-Bomb Pilot Backs Kerrey," *Omaha World Herald* (Nebraska), 20 May 2001.
21 Eqbal Ahmad makes a strong point when he argues, "First avoid double standards... Don't condone Israeli terror, Pakistani terror, Nicaraguan terror, El Salvadorean terror, on the one hand, and then complain about Afghan or Palestinian terror. It doesn't work. Try to be even handed. A superpower cannot promote terror in one place and

reasonably expect to discourage terrorism in another place. It won't work in this shrunken world." Eqbal Ahmad, "Terrorism: Theirs and Ours" (1998) in *Terrorism and Counter-Terrorism* ed. Russell D. Howard and Reid L. Sawyer op. cit.

22 I first made this point in my lecture "American neo-conservatism" *Collège InterArmées de Défense*, École Militaire, Paris, 5 May 2003. General Sherman's "March to the Sea" is generally considered one of the first instances of "total warfare." In regard to the analogy to the 1901 Spanish-American war, American intervention in Cuba and the Philippines, much like intervention in Iraq, was, in part, justified by the human rights abuses and concentration camps of Cuban General Wyler as well as the need to "civilize" the Filipinos, in addition to the fact that President McKinley, like President George W. Bush, thought that God supported the intervention.

23 This point ignores weapons such as B-52s with 2,000 pound bombs or 4,000 pound bunker busters, or 15,000 pound Daisy Cutters used to clear large areas in Vietnam and Afghanistan, or the latter's replacement, the 21,000 pound Massive Ordnance Air Blast (MOAB) intended in part to "terrorize" the opponent into submission, or else proposed new nuclear weaponry designed to penetrate underground bunkers.

24 Taras Kuzio, Al-Qaeda Regroups. State Misuse of the Anti-Terrorism Campaign. RFE/RL Volume 3, Number 5, 13 February 2003.

25 Robert Kagan, *Of Paradise and Power* (New York: Knopf, 2003).

26 First using the term, the Clinton Administration had identified Cuba, North Korea, Iran, Iraq and Libya as "rogue" or "backlash states." See Anthony Lake, "Confronting Backlash States," *Foreign Affairs* March/April 1994. The Clinton administration sought an international "concerted effort" to counter such states; the Bush administration has been more willing to act alone. At the same time, Moscow wondered why Pakistan and Saudi Arabia, for example, were not on the list.

27 This is precisely the kind of "demonization" that Hans Morgenthau warned against in his six principles of realism in his textbook *Politics Among Nations*, op.cit., that, at one time, represented the Bible of traditional "realism" used extensively in US international relations classes, but which has been totally ignored by US policy makers.

28 On "ripe for prevention" see Michael Lund, *Preventing Violent Conflicts* (Washington, DC: US Institute for Peace Press, 1996). On dilemmas of conflict resolution and the concept of "ripe for resolution," see I. William Zartman and J. Lewis Rasmussen, eds. *Peacemaking in International Conflict* (Washington, D.C.: U.S. Institute of Peace, 1997). For case studies see Chester A Crocker, Fen Osler Hampson, Pamela Hall, eds. *Herding Cats* (Washington, DC: US Institute for Peace Press, 1999).

29 Hall Gardner "The Genesis of NATO Enlargement and of War 'over' Kosovo" in Hall Gardner, ed. *Central and Southern Europe in Transition* (Praeger, 2000).

30 On the 1993 Vance-Owen plan, see David Owen, *Balkan Odyssey* (New York: Harcourt Brace and Company, 1995). On Kosovo, see William D. Hartung, "Costs of NATO Expansion Revisited," *A World Policy Institute Brief*, 21 April 1999. http://www.worldpolicy.org/projects/arms/reports/april99.html.

31 C. Fred Bergsten, "America's Two Front Economic Conflict" *Foreign Affairs* March/April 2001.

32 Robert Johnson argues that worse case scenarios have a legitimate, but limited purpose; but national policy should be "based upon the most realistic estimates of *both* capabilities and intentions." The risk is "to assume the worse with respect to *both*." (Emphasis mine.) Robert H. Johnson, *Improbable Dangers: US Conceptions of Threat in the Cold War and After* (New York: St. Martins, 1994).

PART I:
THE STRATEGIC IMPACT OF SEPTEMBER 11

Chapter 1

Asymmetrical Conflict: A Critical Assessment

Marwan Bishara

Introduction

In just the last century, two world wars have made nationalism intolerable as a basis for international *legitimacy*—just as the previous wars of religion finished off religion as the basis of the international order in centuries past. The wars of the nations, from 1914 to 1945, thus killed the nation as an organizing principle for the society of states. World War II, in particular, entirely discredited nationalism; the Cold War then eliminated communism and the idea that the state could play a role as an economic manager.[1]

The fall of the Berlin wall has finally accelerated an American-led process of globalization, which is reshaping the nature of geo-politics in general and along the North-South division in particular. This process has begun to compromise the sovereignty of states and has led to the emergence of a new "market state." In the meantime, the globalization process is re-inventing the nature of war and conflict.

The hostility of US-led neo-liberal globalization towards borders and sovereignty will tend to weaken, destabilize or eradicate states in the south, a process that will generate further chaos and fertilize new breeding grounds for new conflicts, wars and acts of terrorism. The ensuing violence will know no national or geographic boundaries, no regulation and possess no ethical standards. It will possess a logic and values of its own that will defy all conventions of war, as well as the UN Charter. The perpetrators of these acts of violence will not fight "fairly;" they will not exclude any body or any place from its targets, and they will completely reject any judiciary authority.

In return, the burgeoning number of *asymmetrical* threats and actions will further unite northern "liberal democracies" as they appoint themselves as "global governors." The latter will attempt to use NATO, the European Union, and other alliances or coalitions in order to help expedite the erection of new dividing walls, similar to that which was erected during the Cold War, but between the West and North versus the South. The effort to erect new walls, however, will not contain the resulting tensions and conflict; nor will immigration officers or border police deter the latter. As products of globalization, *asymmetrical* threats will not be restricted to certain geographic regions; they will be as global as globalization itself.

Eventually, this globalization-produced instability will transform the "liberal democracies" themselves. Contrary to the prediction of the triumph of the liberal free market democracies above all other historical systems as the so-called "end of history" (Francis Fukuyama's central theme), *asymmetrical* conflicts and threats, as well as *asymmetrical* values, could well transform the liberal market economies into very different systems of relations, perhaps making them more centralized and more authoritarian. This is especially true in the so-called "Third World," where at best illiberal "democracies" could emerge.[2]

New Fault Lines of Conflict

The process of globalization is transforming the international system in two paradoxical ways: On the one hand, it is connecting people, harmonizing standards (at times at the expense of diversity), universalizing ideas, empowering business, popularizing access to information and weakening geographical borders. On the other hand, it is also erecting new barriers between the world's centers and peripheries, between its rich, developed, well-connected "northern flanks" and its southern poor, which are divided regions with ever growing populations and underdevelopment.

The center of the world system is developing fast with innovation and dynamism while the periphery is stagnating (with the exception of China) and sinking into deeper poverty and chaos. This is not the direct result of exploitation, as was the case in the colonialist days, but rather because of the indirect manipulation, competition and domination by the sub-centers of the North.

In certain cases, the process of underdevelopment takes place by the mere placing of a country or region far from the center through boycott or containment or the shifting of financial investments. In other cases, as in the example of eastern Europe, fast track development is guaranteed through the process of inclusion into the center of world system, through integration into the European Union (as well as NATO).

Globalization is also a manifestation of "market totalitarianism." As such, the US-led globalization process has been generating sweeping economic and social processes that are destined to compromise an individual state's ability to manage and regulate its community's economic and political affairs, or to guarantee the economic or physical safety and well-being of its citizens.

As a consequence, people tend to find shelter or meaning in pre- or post- state identities such as religion, ethnicity or cults. Ethnicity is making its way to the center of the political discourse as it looks for legitimacy that has been lost by the state as the former authority. At times, this political discourse uses violence as a means by which to galvanize sentiments and obtain legitimacy.

Geopolitics today observes and justifies the struggle for identity against globalization. It activates cultural "identity politics" and not just socio-economic factors. Since the state has failed to provide well-*being in its fullest sense* for its citizens in the many of the regions of the so-called "developing" world, the struggles have been transferred to a geocultural level that puts "ethnicity" at the top of the list of actors.

Geopolitics has long shown that the 'map of nations' is not the same as the 'map of states'. And as nationality and ethnicity retake the initiative in the face of retreating state sovereignties, geopolitics is influenced as much by ethno-politics, irredentism, as by geography. As globalization united the world into one market place and re-divides along both old/new ethnic lines, the geo-politics of violence is necessarily transformed in the process. Moreover, today's world is shaped by multinational corporations, religions that are organized across continents, transnational pressure groups, as well as communications satellites, as much as by the voluntary military intervention of individual states.

Like the global market, *asymmetrical* war sees no state boundaries; it has no national identity, no geographic location or address, and it sees no limits to potential reproduction. Its outreach is that of the market and its instruments are those of globalization; its targets are the soft or weak points of globalization such as confidence, trust, free flow of goods and services, harmony, etc.

French sociologist Alain Joxe has suggested that:

> Despite its confusion, our civilization can still be mapped. It is, in spite of its universal dimension, still composed of 'neighbors' grouped together on the surface to live on the sphere...At the same time, there is a discreet generalization, a spreading of violence, limits, enclosures, shelters, camps, barbed wire, patrol dogs.[3]

Since America is the leader in the globalization era, its example is instructive for the future. America's conventional/symmetrical type war is in the process of retreating in favor of wars against non-state or failed state actors. The 1991 and 2003 wars against the Iraqi regime of Saddam Hussein belonged to the previous era of conventional petrol-military wars. Thanks to its revolution in military affairs (RMA), Washington's superiority in the conventional warfare will deter any other state leadership from confronting America directly in the battlefield. Saddam's Iraq did not pose any direct threat to America.

Because of its military superiority, Washington reckons that new types of threats to its global power in the post-Cold War era will emerge from remaining "rogue states" as well as from transnational non-state actors: It is believed that both could resort to weapons of mass destruction (WMD). Those threats to the world economic and geo-political center (the US and its NATO allies) will mostly, but not exclusively, originate from the periphery (the underdeveloped regions) and will spring from both internal domestic, as well as external foreign, sources. America's superiority in the last Gulf War of March 2003 will deter its traditional state enemies from meeting it in the battlefields of war, but it will consequently push its opponents towards finding new *asymmetrical* ways of confronting US, European and NATO interests—in down town areas, residential neighborhoods, airports etc.

Asymmetrical conflicts will be exacerbated by the international and domestic fault lines that have been dividing the world's communities, between north and south as well as within prosperous center and their belts of poverty— the periphery around cosmopolitan cities. These conflicts will also be nourished by a number of sources that are internationalized through the process of globalization, such as domestic and regional criminality, cross border smuggling, and economic disparities. They will be further inflamed by religious and ethnic phobias, among other factors, as well as by ultra-nationalism and religious fundamentalism. Their global outreach will be assisted by easy access to technologies and information systems.

Rethinking War

Since the collapse of the Soviet Union and the end of the essentially bi-polar global system, new "unconventional" wars have killed approximately four million people, mostly civilians. Coupled with the spread of apocalyptic and transnational terrorism *these conflicts have largely discredited the semi-sacred Clausewitzian theory of war that has, as a whole, become the encompassing paradigm for the understanding of conflict.*

After Clausewitz's disciples failed to explain guerrilla insurgency, nuclear strategy, ethnic conflicts, narco-violence and international terrorism through the lenses of that Prussian strategist, new strategic thinkers emerged soon after the end of the Cold War to offer un-Clausewitzian ways of thinking about war. Some reckon that (1) when we fight, we produce wealth; others argue that (2) we become the way we fight. A third group believes that (3) war is a question of culture.

In regard to the first thesis, in the *Transformation of War*, Israeli (originally Dutch) historian Martin van Creveld reverses the casual relationship between the actor and the act: how and why people fight, he argues, help to determine their political, economic, and even their social organization.

In regard to the second thesis, the British historian John Keegan tries to study non-European wars in *A History of Warfare* only to show that Clausewitz was, in fact, a Euro-centric. Much like Van Creveld,[4] he begins his book by underscoring his belief that "war is not the continuation of policy by other means."[5]

In the other (but not contradictory) direction, in regard to the third thesis, the futurist American economists Alvin and Heidi Toffler claim in *War and Anti-War*, that the way we make war "reflects the way we make wealth."[6] The core argument of the Tofflers is that a third historic economic transformation is under way (the first was the invention of agriculture, the second, the industrial revolution). The emergence of "Third Wave" economics "based on knowledge rather than conventional raw materials and physical labor" will pave the way to "niche wars;" that is, the military use of space; robotic combat; nano-technology; non-lethal weapons; and cyberwar. In the process, third wave economics will transform all aspects of human life, including warfare.

There is no doubt that the American Revolution in Military Affairs (RMA) has already begun to produce results in above direction. America's superior military advantage over all other states, and particularly its competitors in Moscow or Beijing, and *vis-à-vis* its opponents in the Third World, has reinforced their conviction that there is no conventional military response to America's global power, and there will not be in the distant future. Enter *asymmetry*.

Asymmetrical conflicts—domestic, regional and international—have, in fact, proven far more capable of obtaining their strategic objectives than have more traditional forms of conventional warfare. In fact, the latter has proven a failure since the end of the Second World War. The Arab-Israeli conflicts, the Gulf wars, that Argentine-English war over the Malvinas/Falklands, the Pakistani-Indian conflict, and even America's Korean and Vietnam wars, have, among others, largely proven incapable of fulfilling their political objectives.

By contrast, urban warfare and other forms of unconventional warfare have, however, proved their utility. Whether it has been the Afghani (and Chechen) resistance to the Soviet invasion, or the Lebanese (and Palestinian) resistance of the Israeli invasion and occupation, or the Vietnamese resistance against the American invasion etc, these have all proved capable of winning wars against conventional armies.

If history is any guide, then globalization will further internationalize this form of warfare by non-armies, or else by non-state actors such as guerrillas, mafias, terrorist organizations, narco-drug traffickers, religious fundamentalists and radial nationalists. These organizations are most likely to make their presence manifest in political groupings, but will remain secret in their organization. They will be constructed on charismatic rather than institutional lines, and motivated less by "professionalism" than by fanatical, ideologically-based, or criminal-hierarchical loyalties. New York (9/11), Gaza, South Lebanon, and east Los Angeles and Oklahoma city, Somalia, Afghanistan as well as Sarajevo, Belfast, Colombia, Angola, Congo, represent the new forms of warfare.

Asymmetrical Enemies

Asymmetric wars—especially transnational terrorism and the war on terrorism—have no fixed *champ de bataille*, as asymmetrical enemies find their home in the gray areas of globalization, between the unchecked power of the neo-liberal global economy and the weakened "sovereignty of states." The attacks of 9/11 are *asymmetric* attacks *par excellence*. And by the same token, America's unconventional/asymmetrical and offensive brand of war-on-terrorism against the likes of Ben Laden's Al-Qaeda is a preview of how America will fight future asymmetrical wars using its new "preemptive" doctrine that was officially announced by president Bush in October 2002.[7]

As in all major wars, 9/11 and its aftermath, is an extension of the past as much as it represents a rupture from Cold War style confrontations. Washington had trained Al-Qaeda type fighters in Afghanistan during the 1980s in order to fight the Soviet occupying forces, which had invaded the country in 1979. The alliance between the two was bitterly interrupted when the Soviets pulled out and Americans abandoned the country, only to station huge hundreds of thousands of soldiers in Saudi Arabia. This was considered a betrayal by the "Arab Afghans" (anti-Soviet "freedom fighters" who may be neither Arab nor Afghan) who vowed to carry the fight to the other "Satan," the Americans. As CIA graduates, those Arab Afghans knew how to deal a blow to a super power. Their secretive organization and careful planning has been a testimony as to how well they have been trained by the CIA in the tricks of asymmetrical warfare.

On 9/11 America was caught by surprise. Many of its experts had predicted similar kind of scenarios, but Washington was not ready to fight this sort of war. For decades it spent several trillion dollars in order to prepare for conventional wars against rival states. The collapse of the Soviet Union and the Warsaw pact denied the United States the option of fighting those kind of conventional wars for which it had prepared heavily. Previews of the immediate threats to America's global governance had predicted confrontation with primarily 20th century type enemies armed with 21st century instruments. These threats were defined as any combination of rogue or failed states, and involved weapons of mass destruction and transnational terrorism (excluding cyber terrorism, space threats and so on, from the discussion).

In order to save face, the Bush administration has begun to use its war machine against the new asymmetrical conflicts, and has combined its threats into one strategic "evil." Here, enter the "axis of evil" states, Iran, Iraq and North Korea, whom the Bush Administration has defined as a threat to US national security. They combine the characteristics of a conventional threat, as well as a potential unconventional threat, as the proliferators of WMD and supporters of terrorist groups. (Add to that the fact that these regimes have resisted open borders as well as the free market policies and ideas of the United States and the West in general.) However the "axis of evil" countries are not, by themselves, *asymmetrical* enemies, even if they are regarded as rogue states.[8]

In addition to the "axis of evil," America and its allies or coalition partners have all been looking for ways to tackle the residuals of the Cold War enemies and deter or stop them from using new technologies to attack Western targets and interests. After the fall of the Berlin wall, many of the conflicts that benefited from Cold War patronage as well as in countries such as Columbia, Angola, Afghanistan, Somalia, not to overlook in a number of African and Asian countries, have now found a substitute in a new source of income engineered by narco-trafficking, arms, drugs, diamonds, prostitution, and other forms of smuggling, as well as various criminal activities enhanced by easy access in the global market place.

America and Asymmetry

In the decade following the fall of the Berlin wall, the country who won the Cold War and who was best fit to define and lead the globalization process, the United States, began to translate its neo-liberal global power into global governance through a combined approach of mostly geo-economics management supported by geo-strategic power (i.e. projection of forces) whenever necessary. For eight years, the Clinton administration adopted in principle geo-economic approach to world affairs initially guided by Anthony Lake's doctrine of enlarging markets and democracies.[9]

For decades the US spent trillions of dollars to ensure minimum casualties in any confrontation. Its huge spending in Europe that topped over $100 billion annually, stalemate in Korea and defeat in the Vietnam War where the US spent hundreds of thousands of dollars for each dead Vietnamese fighter and still suffered tens of thousand of dead. But by the early 1990s, in the Persian Gulf war, the US kept American casualties low. With rapid, massive bombardment from afar (the Colin Powell doctrine), the US hoped for zero casualties in future symmetrical or conventional wars. Its missiles and superior fighters, supported with the most sophisticated airborne intelligence, could guarantee such a zero-death result by being capable of inflicting unbearable destruction on the enemy.

Before the end of the end of the Republican administration from 1989-91, Bush administration officials launched a search for a new strategy for America in the post-Cold War era. While the Pentagon continued to develop a new doctrine in the 1990s, those Republicans who launched the search for a new strategy prior to the entry of the neo-liberals into the White House from 1992-2000, continued their parallel research to that of the Pentagon for a geo-strategic based foreign policy in the various think-tanks in Washington, DC.

Targeting the Pentagon and the World Trade Center—America's symbols of its economic pride and military arrogance—was the ultimate asymmetric scenario the Pentagon had in mind when it decreed an emerging post-Cold War geo-politics in the age of globalization. Washington, trying to adapt to an evolving, globalising world, had been in the midst of introducing a revolution in military affairs (RMA). This revolution was not aimed at a particular enemy but rather at any potential threat in a changing world. The configurations of power, however, have changed with globalization and the end of half a century of cold war in the north and hot war in the south.

The Transformation of Threats: From Enemies to Dangers

As the United States accumulates new means to achieve global hegemony as a unique super power, it opens the door for new threats stemming from competitors who need to catch up in order to defend themselves against future hegemony. America therefore has to insure its maximum safety net and precautions within the new power domain and structure that it is in the process of creating. Hence for the time being, Washington continues to compete with a virtual reality, which, in effect, comes down to its own imagination in regard to envisioning scenarios of the new threats to its system of domination. It competes with itself to improve its performance. As Rumsfeld put it in *Foreign Affairs*: "Our challenge is to defend our nation against the unknown, the uncertain, the unseen, and the unexpected."[10] During his presidential campaign, George Bush had already spoke of threats coming from "plutonium merchants, crime syndicates, car bombers, cyber-terrorists, drug cartels, biological, chemical, and nuclear terrorism."[11]

In February 2001, before a Senate committee on world threats, CIA director George Tenet said what struck him most forcefully was "the accelerating pace of change in so many arenas that affect our nations interests."[12] To the US, *asymmetry* means Osama Bin Laden and other international terrorists, mafiosi and drug dealers. But the idea also covers non-state actors like those the US has already encountered in Somalia, Kosovo, and Lebanon in 1983, when a bomb killed 239 US Marines. Those analysts who think the future will only be asymmetrical propose a total rethink of the usefulness of billion-dollar fighter planes and advanced frigates, if two men and a boat could kill 17 men and damage the USS Cole (12 October 2000 of the cost of Aden), or if American embassies in Africa had become such easy targets as in Dar es Salaam and Nairobi.

Asymmetry must, however, be distinguished from *di-symmetry*, meaning a quantitative difference in firepower and force, a strong state against a weak one (the US against Iraq). Asymmetry is about the *qualitative* difference in the means, values and style of the new enemies. Once a power like the US insists on exclusive superiority in world affairs, as well as in conventional warfare, its disadvantaged enemies resort to unconventional asymmetrical means to fight it; they seek to avoid its strengths and concentrate on its vulnerabilities. It is a form of fourth generation warfare, stateless or asymmetric, which to be fought by an opponent who might have a non-nation-state base, linked by an ideology or religion.

From this perspective, America's approach leaves many questions unanswered. Who, aside from Bin Laden, who Washington groomed during the 1980s fight against the "evil empire" in Afghanistan would become the future enemy? It is dubious that mafias and drug-dealers will be targeted: hostilities are bad for business. Unless Washington intends to bomb one of the rogue states, why would their leaders launch a missile against the US when they would be punished like Libya, or Iraq over the last decade? To what extent has America created new enemies, and just how dangerous, beyond the 11 September outrage, are they? How is this terrorism different from that which Arab nations, or certain European countries, have faced over 20 years? Is it a *qualitative* difference or just (if one can say just) *quantitative*?

The above questions cannot be answered within the same logic that governed past US administrations. Ultimately the systems created by the Cold War and the neo-liberal global governance in its aftermath have been a source of conflict. These cannot be understood through a linear Newtonian logic of cause and effect. Rather a globalized and networked world with security and economics that recognizes no borders could only be understood as complex organs or interactive living cells that feed into each other. America's structures and networks of the Cold War and of globalization have been producing their own nemesis that has also been part of transnational systems produced by globalization.

It is the entire international system that needs an overhaul.

Not Fighting Fair

The Pentagon says the new enemies do not fight fair; their strategy, based on conditions in a globalised world, uses all possible sophisticated modern means: communication, transportation, information, psychological terror, international media and the internet. In their arsenal are also such low-tech weapons as penknives, fishing boats, homemade explosives and civilian planes. As we have seen, these work. Even though these enemies must be based somewhere, no permanent location can be assigned to them, because they have no permanent home, their network is dispersed. The world is both their address and area of operation. All the characteristics that the American strategists attribute to the new model asymmetric enemy add up to a profile of Osama Bin Laden.

Asymmetric enemies have a common interest: weakening state sovereignties and boosting international market forces. In this they are like McDonalds, CNN and AOL. All use the gray areas of a globalised world, the gaps in the legal structure; they seek to ensure maximum profits and escape the accountability that results from constitutional or democratic *legitimacy*. In this sense, *asymmetric* enemies are creatures of the neo-liberal version of globalisation. They have more room for manoeuvre than states. That is why the American media describe Bin Laden not just as a political Islamist, rooted in a particular society, but as the representative of a new cosmopolitan Islam that is a global threat, like the pan-Islamist movement of Hassan al-Turabi (now in prison in Sudan). This movement is thought to be confronting the US, to weaken or destroy its power.

Yet should an asymmetric enemy be distinguished from a state and that state's intelligence network? Is it possible to organise a movement of international violence without some state support? It is not clear how a new enemy could reduce its operations to being only "virtual." And even enemies whose heartland is an ideology need physical space somewhere for their logistics and tools. Their bank accounts must be kept somewhere, too.

What about the rogue or failed states? The intervention in Somalia taught the US a hard lesson. When, in October 1993, Hussein Aydid humiliated the US, killing 17 American soldiers, the Clinton administration became convinced that it could not manage, let alone win, a war against militias not accountable to the conventions of a state. Operation Just Cause in Panama in December 1989 was also an asymmetric war, even though it was the largest American operation since Vietnam. It was meant to recapture Manuel Antonio Noriega and it succeeded. The US went on to target Farah Aideed, Slobodan Milosevic and Radovan Karadzic, Mullah Omar—all of whom it considered to be more like bandits than heads of state. Such operations were no different from US operations during the Cold War targeting South American or the Middle Eastern leaders.

The Bush administration had evidently adopted the second approach of regime change or attacks against "rogue states" much before September 11. Its objective was not to dry the swamps that foster terrorism but rather disinfect them. In other words, we are in for a long-term strategy of "ending" uncooperative regimes and doing away with those who are not "with us." Hence, Islamists have become irredeemable and Saddam Hussein and Osama bin Laden constitute irrational menaces to human civilization despite the fact that these two were once Washington's allies against Iranian fundamentalism and Soviet communism. Both Moslem leaders are hostile to America's interests, they were to become part of an "axis of evil" designated by Washington as the successor to the evil empire—the Soviet Union.

So what is new? Perhaps what is new is the possibility of deploying many new non-orthodox methods of prevention and dissuasion that were impossible, or illegitimate, before 11 September 2001. Less than a week after September 11, Congress lifted the ban on assassinating foreign leaders.[13] An upgraded level of American violence was then made possible.

The Geo-Economics of Asymmetry

The geoeconomic school believed that the dynamics of underdevelopment produce economic disparities that feed instability, international crime, and immigration. Using its high stakes in the World Bank and IMF, Washington looked to impose structural reforms in developing countries that would allow economic liberalization and privatization and open the way for the expansion of free market economic and liberal democracy around the world. This was to be the program long sought by Washington during the Cold War and which had become possible after the collapse of the Soviet Union and the Warsaw Pact.

In 1992, three years after the fall of the Berlin Wall, America gave Bill Clinton and his domestic and economic program priority over the Republican post-Cold War geo-strategic program. "It's the economy, stupid" became the slogan of the new era of a militarily victorious America, not only within the continent but also in its foreign policy. The neo-liberals who emerged in the early 1980s as the carriers of the renewal of the democratic party stood behind Clinton and his vice-president, Al Gore. They envisioned a geo-economics based foreign policy. After its victory in the Cold War and the war against Iraq, American turned to the economic dividend of their victory in both the Cold and Gulf War.

As previously mentioned, this new strategy of "enlargement" was best articulated by Anthony Lake, a Professor who served in the Carter administration in the 1970s and who became Clinton National Security advisor in 1992. Their program became the central agenda of the first four years, in expanding democracies and free market economies in the world, especially in Eastern Europe but also co-opting the important rising Asian star, China, into the capitalist mode of production.

The theory of American scholar and Rand Corporation researcher, Francis Fukuyama similarly became the incarnation of a triumphant American capitalism and geo-economics. His leap into the future with huge waves were titled in his famous work, *The End of History and The Last Man* as the final triumph of liberalism and free market capitalism over all other systems as viable means to organize the society. His theory claimed to bypass the actual and residual conflicts of the old world, which we have been living since the fall of the Berlin Wall. The goals of democratic liberalism have translated into reality especially in the ten plus Eastern European countries who were motivated by membership in the European Union and who were obliged to follow the strict criteria of the EU. The Soviet Union and China have also moved in that direction, but have so far fallen short on the American-Western modern of Liberal Democracy.

In the "developing" South, however, these policies have led to contraction in social services, the elimination of subsidies for basic foodstuffs, and the dumping of foreign goods as protection for domestic industries ends. Coupled with state corruption, these policies has amplified the belts of poverty around Cairo, Casablanca, Tehran but also in Moscow, Warsaw and other centers that have become fertile ground for local and international crime and terrorism. Instead of a well-balanced development, informal economies based on corruption, crime, narco-trafficking and other smuggling have become an important segment of those economies and a central source of "alternative development."

Today, a billion people, or almost one sixth of the world's population, live in areas mired in civil or regional wars, or risk falling into such conflict. As many of these conflicts sustain themselves through criminal and other illegal activities, they could easily over spill into rich countries through drugs, disease, terrorism and even immigration.[14] The UN has estimated that drug trade rose to $500 billion or some 8 percent of the world trade or larger than oil. The overall profit from criminal activities has reached $750 billion. Many of the Asian, Africa and even east European countries became involved in this informal economy making it a central engine of development. In countries like Angola, the formal economy was no more 10 percent of the real GNP of the country, the rest is smuggling and crime; while in Mozambique it reached no more than 50 percent of the GNP. Even on places like Kenya and Russia, the in-formal economy climbed to some 40 percent of the GNP.[15]

Drugs, arms and oil are the three most internationally traded commodities in the world. No wonder, the Middle East, central Asia, and Latin America, who intensively produce and consume all three, are seen as potential disaster areas for asymmetrical conflicts in a globalized world, which is at once coming together and drawing apart. So too failed and weakened African states, who are struggling with civil and tribal wars, and who are illegally trading diamonds and minerals and buying arms, are increasingly becoming fertile ground for future continental asymmetrical threats. Somalia, Kenya, Angola and the Ivory Coast are a few recent examples. Those who can smuggle drugs and arms could also smuggle explosives.

The Geo-strategic School

The other school underlined the geo-strategic dimension and pinpointed cultural antagonism as a source of conflict—fundamentalism versus free markets, jihad versus McDonald's, and eventually a "clash of civilizations." Unfortunately, the fixed and dogmatic view of "the other" has easily slipped into de-humanization in time of conflict and slippery slides into war. Not only have we seen bloody ethnic conflicts emerge in the cases of the Balkans, India-Pakistan, Israel-Palestine and Rwanda, etc., but also in North-South relations.

Samuel Huntington, took the opposite route to that of Fukuyama, and instead, foresaw a world advancing forward towards a tribal past in his famous work, *The Clash of Civilizations*. Once the East-West rivalry was over in 1989, the world, specifically the West, would be pushed into a tribal planetary conflict between the big tribes-civilizations, particularly the Christian West, Moslems and the Chinese. (Huntington's central hypothesis is "that the fundamental source of conflict in this new world will not be primarily ideological or primarily economic. The great divisions among humankind and the dominating source of conflict will be cultural. Nation states will remain the most powerful actors in world affairs, but the principal conflicts of global politics will occur between nations and groups of different civilizations. The clash of civilizations will dominate global politics. The fault lines between civilizations will be the battle lines of the future."[16])

As for Thomas L. Friedman, his attempt to propose a geo-economic understanding of Globalization, as the central "big thing," but not necessarily the only thing, as to understand the world we live in with all its ups and downs. He sees a new "system" of globalization at conflict with other older "power politics, chaos, clashing civilizations, and liberalism. And the drama of the post-Cold War world is the interactions between this new system and all these old passions and aspirations."[17] Hence Friedman demonstrates the tensions between those powers of the past whom Huntington's talks about and the forces of the future that Fukuyama decrees: those backlash forces that pull it backwards and those looking to advance liberalism through globalization.

It is, in fact, the conflict between a First Wave that tries to pull the world ahead with it (always trailing behind of course), and the Second Wave of liberalism within the states' power structures, and of course in direct interactions with the First Waves who have hardly joined globalization. But Friedman, a prolific reductionist, insists early on that in reality "there is no more First World, Second World and Third World" and then he adds with certainty "there's now only the Fast World—the world of the wide-open plain—and the Slow world—the world of those who either fall by the way-side or choose to live way from the plain in some artificially walled-off valley of their own, because they find the Fast world to be too fast, too scary, too homogenizing."[18]

As the West has continued to exploit the resources of the Third world, Africa, Latin America and Asia, notably in the fields of oil, minerals and drugs, new low intensity conflicts and wars were proliferated in Africa (diamond wars) in Latin America and Asia financed by narco-trafficking, smugglings and other criminal activities. Certainly the drug smuggling implication in the financing of Al-Qaeda have been evident. The same applies to the Lebanese Hizbollah, Columbian FARC, Angola's UNITA, etc.

The American and the Israeli governments have been taking the works of the Tofflers and Martin van Creveld to plan a future force including training, doctrine, and leader development. America, with its revolution in military affairs is preparing the next wave of warfare, with all that entails in reorganizing the armed forces, revolutionizing the relationships between military and business, developing new weapons and new methods of warfare. Israel, which claims rich experience as a "first wave" country fighting "third wave" societies, has attempted to contribute to the American RMA, through the understanding of asymmetry.

As a result of its 1970-80 partnership or client-patron relationship with the United States, Israel's regional and international policy began to go through major transformation as a result of its continued dependency on the United States at the advent of the 1990s. However, the threat to Israel status *vis-à-vis* the United States as a "strategic asset" by the end of the Cold War only added to Israel's insecurity. The possibility that America would abandon Israel now that the Soviet Union collapsed became an Israeli strategic pre-occupation.

The ensuing of the Gulf War after the Iraqi invasion of Kuwait in August 1990, underlined Israeli dependency on Washington. Not only did Israel need protection against incoming Iraqi Scud missiles, but it was also bound not to retaliate against Iraq because of American exigencies (and US fears of alienating Arab states in the coalition against Iraq) as the commander of the international coalition against Iraq. Since that time, Israeli insecurity has only compounded. America's destruction of Iraq's missile capabilities did not improve Israel's self-confidence. Its dependency on the United States has only deepened.

As the US and Israel began to interact, two strategic American schools of thought emerged with roots in the Israeli experience and with important ramifications on the "Jewish state." One charted a lasting triumph of liberal economy and a new era of American global governance in an age of globalization. And the other envisioned a return to the past conflict of pre-ideological global tribal conflicts of civilizations. The Middle East figured high on the agendas of both American strategic approaches. One the one hand, the geo-economic school charted a map of resolving the conflict and opening an era of a "New Middle East" based on economic cooperation and Israeli economic supremacy. And, on the other hand, there was Israel as a leader in the upcoming American/Western confrontation with the Islamic world.

When the Intifadah broke out in the year 2000, Martin van Creveld insisted that Israel will eventually lose. As it fights the weak, it becomes weaker and eventually the Palestinians would win through attrition. In his words, "... it's always a question of the relationship of forces. If you are strong, and you are fighting the weak for any period of time, you are going to become weak yourself." And he adds "The same happened to the British when they were here ... the same happened to the French in Algeria ... the same happened to the Americans in Vietnam ... the same happened to the Soviets in Afghanistan ... the same happened to so many people that I can't even count them."[19]

Needless to say, Martin van Creveld's thesis is anything but what the Israelis are trying to sell to America, but his perspective deals with Israeli experience between the First and Third Wave countries. As far as van Creveld is concerned, all Israeli measures have failed and matters are only getting worse: "between 1957 and 1967 the number of Israelis who lost their lives as a result of enemy action was just thirty-five. Now we pray for a week in which we shall not lose thirty-five people."

In giving his support to the logic of intifada as the only means to pressure Israel to change its policies (as a ceasefire would provide security for the Israelis, but would not provide statehood for the Palestinians), van Creveld shows how the tactics of the Israeli repression are failing to achieve their ends, and are, in fact, counter-productive, contrary to what Clausewitzian analysis would expect. In regarding the utility of a full military solution such as, blowing up the Palestinian home, or razing the camps, for example, van Creveld argues that "... a home that has been demolished offers even better shelter than a home that stands intact. The Americans in Vietnam tried it. They killed between two-and-a-half and three million Vietnamese. I don't see that it helped them much."

Van Creveld proposes the following as possible solutions:

> A, waiting for a suitable opportunity ... B, doing whatever it takes to restore the balance of power between us and the Palestinians ... C, removing 90% of the causes of the conflict, by pulling out ... and D, building a wall between us and the other side, so tall that even the birds cannot fly over it ... so as to avoid any kind of friction for a long long time in the future.

Van Creveld arrives at the conclusion that option "D" building a wall is the best option, but argues against the idea that Israeli forces should attempt to remain on both sides. He predicts that 95 percent of Israeli settlers will return to Israel, thus pulling out, and accepting a two-state solution. At the same time, building a wall will not at all solve the problem, which will require the two sides to learn to cooperate.

Conclusions: Becoming Like "Them"

Armed forces, as well as the state, are growing obsolete. As territorial states armed with conventional armies prove unable to decisively defeat low-intensity conflict, they will embark instead on perpetual war, which paradoxically leads both the state and the armies to fade away. "The most important single demand that any political community must meet," writes van Creveld, "is the demand for protection." If the territorial state cannot protect its citizens, "then clearly it does not have a future in front of it."

Van Creveld, however, goes further than anything expected. He argues not only that conventional, modern forces will fight against guerrillas and terrorists; but, moreover, as low-intensity conflict becomes the dominant form of armed violence, all armed forces will move toward a guerrilla and irregular configuration. He actually concludes that "we" may become more like "them" instead of how most Americans conventionally think, i.e. that they will become "like us."

In fact for many years, America contended at least officially and diplomatically that its enemies must join the so-called "civilized" world of law-abiding nations. The United States had used the UN and its Security Council to advance its goals all the while Israel was shunned as outlawed state by the international community, which, itself, did not attempt to fully implement international law. Yet, nothing has come out of this double standard but repeated cycles of vengeance. It is time for America to conclude, as Israel did, that it will end up behaving like its enemies, and that it will become just like them—if the "war on terrorism" goes on unabated.

Notes

1   Philip Bobbitt, *The Shield of Achilles: War, Peace, and the Course of History* (New York: Alfred A. Knopf, 2002).
2   Fareed Zakaria, *The Future of Freedom: Illiberal Democracy at Home and Abroad* (Norton and Company, 2003).
3   Alain Joxe, *Voyages aux sources de la Guerre* (Paris: PUF, 1991).
4   Martin van Creveld, *Transformation of War* (Free Press, 1991), ix.

5   John Keegan, *A History of Warfare* (Vintage, 1994), 3.
6   Alvin and Heidi Toffler, *War and Anti-War* (Warner Books, 1995).
7   Dr. Condoleezza Rice Discusses President's National Security Strategy, Waldorf Astoria Hotel, New York, New York, October 1, 2002. http://www.whitehouse.gov/news/releases/2002/10/20021001-6.html. See also, National Security Presidential Directive-17/ HSPD "National Strategy to Combat Weapons of Mass Destruction" (12 December 2002).
8   David Frum, *The Right Man: The Surprise Presidency of George W. Bush* (Random House, 2003). "Gerson wanted to use the theological language that Bush had made his own since Sept. 11, so 'axis of hatred' became 'axis of evil'."
9   Anthony Lake, Assistant to the President for National Security Affairs, "From Containment to Enlargement," Johns Hopkins University, School of Advanced International Studies (Washington, D.C.: September 21, 1993).
10 Donald Rumsfeld, "Transforming the Military," *Foreign Affairs* May/June 2002.
11 George Tenet, "Worldwide Threat 2001: National Security in a Changing World" (7 February 2001), 8. http://www.cia.gov/terrorism/ pub_statements_terrorism.html.
12 Frances Fitzgerald, "George Bush & the World," *The New York Review of Books*, September 26, 2002.
13 *Le Monde*, 18 September 2001.
14 A recent World Bank report underlines the relationship between civil war and low income, economic stagnation and dependency on primary commodity exports. Civil wars fuel global scourges such as smuggling, illegal narcotics, AIDS and international terrorism. In fact, civil war zones are the source of 95 percent of illegal narcotic production. Paul Collier, "How to stem civil wars: It's the economy, stupid," *International Herald Tribune*, May 21, 2003.
15 Mark Duffield, *Global Governance and the New Wars: The Merging of Development and Security* Palgrave Macmillan, 2001, 141–43.
16 Samuel Huntington, *"The Clash of Civilizations?" Foreign Affairs* Summer, 1993.
17 Thomas L. Friedman, *The Lexus and the Olive Tree* (Random House, 2000) p. xxi.
18 Ibid. 46.
19 Jennifer Byrne, Interview with Martin van Creveld Broadcast (20/3/2002) http://www.abc.net.au/foreign/stories/s511530.htm. Citations are from this interview.

Chapter 2

From "Balance" to "Imbalance" of Terror[*]

Hall Gardner

Introduction

The American concept of *deterrence* during the Cold War (and up until the Clinton and Bush administrations) can best be defined as an essentially *defensive stance intended to sustain the status quo*. Deterrence seeks to persuade one's opponent that the costs/risks of a given course of action might outweigh the expected benefits. The purpose of deterrence is not merely to assess the opponent's intentions, but to attempt to ultimately change the opponent's immediate or long-term intentions and *to avert* offensive conventional or non-conventional military actions—by means of manipulating threats.

The official American view states that deterrence depends upon "overwhelming symbols of power and force." It argues for the need to develop retaliatory defense capabilities involving survivability, mobility and agility, and increasingly stealth, including the capabilities to engage appropriate forces in the region of conflict as rapidly as possible. The official view also emphasized the necessity to show willingness and resolve to engage such forces. Although nuclear forces are not the only factor in the deterrence equation, the fundamental purpose of US nuclear forces is to deter an enemy's use of Weapons of Mass Destruction (WMD) and serve as a hedge against the emergence of an overwhelming conventional threat.[1]

The September 11 "terrorist" strikes against the Pentagon and World Trade Center, two "overwhelming symbols" of American military and economic power, were, consequently, strikes against the very deterrent power of the US itself. These actions were thus intended to undermine

---

[*] An earlier version of this paper "From Myth of Deterrence to Myth of Assured Security," was delivered at a seminar held at the *Institut de Hauts Etudes de Défense Nationale*, 6 November 2001, at the Ecole Militaire, Paris.

American confidence in its nuclear and conventional deterrent capability, at the same time that such actions represented a warning of further acts of "terrorism" if the US continued to engage in actions and policies opposed by the perpetrators of this heinous crime.

From Myth of Assured Destruction to Myth of Assured Security

During the Cold War, American nuclear deterrent strategy envisioned: (1) the *threat* to use nuclear weapons *first* if necessary against Soviet conventional force superiority; (2) The maintenance of an adequate second, or even third, strike capability in case deterrence fails.

The term "deterrence" really came into vogue in the 1960s once the Soviet Union had reached strategic nuclear parity or "balance of terror," and the concept of Mutual Assured Destruction (MAD) was developed. The term *general deterrence* thus tended to be associated with the policy of US-Soviet détente plus MAD. Concurrently, it was questioned whether the Washington would provide *extended deterrence*, in regard to an American nuclear defense of Europe (if, in defending Europe, the Soviet Union would strike US territory).

It was at this point that the US moved away from the concept of massive retaliation and toward the concept of "graduated deterrence" or "escalation dominance" or else "flexible response" that threatened the possible use of tactical nuclear weapons in so-called "non-strategic" regions if conflict should move beyond a clash of conventional forces.[2] Rather than responding with overwhelming nuclear force that could result in a devastating second strike attempt by the USSR, the United States would retaliate in a step-by-step fashion that would be proportional to the use of force by the Soviet Union. This fact raised a significant debate: What could then be considered "theater" for Washington, such as East Germany, might be considered "strategic" for Moscow as well as Bonn! There were also questions as to whether the scenario of a tactical nuclear conflict over the two Germany's would remain "limited."

Toward the end of the Cold War, the Reagan Administration argued that *extended deterrence* would work best if the US homeland was made invulnerable to attack from a broad range of potential threats and from a multiplicity of actors with divergent capabilities. Rather depend upon the concept of MAD that may or may not deter a devastating first strike, the Reagan administration began to develop the concept of "Assured Security" which was accompanied by the Strategic Defense Initiative dubbed "Star Wars." In effect, the concept of Assured Security represented a "leap of faith"—in that the United States did not then possess the technological capabilities to develop ballistic missile defenses (BMD).

The Star Wars proposal came into being as a means to outflank the anti-nuclear and nuclear freeze movements of the 1980s that generated a counter-movement based upon a "leap of faith" in US technological capabilities.[3] It represented a move from Mutual Assured Destruction (MAD) to "Assured Security," now called Homeland Defense. In effect, one utopian movement generated another: The political movement for Assured Security shared the abolitionist beliefs of the anti-nuclear movement but sought homeland protection versus potential missile threats.[4]

Moreover, SDI or Star Wars generated another myth: The belief that the threat of Star Wars impelled the "roll back" of Soviet forces from eastern Europe. But here, Soviet concern was not so much Stars Wars but "emerging" conventional technologies or the "revolution in military affairs" (RMA) that made the Soviet tank defense of eastern Europe obsolete. It would be the RMA on the level of high tech conventional forces that would force Moscow to choose between a major high tech build-up or else retrenchment. Despite hard-line Politbureau opposition, Mikhail Gorbachev chose retrenchment, which led not-so-accidentally to Soviet collapse, followed by the still potentially dangerous geopolitical destabilization of the Eurasian continent.

The Cold War effort to hold the planet in awe through the so-called "balance of terror" has consequently led to efforts to circumvent the forces of deterrence through sneak attack—or what the American military has called "asymmetrical warfare." What may be considered "new" is the fact that non-state actors, as well as lesser states, can now acquire WMD and delivery capabilities; lesser states and the so-called "post-modern terrorist" can assemble and threaten the use of tremendous destructive powers, through dirty bombs or through chemical or biological warfare.

In many ways, the Myth of Assured Security has replaced the Myth of Mutual Assured Destruction; an *imbalance of terror* has now replaced the *balance of terror*. And to deal more effectively with *the imbalance of terror* and the "new threats," the traditional Cold War strategy of *deterrence* should be replaced by a new strategy of *multilateral dissuasion,* which involves engaged irenic diplomacy as well as multilateral security and defense commitments, and which focuses more intensely on the root geo-political, socio-economic and ideological causes of the "new threats," rather than concerning itself with primarily with military-technological capabilities of the opponent, as was generally the case during the Cold War.

Conceptual Issues

General Deterrence

In the post-Cold War era, US nuclear deterrent strategy still opposes adaptation of the proposed policy of "no first use" of nuclear weapons. US deterrent strategy warns that any use of nuclear or non-conventional Weapons of Mass Destruction (WMD) will be met with by the use of "equivalent" weaponry or a some form of "proportionate" response. The exact kind of response is purposively kept vague.

General deterrence can also be associated with Clinton policy of engagement ("deterrence" through "engagement.") Yet when the Clinton administration was criticized for not developing Ballistic Missile Defenses rapidly enough to deal with the potential threats posed by Russia, China, as well as so-called "rogue states" or "states of concern"—which can better be depicted as *parvenu powers*—it had essentially two responses.

The first response was that it was possible to negotiate with "states of concern" so as to convince them to eliminate their nuclear systems. The United States and Russia had jointly worked to *dissuade* Belarus, Kazakhstan and subsequently Ukraine, to eliminate their nuclear weaponry that remained after the collapse of the USSR. It was argued that it was also possible to try to *dissuade* states, such as North Korea, from developing nuclear weaponry and ballistic missile capabilities.

The second option was that of threat of *compellence* through *pre-emption*. National Security Advisor Sandy Berger of the Clinton administration argued that the US could possibly engage in pre-emptive strikes—if so-called "states of concern" obtained ballistic missile and nuclear capabilities that threatened US and allied interests.

Although the possibility of pre-emptive strikes were considered against the deployment of Soviet missiles in Cuba, the first steps toward such a formal preemptive strike policy were initiated by the Clinton administration by cruise missile strikes against Baghdad following the attempted assassination of former president George Bush Sr. in Kuwait City in 1993 presumed to be instigated by Iraqi agents. The Clinton administration then struck Al-Qaeda training camps in Afghanistan and a pharmaceutical plant in the Sudan that was (falsely) alleged to have produced chemical warfare agents, following Al-Qaeda attacks against US embassies in Kenya and Tanzania.[5]

President Clinton's Presidential Decision Directive 62 "Protection Against Unconventional Threats to the Homeland and Americans Overseas" took a step in developing a formal policy of *pre-emption*.

Following the events of September 11, the administration of George W. Bush subsequently formalized a *pre-emptive* strategy in its National Security Presidential Directive-17/HSPD "National Strategy to Combat Weapons of Mass Destruction" (12 December 2002) in that the United States requires "new methods of deterrence" against states aggressively pursuing WMD and their means of delivery: "A strong declaratory policy and effective military forces are essential elements of our contemporary deterrent posture, along with the full range of political tools to persuade potential adversaries not to seek or use WMD. The US will continue to make clear that it reserves the right to respond with overwhelming force—including through resort to all of our options—to the use of WMD against the United States, our forces abroad, and friends and allies."

The new tools include conventional and nuclear response capabilities, and an overall deterrence posture against WMD threats that is reinforced by effective intelligence, surveillance, interdictions and domestic law enforcement in the effort to "devalue" an adversary's WMD and missiles and pose the prospect of an overwhelming response to any use of such weaponry. In this regard, American strategic policy seemed to be adopting new strategies of *compellence* and *dissuasion*, in addition to that of *assured security*, despite the fact that the latter appears based *on a leap of faith* that a National Ballistic Missile Defense (NBD) system can be developed that can destroy ballistic missiles either at boost phase or once they are in flight. Concurrently, the US is also developing theatre missile defenses that can be forward deployed to regional hot spots.

Pre-emption versus Preclusion

Due in part to the very uncertainties involved in building and deploying effective BMD systems, the Bush administration may have taken a policy of *pre-emption* one step farther in the development of a *preclusive* or *precautionary* policy in regard to Iraq, that is the destruction of military capabilities and overthrow of a leadership that is believed to *intend* to develop WMD—even before WMD can be fully developed and deployed. These policies are rationalized on the basis that the possibility of attacks using WMD can be so devastating that one cannot simply wait to be attacked in order to retaliate; one must strike first.

Pre-emptive action thus means striking first against a state when war *appears* imminent and unavoidable. *Preclusive* or *precautionary* action, however, means attacking first to prevent the *presumed* rise of a threat some time in the future.[6]

On the one hand, both these concepts, along with that of *humanitarian intervention*, challenge traditional concepts of state sovereignty and international law. In the neo-conservative view, only "democratically constituted" states ostensibly possess the right to intervene militarily in the domestic affairs of other states to check extreme human rights abuses, crimes against humanity, genocide, or else prevent "rogue" leaderships from obtaining WMD. On the other hand, "just war" theory can more readily justify *pre-emptive* attacks on the basis that a threat is truly imminent than it can justify *preclusive* strikes. The latter can only be rationalized by "just war" theory *only if it were absolutely true that all other possible options to resolve the crisis had been tried and failed.* Here, the ethical and legal issues reside in the nature of the judgment of the leadership and its true intent, as the decision to attack first could be based on mis- or dis-information; incorrect interpretation of what information is provided; or else, purely hostile or else predatory motivation.

Compellence can best be defined as a more *offensive* stance intended to reverse the *status quo* or fundamentally alter the opponent's intentions through threats to use force, denial or punishments. In effect, compellence seeks to *coerce* a rival rather than deter or avert the possibility of conflict. Compellence could involve a threat of *pre-emptive* strikes.

Unfortunately, the terms are often confused. Pro-Soviet observers, and strategists of *parvenu* nuclear powers have tended to regard US nuclear strategy and its quest for nuclear superiority as *compellence* not deterrence. Indian strategists, for example, have argued that Moscow's nuclear force was able to *deter* the US and thus prevent it from achieving world predominance; in this viewpoint, those states that intend to challenge US interests should possess nuclear weaponry and ballistic missile capabilities.

By contrast, from the American viewpoint, as long as the USSR was perceived to possess conventional weapons or nuclear *superiority*, the conceptual basis of US nuclear force posture was considered to be the *defensive* protection of the status quo, or "deterrence." In the Reagan years, the United States argued the Soviet Union was moving to nuclear superiority, based upon the criteria of nuclear "throw weight" as well as the deployment of IRBMs (SS-20s) capable of striking Europe and Japan. The Soviets, however, countered that the US was gaining superiority in emerging technologies and revolution in military affairs.

Immediate Deterrence

Even in situations of *immediate deterrence*, the use of agile, alert and rapidly deployable conventional forces was probably more important than the nuclear threat. Nuclear weapons, in effect, represented a *secondary* back-up, and sometimes a bluff, when nuclear states were in dispute and engaged in "brinksmanship." In this view, the Cuban missile crisis was not "resolved" by the nuclear threat but by American conventional and naval force superiority in the Caribbean, impelling the Soviet Union to back off.

Robert McNamara, however, argues that only sheer luck prevented the Cuban Missile crisis from escalating into a nuclear conflict, and thus neither nuclear weapons nor conventional forces really deterred the possibility of war.[7] At the same time, one can argue that the two sides had a mutual interest in containing the conflict. Both sought a number of face-saving measures that helped to mitigate tensions. Moreover, both the US and USSR had a mutual interest in supporting India versus China in the 1962 Sino-Indian war which broke out at roughly the same time as the Cuban missile crisis.

In 1973 Arab-Israeli conflict, the American threat to use nuclear weapons (putting US nuclear forces on world wide alert at Defense Condition Three [DEFCON 3]) was symbolic of US determination, but more to the point was the US willingness and readiness to engage conventional forces. Once again, both sides had common interests in keeping conflict "contained."

The Concept of Dissuasion

In distinction to deterrence or compellence, *dissuasion* involves a mix of rewards and punishments; it involves a range of political, economic and technological options or tools (what I have called *strategic leveraging*[8]). The threat to use nuclear weapons, in this view, should best be regarded as a tool of strategic leverage utilized to gain concessions, threaten potential enemies, and win allies, through the use of "hard" power. It is also possible to bargain and persuade states to adopt policies aimed at more peaceful cooperation through more positive incentives and reinforcements rather than sanctions—or what Joseph Nye has called "soft power" using techniques of "co-option" rather than "coercion."[9]

From the point of view of *dissuasion*, nuclear deterrence merely tells how to *sustain* a hostile relationship in defensive terms but gives no advice as to how to avoid crises or how to resolve conflict. Deterrence also does not examine the crucial role of rewards and compromise in the resolution of crisis or conflict. Deterrence has also been regarded as resulting from either a failure to negotiate differences or else a refusal to negotiate thoroughly.

Dissuasion thus assumes the possibility of bargaining with the potential opponent, and that some compromise over political and strategic interests, values and positions is in fact possible. A number of states such as Argentina, Brazil and South Africa have given up their nuclear programs. South Africa gave up its nuclear program but only after forging peace with its neighbors and taking steps to abolish the system of Apartheid. Kazakhstan and Ukraine likewise gave up their nuclear weaponry; Kiev, in particular, gave up its weapons program under strong US-Russian pressures in exchange for multilateral security guarantees granted by the UN Security Council members in 1994.[10]

North Korea at least *appeared* to be moving toward non-nuclear status as well; yet in January 2003, it announced that it was dropping out of the NPT program (at the same time that US tensions with Iraq began to escalate). Pyongyang cited US threats to engage in "pre-emptive" strikes against it as one of several reasons for dropping out of the NPT treaty. It demanded "multilateral security guarantees" that would involve a three-point package (similar to a proposal by Moscow in January 2003), which included a nuclear free status for the Korean peninsular, a US security guarantee for North Korea, as well as the resumption of humanitarian assistance and economic aid.[11] In essence, North Korea has continued to threaten to develop nuclear weapons in an effort to impel Washington to grant it US security guarantees, accompanied by multilateral assistance. Whether Washington, which has stated its refusal to be "blackmailed" and which continues to insist upon verification that North Korea will not develop WMD, will work to negotiate a settlement, that would, at least in the short run, legitimize Kim Jong Il's regime, remains to be seen. It is not clear that calling North Korea's bluff would be worth the risk.

Critique of Deterrence during the Cold War

Despite the fact that the concept of *general deterrence* during the Cold War included aspects of diplomacy, American diplomacy never intended to make far-reaching compromises with the Soviet Union; only limited compromises were possible. American containment policy, combined with its nuclear deterrent strategy, largely assumed an uncompromising stance on the part of the Soviet Union and consequent refusal to reach in-depth compromise on the part of the United States, as argued by National Security paper NSC-68. (American diplomacy, as it bargained with Moscow, was unwilling to accept a neutral yet unified Germany, or a confederal Germany that recognized East Germany as a legitimate entity, for example, as possible alternatives to unification as a federal state.)

Although Moscow did continue to engage in numerous proxy wars, and supported Communist movements within West Europe and elsewhere, both sides shared common interests in "double containing" or limiting the political-military capabilities of potentially rising powers. The official American deterrence concept accordingly tended to overlook the fact that the US and USSR both possessed a *mutual interest* in *double containing* the power potential of states such as Germany, Japan, as well as China, in addition to the military potential of other developing countries.

The Cold War dilemma was that the US had to both reassure Germany and Japan that it would defend them by deterring the USSR, at the same time that it restrained both Germany and Japan from developing independent military and nuclear capabilities. The latter fact, in turn, reassured the Soviet Union that Germany and Japan would not rise again. In this sense, both Germany and Japan were double contained by tacit collaboration between the US and USSR. The issue raised here is that the Soviet Union was not deterred by nuclear weapons *alone* during Cold War. The fundamental issue was not the threat of "utter destruction," nor was it shared "values" or "rationality;" nor was it "bipolarity."[12]

In this view, neither nuclear weapons nor conventional forces averted the real possibility of war between the US and USSR; rather major power war was primarily averted by tacitly shared US-Soviet interests *against* the rise of potential rivals. In immediate conflict situations, both sides did resort to threats to use nuclear weapons, and did deploy conventional forces—and yet, for the most part, they did not fight directly.[13] Although common values and bipolarity did help maintain the peace, the most salient factor that averted either conventional or nuclear war was the fact that both the US and USSR had mutual and tacit interests vis-à-vis *actual* and *potential* threats despite their more obvious antagonisms. Their relationship was one of *both* conflict *and* collaboration.

Post-Cold War Deterrence

The general theory advanced here is that war between major powers will not necessarily be prevented by technological means alone. In his Foreign Affairs article, *The Delicate Balance of Terror*, Albert Wohlstetter recognized that "without a deterrent, general war is likely. With it, however, war might still occur. This is one reason deterrence is only a part and not the whole of a military and foreign policy."[14]

Deterrence by itself is not sufficient, but major power war can be averted if there are close mutual or tacit geo-political-economic interests between the major powers. Or, if a close entente or alliance relationships can ultimately be forged between those same powers, which are then accompanied by "overlapping" multilateral security guarantees for less powerful states, the possibility of conflict can be reduced.

In the post-Cold War world, however, tacit collaborative relations between the USA and USSR over Germany, Japan and China have been breaking down. The Soviet collapse has resulted in a Pandora's box of potential regional conflict from the Baltic region to ex-Yugoslavia and deep into Central and South Asia, as the latter conflicts, and now that of "World War III in Africa" tend to overlap with the Middle East and Persian Gulf shatterbelt. *Soviet collapse has opened up the door to the possibility of even wider wars—unless the US, EU and Russia (and ultimately China) can forge a broad new concert of powers.*

Moreover, so-called US "unipolarity"—what can be called the "sound of one hand clapping"—has not-so-ironically worked to engender multiple and mobile threats in conditions of *lopsided or highly uneven polycentrism.* In the immediate aftermath of the Cold War, Washington tended to become complacent due to its self-perceived "victory" in the Cold War; it was largely unable to assess, analyze and prioritize the broad range of forces opposed to American and Allied interests. On 11 September 2001 both nuclear and conventional force deterrence failed.[15] The efforts to eradicate Al-Qaeda in Afghanistan in October 2001 largely forced Al-Qaida and the Taliban underground. The 2003 war with Iraq really represented a second phase of the "war on terrorism" but this time the focus was more on the emerging nuclear weapons program, ballistic missile threats and WMD, than on terrorism itself. (Such weaponry has been difficult to locate following the war, indicating either that WMD did not exist, or perhaps has been sold elsewhere.)

Opposing sides may also hold contrary interpretations about the same phenomena: During Persian Gulf war, the utilization of nuclear weapons was never seriously considered but had chemical or biological weapons been used against the United States, a possible nuclear response would have come under consideration. Here, it was argued that the United States engaged in double standards: The use of fuel air explosives against Iraqi bunkers, for example, has been regarded as the use of "chemical weapons" by critics of American actions. This fact opens the door for rationalizing the use of other "non-conventional" weaponry—and accusations against "double standards" in American policy. The issue raised here is that *parvenu* states and terrorist groups may not see any clear and distinctive "firebreak" between conventional, unconventional and nuclear weaponry, as does the United States, at least ostensibly.

Osama Bin Laden has subsequently spoken of possessing his own nuclear "deterrent." Whether this remains bluff, or whether his group—or others—possess a crude dirty bomb capability, or possess tactical nuclear warheads, has not publicly been verified. But his real "deterrent" is the threat to destabilize the present status quo in Islamic states of Yemen, Jordan, Nigeria, Morocco, Pakistan, Saudi Arabia, Indonesia or Egypt, among other states in the Trancaucasus and Central Asia—or to put it more accurately, to beg the US (and the Europeans and the Russians) to destabilize these regions by their own military interventions. The general condition of instability in these regions indicates the possibility of continued confrontation with *asymmetrical* warfare, which can manipulate civilian technologies as innovative forms of warfare—utilizing techniques of "hit" but not "run"—in addition to the threat to utilize chemical and biological weapons, the poor man's atomic weapons.

Much like Che Guevarra's concept of *foco*, in which a band of elite forces could set off a revolution even if the conditions for such a revolution were not entirely "ripe," Bin Laden hopes that the actions of Al-Qaeda—despite their lack of a truly popular base except perhaps in Afghanistan and northern Pakistan—will spark counter-interventions by the US, UK, Russia, Israel, or other powers, that will, in turn, help set off anti-Western movements throughout many Islamic countries. Al-Qaeda's intent is to ultimately spread the conflict and place the control of nuclear weaponry and ballistic missiles in the hands of pan-Islamic forces to counter all states that might be hostile to a pan-Islamic movement. (The fact that Pakistan possesses a nuclear capability makes this a credible threat given the vehemence of pan-Islamic sentiment in the country.)

Nuclear Weapons and the UN Security Council

The underlying concern raised here is that US (and EU) policy has not dealt adequately with the issues surrounding concept of *existential deterrence*, which has been defined as "the aura or menace inherent to the possession of nuclear weaponry whether or not the possessors make specific, defined threats or make elaborate targeting plans."[16] The concept of existential deterrence should be further extended to incorporate concepts of "prestige" and even the *quest for parity*. A major reason for states to acquire nuclear weapons is the fear that no other state will defend the vital interests of non-nuclear states; these states thus seek *instant parity* with the major players (those on the UNSC who possess the sole legal right to nuclear weapons). Non-state actors may also seek such weaponry so as to further disconcert the major powers, who may be unable to deal effectively with such threats.

The point here is that many American strategists have tended to overlook the reason why a number of states, which have been regarded as "deviants" or "rogues," have sought to develop a nuclear weapons capability. They have not closely analyzed how nuclear weaponry tends to be perceived by those "parvenu" states whose possession of nuclear weapons have not been legitimized by the 1967 Nuclear Non-Proliferation treaty. The fact of the matter is that nuclear weapons and ballistic missiles help create a public perception that states that possess such weaponry will not be ignored by the world community and will be treated with more respect. It is also believed that such weaponry and other WMD will help them to assert their regional interests.

In the atomic age, the roots of the tensions that have generated many of the "new threats" thus lie, in part, in the fact that the five UN Security Council (UNSC) permanent members (the United States, Russia, the UK, France and China) have claimed that it is their legal right (and only their right) to acquire nuclear weapons as permitted by the 1968 Non Proliferation Treaty: What is at issue is how of considerations of "balance of power capabilities and perceived political intent" interact more or less positively or negatively with pre-established "international norms."[17] As these five states also happen to be members of the UNSC, non-nuclear powers have demanded what makes it *legitimate* for the five UN Security Council members to possess nuclear weapons, but not other states?

Accusations of "double standards" thus plays a key role in the rise of new threats as well as in the propaganda of "terrorist" movements, who tend to see their cause as just and the other side as supporting "terror." In the case of nuclear weapons, the illegal possession of such weaponry by allies of the major powers appears to be tolerated, if not given overt or covert support, once again raising questions of double standards. Here, Israel vis-à-vis the Arab states and possibly Japan with its high tech capabilities vis-à-vis North Korea, represent cases in point.[18] This fact has accordingly appeared to represent an arbitrary dividing line in the opinion of the nuclear "have nots," who do not possess the technical or financial capabilities to acquire such weapons, but who seek alternative systems of "deterrence" through WMD or support for "terrorist" groups.

Myth of Assured Security

It is only at the end of the Cold War that the United States had begun to utilize a policy of *multilateral dissuasion* in regard to states such as Ukraine and North Korea. (Here, Ukrainian nationalists argued that Kiev should have never given up its weaponry in 1994; at the same, the country still possesses atomic know-how and missile delivery capabilities.)

While Ukraine was offered multilateral security assurances in 1994 from all five members of the UN Security Council to give up its nuclear capability, in addition to financial incentives, a number of states appear to either be (1) announcing their nuclear arsenal in defiance of international opinion (Pakistan and India); (2) building new systems (such as North Korea, Iran, among others; (3) engaging in *non-weaponized deterrence*, that is, deterrence by coming close to building nuclear weapons but not actually deploying (such as Japan); (4) basing deterrence upon uncertainty, i.e. not officially announcing their development, but leading states to believe in their possession (Israel); and (5) engaging in a number of games in regard to nuclear weapons by trying to hide their WMD capabilities despite signing the NPT (possibly Iraq).

A sixth option included the concept of *virtual deterrence* as developed by the Clinton administration which sought to de-alert or de-activate US-Russian nuclear forces as a means to reduce tensions. Yet virtual deterrence can be critiqued in that it really represents a temporary or non-permanent "solution;" nuclear weapons on alert are still required to protect those de-alerted forces. Once geopolitical and political economic tensions mount, nuclear weapons will be put back on alert or re-activated.

Following war with Iraq in 2003, American strategic doctrine also *appears* to be moving away from *deterrence* and toward *compellence* involving "pre-emption" or really *preclusion* (or else pre-caution or anticipated defense) as well as *assured security* through extended systems of theater missile defenses as well as an effort to achieve a national missile defense system. (This latter appears true even though the BMD Maginot line has already traversed by a strike from *within* US territory and could be traversed again by many diverse methods: Neither nuclear weapons nor conventional forces averted the September 11 attack.)

On the one hand, BMD theoretically resolves the international legal question of *compellence* which involves questions of political ethics and international legality in the case of a desired need for a pre-emptive or preclusive strike in regard to the question as to exactly who is the aggressor and who attacked whom first. On the other, due to the fact that there is no guarantee for BMD to function effectively, the concept of pre-emption (or really preclusion and pre-caution) may remain the official dogma—without fully exploring other possible political-military alternatives or options.

It is clear that even if the US had developed BMD systems in the 1960s, no such defenses would have protected it from the September 11 kind of internal attacks. Air marshals on domestic air flights, firmer visa controls (even in regard to friendly Allied states), and greater coordination between CIA and FBI (the political division implemented after World War II so as to prevent the formation of one Gestapo-like super-secret agency), would have been better handled this kind of threat. Other efforts to fight terrorism could include more effective Coast Guard actions against smuggling, drug running, etc., not to overlook the need for stronger cooperation with the intelligence services of other countries, plus the control of illegal financial operations.

Beyond Deterrence

In essence, Cold War nuclear deterrence theory is based on theory of MAD in which each of the most powerful nuclear states each possessed the capabilities to retaliate with a devastating second strike. Deterrence theory tended to develop from classical balance of power (really "balance of terror") theory, particularly once the Soviets reached a rough nuclear parity, hence the terms, *mutual, stable, or balanced deterrence.* (Specific weapons and basing modes, for example, were accordingly regarded as "stabilizing" or "destabilizing." MIRVed systems in hardened silos are generally seen as destabilizing, for example; MIRVed systems in land-based mobile units or undetectable submarines, however, were seen as stabilizing.)

One of the major American theorists of deterrence, Albert Wohlstetter, argued in his seminal essay *The Delicate Balance of Terror*,[19] that deterrence was "not automatic" and that a capacity to retaliate was very difficult to achieve. In Wohlstetter's view, a deterrent force must be economically viable; it must be able to survive an enemy attack; there must be an ability to make and communicate the decision to retaliate. The nuclear deterrent must be capable of reaching the enemy territory, penetrating its defenses and destroying targets in spite of "passive" civil defense measures or protective construction.

In practice, this has meant sustaining both offensive and defensive capabilities. In operational terms, the air and land-based legs of nuclear triad had to be prepared to either fire first or be launched under attack (or even launch on warning); the sea leg of nuclear triad, involving a mobile submarine force, and nuclear bombers in alert appear to be prepared for survival and possessing second strike capabilities. (It has been argued that a sustainable second-strike capability never existed in the real world in that American command and control facilities would not be able to ride out a sustained first strike.[20])

In conceptual terms, it was argued that a nuclear deterrent cannot be effective unless the other side knows that the deterrent force actually exists and what its capabilities actually are. In this perspective, the opponent must know *something* about the nature and capabilities of deterrent force—but not so much that it would weaken that deterrent and facilitate attack. This leads to a situation of "second guessing" in which each side attempts to assess the present and future power capabilities of the other. Some theorists, such as Stanley Sienkiewicz, went a step further and argued that the greater the operational "uncertainty," the greater the crisis stability of the strategic nuclear balance.[21]

Uncertainty is thus a key principle of the deterrence concept: The Nixon-Kissinger administration dropped American opposition to French nuclear deterrent in part because the latter was seen as to add greater "uncertainty" to Soviet nuclear planning, for example. At the same time, however, the concept of "uncertainty" as articulated by Thomas Schelling and other deterrence theorists, leads to other risky concerns, and can lead to *hyper-rationality*, in which all possible worst case scenarios are imagined.

It is recognized that the actual "games" of deterrence may provoke fears and new uncertainties and that the concept of deterrence cannot always assume *rationality* in perpetuity, thus leading to the concept of *hyper-rationality*, or the rational extension of the fears of irrational actions. From Thomas Schelling's perspective, it may, in fact, be "rationale" to threaten and carry out a move that increases slightly the danger of an all-out war. From his perspective, the fear of irrational actions can actually strengthen deterrence, causing the other side to retreat. By contrast, this same argument has been utilized by "terrorists" who, as depicted by Joseph Conrad in *The Secret Agent*, for example, seek to portray an image of madness and irrationality so as to shock governments and populations with violent actions, but who still consider themselves "civilized."

Thomas Schelling himself recognized in *Arms and Influence* that state leaderships in "sheer desperation" may not be deterred and may decide to strike with whatever capabilities they have at their disposal. It was feared that Saddam Hussein might use his arsenal of WMD in 2003, even though he did not fully use all his military capabilities during either the first 1990 Persian Gulf War or during Anglo-American bombing of Iraqi military positions since the 1998. The same question has remained at the forefront in the confrontation with North Korea, at the same time that the US has not uncovered WMD in Iraq after the war, as of this writing.

In this regard, the US really has no equivalent concept to French doctrine of an "ultimate warning," for example, should US interests be threatened with the use of WMD. The American concept is best described by what Thomas Schelling called, "the threat that leaves something to chance."[22] US deterrence doctrine thus assumes that it can continue to up the ante in the hope that the other side will give up its claims and change its views or goals. To "deter" its opponent the US must accordingly possess capabilities of "graduated deterrence" or "escalation dominance."

Question of Uncertainty

The problem raised here is that technological capabilities of nuclear and conventional forces are constantly in a state of flux and imbalance: This makes it unclear whether the ever-revolutionary military technology (which enhances the uncertainty of power and military calculations) will actually strengthen or weaken the general condition of deterrence. In addition to the fact that uncertainty is generated in the nature of ever-revolutionary technological innovation, uncertainty is also generated in the effort to determine the exact nature of the other sides' ultimate intent.

In *Politics Among Nations*, Hans Morgenthau clearly recognized the mythological nature and pretended precision of "balance of power" concepts in that the assessment of the "balance of power" could never be accurately estimated until actually tested in a specific conflict, and in situations that often reveal the *relative* nature of power capabilities. Moreover, the tension between the "pretended aspiration" to seek a "balance" and the actual aim for predominance or superiority essentially made "balance of power" a myth or ideology to begin with.[23] And finally, if states could not counter-balance rivals through intrinsic resources, they could seek to forge new alliances, which in turn, raises new uncertainties, as states even in alliance may or may not coordinate policy. They could also seek out unconventional means of attack so as to weaken their opponents, as did Japan in Pearl Harbor.

The tensions between the perceived or pretended *quest for parity* versus the perceived *quest for superiority* thus made it difficult to "stabilize" or "balance" the relationship between rival nuclear and conventional powers. *Too* great an uncertainty in the perceptions of power capabilities or *projected* power capabilities may result in an opponent taking a significant risk and launching a first strike with either conventional or nuclear forces (or else with new asymmetrical techniques of unconventional warfare). One side may ultimately opt for a preemptive strike or attempt to find other holes in the opponent's defenses *precisely because of uncertainty*, because it is *uncertain* of the future nature of power capabilities of the other state or actor, as the latter develops new more advanced technologies—or adds on new allies who are militarily or economically powerful. One can accordingly argue that the unconventional attacks on the World Trade Center and Pentagon (coupled with the assassination of the General Ahmed Shah Massoud) represented a form of first strike intended to ward off US and EU support for the Northern Alliance in Afghanistan against the Taliban leadership and Al-Qaeda.

Beneath the question of "uncertainty" are the issues of shared values, rationality and mutual interests. In most conceptions, the deterrence concept is based on "shared" or "mutual" values and "rationality." The leaderships of US and USSR were both regarded as "rational" in that they held common values and were generally cautious and risk averse; they sought mutual accords. Despite the *hyper-rationality* inherent in the concept of MAD, negotiations resulting in *limited* compromises were possible. But even here, the US nuclear strategy emphasized "surgical strikes" of Soviet military targets, Soviet strategy emphasized greater nuclear *throw weight* (with greater circular error probability and more bang for the buck) in order to make up for the technological gap between Soviet and American delivery capabilities. Being less accurate, Soviet weaponry would more likely strike *counter-value* targets, i.e. civilian populations.

While the latter question of rationality thus *appeared* to be true in regard to US-Soviet behavior during the Cold War, such "rationality," however, was not an attribute of the conflicts with Vietnam or Algeria, for example. Guerilla wars fought between opponents with highly *uneven* power capabilities during the Cold War revealed that power capabilities may actually be *leveled* in the actual theatre of conflict and in actual combat situations. The fact that the use of power and force is *relative* to the specific combat situation tends to lower the capabilities of the more "powerful" actor, in part due to *relative* willingness of the two sides to prosecute war and accept damage, coupled with the differing aims and goals of the respective sides. Moreover, the mere possession of nuclear weaponry did not deter revolutionary action and acts of terrorism.

The problem is that elites of differing states or political groups in conflict may both be "rational" but still uphold very different priorities (based on differing assumptions) and differing values and differing willingness to accept "collateral damage." Hegel knew this well when he defined genuine tragedy in his critique of King Creon's role in Sophocles' play *Antigone* not as "Right versus Wrong," but "Right versus Right." The key concern raised here is consequently that it may not always be possible to deter *parvenu* states (or terrorist groups) who do not share common values with their opponents, or who are willing to take significant risks (i.e. act "irrationality"). The psychological attitudes, values and processes may furthermore not be the same for *challengers* as for *defenders* of the status quo—particularly given *highly uneven* or *highly lopsided* or *asymmetrical* military capabilities. There may additionally be differences in perceptions and values between those who are closer in proximity to a conflict and those farther away from the conflict.

Two (or more) parties may also not view the credibility of threats on similar or equal terms. They may not know the exact intentions and possible response of the other side; thus they misinterpret those intentions and act provocatively. Moreover, leaders acting under pressure may not react "rationally." Deterrence theory has thus generally assumed an ability to accurately communicate a threatened sanction, which both sides *equally* understand in terms of costs, risks as well as expected benefits (if the sanctions are not acted upon)—but this may not, in fact, be the case with "terrorist" groups willing to take on kamikaze-type activities or sacrifice civilian populations or with *revanchist* leaderships who are either willing to risk "punishment" (in the assumption that they may succeed in their attack) or that are so desperate that they believe that have no remaining options. Put more bluntly, the high tech "terrorism" of advanced weaponry wielded by the most powerful and opulent states may be countered by the dirty low tech "terrorism" of the less powerful, less technologically advanced, and less relatively opulent, and who are willing to engage in wars of attrition.

Critique of Neo-Conservatism

Neo-conservatism or "conservative internationalism" may not be able to deal as effectively with the problem of both state-supported and anti-state terrorism ironically and precisely due to its over-riding concern with the military security of individual states. This is true as it tends to regard security issues in *positivistic* isolation from other forces and actors in the international system, such a non-governmental and international organizations, environmental and health concerns, as well as fluctuations in the global economy. Neo-conservatism thus tends to overplay the military aspects of state security without a full analysis of the interplay between "balance of power," intent, and international norm and between traditional state security and socio-political-economic-ecological conditions.

As traditional military security concerns predominate in neo-conservative thinking, there is little consideration or recognition for issues surrounding complexities of divergent and conflicting *political* differences within the balances of power and force as they relate to political-military *intent*. Neo-conservative strategy tends to exacerbate, rather than ameliorate, the general condition of *uncertainty*, precisely because it intends to set all rival actors "off balance" from a position of military superiority. In exacerbating uncertainty, however, it could likewise exacerbate the root political-military, social-economic and ideological conditions and causes for the rise of terrorism and state-supported terrorism in that it tends to pit one *chosen* side versus another. It tends to presume the other side will capitulate with a show of superior force, which may not prove to be the case. Moreover, by seeking to identify and then eradiacate an opponent, neo-conservative strategy ironically tends to grant that opponent a certain legitimacy that could help it to gain popular and state supports, *thus actually enhancing its long-term ability to resist*. This creates a self-fulfilled prophecy that exacerbates the prospects for more acts of terrorism: Yesterday's martyrs may inspire tomorrow's "heroes."

"No concessions, no compromises" may be publicly stated, but Machiavellian diplomacy may lead to other realities. Dealing effectively with terrorism may accordingly mean a more *empathetic* examination of the goals of the relatively less powerful and the powerless, as they utilize aspects of strategic leveraging, including terrorism, to assert their interests, conflicting values and claims. In addition to the use of force, this means utilizing a wider range of diplomatic, as well as political-economic, tools in order to adjust the geopolitical, as well as social psychological and ideological conditions/relationships, that set the grounds for "terrorist" actions, as well as other acts of resistance. The concept here is to *go around* the terrorists and to isolate them by co-opting their supporters but without actually falling into their trap. It may be necessary to find *tacit* or *indirect* compromises based on mutual geostrategic and political economic interests in which so-called "vital" interests can be redefined. If vital interests, however, cannot be *re-defined*, the result will be either stalemate or continuous acts of terrorism and counter-terrorism.

Neo-conservatism tends to place greater emphasis upon the threat posed by *military capabilities* than on the *actual intent to use those capabilities*. While *immediate* threats must obviously be given the fullest, if not the most urgent, attention, by military and clandestine means, such as the use of special forces, if necessary, there will be no long term abatement of the crisis, unless there is a greater focus placed on the political, socio-economic and ideological factors that underlie the *motivations* and the *intent* to manipulate the new threats. In terms of irenic strategy *in the long run*, issues of "terrorism" and of WMD must be treated as *secondary* to the need to change *intentions*, and *secondary* to the need to develop appropriate regional security conditions that work to prevent both state-supported and anti-state terrorism from all sides, and that seek to prevent groups from obtaining bases of regional and state supports, and that prevent militant groups or *parvenu* states from seeking out countervailing alliances.

As indicated above, the neo-conservative perspective regards the development of WMD as "deviant" state behavior, despite the fact that such weapons have been developed by each of the permanent UN Security Council members. In this regard, so-called "rogue states" are merely following in the footsteps of those states that have declared the *post-facto* legitimacy of their right to acquire and retain nuclear weapons. There is very little consideration given to the issue of double standards and normative faults as perceived (rightly or wrongly) by lesser powers and anti-state actors. Neo-conservatives argue that US preclusive actions in Iraq in 2003, for example, represent a demonstration effect designed to warn other states not to acquire WMD and to pressure states in the region to reform; yet such actions, by creating greater uncertainty, may, in fact, speed up the effort of North Korea and Iran to obtain such weaponry so as to prevent such an attack—unless these states are granted some form of international or bilateral security guarantees as a form of compensation. Similarly, *parvenu* states such as India and Pakistan may seek to make their nuclear capabilities more effective and *useable*.

Most fundamentally, the real risk posed by the new logic of "preemption" and "war on terrorism" is a *hyper-rationality* based on hypothetical worst-case scenarios similar to those of the Cold War that led to the nuclear and conventional arms race and the worldwide proliferation of weaponry, without accepting fundamental compromise with the Soviet Union. Such *hyper-rationality* lies at the roots of Wohlstetter's argument, as well as that his post-Cold War neo-conservative followers, who likewise tend to exaggerate worst case scenarios, and who, just as problematically, at least claim to take the "high moral path" in refusing to take *preventive* steps of tacit diplomatic compromise and concession—as a means to potentially isolate, divide or co-opt "terrorist" or partisan organizations and their actual or potential supporters—in the *a priori* assumption that these individuals, groups or state leaderships are absolutely intractable.

Toward a Concept of *Multilateral Dissuasion*

Contrary to the neo-conservative argument that leading powers such as the US must primarily act through unilateral or bilateral measures, international or multilateral regimes can help provide greater incentives for states, partisan groups (or other anti-governmental actors) to re-define their "vital interests" and thus to find compromise through the promise of multilateral security guarantees, inspections—or through the deployment of multinational peacekeepers, for example, among other multilateral incentives (or threat of sanctions). From this perspective, much as *general deterrence* can not deal effectively with "irrational" actions, involving suicidal "kamikazes," asymmetrical acts of terrorism, accidents, or even the *misinterpretation of warning signals*, a more proactive approach of *multilateral dissuasion* must be attempted that can reduce aspects the uncertainty generated in a highly anarchical global system, increasingly characterized by threats of unilateral action.

Dealing with terrorism, state terrorism and WMD through a process of *multilateral dissuasion* requires finding the appropriate path of secret negotiations though back channels, bilateral or multilateral discussions, or through international regimes. At the same time, it also means recognizing that numerous groups or individuals, who may represent a multitude of conflicting factions, may seek to use all possible means, including acts of "terrorism," to stifle the negotiation process or block compromise that does not suit their interests. Some of the parties whose interests are affected by negotiations may be prepared for compromise, others not. There is a risk that the whole process can be derailed by events such as leaks to the press or terrorist reprisals and hostage taking, etc. A prime target of partisan groups are not only those who attempt to eradicate, repress or prosecute them, as these individuals ironically tend to actually demonstrate the proof of militant critiques through acts of repression and violence, but even more conspicuously, the prime targets are those who wish to broker a compromise that appears to undermine the fundamental values and goals of hard line true believers in the cause, by means of co-opting actual or potential followers.

In order to help build international consensus, and to counter the potentially destabilizing effects of accusations of "double standards," multilateral diplomacy may need to be accompanied by concrete, visible and far-reaching social-economic and political reforms by the state actors themselves, reforms that are tacitly designed to compromise over some of the *legitimate* aspects of a revolutionary critique.[24] In theory, this can be accomplished by co-opting various elements of the general population and by isolating the more militant and least compromising critics of a particular regime. The failure of a particular government to engage in significant and worthwhile reforms, or else the failure to thoroughly pursue those reforms, however, could lead to the ultimate victory of anti-government partisans—or, to a stalemate in which efforts to repress the militant opposition result in acts of terror and counter-terror in which no one appears to win except those who desire stalemate.

From this perspective, the mere *threat* to use force may not be sufficient to prevent states from acquiring WMD; such threats may actually accelerate efforts to develop or purchase such weaponry, or engage in acts of "terrorism," thus exacerbating the security dilemma inherent in hyper-rationality. It is furthermore dubious that the sources of "terrorism" themselves can be eliminated unless the general socio-political-economic—and geopolitical—conditions that help form the breeding ground for partisan or "terrorist" activities are either eliminated—or else somehow *ameliorated*. More explicit defense and intelligence cooperation between US, EU and Russia can thus be effective against the immediate threat of "terrorism" in the short run, but in order for there to be a lasting change that ultimately removes the very sources of the "threat," there must be deep structural change, both in the nature of political-social-economic conditions—as well as in the nature of regional and international alliance and geopolitical relationships.

Conclusion: Toward *Multilateral Dissuasion* as Key Concept

Deterrence has been critiqued as:

1) *Immoral:* Deterrence may require a devastating nuclear counter-value strike against civilian populations. The nuclear threat has been opposed by religious leaders of many faiths as well as by retired military leaders.[25]

2) *Impractical and highly risky, if not non-existent:* Deterrence assumes that one state can absorb a first strike and still retaliate, but nuclear deterrence (conceived as an adequate and sustainable second strike capability) never existed in the real world in that American command and control facilities would not be able to ride out a devastating first strike.

3) *Ineffective:* Deterrence has not prevented revolutionary (Vietnam, Algeria, Afghanistan) or conventional wars waged by non-nuclear states against nuclear states (Argentina and UK over Falklands/Malvinas); nor have nuclear weapons prevented significant conventional force confrontations between nuclear powers, such as Russia and China during the border clashes of the late 1960s. The possession of rough nuclear parity by India and Pakistan has not stopped acts of mutual subversion.

4) *Not credible:* Those states that possess nuclear weapons states are not about to use those weapons in most circumstances or even in conditions of "flexible response." The opponent will thus take the risk that the nuclear power will not opt to use the so-called "ultimate weapon" and that it will remain "self-deterred."

5) *Illogical:* Deterrence compounds uncertainty through the ever-revolutionizing technology and through *hyper-rationality* based on worst-case scenarios. It is seen as setting into process an absurd build-up and counter-build-up based on both inter-service rivalries as well as an heightened assessment of the "threat" from the Soviet Union during the

Cold War or other *parvenu* states or "terrorist" organizations. The problem is that the military technocracy has largely been divorced from politics and is largely immune to political manipulation.

6) *Genetically genocidal:* Compared with the health risks of most weaponry, radioactivity from nuclear weapons poses the greatest threat to the human gene pool and ecosphere.[26]

In post-Cold War circumstances, the United States has no single script to follow. A number of scenarios involving the spread of nuclear weapons that will ultimately affect the concept of deterrence have been posited: Is it truly possible to sustain the status quo involving a two-tiered level of nuclear *haves* and *have nots* (in which the UN Security Council members possess nuclear weapons while other states are not legally permitted to possess such weaponry)?

Or is a more *managed* proliferation possible?[27] If the latter should prove to be the case, which states should be permitted nuclear weapons? Will the "gradual" spread of nuclear weapons ultimately result in a system of "unit veto?" Will "national" or so-called "theatre" BMD systems help slow down the spread of nuclear weapons? Or will they result in a massive nuclear weapons and missiles build-up designed to penetrate such systems?

Or, on the contrary, is the abolition of nuclear weapons still possible? Nuclear abolitionists oppose Ballistic Missile Defenses arguing that such systems will result in a proliferation of counter-systems. At the same time, they tend to vacillate between positions seeking the abolishment of nuclear weapons versus positions advocating minimal deterrence (in the assumption that hard-line states may continue to refuse to abolish nuclear weaponry). Robert McNamara has argued that absolute *parity* in nuclear weapons, for example, is not necessary due to the vast destructive nature of just a few nuclear warheads; the US should seek a minimal deterrent, if it cannot abolish nuclear weapons altogether.

A minimal nuclear second-strike capability (sometimes called "pure deterrence") is seen as problematic in that it involves no element of *extended deterrence*. At the same time, the need for extended deterrence could become less pressing, that is, if the UK and France built up their own nuclear capabilities to the point that they can help defend an expanding Europe as it enters into former Soviet space. Extended deterrence also becomes less pressing if the EU reaches out to entente or alliance relationships with Russia and/or China, and thus lessens its dependence upon the US. But this approach, unless it is coordinated with the US, and involves multilateral overlapping security guarantees, risks a split in the Atlantic Alliance, and raises US fears of "decoupling" and "duplication."

Nor does the concept of minimum deterrence involve aspects of compellence or of dissuasive aspects of strategic leveraging. Minimal deterrence is regarded as precluding the need for elaborate defense, but still needs to assure survivability of nuclear capability. It is furthermore dubiously capable of dealing with emerging powers and political movements that may not feel threatened by any nuclear deterrent. The total abolishment of nuclear weapons has thus been proposed; but it seems the genie is out of the bottle. The best way such genetically genocidal weapons can be reduced is by the formation of a concerted alliance of major powers that include US, UK, France, Russia and ultimately China. The latter can then use powers of *multilateral dissuasion* to reduce and ultimately eliminate such weaponry through the promise of overlapping security guarantees, much as the case of Ukraine has shown in 1994.

But as long as such a grand concert seems a long way in the making, nuclear weapons appear here to stay. Nuclear weapons capabilities have now been accompanied by steps to develop National Missile Defenses (NMD) and Theatre Missile Defense (TMD) systems. The new post-September 11 strategic concept of *general deterrence* thus represents a mix of offensive and defensive systems, involving both "deterrence" and "assured security." The strategies of *pre-emption, preclusion* or *pre-caution* have also been developed. Yet it must be admitted that neither nuclear weapons nor conventional forces deterred the "suicidal" attacks upon the World Trade Center and the Pentagon. And had Ballistic Missile Defense (BMD) systems been operating, such systems would not have stopped those attacks either. *Thus the key issue raised here is that National Missile Defense, coupled with strategies of pre-emption, preclusion or pre-caution, risk exacerbating the general conditions of instability, and may actually boost the willingness of major powers, parvenu states, as well as "terrorist" groups to strike either preemptively, or else clandestinely. These strategic concepts may actually provoke further conflict and uncertainty rather than ameliorating or resolving tensions and the general condition of uncertainty.*

In regard to Russia, the new strategic concept involving general deterrence with proposed offensive/defensive measures, plus pre-emption and preclusion, can be regarded as being capable of destroying Russian strategic ICBM systems (threat of first strike)—assuming Washington does develop a concept of *assured security* involving a homeland defense system or NMD—as it has threatened. But, at the same time, however, Russia could accept such a BMD system if it is limited and merely capable of protecting against accidental launches and threats of lesser powers involving weapons systems of shorter ranges. Accordingly, although Russia opposes the US conception of NMD, Moscow appears more willing to accept Theater Missile Defense (TMD) as long as its own strategic missiles are not threatened by a potential first strike. At the same time, Moscow may be more willing to accept a TMD system if it involves power sharing, and helps to define and develop the parameters of such a system, a long with the Europeans (thus involving *cooperative/collective security*).

China, however, thus far appears less willing to accept either US-based NMD or TMD. This is because TMD systems could be deployed to provide *extended defense* to Taiwan, which is regarded as a strategic, and not a so-called theater, question for Beijing. China's threat to resist US efforts to deploy TMD systems by deploying up to 200 long range nuclear missiles, capable of striking the US itself, coupled with a blue water navy is intended to gain leverage vis-à-vis Washington. Another option for China, however, could be to "bandwagon" with a burgeoning coalition of the US, EU and Russia, depending upon assessment of its geopolitical interests, and whether or not a negotiated compromise can be found over Taiwan, North Korea, among other issues.

Yet another factor preventing a further reduction of US-Russian nuclear weapons from between 1700-2200 as proposed by Washington is the fact that the US and Russia can not "build down" too deeply because it would be easier for China to "build up"! China may thus need to be included in multilateral strategic arms reduction and BMD negotiations—at some point in the not too distant future. Beijing has requested negotiations over the militarization of outer space.

Both the anti-nuclear and pro-BMD movements thus represent utopian visions that ignore the emerging reality of a panoply of offensive and defensive weapons systems as *real war* fighting forces that are in the process of being developed. Anti-nuclear and pro-deterrence proponents, who oppose BMD, argue that despite its proposed intent, BMD systems will lead to an increase in nuclear weapons which will be intended to penetrate missile defense shields—rather than result in a reduction of such weaponry. This could be true if China continues to build up its nuclear weapons capability as threatened. Yet anti-nuclear and deterrence proponents offer no viable alternative either. They do not really explain how the security of states is to be maintained, and conflict is to be prevented—even if nuclear weapons can ultimately be abolished.

To be more effective, the American concept of general deterrence must involve more balanced relationship between *strategic denial*, *compellence*, and most importantly, *diplomacy* and *multilateral dissuasion*. On a deeper level, the struggle against "terrorism" and the taming of *parvenu* states must involve the development of new regional approaches to security involving concerted multilateral interaction of major powers with regional actors, involving overlapping security guarantees and regional security communities. (See Hall Gardner, Introduction and Chapter 8.)

Multilateral dissuasion strategies must be designed for specific purposes and take into account diverse and conflicting *value* hierarchies of numerous potential regional opponents. What dissuades one government or actor may not deter another in a specific conflict; what succeeds in one geohistorical context may not succeed in another.[28] Dissuasion must lead to new forms of confidence building measures and mutual security guarantees for both states and partisan groups in order to incline the latter toward resolving disputes and conflicts in a multilateral context. The positive benefits of cooperation must be clearly outlined.

The general deterrence issue can be *partially* resolved by bringing more states into a larger alliance or coalition after negotiation of significant geopolitical and economic differences. Russia need no longer be "deterred" nor "dissuaded" if it is brought into NATO in a new form of membership involving the implementation of the adapted 1999 Conventional Force in Europe Treaty, as well as START II and then START III accords, for example. Steps to forge a BMD for the entire Euro-Atlantic community utilizing a mix of US, European and Russian technologies should also be taken. The key question here is to what extent will US-EU-Russia be able to share BMD technology—as well as coordinate strategy! More broadly, a US-EU-Russian *Transatlantic Political-Economic and Strategic Council* should be implemented, that could coordinate the strategic nuclear and conventional force relationships, and peacekeeping and force deployments for the entire Euro-Atlantic Euro-Mediterranean areas. (See Hall Gardner, Chapter 8.)

Notes

1   The Air Force Doctrine Document 23, Secretary of the Air Force 26 August 1994, Federation of American Scientists, www.fas.org: "General Strategic deterrence is, and has been, a key foundation of US National Military Strategy. The world is continuing to move from bipolar to multi-polar, and regional actors are now more likely to acquire and employ Weapons of Mass Destruction (WMD). These factors ensure that nuclear deterrence will remain a top priority for the US in the foreseeable future."
2   The failure of deterrence could first lead to low-intensity conflict; 2) limited or "theater" war utilizing "graduated deterrence" or "flexible response." The latter could include a nuclear warning or demonstration "shot across the bow" or the use of tactical nuclear weaponry in regions that one does not expect a strategic response (i.e. a direct attack on American territory.) Strategic nuclear war could begin with selective counterforce targeting, followed by targeting of command and control centers.
3   Frances Fitzgerald, *Way Out There in the Blue: Reagan Star Wars and the End of the Cold War* (New York: Simon and Schuster, 2000).

4   As Richard Perle put it: "I once had occasion privately to discuss the idea of eliminating all nuclear weapons with President Reagan. I said I thought the Soviets would cheat and probably others as well. So do I, he said. That is why it could be done only after we had a fully effective SDI in place." Testimony of Richard Perle, Subcommittee on International Security, Proliferation, and Federal Services of the Committee on Governmental Affairs United States Senate One Hundred Fifth Congress First Session, February 12, 1997.

5   "Statements aside, the fact remains that this is the first time the US has: (1) launched and acknowledged a preemptive strike against a terrorist organization or network; (2) launched such a strike within the territory of a state which presumably is not conclusively, actively and directly to blame for the action triggering retaliation; then (3) launched military strikes at multiple terrorist targets within the territory of more than one foreign nation, and (4) attacked a target where the avowed goal was not to attack a single individual terrorist, but an organizational infrastructure instead. Moreover, in the case of the facility in Sudan, the target was characterized as one that poses a longer term danger rather than an immediate threat." See Raphael F. Perl, "Terrorism: U. S. Response to Bombings in Kenya and Tanzania: A New Policy Direction?" (Congressional Research Service (CRS) *Report for Congress*, The Library of Congress Washington, DC: 98-733F Updated September 1, 1998).

6   See Carl Kaysem, John D. Steinbruner and Martin B. Malin "US National Security Policy: In Search of Balance" in *War with Iraq: Costs, Consequences, and Alternatives*. Here I prefer the terms pre-caution or preclusion to "war prevention;" this is because all pre-emptive or preclusive action *presume* that a threat may be actualized in the immediate or near future, without an absolute guarantee. Richard Perle, for example, argues that pre-emption can be justified if the threat is *imminent*, using the 1981 Israeli bombing of the Iraqi Osirak nuclear reactor as an example. Perle defines *imminence* as the point in which "a threat becomes unmanageable ... In the case of Iraq, we're talking about stopping the further development of nuclear weapons, we're talking about new systems of delivery for the chemical and biological weapons Saddam already has, including systems with much longer range. What is imminent about Iraq and what may be imminent in some other situations requires you to look back and decide when a threat becomes unmanageable." http://www.newamericancentury.org/iraq-20030224 htm. The problem with this argument is how to determine whether and when such threats become truly "unmanageable" and precisely what are the most appropriate means to deal with those presumed threats. One can question whether the Osirak "threat" was, in fact, "imminent" and whether the means used may have actually sped up the Iraqi nuclear program to counter the Israeli program. Could a call for international inspections have worked then? Moreover, as the US has been unable to uncover Iraqi nuclear weapons, one wonders if an imminent threat actually did exist, or did the weapons move location as a result of the US intervention?

7   Robert McNamara, see Global Security Institute. http://www.gsinstitute.org/projects/new/military.html.

8   Hall Gardner, *Surviving the Millennium* (Westport, CT: Praeger, 1997).

9   Joseph S. Nye, Jr., *The Paradox of American Power* (Oxford: 2002), 9.

10 On joint US-Russian efforts to remove non-Russian nuclear weaponry from former Soviet bloc states see, Hall Gardner, *Dangerous Crossroads* (Westport, CT: Praeger, 1997), and *Surviving the Millennium op. cit.* See also Condoleezza Rice "What Does Disarmament Look Like?" *USA in Review* January 27, 2003. http://www.usainreview.com/1_27_Rice.htm.

11 David Shambaugh "China and the Korean Peninsula: Playing for the Long Term" The Washington Quarterly 2003 Spring Vol. 26, No. 2; Pg. 43; Colin Robinson, "Stand-off

with North Korea: War Scenarios and Consequences" *Center for Defense Information* www.cdi.org *Xinhua General News Service*, 24 January 2003.
12. See my argument in *Surviving the Millennium*, op. cit.
13. On exception might be the Korean War in which Russian pilots flew in Korean jets, but both sides kept this fact secret so as not to escalate the conflict.
14. Albert Wohlstetter, "The Delicate Balance of Terror," 6 November 1958 reprinted: http://www.rand.org/publications/classics/wohlstetter/P1472/P1472. A critique of Wohlstetter's work is highly relevant in that neo-conservatives Richard Perle and Paul Wolfowitz, key officials of the George W. Bush administration, are regarded to be protégés of Albert Wohlstetter. (Alfred Wohlstetter, R.I.P. January 16, 1997. http://www.polyconomics.com.)
15. Vice-President Richard Cheney described the concept of deterrence in this way: "They have nothing to defend," he said. "You know, for 50 years we deterred the Soviets by threatening the utter destruction of the Soviet Union. What does Bin Laden value? There's no piece of real estate. It's not like a state or a country. The notion of deterrence doesn't really apply here. There's no treaty to be negotiated, there's no arms control agreement that's going to guarantee our safety and security. The only way you can deal with them is to destroy them." Cited in *Bob Woodward* "CIA Told to Do 'Whatever Necessary' to Kill Bin Laden" *Washington Post*, October 21, 2001, A01.
16. McGeorge Bundy, cited in Jonathan Schell, *The Gift of Time: The Case for Abolishing Nuclear Weapons Now* (New York: Henry Holt, 1998).
17. Hall Gardner, *Surviving the Millennium*, 27.
18. Israel may possess as many as 75-130 weapons, include warheads for mobile Jericho-1 and Jericho-2 missiles, as well as bombs for Israeli aircraft, and may include other tactical nuclear weapons as well. See also Ekovich, this book.
19. Albert Wohlstetter, op. cit.
20. Bruce Blair, cited in Jonathan Schell, *The Gift of Time: The Case for Abolishing Nuclear Weapons Now* (New York: Henry Holt, 1998).
21. Stanley Sinkiewicz, "Observations on the Impact of Uncertainty in Strategic Analysis," World Politics, XXXII (Ocotober, 1979), 98-99.
22. Thomas Schelling, *Arms and Influence* (New Haven, CT: Yale University Press, 1966).
23. Hans Morgenthau, *Politics Among Nations* (Boston: McGraw Hill, 1993); George Liska, *Quest for Equilibrium* (Baltimore: Johns Hopkins University Press, 1977).
24. Here, for example, Saudi Arabia announced in February 2003 that US troops would pull out of Saudi Arabia following the war with Iraq, a key goal of Bin Laden.
25. See statements by military and religious leaders, "Joint Nuclear Reduction/ Disarmament Statement and Signatories" *Global Security Institute* http://www.gsinstitute.org/ projects/new/military.html. "We... believe that reliance on a nuclear deterrent in the long run calls into question our stewardship of God's creation. In the short run, effective diplomacy may well require reciprocal and phased reduction of nuclear weapons over some period of years. While we have a variety of perspectives on the language and ethics of nuclear deterrence, none of us would support any role for nuclear *weapons except possibly to deter the use of nuclear weapons by others.*" Of course the last phrase is the root of the problem!
26. Gardner, *Surviving the Millennium*, op. cit.
27. John Mearsheimer, "Back to the Future," *International Security* 15:1 (Summer 1990).
28. Raymond Aron, "The Evolution of Modern Strategic Thought" in *Problems of Modern Strategy: Part I Adelphi Papers* (London: IISS, February 1968).

PART II:
THE FUTURE OF NATO

Chapter 3

Thinking About and Beyond NATO

Simon Serfaty[*]

Entering 2001, the two summits scheduled by the North Atlantic Treaty Organization (NATO) and the European Union (EU) for late 2002 were expected to start the final phase of the Euro-Atlantic vision that had been launched after World War II, and pursued throughout the Cold War. The central dimension of these summits was an institutional enlargement to a large group of countries liberated by the collapse of the Soviet empire a decade earlier. Such parallel enlargement of NATO and the EU would build a more complete Euro-Atlantic community of common interests and compatible values, especially as an overlapping set of European members would facilitate relations between NATO and the EU, as well as relations between the EU and the United States. In Warsaw in June 2001, newly elected President George W. Bush urged, during his first official European trip (and, remarkably enough, his first trip to Europe ever), to end the "artificial lines that still divide Europe." These were lines that stood among European countries, but also between NATO and the EU and between both and Russia.

Thus, the "vision thing" that had been absent during the previous decade was addressed unexpectedly: the post-Cold War era did not demand any new vision, so long, at least, that the old one had not been finalized. Admittedly, both sides of the Atlantic did not have a common view of the Euro-Atlantic finality to which they might aspire. But their differences could be dismissed as a recurring pattern in U.S.-European relations. Since April 1949 for the Washington Treaty, and since March 1957 for the Rome Treaties, no common view has ever been held among the members of the Alliance or the then European Community, irrespective of size. Indeed, by

---

[*] Simon Serfaty first published this article as "Europe Enlarged, America Detached?" in *Current History*, vol. 102, no. 662 (March 2003), 99-105. The editor would like to thank Bill Finan for permission to republish it. The article was thus completed prior to US-UK intervention in Iraq.

the summer 2001, the shouting match that had been heard in the spring over a wide range of security and societal issues seemed to subside. The pattern had been seen before: A new U.S. president who progressively adapts his campaign rhetoric to the realities he uncovers, and European allies who progressively move away from the caricature they drew of the incoming American president relative to his predecessor.

Initially, the events of September 11 (9-11) brought the two sides of the Atlantic closer together. Europe's spontaneous display of solidarity reflected a steadfast commitment to making of its alliance with the United States a community of action whenever its members' shared interests and values were at risk. Confirming Europe's commitment was an institutional triple play that was truly unprecedented: NATO's immediate invocation of Article V, a quick EU declaration of "complete solidarity," and France's and Britain's role to ensure a unanimous declaration of support from the United Nations.

These lofty expectations did not endure the diplomatic turbulence of the year that followed, however. Beginning with the President's State of the Union speech on 29 January 2002, the two sides of the Atlantic seemed to be drifting away amidst parallel charges of Europe's anti-Americanism and America's anti-Europeanism. In Afghanistan and wherever else the wars of 9-11 might go, NATO became an afterthought—a "spare wheel," suggested its Secretary General, George Robertson. In the summer, the offensive rhetoric heard during Chancellor's Gerhard Schroeder's campaign for re-election in Germany provided a catalyst for an American exasperation with, and anger at, countries the United States have saved from themselves and others throughout much of the twentieth century. It also pointed to a potentially dangerous split within the EU between a peripheral ring of Atlanticist states, let by Britain, and a continental core of European countries, led by France and Germany, with both competing for the allegiance of new NATO and EU members in the East. In the fall, the relationship was said to be lacking a common view of the world. Worse yet, allegedly settled unto different planets, Americans and Europeans were separated further by a growing capabilities gap that prevented common action even when values or interests might otherwise be shared, however unevenly.[1]

Rumors of an impending death of the transatlantic partnership are hardly new. For the past 50 years they have drowned the facts of mutually beneficial cooperation between America and its European allies, as well as among them. In the end, however, these rumors never amounted to much. Although these are the facts of history, such memories of past discord should not be cause for complacency. The current divergences are troubling and possibly dangerous because the conditions that surround them are indeed novel and potentially existential. Even as (and because) the Copenhagen Summit of December 2002 brought the EU closer finality, the Atlantic Alliance must be thought anew; but even though the Prague Summit of November 2002 helped revive NATO, a new Alliance of which NATO remains the embodiment is not yet in sight. In short, underlying the current transatlantic rift are three conditions that have to do with the rise of "Europe," the decline of NATO, and the emergence of a new security normalcy in interstate relations. Each of these conditions alone would have a significant impact on the terms of transatlantic engagement, but together that impact is magnified beyond the traditional norms of past tensions.

All That Europe Can Be

To start with, there is the matter of the European Union: because of it, Europe, as Americans have known it since 1917, is dead and beyond resurrection. Some, admittedly, remain in a state of denial as they still predict, and even await, the revival of the traditional nation-states whose sovereignty within impermeable boundaries was well worth a war or two.[2] That prospect, however, is nil. It ended when the rise of institutions that were created to save the nation-states (from each other, as well as from themselves) progressively eroded their members' national content instead. "To understand," wrote Isaiah Berlin four decades ago, "is to perceive patterns."[3] Patterns are not shaped by theory but asserted by history. The pattern that has grown out of Europe's history over the past 50 years could not be more evident. With nation-states reinventing themselves as member states of the Union they form, or which they hope to join, the EU is achieving a new territorial and even political *synthesis* that is making much of the continent whole after NATO helped make it free. The single currency that was launched in January 2002, the enlargement to 10 new members that was announced in December 2002, the constitutional convention scheduled for the spring of 2003, and the Intergovernmental Conference (IGC) that will take place in 2004 are the identifiable plays of an end game known as finality. The agenda is not new—deepen in order to widen, widen in order to deepen, and reform in order to do both—but its scope and urgency are.

The final transformation of Europe should make Americans proud. The deconstructed Old World that twice in slightly more than one generation organized its own collective funeral is now being consolidated *à l'américaine*. To a large measure, this transformation is due to inspired U.S. policies that showed, during 15 glorious weeks in the spring of 1947, how the peace could be won historically after the war had been won militarily. Indeed, the new Europe is more peaceful, safer, more affluent, and more democratic—in short, more stable and, why not, more likable—than at any time before. Even the unfinished security business inherited from earlier wars but still feared after the Cold War has receded because the bait of institutional enlargement has acted as a catalyst for reconciliation and reforms. Yet muting a legitimate U.S. satisfaction over Europe's current condition, there is growing exasperation over what is still missing now and even some apprehensions over what might be about to emerge.

For the growing number of Americans who have at last ceased to view "Europe" as an institutional fake, causes for apprehension are varied. Most generally, an ever more united and progressively stronger Europe could conceivably rise as a "counterweight" to U.S. power. As the Cold War was ending, Samuel Huntington was quick to forecast Europe's future as "the preeminent power of the 21st century." In 2002, the theme has become more common, with the EU widely seen by Joseph Nye as "the closest thing that the United States faces" for a world in which, suggests Thomas Friedman, "two United States are better than one." At its best, such a Europe might explain its interest in assuming a bigger role in the world as an obligation to protect Europe from America, but also America from itself.[4] At its worse, however, the increasingly assertive and even adversarial use of its newly regained weight would leave Europe as an alternative to U.S. leadership at the possible cost of U.S. interests. This latter prospect is all the more troubling as Europe might wish to pull its weight before it is ready, thus leaving Americans once again with the burden of finishing what Europeans would have started but could not complete. In other words, the new Europe cannot claim to do all it wants so long as it has not become all it can be, especially in the area of military capabilities and political unity. Pretending otherwise and viewing this moment as Europe's time would risk exposing the EU as a mere "counterfeit" of the superpower it claims to be.[5]

In coming years—through the 2003 constitutional convention and past IGC 2004—Americans will have to be convinced that the new Europe will be the "counterpart" successive U.S. administrations have awaited, rather than the counterweight or counterfeit they might resent or from which they could suffer. To achieve that lofty goal, much will be needed from both sides of the Atlantic. For Europeans, it is high time to take their own commitment to integration seriously—in other words, to do what they say after they have said what they will do. This is especially true in the area of foreign, security, and defense policy about which "headline goals"—for both capabilities and structure—should also come with robust deadlines if they are to gain the credibility they deserve. In addition, while thus crawling toward their institutional finality, Europeans should also acknowledge the U.S. role in the development of their Union. More specifically, the U.S. role and privileges as a non-member member state of the EU should be made an intrinsic part of Europe's finality debate—including, for example, the presence of a handful of American observers drawn from the U.S. Congress to the constitutional convention presided over by Valéry Giscard d'Estaing.

Only with a tangible acknowledgement of the U.S. role can the EU be engaged more directly than has been the case to date—on the same grounds as the bilateral relations maintained by the United States with each of the main EU members. Admittedly, U.S.-EU relations cannot substitute for bilateral relations so long as the Europeans themselves do not complete their Union. Yet, it is already possible to view the EU as the sixteenth member of the 15-member union—a virtual member that influences its partners no less than they influence each other. The pre-summit invitation extended to President Bush by the European Council during the Swedish EU presidency in June 2001, was a first step toward such a privileged U.S. status relative to, and even within, the EU. There should be more of such consultations not only at the highest political levels but also at lower levels and for each of the various bodies that "represent" the EU. But, to repeat, the dynamics of U.S.-EU relations will remain conditioned by what EU members do with and for their Union more than by what the United States seeks from each of them within or outside the union to which they already belong or which they hope to enter.

All That NATO Is Not

While the Atlantic Alliance is affected by the transformation of post-World Wars Europe, as Americans came to rediscover it after 1917, the post-Cold War North Atlantic Treaty Organization has also evolved. Most fundamentally, NATO, as its members relied on it after 1950, is finished. Although such a conclusion had been emerging after the war in Kosovo demonstrated the limits of NATO as a community of action, the events of 9-11 clearly reinforced it and the war in Afghanistan, which kept the Organization at a distance, made it explicitly marginal and seemingly irrelevant.

Since 1991, the United States and its 15 partners in Canada and Europe had sought to prepare NATO for the new security environment engineered by the collapse of the Soviet Union. A modest adaptation of

NATO, as well as its enlargement, was expected to expand the Western zone of stability to the rest of the continent. The war in Bosnia, and the escalation of violence elsewhere in the Balkans, made the process increasingly urgent, leading to the 1999 Washington anniversary summit, when the ongoing war in Kosovo justified further a first wave of three new members. After that, the 2002 summit in Prague was progressively viewed as a point of arrival for the final post-Cold War transformation of a NATO that would be opened to a second and larger group of new members.

How much such a transformation mattered for its members' security was unclear. A NATO at 19 was now meant to have a reach beyond the European continent, and even a "NATO at 20" that would partner more closely with Russia was not expected to gain the global reach that the Clinton administration had sought in early 1999. Nonetheless, within Europe the bait of enlargement proved decisive to settle some unfinished security business as applicant states resolved long-standing territorial and ethnic disputes in the name of the organizations (including the EU) that they hoped to join. To that extent, post-Cold War NATO demonstrated that it was still an effective tool of deterrence. But after the Kosovo war also demonstrated the difficulties of waging war by committee, NATO seemed on its way to being turned into a Cold War relic—an ever larger, passive, and shallow community lost without the Soviet threat and overwhelmed by the predominance of U.S. power.

Accordingly, on the way to the Prague Summit, the second wave of NATO enlargement seemed to raise little interest. Allies in Europe, openly focused on the EU and its ambitious agenda, were ready to follow the U.S. lead as of the moment when that leadership would be exerted. In the United States, however, the attention was also elsewhere—in the Middle East but also in Asia where China was viewed as the most dangerous challenger for the future. Admittedly, Russia might object to another NATO enlargement, especially when coupled with President Bush's emphatic interest in missile defense and deep cuts in offensive strategic capabilities. But Russian president Vladimir Putin also seemed resigned to these assertive displays of U.S. preponderance, especially after he was elevated to the status of a "soul brother" during their first meeting in Ljubliana, Slovenia, in June 2001.

Yet what an enlarged NATO would do, and where—and how it would be adapted, and when—was left unclear. That NATO could no longer make decisions by consensus, and that security could no longer depend on increasingly cacophonic "coalitions of the willing," was already true before any enlargement to the East, as shown during the protracted debates over Bosnia, when NATO had "only" 16 members. In 1999 a surplus of "willing" partners made the war in Kosovo a challenge to common sense, especially as too many of the willing were not capable, while many of the most capable were also the least responsive to the will of the coalition. Even without September 11, and before further enlargement in Prague, unilateral decisions by the United States on behalf of its NATO allies had become more difficult to impose, and an ever more united Europe with a security identity it could call its own was bound to increase that difficulty exponentially.

In addition, because most of the new NATO members were small, weak, or poor, the capabilities gap within Europe would be growing no less dramatically than the capabilities gap between Europe and the United States—between Latvia and France, say, no less than between France and the United States. In any case, the gap was no longer defined by the availability and quality of military capabilities, but also by the will to use them assuming the ability to agree on the areas, in and out of Europe, where these capabilities might be used. Previously, it was America's will to use military force everywhere that had been questioned. Now, it is Europe's will to use them anywhere that was in question: weakness encourages appeasement, or at least a quest for "solutions" that avoid the use of force even at the cost of additional, occasionally unwanted, and often self-defeating compromises.

In Afghanistan, the NATO allies expected that their offer of solidarity entitled them to an active role in the war that they were willing to enter but unable to fight because of their own insufficiencies relative to the U.S. own self-sufficiency. Yet, reports of an American neglect of Europe's offer were no less exaggerated than related accounts of European dissatisfaction with such alleged neglect. The NATO allies were not underused by the United States: it is their uses—in part military, but mainly non-military—that were understated on both sides of the Atlantic. What the United States can do is necessary—indeed "indispensable," as Secretary of State Madeleine Albright once put it. But it is not, and is unlikely to become, sufficient: there is far too much instability around the world to be managed by the United States alone—blowbacks inherited from earlier conflicts everywhere and over time. The same is true of NATO. During the Cold War, one organization was enough to attend to the common defense of the West: one enemy, one alliance, one theater, and one hegemonic leader. This was U.S. unilateralism with a NATO *prix fixe*. Now, the security environment is more diffuse, the war more strange, and the enemy more elusive—everywhere and nowhere, about everything and for nothing. Whether at one (the United States), at 20 (with Russia), at 26 (after Prague), or at many more (past 2004), NATO alone will not suffice: however necessary the alliance may be for military purposes, it is not, and never was, a full-service institution. It is Western multilateralism *à la carte*—a bit of this institution and a bit of that institution, simultaneously or consecutively, and designed to constrain or engage their leading members.

Admittedly, other NATO countries must spend more on defense—and past the French and German elections there are indications that they will, at least to an extent. The shared goal is not only to remain "interoperable," but also to maintain appropriate levels of "co-operability" without which the alliance would be too unbalanced to gain the global scope it now needs and was given at the Prague Summit. But the criteria of co-operability are not met only with levels of defense spending. They are also met by what NATO countries in Europe can do in relief of their senior partner during the latter innings of a particular contest. Working through the EU, the European allies have the economic capabilities to reward and sanction; they have the political tools to stabilize and punish; and they have the know-how to negotiate and isolate.[6] Like sheer military power, these capabilities, these tools, and these skills are hardly sufficient to initiate action—but they are undoubtedly necessary to end it.

In short, on the way to Prague enlargement ceased to be NATO's central issue and it even ceased to be a contentious issue for Russia. Indeed, it ceased to be an issue at all: bigger might or might not be better for the Organization, but that would be of little significance if NATO itself was not made better and became all it can be as an organization with a global reach. Unless it was decided to let a larger NATO wither away, the NATO agenda therefore needed to be broadened *à la* EU. For enlargement to be effective the Organization also needed a new mandate and more capabilities, as well as a reform of its structures and governance. In other words, for NATO, too, the agenda became widen in order to deepen, deepen even as you widen, and reform in order to do both. Accordingly, in Prague NATO did not merely complete the post-Cold War process launched by its 16 members in Rome in June 1991. It also pointed to the rise of a new NATO whose 26 members would rely on new capabilities equipped for global action and placed under the control of new command structures designed to give the Organization the means and reach needed to wage a global war on the new enemy.

Defining the "New Normalcy"

The limits of NATO as the security institution of choice, but also its unparalleled potential over that of any ad hoc alliance were reinforced by the events of September 11, 2001, and the "new normalcy" of "post-modern conflicts" it threatened to inaugurate. Central to the uncertainties that surround NATO and its purpose is a fundamental difference between the allies over the meaning and implications of these events.[7]

The semantic contest that began almost at once between America and its European allies reflected a clash of historic experiences that became increasingly open in 2002.[8] For Europeans, notwithstanding the spontaneous emotions generated by the extraordinary sight of their bleeding, crippled, and even frightened senior partner, these events were, in a sense, predictable—history as usual. Hegemonic powers cannot live their moment of preponderance without pain. Indeed, judged by standards set by history, the pain endured by America on September 11 was relatively minor—a few minutes worth of casualties on a bad day in Europe, in 1916 or 1940. Understood as an act of terror, that pain pointed to a way of life that European countries have faced and defeated many times, from Northern Ireland to the Basque region—although the standards of September 11 were especially disconcerting since, in Jacques Chirac's words, "next time it might be us." Still, having properly demonstrated their sympathy, Europeans could invoke the *déjà vu* of history to reassert the *déjà dit* of the need for consultation with the allies and for patience in defeating the enemy.

For Americans, however, such logic hardly applied. Pain may well be the way of history, but it is not the American way. Wars are expected to be waged "over there" where the forward deployment and use of superior American power keeps them by containing foes and even, on occasion, friends too. "Over here," there might be acts of terror initiated by misguided high school teens or nihilistic misfits. But these acts would be home bred, not exportable to the nation by evil forces abroad. On the whole, so it has been since the War of 1812, and for 189 years subsequent attempts to violate America's territorial invulnerability were stopped and countered forcefully, whether far away in the Pacific (after Pearl Harbor) or closer in the Caribbean (after the Cuban missile crisis). Under such conditions, the war that erupted in Afghanistan, where the culprits hid, was more than America's "first war of the twenty-first century" (as President George W. Bush dubbed it)—it was indeed the first war in at least half a century which America could truly call its own. The U.S. goal was not to protect or avenge others but to avenge and protect America's citizens and its institutions. It would therefore be fought the American way: admittedly brutally, until unconditional surrender or unmitigated annihilation, and somewhat unilaterally, with coalition members used on the basis of need rather than because of stated availability.[9]

But this transatlantic clash of history is not limited to the experiences enjoyed by the New World relative to, or occasionally at the expense of, the Old World. It is also rooted in the differing interpretations that were and continue to be made of the most effective way to contain the threats unveiled through the attacks on the World Trade Center and the Pentagon. As Eric Hobsbawm noted on the eve of the twenty-first century, "single, specific events ... are unpredictable," but even *post facto* the real task for historians and analysts "is to understand how important they are or could be." That certainly is true of the events of September 11: however unpredictable these events may have been, it would be wrong to shy away from assessing their consequences.[10]

Europe's vision of the "new normalcy" does not fit the U.S. view, let alone its preference. For many in Europe, the perpetrators of this act of violence, already helped by their enemy's blunders and also by chance, aim mostly at the United States and the local conditions it permits or even creates. Accordingly, it is important to influence U.S. responses whose motivation might be legitimate but whose consequences would be felt in and beyond Islamic countries, including in European countries where the risks of a cultural spillover are especially high. Thus, the Euro-Atlantic community of interests perceived in the immediate aftermath of September 11 have come under threat since President Bush began to emphasize the other dimensions of an "axis of evil" that included, but was hardly limited to, Iran (and North Korea) as well as Iraq.

However, with America's traditional margin of security now bridged, there is less room for ambiguity and indecision, at home as well as from the allies. The threats posed by weapons of mass destruction that have been, or are, acquired by intrinsically hostile groups or evil states are real, lethal, and unacceptable. "The depth of the hatred," said President Bush in his State of the Union address of January 29, 2002, "is equaled by the madness of the destruction they design." The hypothesis is too daunting to be checked for accuracy after the fact. The madness will have to be denied before the hatred can be cured, thereby making it necessary to "be ready for preemptive action when necessary to defend our liberty," as the president put it more cogently in his address in June 2002 at West Point.

This is the defining question that was raised on September 11, 2001, when four hijacked planes and 19 criminals ended America's sense of territorial invulnerability. The risk had been perceived by America and its allies—it was one of these "other risks of a wider nature" first envisioned in NATO's 1991 Strategic Concept, and reasserted next in its 1999 Strategic Concept. It is an existential risk written with the invisible ink of an unpredictable future. It carries with it the related risk of an undeclared cultural war that would prove irreversible for the many after it might have been precipitated by the suicidal acts of the few.

The response of Western powers to that risk should not be to go it alone but to go it together. While "Europe must understand we are ready and able to act without them to fight this new war," as Richard Perle put it,[11] the United States is probably neither ready nor able to end this war, even if it continues to win every military engagement it faces or launches. September 11 should be catalyst for a renewal of the West as a community of action that is shaped by interests that are common even when they are not always equally shared. What it needs, and must seek in and beyond each of the two central institutions that comprise it, is more, not less, integration. Among themselves as a mutually shared right of first refusal, but also with new associates and partners, the NATO countries should be able to agree on some immediate priorities and certain key principles on how to define and counter these new threats, as well as on what to do during the days after these threats have been defeated or even preempted. As Samuel Huntington has stated, "the idea of integration" is "the successor idea to containment." More specifically, integration is "about locking [the allies] into these policies and then building institutions that lock them in even more."[12] This is the idea that was launched along two parallel paths after World War II, and refined—deepened and enlarged—throughout and since the Cold War. It is also the idea that can now be completed by and between the United States and the states of Europe in the context of the new normalcy envisioned after the Cold War for the twenty-first century. The goal is not merely to do something, let alone everything, together, but to make sure that together, everything, or even something, gets done.

Notes

1   Robert Kagan, "Power and Weakness," *Policy Review*, No. 113, June–July 2002: 1.
2   Nothing lastingly new in Europe, insists John Mearsheimer when he writes, ominously: "Almost every European state, including the United Kingdom and France, still harbors deep-seated albeit muted fears that a Germany unchecked by American power might behave aggressively." (*The Tragedy of Great Power Politics* [New York: W.W. Norton, 2001], 2.)
3   Isaiah Berlin, *Four Essays on Liberty* (New York: Oxford University Press, 1969), 52.
4   Samuel Huntington, "The U.S.—Decline or Renewal?" *Foreign Affairs* (Winter 1988-89), 93. Joseph Nye, *The Paradox of American Power, Why the World's Only Superpower Can't Go It Alone* (Oxford University Press, 2002), 29. Thomas Freedman, "I love the E.U.," *New York Times*, June 22, 2001.
5   For example, see Charles A. Kupchan, "The End of the West," *The Atlantic Monthly*, November 2002, 42-44, and "The Last Days of the Alliance," *Financial Times*, November 17, 2002.
6   Christopher Hill, "The EU's Capacity for Conflict Prevention," *European Foreign Affairs Review*, Vol. 6 (2001): 329.

7   The reference to a "new normalcy" was first made by Vice President Richard Cheney. Quoted by Bob Woodward, "CIA Told To Do Whatever Necessary To Kill Bin Laden," *The Washington Post*, October 11, 2001, 22. Also, Lawrence Freedman, "Post-Modern Conflict," *Financial Times*, September 12, 2001.
8   Eliot A. Cohen, "A Strange War," *The National Interest*, No. 65-8 (Thanksgiving 2001): 3. For a lengthier discussion of some of these concluding themes, see my own "The Wars of 9/11," *The International Spectator*, Vol. 36 (October-December 2001): 5–11.
9   "Leadership demands a Pagan ethos," pleas Robert D. Kaplan, as he acknowledges, or boasts of, "the imperial reality" that "already dominates our foreign policy" and which demands that "power politics [be placed] in the service of patriotic values." (*Warrior Politics* [New York: Random House, 2001], 145, 154.)
10 Eric Hobsbawm, in conversation with Antonio Polito, *The New Century* (London: Abacus Books, 1999), 1
11 Quoted by Vago Muradian, "NATO Remains Key, But U.S. Ready To Fight Antiterror War Without Europe," *Defense Daily International*, February 8, 2002, 2.
12 Quoted by Nicholas Lemann, "The Next World Order," *The New Yorker*, April 1, 2002, 46.

Chapter 4

NATO's 2002 Enlargement: US-Allied Views on European Security

Marco Rimanelli

Introduction: NATO Enlargement vs. "New Threats" ("9/11," Iraq, North Korea)

During both World Wars and Cold War, Europe's security has been entwined with America and the NATO Alliance as the cornerstone of the last 50+ years in protecting a widening Transatlantic area of 19 Allies, 10 Aspirants and 16 Partners (made up of "neutrals," ex-Communist foes of East Europe and ex-USSR), with shared Western values (democracy, freedom, market economy), US leadership and its nuclear umbrella. The Cold War forced together both victors and foes of World War II into a US-led collective defense against the USSR in any World War III, while bridging the Allies' old nationalist hatreds through politico-military cooperation among equals. After the 1989-91 collapse of Soviet-Communist rule in East Europe and USSR, most ex-foes sought dual integration in NATO and the European Union (E.U.) to guarantee national security and economic integration in a US-led West.

Today, the US-led Euro-Atlantic security architecture institutionalizes cooperation with neutrals and ex-Communist states in the OSCE, NAC/Euro-Atlantic Partnership Council, NATO-E.U.'s European Defense Identity (ESDP), as gateways to NATO's Enlargement to 13 Aspirants, once they qualify politically, militarily and economically (Membership Action Plans). Like NATO's 1999 Enlargement to Poland, Hungary and the Czech Republic, also the November 2002 Prague Summit sifted through 10 Enlargement options to accept 7 new Allies ("Mini-Bang": incorporating the military better-prepared Slovenia, Slovakia, Lithuania, Estonia, plus weaker Latvia, Romania and Bulgaria), with US support twice overcoming Allied reservations and Russian opposition. Both

Aspirants and new Allies are also striving to join the E.U., with its Copenhagen Summit in December 2002 accepting 10 new members by 2004 (and the 4 weakest Aspirants delayed to the decade's end). Thus, the post-Cold War new "Europe" strengthens its unity through a dual Enlargement identity (military integration in NATO and economic one in the E.U.), to jointly preserve Transatlantic bonds with America, regional stability, NATO-ESDP security cooperation and Balkan peace-keeping.

Paradoxically, as these enlargement successes make Europe finally whole and militarily secure in the post-Cold War, both NATO and the E.U. suddenly face escalating strains against unconventional "New Threats." The "9/11" attacks by pan-Islamic terror-networks and proliferant "rogue-states" (mostly Iraq and North Korea) compete in threatening America and Europe with hard-to-detect terrorist strikes and soon missiles armed with weapons of mass destruction (WMDs: chemical, biological, nuclear). Europe's disarray is the result of both the E.U.'s desperate resolve to pursue at all cost only fruitless diplomatic negotiations, while NATO's relevance as a war-fighting Alliance has been dramatically undermined by domestic-driven anti-war vetoes from Germany, France and Belgium, backed by Russia and China, to stymie within NATO, the E.U. and U.N. any American drive to totally destroy the Iraqi regime in 2003 (all opponents argue that U.N. inspectors need more time to disarm Iraq and avoid a "pre-emptive" US strike). Both NATO and E.U. leaders fear that the bitter divisions in NATO (which aborted a US-backed plan on war-preparations and to protect Turkey against the threat of Iraqi attacks) would also split the E.U., preventing both organizations from forging a single European voice on the Iraqi threat. Most NATO-E.U. members (especially Great Britain, Portugal, Denmark, Italy, Spain and new East European Allies) backed America's military plans and bitterly opposed the hold-outs (France, Germany, Belgium, Austria, Sweden, Luxembourg, backed at the U.N. by Russia and China) who sought more time for U.N. inspectors in Iraq, rather than war. Like few other crises in the past, it has been this chasm in resolve and cooperation over "New Threats" between America and few key Allies, which dangerously weakens the fabric of common transatlantic security.[1]

NATO from Cold War to Collective Security and Enlargement, 1949-1999

The end of the Cold War and the USSR forced NATO to evolve from collective defense (Art.V) to collective security (Art.IV), regional stabilization and "Out-of-Area" peace-keeping in a broad Euro-Atlantic region, while slowly integrating "neutrals" and ex-foes (East Europeans and ex-USSR):

1) Since 1990 NATO's collective security guarantees peace on a broad Euro-American area including the ex-USSR (with peace-keeping in Bosnia, Kosovo, Albania, Macedonia and Afghanistan).
2) NATO fosters a "Europe whole, democratic, free" and tied to the US., by enlarging twice in 1999 and 2002 to most Aspiring Allies, while supporting politico-military-economic reforms and cooperation with 30 "neutral" and ex-Communist states (Euro-Atlantic Partnership Council).
3) After the "9/11" Islamic terrorist attacks of 2001 in the US., NATO has invoked for the first time its Art.V defense clause to support the US-led global coalition war against terrorism and peace-keeping in Afghanistan, thus institutionalizing "Out-of-Area" missions beyond Europe.

NATO's strategic evolution is based on the "Open Door" and 1999-2002 Enlargements to 10 Central-East European Aspirants (with others in a later Third Enlargement), who were EAPC members with democratic values, market economies and minimal NATO military interoperability as "producers of security" (Partnership for Peace military cooperation, Balkan peace-keeping, Membership Action Plans). At the 2002 Prague Summit doubts among many experts and Allies (like Great Britain and Germany) on several Aspirants' viability were quelled by the "9/11" Crisis, America's fight on new international crises and the lack of a USSR-type conventional threat.[2]

Already during the Cold War NATO expanded from 12 members in 1949 to 14 in 1952 (Greece, Turkey), 15 in 1955 (West Germany) and 16 by 1982 (Spain) building large conventional defenses and geo-strategic links to far-flung allies against a compact Soviet bloc. However, in the early-1990s both America and Europe recoiled at accepting as members 13 ex-Communist Aspirants:

1) NATO's inter-government consensus and US leadership lacked blueprints for enlargement, while having to recast its politico-military mission from anti-USSR collective defense to "Out-of-Area" collective security to avoid collapse of its down-sized militaries and cohesion if too many Soviet-trained ex-foes quickly joined without adapting combat-doctrine, standardization and resources.
2) NATO also feared that a rapid Eastward Enlargement to ex-Communist Aspirants would destabilize the region if a semi-democratic Russia collapsed while opposing NATO Enlargement.

3) East Europe is a "no-man's land" between weak pro-Western semi-democracies and violent post-Communist national-populists, with NATO paralyzed by Yugoslavia's Civil Wars (1991-2001).[3]

Both Presidents George Bush Sr. and Bill Clinton wanted to avoid isolating a fallen USSR/Russia, and favoured until 1994 conflict-resolution in a post-Cold War Europe: by using the Conference on Security and Cooperation in Europe (OSCE), and NATO's North Atlantic Cooperation Council (NACC), they guaranteed US-Russian involvement in a 46 member-strong Transatlantic and Euro-Asian security system (including Allies, "neutrals" and ex-Communist states-East Europeans, Russia and all states after the USSR's disintegration in December 1991). Instead, despite rejection by the US and NATO since 1991, the 12-strong "Visegrad Group" (Poland, Lithuania, Hungary, Czech Republic and Slovakia, soon joined by Estonia, Latvia, Romania, Bulgaria, Slovenia, Albania, Macedonia and Croatia) repeatedly sought security in NATO (Art.V collective defense and US nuclear umbrella) against fears of future Russian expansionism and regional ethno-nationalist conflicts.

The US also favored the E.U.'s politico-economic integration and expansion to Aspirants as a substitute for NATO's more controversial Enlargement: the E.U.'s December 2002 Copenhagen Summit accepted 10 of 14 Aspirants by 2004 (Czech Republic, Cyprus, Estonia, Hungary, Poland, Slovenia, Malta, Lithuania, Latvia, Slovakia), with weaker Aspirants delayed after 2005 (Croatia, Romania, Bulgaria, Turkey). But the E.U. could not offer Aspirants credible security protection. Thus, dual NATO-E.U. membership always remained the goal of the "Visegrad Group," especially once regional conflict-resolution collapsed during the bloody Yugoslav Civil Wars (where Belgrade's Great Serbian dream and "ethnic cleansing" killed 300,000 and left hundreds of thousands refugees).[4]

NATO's Twin Enlargements: US, Allied and Aspirants' Views, 1999-2002

US Leadership in 1999 vs. 2002

1) Given chronic Allied divisiveness in both Enlargements (1999-2002), NATO decisions were dominated by Washington. In 1993-1994, President Bill Clinton was swayed by Germany, Poland and Czech Republic to integrate in the West all democratic Central-East European states. In 1994-1997, Clinton's secured bipartisan and Allied support for NATO's

Enlargement, despite critics' fears of a new Cold War with Russia and high costs of integrating many weak Aspirants:

2) NATO's 1994 Brussels Summit integrated all NACC and OSCE members in NATO's new Partnership for Peace defense cooperation, but only those fully committed to Transatlantic values and security would become new Allies through the 1995 *Study on NATO Enlargement*'s strict criteria: democratization; 1994 Partnership activities; politico-economic reforms; pro-Western policies; pro-NATO military contribution for peace-keeping; geo-strategic and logistic assets.[5]

3) All "Visegrad-12" Aspirants sought quick bloc integration, but only Poland, Slovenia, Hungary, Slovakia and the Czech Republic were worth integrating (also due to Germany's advocacy).

4) In 1993-1995, NATO was too deeply fractured to act either on Enlargement or "Out-of-Area" actions in Bosnia, until the 1995 US-NATO and Croat interventions against the Bosnian-Serbs imposed NATO's peace-keeping (IFOR-SFOR) and a tense regional peace (1995 Dayton Accords).

5) Moscow and Kiev's 1997 alignment with the West (Partnership for Peace; NATO-Russia Charter; NATO-Ukraine Charter, Balkan peace-keeping), diluted Russia's bitter opposition to NATO Enlargement and forestalled any renewed Cold War. Although Russia remains the most volatile of NATO's Partners and suspended bilateral relations in 1999-2000, this was due to NATO's 1999 Kosovo War against Yugoslavia and not by NATO's 1999 Enlargement (Washington Summit).

6) In 1999-2002, NATO focused on Aspirants' MAPs (performance; military doctrines; realistic priorities; domestic support for politico-military-economic reforms), while admitting that all need a decade to complete reforms. The Aspirants in turn, sought to balance strict MAP military goals with "informal criteria" (democracy, economic transformation, Partnership, geo-strategy).

NATO's Prague Summit (24 November 2002) strengthened Transatlantic security, US leadership and "Out-of-Area" peace-keeping (Balkans and Afghanistan), while continuing the 2001 Anti-Terrorist War and Europe's democratic unification through parallel NATO-E.U. Enlargements. Also in 1999-2002, lack of Allied leadership on NATO's second enlargement (including Germany and France, active in 1997-99) forced US diplomacy to cultivate bipartisan support and defuse Allied concerns that a large 2002 pool of new members would alienate Russia, cost too much and leave NATO unwieldy. Like earlier NATO summits, Prague also ensured that "left-out" Aspirants continue to strive for membership and not become demoralized, undercutting pro-Western reforms.[6]

Allied Views in 1999 vs. 2002

Most Allies initially resisted US proposals (1994-1995) to enlarge NATO to ex-Communist states, and during NATO's First Enlargement debate (1997-1999) remained divided:

1) the 1999 agreed "Minimalist Mitteleuropean Option" advocated by Germany and US for three better-prepared Aspirants (Poland, Hungary, Czech Republic), defused a NATO-Russia clash on the Baltics and Allied discord on unprepared, democratically-weak Romania, Slovakia, Bulgaria and Slovenia;
2) a "Maximalist Mitteleuropean Option" with 6 Aspirants (the three above plus Slovenia, Slovakia, Romania);
3) a "Central-East European Option" to 10 of 12 Aspirants (an early "Big-Bang" including the three controversial Baltic states and Bulgaria, but not unstable Albania and Macedonia).

NATO's "Open Door" later assured future memberships for all "Left-outs" once the "Perry Principles" (objective readiness benchmarks under NATO's "19+1" reviews and annual MAPs) did streamline Aspirants' politico-military reforms, military budgets, resource-allocations, training, peace-keeping and human rights. Despite misgivings that the MAPs would indefinitely postpone a Second NATO Enlargement, by the 2002 Prague Summit these military criteria had turned most new Allies and Aspirants into "producers of security" (US pressures allowed also latitude for geo-strategic criteria):

1) America, Germany and other Allies supported in 1997-1999 the stronger Visegrad-3 (Poland, Hungary, Czech Republic), as Clinton's poster-children for a true "Europe Whole and Free," given their politically important ethnic brethren in US elections and better-prepared militaries. Since 2001 America has pushed Allies on a Second Enlargement (Slovenia, Slovakia, the three Baltic states, and recently also Romania and Bulgaria) quietly cultivating domestic bipartisanship, while defusing Allied concerns and Russian opposition through new US-NATO-Russian cooperation (WMD proliferation, nuclear arms control cuts, anti-Terrorist War, Afghanistan, Iraq).
2) Germany, the most vocal 1990s Enlargement supporter, was "softer" than perceived: it sought secure eastern borders through Polish-Czech dual NATO-E.U. membership, but wavered when Russia opposed Enlargement.

In 1999-2002, the new domestic-oriented Schroeder government (SPD) eschewed a leading role in NATO's Second Enlargement, given its secure borders after the 1999 entry of Poland, Czech Republic and Hungary, which pushed Russian forces into Belarus. Berlin supported only Slovenia and Slovakia (NATO's vital geo-strategic links to Hungary), but rejected Baltics (indefensible and opposed by Russia) and Balkan Aspirants (poor, unready, unstable).[7]

3) All Allies acknowledged Bulgaria's and Romania's help for NATO's logistical and peace-keeping in Bosnia, but in 1997-99 only Southern Allies (France, Italy, Greece, Turkey) supported also admitting Slovenia, Romania and Bulgaria to balance NATO's shift towards mostly Northern new Allies and Aspirants (allegedly under Germany's sway). But US-Allied support waned, given these four Aspirants' shortcomings (stalled politico-military reforms; excessive reliance on geo-strategic criteria as "consumers of security"; political instability; weak democracies; and weaker market economies). Yet once NATO's 1999 Washington Summit excluded them, the Allies were embarrassed into requesting the "Left-outs" and Croatia's logistical aid during the spring 1999 Kosovo War. By 1999-2002 most Allies remained torn on rewarding Slovenia, Romania and Bulgaria, with strong support from France, Italy (both critical of the 1999 "unilateral" US decision favoring the Visegrad-3 and playing a low-key now), Hungary, Greece, Turkey and Spain.

4) In 1999 Canada, Belgium, Netherlands, Luxembourg, Spain and Portugal did not oppose the "Visegrad-3," Slovakia and Slovenia, while in 2002 they supported just Slovenia, Slovakia and Lithuania. But all agreed to follow US leadership with the 3 Nordics, Poland, France, Italy, Hungary, Czech Republic, Greece and Turkey, once "9/11" geo-political threats and Russia's muted opposition made acceptable a "Mini-Bang" of 7 Aspirants (with the Baltics), despite uneven MAPs.

5) In both Expansions only the Nordic states (Denmark, Norway, Iceland) supported entry for the three Baltics, but most Allies (including the 5 major Allies, US, Britain, Germany, France, Italy) opposed them as unready and provocative for Russia. Until 2001 their position remained unchanged, hoping the Baltic states would first join the E.U. before admittance in a future NATO third Enlargement. By 2002, the new Bush Jr. Administration quietly pushed the Allies to accept a "Mini-Bang" Option.

6) In both Enlargements, the UK rejected all Aspirants as unready and too costly (Slovenia and Slovakia were reluctant choices in 1999–2002), but once marginalized London did not veto either NATO's 1997 Madrid consensus on the Visegrad-3, or Prague's 2002 accord on 7 new members.

7) In both Expansions all Allies rejected Albania and Macedonia (plus

Croatia, not yet an Aspirant in 1999 but a 2002 late-comer) as chronically unstable. But all support a Third NATO Enlargement to Croatia and "Neutrals" to finish Europe's dual NATO-E.U. integration of respective members. In any distant Fourth Enlargement, only Turkey, Poland, Greece, Romania and Bulgaria would support Ukraine in NATO and E.U., while most Allies oppose Moldova, Bosnia, Kosovo, Yugoslavia, Russia and ex-Soviet states (all weak, unstable and unready). Allies also fear NATO's effectiveness weakening as a new OSCE saddled with Russian "permanent objections."[8]

Aspirants' Views in 1999 vs. 2002

Since 1991, 13 ex-Communist Central-East European Aspirants sought dual identities as NATO-E.U. members against Russia and rival neighbors, but converting national economies to Capitalism for E.U. integration left NATO's security integration constrained at lower defense budgets. NATO's 1997-1999 First Enlargement saw military criteria lagging behind political and geo-strategic ones (defenses and democratization) for key Aspirants (Poland, Hungary, Czech Republic, Slovenia, Slovakia, Romania). Poland has the largest, best ex-Warsaw Pact military, but all Aspirants' forces declined since the 1989 collapse of Soviet rule, until NATO Enlargement propelled them to modernize, with NATO interoperability and peace-keeping, while minimizing clashes with Russia by holding in Germany Alliance forces and tactical nuclear weapons:

1) Stronger "Visegrad-3" (Poland, Hungary, Czech Republic) Allies protect Germany and NATO's eastern borders up to Russia, Belarus' and the Balkans. As new Allies, the Czech Republic and Hungary backtracked on the 2% GDP defense spending promised upon joining NATO ($1.1 billion and $0.7 bn. respectively in 2001), with only Poland at 1.2%-to-2% GDP ($3,2 bn.).
2) Since 1999, the three new Allies have been slowly completing integration: their Warsaw Pact forces are still too large and armor-heavy (Cold War doctrine for World War III) compared to needed air-lift and rapidly-deployable forces (post-Cold War peace-keeping), while competing socio-economic priorities and lack of coherent planning erodes military budgets.
3) Gaps in planning and resources slow military reforms, while cutting forces by 2006: Hungary with 10 million people and $47 bn. GDP is cutting its 52,000 men to 37,000; Poland with 38.8 million and a $160 bn. GDP is cutting its 201,000 manpower force to 150,000; and the Czech

Republic with 10.2 million and $52 bn. GDP is cutting its 57,000 men to 40,000.⁹

4) The "Visegrad-3" shared a history of anti-Communist insurgency and democratic politico-economic growth after the 1989 Revolutions, reflecting NATO's own democratic bias since the 1974-1975 demise of Allied Fascist régimes in Greece, Portugal and Spain. Thus in 1999, NATO sacrificed geo-strategic links to Hungary by "delegitimizing" Slovakia and Romania once they became politically unstable under the anti-Western, anti-reformist Meciar and Iliescu governments, as well as Slovenia for her policy as "consumer of security" based only on geo-strategic assets.

5) Public support for NATO Enlargement and missions remains shallow in most new Allies (except Poland) and ten Aspirants (at 50%), because their governments failed to prepare their peoples to the long-term costs and duties of NATO membership. Thus, temporary decline in popular-élite support followed the shock of being involved overnight in NATO's 1999 Kosovo War, but pro-NATO support has rebounded since, and is strongest in Poland, Hungary, Lithuania, Croatia and Albania.

Better-ready Group

Many newly-independent Aspirants must craft military structures from scratch, while Croatia's grew during the 1990s Yugoslav civil war, and all remain less-ready on MAPs (Slovenia, Slovakia and Lithuania are best) than the three new Allies of 1999. Aspirants experience even stronger discrepancies in forces against new threats to Europe and NATO: limited budgets (below NATO's goal of 2% GDP), contrasting national priorities, and pressures to complete military reforms of obsolescent forces. Few Aspirants' military have English-fluency or NATO experience, and lack performance-oriented personnel policies (rather than patronage-driven careers), while politicians and populations distrust the military, mostly given their repressive role during 44 years of Communist dictatorship, and misperception of a lack of post-Cold War threats.

1) Slovakia peacefully seceded from Czechoslovakia in 1992, with 5.4 million people, $19.6 bn. GDP, 33,000 men and $0.3 bn. defense budget in 2002. Bratislava has very limited air-lift or force-readiness, and needs constant prioritization of its limited resources (1.8% GDP), despite military reforms tutored by the US, Britain and the three new Allies. Meciar's electoral loss in 2002 guaranteed NATO's acceptance of Slovakia's at the 2002 Prague Summit.

2) Slovenia, the smallest ex-Yugoslav new state in 1991, was unprepared militarily during NATO's 1999 First Enlargement, relying on its geo-

strategic location between Italy and Hungary. With 2 million people, $18.6 bn. GDP, 7,600 men and $0.2 bn. defense budget in 2002, it has developed a solid civil-military interface but military reforms remain slow, without sea- or air-lift and low military readiness, except Aviation and Reaction Forces.

3) All three Baltic states—Lithuania, Estonia, Latvia—were ex-USSR Republics with forces inside Soviet units, so since independence in 1989 new national militaries were built with US and Nordic aid by pooling resources (BaltBat peace-keeping battalion; Baltic Defense College; BALTNET radars). By 2002 Lithuania and Estonia had the better MAPs, making Baltic membership difficult to dismiss compared to their 1999 weak military. In 2002, Lithuania has 3.6 million people, $11.2 bn. GDP, 12,200 men and $0.2 bn. defense budget; Estonia 1.4 million people, $5.6 bn. GDP, 4,500 men and $0.08 bn. defense budget; and Latvia 2.3 million people, $7.2 bn. GDP, 6,500 men and $0.02 bn. defense budget. But the Baltic states remain indefensible against Russia without large NATO redeployments or nuclear deterrence.[10]

Lesser-ready Group

The US and Allies agonized on Romania's and Bulgaria's worsening politico-economic-military weakness, despite MAPs and Clinton's unofficial promise to reward their aid for NATO's 1999 Kosovo War (strongly opposed domestically), while Croatia remains still too raw.

1) Romania and Bulgaria must reduce large old Warsaw Pact-type armored forces, while applying NATO doctrines and defense-planning to their role as NATO's vital geo-strategic land-link between Hungary, Greece and Turkey. In 1999–2002, both Aspirants and Slovenia, have engaged in far-reaching defense reforms and new civil-military relations, but have limited air/sea-lift or even rail-transport. The military have low readiness, except the well-prepared Romanian Surveillance and Reaction Forces and Bulgarian Rapid Reaction Forces—however both can only deploy small peace-keeping forces while reforms remain hampered by limited resources. By 2004, Romania with 22.2 million people, $38.4 bn. GDP and $0.8 bn. defense budget, is cutting forces from 150,000 to 112,000 men. Bulgaria with 8.2 million people, $12.8 bn. GDP and $0.3 bn. defense budget, is cutting forces from 82,000 to 40,000 men.

2) Croatia has a strong pro-Western stance (supporting NATO in the Balkans against Yugoslavia in 1994 and 1999, and U.N. war-crime trials), 4.4 million people, $19.4 bn. GDP, 58,300 combat-hardened men, $0.5 bn. defense budget and vital geo-strategic location (which led to quick

integration in the Partnership for Peace in May 2000). Yet despite Zagreb's aggressive quest since 1991 to quickly join both NATO and E.U., her late entry in 2002 as tenth Aspirant did not sway neither NATO at Prague, nor the E.U. 2002 Copenhagen Summit. Instead, Zagreb will be the leading NATO-E.U. Aspirant in a Third NATO Enlargement by mid-decade with E.U. "neutrals" (Austria, Sweden, Finland, Ireland), NATO "Left-outs" (Albania, Macedonia), and non-E.U. Allies (Romania, Bulgaria, Turkey).

Unready Group

The rebuilding of Albania's collapsed economic and political system, coupled with Albanian ethno-nationalist insurgency in Macedonia, make both nominal MAP Aspirants, with long-term NATO peace-keeping to stabilize them—AFOR in Albania; "Operation Amber Fox" in Macedonia—before they can ever become new Allies in a Third or later NATO Enlargements:
1) With 3 million people, $3.8 bn. GDP and $0.1 bn. defense budget, desperately poor Albania has still to recover from 45 years of the most backward Communist dictatorship, plus a lost decade of a disastrous transition from Communism since 1989, the politico-economic collapse of the country in 1997, its "tutelage" under Western peace-keepers, and the temporary inflow of 500,000 Kosovar-Albanian refugees during 1998-99. Without a military, Albania opened itself to NATO's operations during the 1999 Kosovo War against Yugoslavia, and under the MAPs will have a reconstructed 19,000-strong military by 2006.
2) Macedonia, with 2 million people, $3.6 bn. GDP, 16,000 men and $0.07 bn. defense budget, is beset by secessionist Albanian guerrillas, despite NATO peace-keeping. Creating new civil-military structures and prioritizing limited resources dominates their national security.[11]

NATO's 2002 Enlargement: Challenges and Advantages at Prague

Since 1997, NATO Enlargements were conditioned by European fear of a NATO-Russian clash on integrating ex-Communist satellites and ex-Soviet states ("red lines"). NATO's Second Enlargement (1999-2002) saw the Allies split again over 10 options (0; 2; 2+1; 4; 4+1; 2+3; 7; 7+1; 10), but without Germany's key support, most Allies accepted minimalist options (2; 2+1)—better-prepared Slovenia, Slovakia, Lithuania—which morphed by 2001 into the "North-South" options (4; 4+1)—Slovenia, Slovakia, Bulgaria, Romania and maybe Croatia. But since mid-2001, US support of Baltic inclusion drove NATO's debate towards larger options (2+3; 7), while rejecting "Postponement," "Zero Option" (0) and "Big-Bang" (7+1; 10). The June 2002 approval of US Senate funds for NATO's integration of 7 new Allies, allowed the US to gain Allied consensus at the 2002 Prague Summit for a "Mini-Bang" (Slovenia, Slovakia, Lithuania, Estonia, Latvia, Bulgaria, Romania—excluding Croatia, Albania and Macedonia), while boosting new capabilities (rapid-deployment forces; airlift; precision missiles; Missile Defense; civilian defense, cyber-security) and NATO-Russia anti-terrorist cooperation.

1) Geo-Politics—US Leadership and a United Europe: America's "post-Cold War Europe" supports NATO-E.U. cooperation to unify Europe as a peaceful, democratically stable region extended to the ex-Communist East, while rebalancing Transatlantic relations through "Out-of-Area" peace-keeping and ESDP Cooperation. NATO's 1999–2002 Enlargements were mostly influenced by US leadership (given Allied "softness"), and consolidate US leadership in Europe through new Allies and Aspirants' Atlantic loyalty versus any "E.U.-Caucus" by older NATO-E.U. dual members (a view made more apparent by the recent Franco-German opposition to a US attack on Iraq).

2) Geo-Strategy I—Land-links and Alliance Contiguity: For the first time in history, NATO's Second Enlargement secured complete regional contiguity via geo-strategic land-links among all Allies left isolated by earlier enlargements: from Norway and the Baltics (bypassing Russian Kaliningrad) to Greece and Turkey through Eastern Europe, Romania and Bulgaria.

3) Geo-Politics II—European Unification and Stabilization with Dual NATO-E.U. Enlargements: NATO and the E.U. stabilize both members and Aspirants as democratic, market economies and peaceful Allies, enlarging European unification, reforms and security to the Balkans and Baltics.[12]

4) Geo-Strategy III—E.U. Enlargement and ESDP cannot replace NATO: Both NATO and E.U. contribute to European security—one militarily, the other economically—but the E.U. cannot assure the Aspirants' defense. NATO-E.U. crisis-cooperation (ESDP's 60,000 to 180,000 forces in few years) works on terrorism and Balkan peace-keeping (as NATO turns over some missions in 2003), with exclusive ESDP leadership only "where NATO as a whole chooses not to engage."

5) Geo-Strategy IV—Future Enlargements: NATO's "Open Door" allows any Partners from the EAPC and Organization on Security and Cooperation in Europe (OSCE) to apply for NATO membership, while after "9/11" only a blurred line separates "European" and "Euro-Asian" members. A later

NATO Third Enlargement to 33+ Allies will complete Europe's integration to "Left-out" Aspirants (Croatia, Albania, Macedonia) and E.U. "neutrals" to avoid isolation after Baltic entry and NATO-ESDP cooperation (Austria, Sweden, Finland, Ireland, Cyprus, Malta), while opposing unstable ex-Soviet states (Ukraine, Georgia, Azerbaijan, Armenia, Moldova).

6) High NATO Enlargement Costs Myths: NATO incurs costs to adapt structures to new Allies, but individual costs to the US and Allies were minimal in both Enlargements, confounding critics, thanks to Partnership for Peace and MAP funds to modernize Aspirants. NATO also sees new Allies in the post-Cold War not needing costly war-fighting capabilities, but rapid mobile forces.

7) Size and Voting: Can NATO retain cohesion and combat-readiness as a consensus-based Alliance when Enlargements and voting balloon members to 19 (Washington 1999), 26 (Prague 2002), or even 33+ (2006?)? The last three US Ambassadors to NATO (Hunter, Vershbow, Burns) dismiss criticism that enlarging NATO hampers consensus: instead all non-Art.V NATO decisions were recently streamlined, preserving "veto" equality for all members, while Alliance combat cohesion will rely on "coalitions-of-willing" using NATO assets in "Out-of-Area" operations (non-Art.V) where not all Allies participate (1990-1991 Desert Storm against Iraq; 1997 Albania; 2003 Iraq).[13]

Conclusion: Prague's 2002 Enlargement Success Versus Europe's Disarray on "New Threats"

Two World Wars, the Cold War and post-Cold War prove beyond doubts that US involvement and leadership has stabilized and pacified Europe, with NATO preserving Euro-American Transatlantic security: 1) NATO deterred the Soviet threat of World War III and Communist subversion; 2) peace-keeping missions in the Balkans (Bosnia, Kosovo, Albania, Macedonia) and Afghanistan prove NATO effectiveness in difficult post-Cold War crises; 3) NATO's geo-strategic Enlargements (1952, 1955, 1982, 1999, 2002) strengthen European security, peace and democracy on the periphery.

NATO's 2002 Prague Summit on a Second Enlargement gave to the Bush Jr. Administration both the political and strategic opportunity to complete Europe's security integration through US/NATO leadership, despite Allied doubts and entrenched Russian opposition. The choice of large vs. modest 2002 Enlargement had to balance both bold geo-strategic vision ("Europe united, peaceful and free") and politico-military accountability (MAP modernization) to spur Aspirants' reforms and military inter-operability with NATO (on old geo-strategic gains), compared to the risk of nativist anti-Western backlash in Central-East Europe. The Prague summit's broad, regional "Mini-Bang" (7 new Allies with the Baltic states) allows NATO to expand Allied resources, influence US-European burden-sharing (most Allies spend below 2% GNP on defense), control ESDP, while countering a "E.U.-Caucus" in NATO.[14]

However, several experts worry that NATO's 2002 Enlargement to 26 members integrates too fast, too many weak new members, turning it into a hollow, "toothless, political institution" unable to increase military capabilities compared to rising security commitments (despite a new NATO-Russia Council and pledges for new NATO Rapid-Deployment forces). During the Cold War, European domestic social priorities routinely undercut national and NATO defense spending; thus the 2002 Enlargement to Slovenia, Slovakia, Lithuania, Estonia, Latvia, Romania and Bulgaria doubles NATO's militarily "free riders" under the US security umbrella (given the minimal role of Iceland, Luxemburg, Denmark, Portugal, Greece, Hungary and Czech Republic). NATO must distribute military capabilities through specialized, modern, multilateral force-planning, while consolidating links with the E.U. on counter-terrorism, ESDP and peace-keeping. A 26+ Alliance must also revise voting rules to improve decision-making, limiting consensus to Art.V collective defense and new Enlargements.

These policy changes are most urgent after "9/11" exposed NATO and Western vulnerability to uncontrollable "New Threats" (Islamic terrorism; WMDs; Iraq; North Korea; Iran). But many in Europe and America again question NATO's military relevance and US "unilateralism," given US-European disagreements and Franco-German anti-war vetoes (backed by few other Allies, plus Russia and China) against the US-led war in Iraq in 2003. Especially troubling is the stark Franco-German anti-war opposition, which cuts at the heart of traditional Transatlantic solidarity: seeking to salvage his razor-thin governmental majority against massive economic woes, SPD Chancellor Schroeder's vehement pacifist rhetoric since 2002 has sacrificed traditional US-German bonds by gambling his retention of power on strong pacifist undercurrents in Germany (and in the ex-East German Länder); in France instead, Conservative President Chirac's overwhelming hold on power has given fresh impetus to Paris' international ambitions, rationalized under the diplomatic rhetoric that U.N. inspectors need few more months in Iraq and that France and the "International Community" oppose any pre-emptive war against Saddam as both unnecessary and untimely yet. All this increasingly bitter divisiveness did not stop US politico-military plans against Iraq, but only strengthened the Bush Jr. Administration's perception of NATO as another multilateral institution "constraining" US global interventionism against unconventional "New Threats." Although Ambassador Burns stressed that NATO remains the military core of any US-led global coalition, rather than its exclusive component, the 2003 Franco-German vetoes on NATO assets for Turkey and against a US-led coalition war on Iraq risked undermining all of NATO's common security gains during the last 50+ years. Thus, if NATO shall remain the key US-European and Western politico-strategic conduit for international security in the XXI Century, all Allies must agree to quickly "muscle-up" their forces alongside America, while the USA must balance national and Transatlantic security. Otherwise, both sides shall regret Europe's pacifist blindness, NATO-E.U. impotence and America's failure of collective leadership.

Notes

1 *Enlargement of NATO: Poland, Hungary & Czech Republic in NATO Strengthens U.S. National Security* (Washington: State Department, 1998); Sabina Crisen ed., *NATO & Europe in 21st Century* (Washington: Wilson Center, 2000); Constant Brand, "E.U. Warns Iraq Rift May Disrupt Summit," Associate Press Wire Service (12 February 2003).

2 Marco Rimanelli ed., *NATO Enlargement 2002: Opportunities/Challenges* (Washington: National Defense University, 2001); Martin Smith & Graham Timmins, *Building Big Europe: E.U.-NATO Enlargements* (Aldershot: Ashgate, 2000).

3 David Yost, *NATO Transformed* (Washington: U.S. Institute Peace, 1998); Ron Asmus, "Clinton Administration & NATO's Enlargements, 1993–99," lecture Johns Hopkins University-SAIS, Washington (6 February 2001).

4 *NATO Handbook 50th Anniversary* (Brussels: NATO, 1999); Fraser Cameron, "Making E.U. Enlargement Work," *EES News* (Washington: Wilson Center, 2001); John Borawski, "NATO Enlargement & Russia," *Perceptions* (n.2, 1996).

5 *Study on NATO Enlargement* (Brussels: NATO, 1995); I.A.I., *Future of NATO* (Roma: International Spectator) n.2 (1999); Nicholas Burns, "NATO & New Era," AUP Conference "New World, New Europe, New Threats" (Paris: 2001); D.S. Yost, *NATO Transformed*, 70–301.

6 Steven Larrabee, "NATO Enlargement after the First Round," I.A.I., *Future of NATO*, 73–85; Jeffrey Simon, "Next Round of NATO Enlargement," *Strategic Forum*, n.176 (2000); Giano, *NATO Dossier* (Roma: 2000).

7 M. Rimanelli ed., *NATO Enlargement 2002*, 51–55; Zbigniew Brzezinski, "NATO: Dilemmas of Expansion," *National Interest* (Fall 1998); Ira Straus, "Russia in NATO? It can be Done," *Moscow Times* (4 October 2001).

8 Gale Mattox & Arthur Rachwald eds., *Enlarging NATO: National Debates* (Boulder: Rienner, 2001); Jeffrey Simon, "NATO's Membership Action Plan & Defense Planning," *Problems of Post-Communism* (n.3) vol.48 (2001).

9   Stephen Cambone ed., *NATO in European Stability* (Washington: CSIS-NATO, 1995); IISS, *Military Balance, 2001–02* (London: Oxford University Press, 2001); Jim Goldgeier, *NATO Enlargement Decision* (Washington: Brookings, 1999).
10 Jeffrey Simon, *NATO's Membership Action Plan & Next Round of Enlargement* (Washington: Wilson Center, 2000), 7–26; *Illuminating the "Gray Zone": NATO Enlargement* (Washington: Wilson Center, 1997).
11 Sabina Crisen ed., *NATO Enlargement & Peacekeeping* (Washington: Wilson Center, 2001); Simon Serfaty, *Stay the Course: European Union & Atlantic Solidarity* (Washington: CSIS-Praeger, 1997).
12 Tom Szayna, *NATO Enlargement, 2002–15* (Washington: RAND, 2001); Heather Grabbe, "Sharp Edges of European Security" (Paris: WEU, 2000); "ESDP after Helsinki's Summit" (Brussels: NATO-E.U. Parliaments, 2000).
13 Kori Schake, "NATO Chronicles: New World Disorder," *JFQ* (Spring 1999); Sean Kay, "Heading Nowhere?" *International Herald Tribune* (10 May 2002).
14 Markus Meckel, "Key Issues for Future Transatlantic Relations" (Brussels: NATO Parliament, 2001); Josef Joffe, "America & Euroweenies: Future Transatlantic Relations" (New Atlantic/AEI, 2002); N. Burns, "NATO & New Era"; Associate Press Wire Service, "France, Germany, Belgium Block NATO Plan on Iraq" (10 February 2003); BBC interview to French Foreign Minister Dominique de Villepin (2 March 2003).

Chapter 5

Looking Down the Road: NATO-EU Relations in the Age of Intelligence and the "Age of Access"

Alexis Debat

Recent comments about the state of the Transatlantic relationship have started to adopt the kind of apocalyptic lexis that is usually heard in emergency rooms. Here it is branded as "strained," "ailing" or even "dead." Public spats over the war in Iraq have indeed been spectacular. But this sense of drama and the fatalism displayed about the so-called rift in "values" defining this vital link for international security should not be exaggerated. There is no shortage of disagreements on Iraq, the Israeli-Palestinian conflict, trade, the role of multilateral institutions, and so on. But these are far from new. What is, is the fact that commentators are now confusing a philosophical "transatlantic syndrome" (another battle for the "new world" label) that started with the Mayflower with a tectonic shift within the Atlantic alliance. Beneath this background "chatter" and decades-old rhetorical guerrilla between "Le Monde" and "The National Review," the foundations of the transatlantic relationship—its power and commitment to market democracy—remains as much today the backbone of global wealth and international security as it was 50 years ago. Most polls conducted on both sides of the Atlantic clearly show that not only Americans and Europeans treasure the same fundamental values, but agree upon the threats and the way to cure them – multilaterally. And despite their constant bickering, European and American elites from both sides of the political spectrum still look at each other with awe. But the Cassandras in Washington, London, or Brussels are right to point that the arrangements and institutions linking United States and Europe are gradually but fundamentally evolving in a way that neither side of the Atlantic have anticipated, but that both probably find mutually satisfies their needs.

For example, by alienating most of the world's public opinion in its first three years in office, the Bush administration's "supply-side" foreign policy has opened a tremendous field of diplomatic opportunities for continental Europe, with its traditional—if sometimes overrated—multilateralism and "polite realism." Similarly, the redefinition of NATO's traditional role after Kosovo and the U.S. government's dwindling interest in such "entangling alliances" opens an entire new space for the European Security and Defence Policy to fill out.

Far from marking the beginning of NATO's "death," as portrayed by some conservative commentators, this reorganization of responsibilities and "burden-sharing" of the old continent's security means that the Atlantic Alliance is shifting its weight away from some of its traditional responsibilities (fight and win wars) and into others (build a security community). While already upon us, the process's future is far from secured on the positive side of the debate. European nations that form the core of the European Security and Defence Policy (France, Germany, the U.K., Spain and Italy) have to step up to these newfound responsibilities, not only by harmonizing their often differing interests and norms of behaviour in the region, but also, of course, by building the "right" capacity to ensure its own security. Much of the debate about ESDP's future has legitimately focused on this relative issue, and has emphasized the surprising discrepancy between European intentions and the reality of their financial commitment. With all due respect to their legitimacy, the regular complaints about Europe's "weak" defence budgets do not exactly address the real questions that underwrite the future of European security and its relation ship to NATO in a new strategic era of shared responsibilities, shared capabilities, expanding challenges, and limited resources.

An Age of Intelligence ... And Limited Capacities

Among their many driving forces, the 1990s and early 2000s were shaped by the sometimes painful transformation of American global leadership in the face of many new geopolitical, economic and technological developments. The simultaneous decline in value of nuclear weapons to foster security, as well as the maturation of decades and tens of billions of dollars of investments in civilian and military research in the field of information gathering and processing, forced Washington's policymakers into a "grand makeover" of American leadership. The logic was unbeatable: by ripping the benefits of its technological and intellectual monopoly in information and semiconductors technologies, the US government could shift the pillar of its influence within Cold War alliances from the irrelevant "nuclear umbrella" to the "information umbrella." As it became clearer that more military operations would now be conducted in a

WMD environment, the capacity to gather, process and disseminate information in near-real time, i.e. "intelligence" in its broadest sense—awareness—quickly emerged as a cornerstone of US military leadership.

By acting both as a wake-up call for the American political establishment and a strong diplomatic lever for Washington in its alliances in Europe and elsewhere, the terrorist attacks of September 11 marked the sad triumph of this strategic hypothesis. As a decentralized collection of "nodes" with hardly any center, Al-Qaeda emerged as a "terrorist internet" which disruption would call upon a "network-centric" approach now embodied in the Pentagon's controversial "Total Information Awareness" program. The event also confirmed the absolute necessity for intelligence processing and sharing (the root of the 9/11 "failure"), a focus that the US military validated on the battlefield with its impressive display of "network-centric warfare" during both "Operation Enduring Freedom" and "Operation Iraqi Freedom." All of these new trends concur to validate a profound strategic shift: the global security environment has now entered an "Age of Intelligence" dominated by networks, and where the capacity to identify an enemy/competitor, process and disseminate strategic or tactical intelligence about it through a secure network in near real-time is the key to the capacity to "win wars" in the broadest and newest possible sense, which is not only to coerce and defeat, but to do so at the smallest possible economic and human cost.

This fundamental shift from a "platform-centric" to a "network-centric" approach only strengthens the role of the US military and intelligence "archipelago" (there is no "community") as the processing center of a complex international intelligence network involving dozens of allies, as well as thousands of technological systems and human informants.

The implications of this strategic revolution for the Atlantic alliance are extremely significant.

The sheer horror of 9/11 sent shockwaves throughout the world and gave the US a much-needed influx of moral authority to lead the global war on terror. Within hours of the attacks, European leaders pronounced their "unlimited solidarity" with the United States, and NATO allies invoked the nearly forgotten Article V mutual defence article of the North Atlantic Treaty. But far from taking on that historic moment to elevate the Alliance as a crucial "node" of its global anti-terror network, Washington politely turned down NATO's offer to use its committees and troops to conduct this new conflict—even though a good deal of it had to be fought in Europe—preferring to gather a more informal and flexible "coalition of the willing."

Far from being surprising, this reaction was the first time that the US government had to put bluntly one of America's biggest doctrinal shifts since the end of the Cold War: its increasing reluctance to accept binding constraints on its sovereignty within alliances, especially when its soldiers are at stake. Few in Europe have measured the extent of the "trauma" that the organization's first (and last?) war in Kosovo represented for the Pentagon, which for the first time had to submit not only its contingency planning but its day to day tactical initiatives to the veto of its 18 allies. Few, if any, have since measured the sweetness of this irony: by running absolutely contrary to the lessons the US has learned from its contemporary military history, NATO's principle of "war by committee" condemned one of the organization's main functions: collective defence. Europe is a land of diplomats; America is a country of soldiers.

Even the Alliance's most recent history validates this reality. With its scheduled extension to 26 members from the Baltic to the Balkans, its partnerships several other nations in central Asia, as well as its growing focus on cooperation, research, and discussion, NATO is gradually shifting its emphasis away from collective defence and war fighting towards its second function: "multilateral security." In the process, the organization itself is turning into what the European Union was before the 1992 Maastricht Treaty: a forum where security policies and standards would be discussed and harmonized. From Washington, this "Europeanization" of NATO—which George W. Bush's enthusiasm for expansion clearly embraces—is also strengthened by a very simple cost-benefit calculus once again hammered home by the military campaign in Afghanistan: because Europe's capability in the field of "high-intensity operations" lags so far behind the United States, and is still not interoperable with its own forces, the Pentagon simply do not need its European partners for other than the painstaking and expensive low-intensity missions (patrolling, peacekeeping, nation-building) it does not wish to accomplish. The good news is that these missions are now being officially picked up by Washington's European allies.

But instead of being celebrated on both sides of the Atlantic, this tacit agreement on future "burden-sharing" in Europe was welcomed with mutual suspicion and even recriminations in Washington about the "gap" between the European Security and Defence Policy's stated goals and its members' concrete commitment to improve its military capacities.

The old continent's relative approach to military power—some say "lack of interest,"[1] which is overstated—stems from its scarce resources, limited security responsibilities, and its governments' historical trust in its diplomats and strategic thinkers' intellectual constructions. That means European governments only prepare for the most likely, whereas the US military consistently develops contingency planning and military capacities for the entire spectrum of threats. But that fundamental difference cannot fully justify the much-debated "capabilities gap" between Europe and the United States, especially at a time when Europe is now collectively committed to taking on new military responsibilities. As defined by the 1999 Helsinki summit's "Headline Goal," that means that Europe will be able to deploy and sustain (for at least one year) military forces of up to 60, 000 troops to undertake the full range of the "Petersberg tasks" (peacekeeping, crisis management and combat) set out in the Amsterdam Treaty of 1997. This commitment comes in time to take over the kind of operational responsibilities that the Pentagon does not want to bear anymore. More: it has been backed up by clear initiatives. To achieve this "Headline Goal" capacity, a series of European consortia have emerged and combined to plug the capabilities gap where it is most needed: in the areas of force projection, sensors and tactical strike platforms. Germany, for example, is taking the lead on strategic lift, while Spain focuses on air-to-air refuelling, and the Netherlands is pushing for joint provision of precision-guided munitions. The U.K. has adopted a similar approach through its clever "Tower of Excellence" program, by which it focuses its scarce research and procurement effort on a handful of "strategic" areas.

As needed as it is, this enterprise misses the bigger picture, and fails to address the hardest questions. Developing and buying new platforms alone will not do the trick in the Age of Intelligence, where capabilities matter less than their capacity to be integrated in real-time in a network as parts of the same body. If anything, Operation Enduring Freedom has shown that what now matters most to battlefield commanders is not simply to mobilize the highest-tech platforms but the highest-tech network to compile and process variously formatted high-tech (UAVs), medium tech (so-called "legacy systems") and low-tech (Northern Alliance guerrillas, US Forward Air Controllers) intelligence collection assets in real time, a process once called "sensor to shooter." But even amid fresh talks of a European Security and Defence Agency (ESDA) to foster joint weapon systems procurement, and a European Security and Defence Research Agency, to handle research and development (along the same lines as the American DARPA), any European push to modernize its military should be wise to focus on the areas and systems where it is the most need, but steer clear of the kind of tactical intelligence "network of networks" that it took the US decades and hundreds of billions of dollars to develop. Even if it draws on its impressive lead in some communication technologies, Europe cannot afford to duplicate such an effort on "network-centric warfare" at a time when military R&D funding throughout the continent is now barely 60% of what it was during the early 1990s. Europe cannot, and it should not, resist American leadership in this field, but embrace it. To exist and grow in the Age of Intelligence, its common foreign and security policy needs less a strong and self-sufficient military capacity than a relevant one.

An "Age of Access" ... And Synergy

Three years ago, the American economist Jeremy Rifkin came forward with another provocative and far-reaching volume, *The Age of Access*, in which he announced the decline of property as a basis for capitalist exchange and the emergence of a new vector for the creation of capitalist value added access:

> In the new era, markets are making way for networks, and ownership is steadily being replaced by access ... This doesn't mean that property disappears in the coming Age of Access. Quite the contrary, property continues to exist but is far less likely to be exchanged in markets. Instead, suppliers hold on to property in the new economy and lease, rent, or charge an admission fee, subscription, or membership dues for its short-term use. The exchange of property between sellers and buyers ... gives way to short-term access between servers and clients operating in a network relationship.[2]

Such seductive thinking went totally unnoticed in the European defence and foreign policy community, even though it had to face similar challenges of procurement v. access, duplication v. delegation, in the context of the reflection on Europe's new responsibilities and capabilities in the larger community of NATO. Far from being irrelevant to this debate, Jeremy Rifkin's hypothesis throws a provocative light on all of these specific challenges by illustrating the same kind of transformation in the concept of "power" brought about by the Age of Intelligence. In both environments, political power stems less from the accumulation of physical assets ("property") but from the access to a capacity to articulate them in a fast and secure network environment. That logic holds a lot of wisdom ... and discomfort on this side of the Atlantic. It thus implies that not only European nations should avoid duplicating the American informational "network of networks," but should embrace Washington's leadership in this field by focusing their scarce resources in building the right access (i.e. the "plug") to this network. According to this hypothesis, NATO would a find a new relevance in the Transatlantic relationship by working as a kind of "Intelligence Service Provider" serving as an interface to the American "network of networks," where Europeans could "plug" their own sensor and shooter platforms to achieve the capacity to conduct high-intensity operations in the Age of Intelligence. By assuming responsibility for the first and the last leg of the "kill chain" and delegating the middle part—the network—to NATO, European nations would not only see their capability multiplied greatly and at a relevant cost, but preserve their strategic industrial base, which is heavily platform-centered.

While already in the making in some high-level policymaking circles on both sides of the Atlantic, this revolution in "burden-sharing" is far from assured. Such close allies as the UK and the US still do not even have the same labels for network-centric warfare.

Breaking down the barriers to such a level of interoperability between the US and its European partners will ultimately involve that both Europeans governments and the US administration overcome their respective mental and political hurdles and take painful initiatives to address and resolve the serious shortcomings in NATO C4ISR integration.

The scheduled replacement of the disappointing Defence Capabilities Initiative (DCI) with the more ambitious Prague Capabilities Commitment (PCC), as well as the American initiative to establish a NATO Response Force (NRF), provides Europeans and Americans policymakers with a unique opportunity to make such a "leap of faith" and accept each other's respective leadership in particular areas of C4ISR and strike technology. Such cooperation implies a strong effort in cutting down on the wide array of standards that govern the Pentagon, NATO, and the European Union, as well as agreeing on a set of realistic—and generally accepted—hardware and software interface standards which, when coupled with information exchange requirements, provide a framework for such evolutionary enhancements. The US government should also be more open in the exchange of information with Europeans on the details needed to make their weapon systems compatible.

More broadly, this commitment to interoperability on both sides of the Atlantic also means that Washington should start loosening its export control regulations, which are interpreted in Europe as a sign of bad will on the cooperation front, and start opening its market not only to joint ventures, which are becoming so numerous that they pre-empt major transatlantic mergers, but to truly integrated Transatlantic consortia. There have been several positive initiatives since the development of the Joint Strike Fighter showed the benefits of flexible standards and open-system architectures to foster Transatlantic systems integration. Northrop Grumman and a group of European companies are already working on an alliance air-to-ground surveillance programme that will combine elements of the US Multi-Platform Radar Technology Insertion Programme with the

European Stand-Off Surveillance and Target Acquisition Radar technology. For their part, European defence companies have made great strides toward integrating operations, and most EU governments are beginning to seriously embrace the need to harmonize their standards to make them interoperable with NATO's. But defence contractors need to go even further to acknowledge this revolution.[3]

While remarkable, these inroads are still walking a tightrope, and a truly interoperable Transatlantic force will have to overcome several other political, financial and technological hurdles. Instead of focusing on a "big bang" solution to interoperability, Europe and the US should favour a gradual approach, and start building this capacity on operational "niches" of common concern, such as Combat Search-and-Rescue (CSAR) missions behind enemy lines, for which European countries are ill-equipped. Already, the partners of the European Air Group (Belgium, France, Germany, Italy, the Netherlands, Spain and the UK) are trying to improve interoperability by sharing knowledge of procedures and equipment.

It will no doubt take time for governments on both sides of the Atlantic to fully embrace these necessities and save both NATO and ESDP from irrelevance. But at a time when Europeans and Americans are again gearing up for a long, drawn-out fight to defend (Al-Qaeda) or impress (Iraq) their mutual values, and besides recriminations or frustrations expressed here and there, the fate of both institutions seem once again inextricably tied up in the same challenge: building the foundations of a unique consortium of awareness and capacities, an "Axis of Intelligence" that would remain the backbone of world stability for the bumpy road ahead.

Notes

1   See: Phil Gordon, "Bridging the Atlantic Divide," *Foreign Affairs*, January 2003–February 2003.
2   Jeremy Rifkin, *The Age of Access* (London, Penguin Books, 2000), 4–5.
3   The American defence and electronics giant Raytheon provides an example of how the private sector can help coming to grips with new challenges posed by the Age of Intelligence and the "Age of Access." Raytheon, like other large, defence-oriented aerospace companies, knows the future is inextricably tied to what is often called network, or information-centric warfare, and that any large US corporation's long-term success will depend less and less on new missiles or aircraft designs. Instead, the company is shifting its core business to developing and linking new technologies such as laser and microwave weapons, multi-spectral sensors and complex algorithms that can sift the crucial pieces of intelligence from masses of surveillance data. Raytheon has decided to treat platforms as interchangeable pieces for carrying various parts of an integrated "kill chain."

Chapter 6

The EU and NATO Enlargement: A Russian View

Nadia Alexandrova Arbatova

In the West both EU and NATO enlargement have been presented as complementary processes, while in Russia these processes are being regarded as the opposite ones. As it seen from Moscow, these two processes reflect the post-bipolar dichotomy of Europe that has two dimensions—EU and NATO. Being compatible in the Cold War times because of Europe's dependence from the US in the field of security, they became contradictory after the collapse of Communism, which removed the very threat of global conflict.

European integration including the EU enlargement to the East is assessed by Moscow as a natural process in the post-bipolar Europe's evolution. It is all the more so, since Russia contributed more than other countries to the removal of the Soviet threat and to the end of bipolarity: the Soviet Union would have never collapsed so quickly without efforts of Russia which became the main driving force for the dissolution of the USSR. But being secessionist in relation to the Soviet empire, Russia was integrationist in relation to Europe. And regardless of different assessments of Russia today, one cannot but recognise that if the USSR occupied Eastern Europe and the Baltic republics, it was Russia that brought freedom and independence to these states.

The end of bipolarity and the strategy of Russian leadership directed at building a functioning democracy and implementing a market economy removed the political and ideological division in Europe. Both the Central and Eastern European (CEE) countries and Russia started to move (although with a different speed) in one direction. Unlike NATO, the EU has not been just the creation of the Cold War, but rather the embodiment of natural and objective trends in Europe's evolution. And this is essential for the comprehension of Russia's attitude towards EU integration, in general, and EU enlargement, in particular.

The fundamentals for EU-Russia co-operation are really sound. The European Union has become Russia's main trading partner and an important investor in Russia's economy. European Union countries account for 40% of all Russian exports and 50% of all foreign investment in Russia. However, the trade volume between EU and Russia is only one third of what it could be, judging by the amount of Russia's GDP and the geographical closeness to the EU markets.[1]

There are no sharp conflicts of security interests between Russia and EU. On the contrary Russia and Europe are sharing common security and foreign policy interests related to the post-bipolar challenges emanating from conflicts in the post-Communist space and the emergence of a new phenomenon—the Islamic dimension of European security.

The partisans of NATO's enlargement eastwards in the West are claiming that the EU enlargement will create for Russia more problems than NATO's expansion. It has been recognised in Russia that three major transformations in Europe—EU single market, EMU, and EU enlargement—are likely to affect Russia deeply.[2] Yet their possible consequences suggest that the combined macroeconomic effects on Russia will in general be favourable, although their near and medium-term impact might confront Russia with additional problems: increased EU protectionism or discrimination against Russia's exports of finished goods, difficulties for Russia's access to Central European markets, the problem of Kaliningrad Russia's exclave, which raises, with the EU enlargement to the Baltic states, the question of free access and transit to the area. But most of these problems are of natural origins, and if Russia wants to continue its domestic reforms it will have to resolve these problems anyway. Some of the differences can be neutralised by agreed measures between the Russian government and the EU, others by Russia's efforts to improve its trade relations with the CEE candidates for EU membership.

Russia's relations with NATO have passed several stages after the demise of the USSR—from euphoria and great expectations in early 1990s to mutual dissatisfaction and mistrust in the late 1990s. After 1993, NATO's enlargement eastwards can be seen and assessed as the embodiment of fundamental differences between Russia and the leading Western countries in the field of security in Euro-Atlantic space. In its traditional shape NATO became inadequate to the post-bipolar realities.

Nothing was created to replace the old security system after the end of the Cold War. There was no common approach to the post-bipolar borders in Europe, and it was easier for the NATO countries to come back to the old, traditional definition of Europe dividing the latter between the CEE countries and Russia. NATO's enlargement resulted from this division of Europe, when the post-Communist space was divided between two security institutions—NATO and OSCE. The former became responsible for the CEE countries, the latter for the post-Soviet space.

For Russia, NATO's decision to expand eastwards was the end of the short period of NATO's readjustment to the post-bipolar realities. Russia's grievances and suspicions about the goals of NATO enlargement can be explained by the fact that Russia was deceived by NATO several times.[3] First, when the Partnership for Peace (PfP) was offered Russia as an alternative to NATO extension. Second, when the founding father of NATO enlargement, Lawrence Eagleburger said in the mid-1990s that "everyone who thinks about taking the Baltic States into NATO needs his head to be examined, because it would create serious problems in NATO relations with Russia."

Undoubtedly Russia made a lot of mistakes after the dissolution of the USSR. It completely ignored the necessity to establish new relations with the former Soviet allies that found themselves in a situation of political and economic turmoil, frightened by the collapse of Yugoslavia and by the prospect of other ethnic conflicts in their neighbouring countries. It is responsible for mismanaging its economy, military reforms and conversion. It has nobody but itself to blame for the lack of a realistic new Russian military and political doctrine for European security. And, finally, by its ill-conceived policy in Chechnya, Russia reinforced the fears of the CEE nations as well as their desire to join NATO as soon as possible. At the same time, Russia's mistakes, however grave they may be, cannot justify NATO extension eastwards which has created the first serious problem in the post-bipolar international relations.

NATO enlargement can be assessed as a final victory of traditional perceptions of, and approaches to, European security in spite of all official statements on indivisibility of European security after the end of the Cold War. Turning from the external vulnerabilities to the security of the CEE countries, it does not appear that the territorial defence of these countries is an immediate problem; there are no direct territorial threats perceived by any of them. More immediate challenges to Europe's security are likely to arise from the spill over of conflicts that may occur on its southern, south-eastern or eastern peripheries. Another factor of risk is related to the emergence of a new dividing line in Europe, which may reverse the positive trend of reorientation of forces to different contingencies and missions than a large-scale East-West war in Europe and become a border of new hostility and confrontation. And, finally, the last challenge is the failure of democratic reforms in Russia, which could be exacerbated by developments outside Russia, with serious foreign policy consequences.

So, NATO's expansion eastwards can be also assessed as the West's disbelief in Russia's democratic future, although NATO's leadership never publicly recognised the anti-Russian bias of this process. But the initially negative reaction of the new CEE members of NATO to the idea of "the Committee 20" which would admit Russia to the decision-making process in NATO is the best evidence to this anti-Russian bias.

NATO's official explanation was the need to erase the Cold War borders in Europe and facilitate the CEE countries' return to European family. That is why the EU enlargement and NATO's extension were being presented as two complementary processes. However, the EU enlargement suits much better the goal of Europe's reunification. The assets that the EU enlargement could bring to Europe contribute to a more balanced grouping of interests and preferences. Meanwhile, NATO enlargement is a policy that could bring greater security for a few more nations but at the cost of repartitioning the continent into Western and Russian spheres of influence.

It would be wrong to confine the problem of NATO enlargement to the east only by the growing security gap between Russia and NATO. It is also a product of NATO's deep internal identity crisis initiated by the end of bipolarity. Not only the so-called Communist bloc, but all institutions created for the Cold War confrontation, have been affected by the end of bipolarity. With Soviet demise, NATO's traditional goals—to keep the Soviet Union out of Europe, the Germans down, and the Americans in— became irrelevant.

The Soviet threat was the main factor, which provided a kind of glue for Euro-Atlantic partnership in the old times. But post-Soviet Russia, however imperfect it may be, cannot play the same unifying role for Euro-Atlantic solidarity. Russia's military weight has diminished dramatically and, with all concerns about its unpredictability, it cannot be assessed as a direct threat to the West. This has been all the more the case after September 11 since Russia sided with the West against the threat of terrorism. As for the German factor, this goal lost its importance a long time ago. Germany has been a democratic state for many decades, one of the main driving forces of European integration, and even if there are some concerns about economic and political ambitions of Germany, they lie outside of NATO's framework. The third traditional goal of NATO—to keep Americans in—is still being regarded as the most important one. However, the main reason of the US presence in Europe was the threat from the East and Europe's dependence on the US in countering this threat. The end of bipolarity removed the threat of the global conflict and became a catalyst for European integration in the field of common foreign security and defence policy (CFSDP).[4] This has been all the more so, since after

September 11, the US has been putting the emphasis on the fight with terrorism on the global level, meaning that the US presence in Europe will shrink, and the US will react to Europe's security needs only selectively.

The demise of the USSR dealt a heavy blow to NATO in its traditional shape having been deprived of its main *raison d'être*. NATO was being faced with a difficult choice to find new missions or disappear. The former would require from NATO to start a process of radical re-assessment of its traditional goals and missions and adaptation to new realities. If NATO had followed this way, it would have been transformed into a new all-European security institution, which in contrast to OSCE, would have military potential to perform the post-bipolar missions— prevention of ethno-religious conflicts, humanitarian and rescue operations, peace-enforcement and peace-making. But NATO's evolution in this direction would raise the question of the post-bipolar European security— that of Russia. Without Russia's inclusion, NATO is doomed to stay in its traditional shape but in a totally new international environment that lacks the old threat that helped to mobilise the Euro-Atlantic partnership.

NATO enlargement has been chosen as a new mission for NATO that could give it a new life but not without radical changes. Russia was offered the Founding Act and Permanent Joint Council (PJC) which were supposed to appease Russia and reconcile it with a new reality but which did not pass the first serious test—the Kosovo crisis. The ultimate irony was that this military campaign was the first act of the enlarged NATO that reinforced the concerns of Russian public opinion and political elite.

NATO intervention in Yugoslavia has undermined the NATO-Russia Founding Act, which regardless Russia's dissatisfaction, provided certain assurances against a new conventional and nuclear deployment on territories of new NATO members. The geostrategic position of NATO's next would-be members—Estonia, Latvia and Lithuania—which are connected with NATO by the narrow Suvalki corridor (100 kms wide) located between Kalinigrad oblast and Belarus raises a question of credibility of NATO's mutual defence obligations if NATO forces were not permanently deployed on the territories of the Baltic States. This fuels Russia's suspicions about intentions of NATO in this region. If it happened, it would be extremely destabilising because a supersonic nuclear-capable aircraft from the Latvian airfield could reach Moscow within 15 minutes and Saint Petersburg—within several minutes. Even the risk of such developments—if the NATO-Russia relations should continue to deteriorate, might result in Russia's nervous and spontaneous decision to field tactical nuclear weapons in the Kaliningrad oblast.[5]

The tragic events of 11 September 2001 opened a new page in the post-bipolar international relations. These events had a strong impact on Russia's foreign policy having confronted President Putin with a necessity to make a clear choice—either to side with the US and its allies or to hold aloof and confirm Western concerns about incompatibility of Russian and European values. The answer to this question given by Russian leadership on the morrow of September 11 was clear and unequivocal—Russia is together with the civilised world against terrorism. Moreover, for the second time in our recent history—after the World War II—Russia, Europe and the US have a common enemy. If this approach were to be shared by everyone, it could drastically change Europe's security landscape and provide NATO with a new *raison d'être* that was lost with the end of bipolarity. President Putin said during his trips after September 11 to Germany and Brussels that Russia is rooted in European values, that under certain conditions Russia could go farther in anti-terrorist co-operation, and finally, that Russia will not be against NATO's expansion to the east if Russia is part of this process. "Of course we would reconsider our position with regard to such expansion if we were to fail to be involved in such process," Putin said in Brussels.[6] Unfortunately, despite all hopes there was no real break through in the Russia-NATO relations. Despite praise for Russia's role in the anti-Taliban coalition, NATO and the US still do not appear ready to treat Russia as a full-fledged partner.

Summing up, there exist three paradoxes of NATO. First, on the one hand, NATO's military power is quite sufficient for inducing fears into the states that are not part of the Alliance, on the other hand, its military power is not sufficient for performing new missions. Moreover, since it was repeatedly said that the NATO and EU enlargement processes are complementary, with new possible tensions between Russia and the US/NATO, the process of NATO's enlargement could have a negative impact on Russia's vision of the EU enlargement which could be assessed in this case as a Western strategy of hostile encirclement of Russia.

Second, on the one hand, the US does not want its Allies to doubt its leadership in NATO, on the other hand, it is shifting the emphasis to new missions, in the first place to the fight with terrorism on a global level while simultaneously reducing its commitments to Europe. Third, on the one hand, NATO does not want to involve Russia in Euro-Atlantic space of co-operation as a full-fledged partner; on the other hand, it will not survive in its traditional shape. If NATO's leadership does not re-think its strategy it will be gradually marginalized in Europe. September 11 has only confirmed NATO's irrelevance, the Article V pledge being primarily a symbolic gesture while the US conducted a military operation largely alone with support from the British.

The same can be said about the Iraq crisis that presented new evidence as to the nature of US unilateralism and NATO's marginalisation in the international affairs. The Iraq crisis has also shown that the CFSP in the EU is far from being complete. But there is one important lesson from Iraq that is worth much thinking on its own. For the first time, the dividing line did not go between the East and the West but between Europe and the US, and Russia emerged in this crisis as part of Europe. This can be assessed as the real end of bipolarity.

Although current Russia-NATO/US co-operation is still very superficial, after September 11 it has created a benign international environment for co-operation between Russia and Europe on security issues that is more needed now than ever before. Sustainable self-restraint, which has always characterized Russian-European relations, will not last forever, and it would be naive to rely only on this phenomenon. Both Russia and the West have already lost a lot of opportunities after the end of bipolarity and it would be unforgivable if Russia and the EU lost the last one. Russia and the West should transform their present relationship into a real strategic partnership directed at avoiding new dividing lines in Europe and at establishing confidence in Russian-Western relations. In order to do this, the question of Russia, and namely of its place in the post-bipolar European security arrangements, should be resolved. This proposal is quite realistic, assuming values are not held hostage to geopolitics.

Notes

1   Hans-Hermann Hohmann and Christian Meier, "Conceptual, Internal, and International Aspects of Russia's Economic Security" in "The Intersection of Economics and Politics in Russia" in *Russia and the West: The 21st Century Security Environment*, ed. Alexei G. Arbatov, Karl Kaiser and Robert Legvold, EastWest Institute (M.E. Sharpe: New York, 1999), 88.
2   Efim S. Khesin, "The Intersection of Economics and Politics in Russia" in *Russia and the West. The 21st Century Security Environment*, ed. by Alexei G. Arbatov, Karl Kaiser and Robert Legvold, EastWest Institute, (M.E. Sharpe: New York 1999), 119.
3   See Nadia Arbatova, "NATO's Enlargement: How to bypass Russia?" in "Nuclear Control," *PIR-Center*, Moscow, December, 2001 (in Russian).
4   Nicole Gnesotto, "Terrorism and European Integration" in *Newsletter*, Institute of Security Studies, Western European Union, Number 35, October 2001, 1.
5   "Russia and the West. The 21st Century Security Environment," ed. Alexei G. Arbatov, Karl Kaiser and Robert Legvold, EastWest Institute (M.E. Sharpe: New York 1999).
6   Gareth Jones, "Putin Softens Stance on NATO," in *The Moscow Times*, October 4, 2001, 1.

Chapter 7

A MAP for Russia

Ira Straus

After September 11, 2001, the question of Russia joining NATO, which has been a live issue for the Russian elite since the beginning in 1991, began to come to life in the West as well. A dangerous new enemy was extant. Americans saw how much they needed to unite with Russia against this enemy; a consideration that tended to displace the earlier belief that NATO, in order to justify its existence, needed to treat Russia as its enemy.

A Russia-in-NATO outcome may be strategically inescapable in the long run; it has meanwhile been approached slowly, resisted at each step yet brought nearer with each step. Strategic necessities, coupled with the logic of Russia's Westernization, are likely to impel the forward movement to continue; a feeling that it is absurd is likely to remain widespread and impel the resistance to continue.

This raises the question of whether the process will proceed in a skillful way, i.e. a way that actualizes most of the enormous potential for Russia and the West to help each other strategically and ends the held-over Cold War practices of undermining each other. Skill also means doing it in good time, for dealing with the awesome threats already presented to both sides by mass terrorism and weapons of mass destruction—threats that Russia and the West had both played their part in proliferating during their decades of mutual competition for clients and influence around the world. Skill finally means doing it in a way that "works" for both sides—works for Russia politically, as an anchor to Westernization; works for NATO structurally, avoiding institutional damage in the process.

Thus far such skill has not been in evidence. If it is to be seen in the future, a solid Membership Action Plan (MAP) will be needed, one that deals with the unique issues raised by Russian membership.

Background: Public Support for Russia-in-NATO, Elite Ambivalence

The American public has massively but passively supported inclusion of Russia in NATO throughout the 1990s, according to poll after poll on the subject.[1] However, much of the elite was for a long time skeptical, both of Russia's intentions and of NATO's capacity to survive such a change; and it is the elite that take the initiative in such complicated matters of international organizational restructuring.

What was new after September 11 was that the prospect began to penetrate the "realist" sector of the Western elite as well as the "idealist" sector and the general public. There was a new and very dangerous enemy; the hypothetical potential future threat from Russia paled by comparison. It was Russia, alone among America's allies and potential allies, that was providing indispensable help in the war against terrorism in Afghanistan. This gave pause to those who previously equated realism in NATO affairs with an anti-Russian orientation. Uniting with Russia no longer had to be a matter of idealism; it could take on a hard-core coloration of uniting against a common enemy.[2]

However, a case against Russian inclusion in NATO had meanwhile been built up by stages in the course of the 1990s—more by an accretion of fears and suspicions than of sound arguments, but the fears were nevertheless expressed in the form of arguments, which built one atop another. The accumulated bundle of counter-arguments spread widely among elites. And the elites could block any action; the diffusion of a bundle of fears among them served to create a system of blockage.

The system of blockage against Russia weakened after September 11, 2001. A heightened awareness of the need for inclusion of Russia in the Western security system led in November of that year to initiatives for closer engagement of Russia with NATO, without however actually including Russia at the main NATO table. These initiatives, the most important of which came from Prime Minister Tony Blair, enjoyed a brief period of ascent, and then went through a longer phase of getting delayed and whittled down, as they ran up against the old anti-Russian arguments still circulating within the elites.

The more serious of the old arguments can be summarized as a belief in the impossibility of including Russia in NATO without destroying NATO in the process.[3] Two reasons are given for this belief: (1) that inclusion of Russia would destroy NATO's identity, which is based on enmity to Russian power, (2) that it would confound NATO's institutional functioning, by giving the enemy a veto. We will deal with both of them, directly and indirectly, in this paper, and offer models for a functioning NATO that includes Russia. Moreover, we will provide scenarios for getting Russia and the West past the political and psychological barriers to their collaboration. First, however, let us review the logic of the new situation, which will show why it is necessary to proceed beyond external cooperative relations to internal integrative relations.

Mr. Putin and the New Geopolitical Configuration

The European leader with the most thoughtful, alliance-focused appraisal of the post-September 11 situation was a non-ally, Vladimir Putin. His approach was unusual among high officials; he called, not for a minimal adaptation, but for one commensurate with the challenge. He was a KGB trainee, accustomed to think of a security problem as a hands-on matter requiring a fully adequate response. And his country had gone through a revolution—a process that encourages people to think new thoughts commensurate with new situations. Other countries, spared the trauma of revolution, had been spared the benefits of new thinking. Their foreign policy had been lagging behind the new realities ever since 1991.

In the aftermath of September 11, Mr. Putin made five interrelated points: (a) that the anti-terrorist camp must be solid, in particular (b) that the terrorist movements must not be allowed to continue running back and forth between the great Northern powers or playing upon their differences, as in the 1990s, (c) that Russia is, in its underlying nature and in its preferred destiny, a part of Europe and the Western camp, (d) that Russia's joining NATO would be a basis for achieving reliability in the common diplomatic front of the Northern powers, and a solution to Russia's security dilemma in Europe—an adequate solution, eliminating the problems created for Russia by NATO expansion, even if not the optimal solution in the view of Russia, which would prefer a new order based on the OSCE, and (e) that NATO should start talking with Russia about the terms of Russian entry into NATO. He added that it was none too soon to begin; Russia and the West had lost ten years on this matter since 1991.

The last point seemed particularly poignant. America paid a heavy price on September 11 for having failed to use the larger opportunities of the 1990s in regard to Russia on the one side and the anti-terrorist struggle on the other. The terrorist milieu grew tremendously in those ten years. It was able to continue playing the two former Cold War rivals off against one another in the Islamic world. This would not have happened if Russia and the West had organized together strategically after 1991. Instead of

NATO being used as a venue for organizing them together, it was used as a venue for expanding on terms that *de facto* excluded Russia and, step by step, alienated it. The process of mutual alienation was carried a step further by the proponents in America of a new "Great Game" and "New Silk Road" in Central Asia and the Caucasus, i.e. a competition against Russia for influence in the region.[4] Several aging geopoliticians, seemingly nostalgic for Cold War scenarios, joined in this new "game." When the Taliban movement was fighting its way to power, America quietly accepted it as something useful against Russia in the Great Game. After 1998 the US slowly came around to Russia's view of the Taliban, but the two sides could never agree on active anti-Taliban measures; each remained suspicious of any military moves by the other. Instead they agreed on ineffective UN resolutions and passive economic sanctions. This left Bin Laden to move first with active measures. Thousands of New Yorkers paid the price on September 11. The rubble of the World Trade Center was the rubble of the Great Game. It was, one might hope, the last game of the Cold War.

East-West and North-South

Putin, with his KGB background, has seen the dangers of the East-West competition more clearly than have most Western commentators. Like a good policeman, he wants to cut out the space for the terrorist movements to run back and forth between the Northern countries, the space where they could look for sponsors or protectors or simply recuperate. This captures the crux of the failure of the 1990s. The West and Russia to a large extent continued the Cold War game of each side playing "its" radical Moslems against "the other side."[5] Meanwhile the terrorists and rogue states were also playing Russia and the West against each other. Who was using whom? Famous old geopoliticians in Moscow and Washington assumed they were using the Islamist extremists as pawns in a bigger global game, but it turned out that they were the ones being used: their own games proved petty and well-nigh irrelevant, while the games of the Islamists proved critically important on a global scale. Both Russia and the West lost in this game; the winners were the extremists and terrorists.

Something like this had already taken place during the Cold War: the same ruthless competition for clients took place, with Islamists and other extremists profiting in the interstices, in the 1970s and 1980s. However, there was a reason for the Cold War in its time: the two sides really did represent opposing projects for the world and the Cold War was the main game playing on the global scale. The 1990s version was like an echo of the Cold War game, history repeating itself as farce—a costly farce.

Throughout the Cold War, both East and West built up new powers and movements in the South as counterbalances and troublemakers for one another. Both sides competed in fanning anti-imperialism against the other and in trying to link themselves to Third World nationalism. As the Cold War dragged on, the utility of this method of play declined, while the dangers from the new forces kept mounting. It was the recognition of the uncontrollability of China and the danger it posed to Russia that led Khrushchev to a turn back toward European civilization. The new forces were even harder to control in the Islamic world, with its multiple fracturing and religious discontent; the Cold War competition entailed a competition in fanning Arab and Islamic nationalism. It laid the basis for the oil nationalizations and embargoes and the rise of OPEC. With the Iranian revolution and the appearance of Islamist ideology as a major force, the dangers in the game grew dramatically. In 1979, some analysts on both sides pondered openly whether it would not be better for each to let the other have a free hand in its area of nemesis, Russia in Afghanistan, the US in Iran. But this was not to be; the Cold War was still on, and the two sides were still doing deals with many a devil against one another.

In 1991, with the disappearance of the Soviet Union, the basic causes of East-West competition disappeared; any residual reasons for competition paled before the reasons for dealing jointly with the new threats. East and West had a huge backlog of dangerous forces in the South that they had built up in their decades of mutual opposition. They needed to work together on cleaning up these forces to the extent still possible. Instead, they reverted at times to the practice of mutual troublemaking, particularly in the 1995-98 period.

To have prevented this backsliding, favored by numerous adversarial instincts and habits, they would have had to organize together for active two-way collaboration on the international plane, not just passive one-way applause for the reforms on the domestic plane inside Russia. If they are to prevent it from happening again, now that the problem has had an extra decade to metastasize, they will need to organize together in an even more substantial form for active strategic collaboration on the international plane.

It turned out in the 1990s that it was not enough for the two sides to proclaim themselves partners in abstract general rhetoric: this failed to overcome the ingrained structures of mutual opposition on the operational level. Conversely, it is not enough—although it is a real step forward—that after September 11 they acted as allies in practical fact during a particular emergency in Afghanistan. For sustainability of the new relation, a synthesis of the general partnership and the particular active alliance is needed. In other words: to deal with the long-term global challenges that they mutually face, Russia and the West need unity that is concrete and active, yet across-the-board, and reliable over the long-term.

It is a verity of international relations theory that such a degree of unity does not come easily. Mutual reliability and a compatible strategy is not the default behavior among separate sovereign powers. From Hobbes and Hamilton to Haas, from Madison to Monnet, from Justice Marshall to General Marshall, it has been understood as requiring institution-building and community-building.[6] Institutions need to be not just *pro forma*, but adequate to provide confidence of mutual security, subsume the security planning of the parties into a common planning process, establish effective arrangements for common or coordinated implementation, and eliminate the need for making plans for fighting against one another (Deutsch). The community of interests must be both organic, that is, based in natural observable commonalities of socio-political structure and purpose, and constructed, in order to overcome the Hobbesian habit of mutual opposition. For the constructed part, a major effort must be made to reconcile previous divergent conceptions of the national interest or purpose. This is something that requires "fusion of interests" (Monnet) or "upgrading the common interest" (Haas), not just compromise or "splitting the difference."

In the case of Russia and the West, one of the specific needs, as we have seen, is to stand together in such a way that hostile forces cannot expect to find any space between East and West or any chance to play upon the numerous minor contradictions that always exist between different countries. Such solidarity will be convincing only if the countries at issue develop a conception of common interests strong enough, over a wide enough range of security and geopolitical issues, that the world will understand that their commonality of interests is not only objectively far greater than their opposing interests—a fact that was widely recognized in principle after 1991, when it was sensed that, with the ideological conflicts having ended, what was left was a natural community of interests among all the industrialized and Europeanized countries, yet was soon lost in practice in the haze of renewed competition over the secondary opposing interests—but will henceforth be better prioritized and more effectively operationalized than any opposing interests they might retain. For this, they need to develop a joint strategic concept and security doctrine. And they need to embed the agreements and practices of collaboration in joint institutions commensurate with the scope of those agreements and practices.

In brief, the countries involved need to develop shared conceptions of interest and of global perspective, and institutions of cooperation adequate to carry and sustain those conceptions.

NATO–The Only Institution Commensurate with the Need

In the strategic sphere, the only international institution that comes close to being commensurate with the scope of the problem—the only one that has shown the capability of providing mutual reliability in the reconciliation of its members' security interests and in mutual support rather than mutual undercutting—is NATO. The UN is virtuous, but like the League of Nations which could never reconcile France and Germany, it is not enough. OSCE is virtuous but can never be seriously strengthened—not unless it is by closer cooperation with a NATO that, by incorporating Russia, comes to approximate OSCE in its geographical shape. The dream of relying upon a novel East-West institution is a delusion, for the "East" of the Cold War decades is not a separate civilization. It is only in the West-West world, duly extended and amended, that the East-West rapprochement can find its fulfillment.

What kind of relation of Russia with NATO could be "sufficient"? Membership of Russia in NATO would be sufficient; it would be an organic or internal relation. But Western elites have tended to feel it is impossible. Many Russians share that feeling, if only because of the resistance to it in the West.

This combination of a sense of need with a sense of impossibility has created a kind of market for finding a new form of link between Russia and NATO, something that would be at one and the same time sufficient and feasible. What has traded on this market has been ideas for something more than the existing inadequate external links, but less than the seemingly impossible internal link of full membership. Most of the ideas traded on the official level in this market have taken the form of enhancing the external links, although in logic they could equally well take the form of rethinking the meaning of an internal membership link and adjusting its content so that it would no longer seem impossible.

Proposals for enhanced external links have offered a tempting substitute for an internal link; tempting, but insufficient. As with the idea of relying on OSCE or the UN, the voice of temptation is deceiving; in the long run inorganic arrangements will always prove inadequate. Nevertheless, in the short run, they can serve an essential purpose, as stepping stones toward another shore. However, this purpose tends to get served well only if they are conceived as stepping stones, not as stopping points. If stood upon too long as a substitute for arriving at the opposite shore, they tend to prove too slippery and narrow to keep the partners from falling into the water. They are properly a launching pad for something more. When the launching pad is mistaken for the landing point, nothing moves. Before long, it is once again observed that the arrangement is insufficient. Real-life strategic crises intervene, disrupting the gradual accumulation of low-level cooperative exercises. Recriminations mount anew on both sides. This has already happened on several occasions in the Russia-NATO relationship, confounding the predictions of careful step by step cumulative progress.

Only a goal of Russian membership in NATO can solve the problem. 'Accept no substitutes': it is not just an advertising slogan, it fits the issue.

The NATO-Russia Council: A Step toward Membership, a Substitute for Membership, or a Waste of the Historical Moment?

Yet there is one substitute that is worth pausing to consider. It is the attempt, based on the initiative of Prime Minister Blair of Great Britain at the end of 2001, at inclusion of Russia in a new NATO-based joint Council as an equal participant in the discussions, without however becoming a member of NATO. The difference from the previous substitute—the NATO-Russia Permanent Joint Council—was that the new Council would be charged with jointly discussing issues from the bottom up, rather than waiting for the NATO members first to reach a common position and then present it to Russia as a *fait accompli*. In other words, Russia would gain something equivalent to an organic position inside the discussion process of NATO on at least some of the issues before the Alliance, without however having the organic status of membership.

If this proposal had been adopted and implemented energetically at the end of 2001, as originally intended, it might well have led to an organic working relationship among the NATO countries together with Russia as active allies in the global struggle against terrorism. There was an enthusiasm in the air at that moment for the new relationship as comrades-in-arms against the Taliban. That active alliance relationship might have come to be extended to a wider set of issues, if the institutional set-up for it had been put in place at the time and taken its tone from the fast-emerging alliance work.

But it was not to be. The proposal was delayed and proceeded to get whittled down considerably. Supporting it were Britain and many of the old members of NATO, along with the US State Department and, initially, the President; resisting it were the three new NATO members from central-eastern Europe, along with Germany and the Secretary of Defense of the United States. The decision was put off, the moment of enthusiasm passed on both sides, and the whittling down processes got underway. Later, it became a matter for Russia-West negotiations, which proved somewhat rancorous; the Russian Foreign Minister, Igor Ivanov, warned that it was coming down to just a "cosmetic" change. In May 2002, a new "NATO-Russia Council" (NRC) was finally established, but many commentators wondered whether it was really much advance over the previous Permanent Joint Council (PJC). It did not have nearly the impact it would have had at the end of 2001. Nevertheless it did provide space for joint threat assessments, which could pave the way for further steps in reconciling perspectives. It was only another transitional step, but a constructive one that opens more doors than it closes.

On What Schedule?

If there is no space for permanent substitutes but only for transitional steps and ultimate goals, is there at least space for delay in discussing the goal, while letting the transitions do their work? Yes, but conditionally: transitions can be recognized as transitions only if the goal is accepted; otherwise there is little assurance that people will be ready to move on from them or know in what direction to move. For those who need to get to the goal, transitions can be accepted without reservation only if it is agreed that they are to lead to the goal. Russians do need the goal of membership: this is the only way for them to have confidence that their interests and voice will ultimately be entrenched and respected as much as those of any NATO member country. In a different sense, both sides need the goal as a basis for thinking that cooperation could become reliable, enduring, and commensurate with the scope of the common dangers.

Prior to September 11, the Secretary General of NATO, Lord Robertson, said that perhaps a Russian membership could be discussed "in the next two decades."[7] After September 11, Secretary of State Colin Powell said that maybe it could be discussed a year hence. Everyone understood that Powell was saying this as a way of putting off the question, which had suddenly become a live one on the international scene. It was tremendous progress, that one year's wait was recognized as a dilatory response; but not enough. The iron needed to be forged while it was hot. Otherwise, a year hence, the sense of crisis would recede, and people would relax and once again say, "well, maybe in a couple decades ..."

Today it will be more difficult; the year has passed, and the initial crisis and the early enthusiasm have indeed receded. Yet it remains necessary to begin the discussion and the planning for Russian membership in NATO: this is still critical for achieving reliability over a long term and across a wide array of issues. The fraying of the unity of the coalition over post-Afghanistan issues—Iraq, Korea, Georgia, etc.—will, if accepted passively, come with time to be treated as proof that nothing more can really be done, due to innate differences in national interest; just as renewed Franco-German divergences would have occurred and would today be treated as inevitable and insuperable if innovative initiatives for integration had not been taken in 1947-54.

The post-Afghanistan divergences are better seen as proof that the coalition structure has not gone far enough and needs an infusion of new form and substance. It would take time for such an infusion to be completed, but only by beginning it can the two sides gain confidence that they are going to stay together for the long term. Such confidence is a prerequisite for focusing, when new issues come up, on primary shared interests and strategies rather than on secondary, tactical differences. For example, only by forming a shared general strategy on all "rogues" can they avoid a re-divergence as they come to dealing with Iran, Iraq, North Korea (America's rogues, Russia's old clients), Saudi Arabia and Pakistan (Russia's rogues, America's clients).[8]

Even before the NRC was in place, Russians had begun speculating that, the high point of the Afghan crisis having passed without being seized for any dramatic institutionalization of relations or entrenchment of Russia's role within the joint councils of the West, the alliance would not endure. "They paid attention to us when they needed us"—so ran the refrain in Moscow—"they asked us to support them and gave an impression of multilateralism; now, with the denunciation of the ABM treaty (or the positioning against Russia in Georgia, or ...), they don't even bother to consider our interest, it is back to business as usual."

How, then, to proceed? If the deed becomes more difficult now that the dust has partially settled, perhaps this also provides space for proceeding with developing a sound and sober plan. The question is twofold: the process of Russian entry into NATO (the form) and the terms of entry (the substance of the matter). Let us consider them each in turn.

The Contents of a Russian Membership Action Plan (MAP) for joining NATO

A. The Process/Form

A three-stage process[9] would be needed to get us from here to there:

Stage 1. Russia and NATO decide to discuss terms of Russian entry into NATO. Both endorse in principle the goal of Russia-in-NATO, contingent upon subsequent agreement on terms that are mutually advantageous.

Stage 2. Two parallel discussions/negotiations proceed, on two interrelated subjects:

a. on the institutional terms for Russian entry into NATO. The results must be acceptable to both sides, therefore must be advantageous to both sides. They also should be terms that are relevant and necessary, not discriminatory without adequate reason. They should not be arbitrary, or insist on conditions such as prior progress on standardization of weapons that have been somewhat irrationally imposed on other new entrants and would be even more irrational for Russia. They should be realistic in the sense that they could be fulfilled in this era, preferably in a matter of a couple years, not decades: brevity is needed to provide a realistic sense of confidence, although it cannot come at the expense of the terms also being realistically to the mutual benefit.

b. on a joint strategic concept or security doctrine, reconciling the global strategies of the two sides. This would be a sort of "political platform" for Russian entry into NATO. It would provide a conviction on both sides that they really should and can be allies. It would also provide an ample supply of tasks for joint effort.

Both reason and evidence indicate that the reconciliation of doctrines and interests can be done. Objectively there is a basis for it in the commonalities of interest between the two sides, which are far deeper than the opposing interests now that the ideological opposition is ended. Methodologically, there is already a joint NATO strategic concept, alongside national security concepts in each of its member countries; this provides a partial model of how it can be done. On the Russia-NATO level, it has been attempted successfully as a simulation.[10]

The present-day NATO and Russian strategic concepts were both prepared separately, without an overarching NATO-Russia process to produce a composite or reconciled doctrine, and were adopted in 1999 and 2000 respectively. Both sides took alarm at the other's new doctrine, partly because of specific provisions in them but primarily because of the mere fact that they were developed separately: accordingly it was possible for each side to become suspicious of any provision in the other side, not having been a party to the debate on it. The separate procedure was a blunder.[11] Afterwards the two tried to "reassure" one another about the new doctrines, and NATO circles portrayed this communications process as evidence of the success of the Russia-NATO dialogue. However, this method of reassurance was not very effective prior to September 11, 2001. After that date, other fears took precedence, but some of the old ones survived and re-emerged a few months later.

The problem is not to give reassurances after the fact about separately-formed strategies, nor merely to compromise and get a diplomatic softening of the rough edges of the separately-formed doctrines, but to form a common doctrine and common strategy. Separate strategies formed independently will almost inevitably clash, and a mere compromise over some of their differences would mean watering down the coherence and energy of the strategic effort on both sides, not shaping a stronger joint strategy. The process of forming a common doctrine and strategy is necessarily more profound than this. It means going to the roots of the issues jointly, rather than trying to reconcile after the fact the disconnected results of separate national processes of going to the roots. It does not focus so much on compromising differences of interest as on upgrading the common interest, and reconfiguring interests along a shared line of orientation.

The process consists, in its bare essentials, of making a joint assessment of the threats facing the participating countries, followed by a joint assessment of their possible responses, and how they can support one another in responding or can act together. NATO regularly goes through this process to form a joint concept, which is how it is able to keep the allies working on the basis of a common security perspective; the common perspective in turn proceeds to inform each country in the working out of its own national doctrine. Russia and NATO need to go through this process together. The NRC provides a venue for doing this, since as we have noted, threat assessment is on its agenda. If the assessment is raised from piecemeal, reviewing threats as they arise, to global—reviewing all major threats and potential threats, weighing the fundamental and secondary interests on both sides, forming joint strategies that focus on the fundamental shared interests, aligning the two sides along a common orientation, capped with doctrinal language stating a joint global strategic concept, and then compromising on what remains of differences in secondary interests—then the NRC will have raised the alliance to a qualitatively new level.

If these two dialogues are successful, then we will have both an understanding of the terms for Russian entry into NATO and a political-strategic platform for Russian entry. If the terms are such that they can be met on both sides in this period, we will have everything in place for ...

Stage 3. Concluding an agreement on the terms of the "Russian MAP," proceeding with all due speed in implementing the MAP[12] and drafting the protocol for Russian accession to NATO. This protocol could not be merely pro forma, as have been the protocols for small countries. Rather, it would include—as happened the last time the Alliance expanded to include a great power (Germany)—substantive provisions: references to the new joint strategic concept, references to other mutual declarations and commitments, and adjustments in NATO to make itself fit to encompass Russia and carry on effectively thereafter. The latter adjustments might include: strengthening NATO's political side, adding new decision-making procedures so it can manage Russia in good moods and bad, and modifying its name to add a reference to Europe or Eurasia.

B. The Terms – The Substance of the Matter

The main substantive issue is the form and degree of Russian influence in NATO decision-making.

All the other widely-discussed criteria and problems are secondary by comparison. Most of them can be dealt with as a matter of course by diplomatic negotiation once the primary problem is resolved. Some of the alleged criteria are completely irrelevant.

What the issue is not: The problem is not for Russia to adapt to NATO weapons standards; this idea, stuck into the NATO expansion plans of 1995 and 1999, has no legal foundation as a criterion for membership. It also has minimal importance for the case of Russian membership. Standardization and efficiency mattered greatly in NATO during the Cold

War, when the two sides had a rough parity. Today, when Russia and NATO enjoy overwhelming superiority as long as they are on the same side, what matters is for Russia and NATO to stay on the same side and to be reliable about giving each other diplomatic and logistical support, not to get 100% efficiency in any actual fighting.

Nor is the problem for NATO to become a "political alliance" instead of a military alliance. Russian diplomats have been using this formulation for years,[13] but it is self-contradictory. NATO would lose its present importance as a political alliance if it dropped its military side; it would just be a talk shop. The North Atlantic Council (NAC) is an important political forum because it is the director of an important structure of military cooperation. Strengthening the political side of the NATO alliance—enhancing the decision-making capabilities of the NAC, the role of the NATO Parliamentary Assembly (NPA), and the resources and role of the Secretary General and the international civil staff—is indeed a valid goal, one which could produce a more balanced alliance that would be more to the taste of Russians and more sustainable over the long haul; but weakening its military side is not a way to go about that goal.

What the issue is: The crux of the problem is for the North Atlantic Council to adapt in decision-making flexibility so as to be able to include Russia without giving it a veto. Flexibility is a strength, especially in the new era when what is needed is joint policy-making in a strategically fluid world, joint diplomacy, and a capacity both to respond promptly to a threat or conflict and to promptly revise the response as conditions on the ground change. As the NATO spokesman, Jamie Shea, said during the Kosovo war, NATO used to be a preparation organization; now it has to become a performance organization. For performance it needs flexibility, not the rigid method of consensus.

NATO is hampered by its old rhetoric on consensus from the Cold War era. When asked whether it would not be better to use more efficient ways of operating, NATO officials used to draw themselves up stiffly and roll off set formulations such as, "unanimity is a strength of NATO not a weakness," "NATO has no element of supranationality," "all decisions must be made on the basis of consensus in the Council," "every country has an equal voice on the Council." All these formulations are misleading in varying degrees, and NATO has in the long run not helped itself by making out of them a kind of required jargon in Alliance discourse.[14]

What this means for the future is that the necessary adaptations on NATO's side for inclusion of Russia are adaptations that can be made on the basis of a simple decision within the North Atlantic Council. New procedures can be established informally, as a supplement to existing options and procedures. There is no legal necessity for a treaty amendment. Perhaps a comment on decision procedures should be added to the next protocols of accession in order to underline the point that no one is being given a veto, but this would be a matter of educating people and of staking out diplomatic turf, not a matter of law.[15]

Accordingly, the key, truly relevant adaptation for Russian membership can be made on short notice—in principle, in a single Council meeting. In practice it would require some months of discussions within the NATO Council to agree on some new informal options for procedures on making decisions, but it does not require waiting 10-20 years. Some other, lesser adaptations would remain to be completed, and working out the terms of Russian membership would take some time, along with implementation and ratification, but we are looking at a total process that, given a serious desire to do it, could in principle be completed in a year or two—or even less time, if further mass terrorist events were to lead to its being seen as a matter of life and death and it were done on an emergency basis. The long delay in thinking seriously about it, from 1991 to the present, does not mean that there has to be an equally long delay after thinking gets underway.

Ratifiability

There would remain the task of convincing the American people, the Russian people, and the other allies to ratify the protocol of accession.

The American people are already sold; polls have invariably shown them favoring Russia's joining by solid majorities, the smallest margin being 51% for, 40% against, the largest 65% for, 30% against. The Russian people have been split, slightly on the negative side; polls have shown variously 27% for, 31% against; 30% for, 40% against.[16] All these polls took place prior to September 11; presumably opinion has shifted to a more favorable posture on both sides.

Getting stronger support from the Russian people should not be difficult. The main specific Russian objection to NATO is that Russia is not included and that NATO proceeds without listening seriously to Russia. Thus far NATO has suffered from bad public relations within Russia for the very reason that it excludes Russia. It has been a vicious circle, temporarily ameliorated by the NRC but still in existence. An agreement on Russian entry into NATO would cut the vicious circle. The elite would have little trouble explaining to Russian public opinion that the reasons for being anti-NATO have gone away. The public tends to be suggestible and to follow the elite on such questions. It has not been done yet, because the elite has learned from experience that it will suffer a politically damaging humiliation by the West, if it ventures to suggest anything more in NATO-Russia relations than what is already accepted at NATO as a living option. Nevertheless, ever since 1991 the mainstream of the Russian elite has always wished on the whole for entry into NATO, initially on a base-level as a "political member" like Spain when it first joined. This is partly because it wishes for Russia to play a large and constructive role in the new world order, partly because it sees the alternative as far worse: isolation and marginalization.

Changing the anti-Russian opinion of the Eastern European countries and securing their ratification for Russian membership would be more difficult, but the capacity of NATO to generate "consensus" from the new members is strong if the will is present. Moreover, there is a quasi-legal obligation that could make the matter manageable. When these countries joined NATO, they made a pledge not to veto further accessions from the PFP area: this was part of the package of terms for their membership, written into their MAP. For them to try now to veto Russia would be to place the legitimacy of their own membership in question. It is striking that some of them, such as President Havel of the Czech Republic, have in fact done this anyway; but if the core of NATO were to object seriously to this, as it did to the similar threats of former President Orban of Hungary against Slovakia, it would have a strong effect. (In Hungary, it ultimately helped get Mr. Orban voted out of office, and meanwhile caused the government to dismiss Mr. Orban's statements as mere private off-hand comments not reflecting state policy.)

There are still some in Eastern Europe who remember that they owe their freedom to the Russian democrats, and that they had in 1990 taken initiatives for building a common Euro-Atlantic home including Russia. It would not be hard for them to return to the 1990 moral framework and accept Russia's inclusion; not as hard as it had been in the 1950s for France to change its mind and accept Germany into NATO. France was dead set against including Germany; it thought that this was contrary to the whole idea and purpose of the Atlantic Alliance. And, as an original Ally in the two World Wars, it had some legitimacy—more than the Eastern Europeans—for claiming to define what the Alliance was all about. But, with a combination of persuasion and pressure, the US got France to waive its objections, and a few years later France realized that it was much the safer for having Germany inside the alliance than out. The new Eastern European members will someday discover the same thing: that the best basis for their security from Russia is to have it integrated into the Alliance.

Selling It More Profoundly

To be sure, there is the deeper matter of selling Russian membership to the soul of people, not just gaining their assent formally. People still have a superficial conception of what NATO is, one that leaves them with a sense of cognitive dissonance about Russia joining NATO. In East and West alike, it is often said: "Wasn't NATO formed to oppose Russian power? Wouldn't Russia's joining make it irrelevant?" This formulation is sorely mistaken, but it is widely accepted as if it were the plain truth.

What is wrong in it is that it is based on a fundamentally skewed historical perspective. It is indeed based on history, but its version of history looks back only to 1949. This amounts to forgetting about the formation of the Atlantic alliance in earlier decades, during the two World Wars, when the enemy was Germany not Russia.

Even for 1949, it uses a merely external perspective for understanding the formation of NATO, or as one might have said in Soviet times, "a vulgar petty bourgeois empiricism, not even attempting to penetrate to the inside of things and their causes." Viewed from the outside, NATO was indeed formed in response to an external threat, the Soviet Union; thus, it would seem it was institutionalization of the Western side of the Cold War; thus it could have no other purpose than Cold War against the Soviet Union. But in that case it should have disappeared after 1991; it hasn't disappeared; ergo something is missing in this view.

What is missing is the internal view of the thought processes and purposes of the makers of the alliance, a view of its organic roots and multi-stage development, its intention or "teleology," the genetic code of the alliance. Missing are the reasons why its founders wanted to respond to the Soviet threat by forming a permanent peacetime institutional alliance structure rather than just an *ad hoc* coalition based on a particular diplomatic convergence. The latter would have been the normal default response, as was seen when a new coalition was formed in 2001 among a large number of countries in support of the anti-terrorist war in Afghanistan. Why was it not used in 1949? The answer is that the founders were not born in 1949. Their greatest life experience was not the Soviet threat but the two world wars. They had seen their countries saved by the Atlantic alliances of 1917 and 1941. They had lived through the interwar years with all its mistakes. By 1941 they had drawn an entire series of "lessons of the interwar years," the most important of which was the necessity of institutionalizing Atlantic unity and avoiding another US withdrawal into isolationism.

Viewed internally, NATO was the institutionalization of something other than the Cold War; it was the institutionalization of the pre-existing Atlantic alliance that had already been developing for half a century. This is what explains why NATO was made more than an *ad hoc* coalition. It is what explains why the Alliance endures. What the North Atlantic Treaty institutionalized was a generic Atlantic alliance, based on commonalities of the allies which enabled them to perceive the line-up of friends and enemies basically the same way as one another from beginning to end of the twentieth century, despite the tremendous permutations in the global diplomatic equations in the course of that century.

The Alliance was never fundamentally dependent on the Cold War or on Soviet Russian enmity for its *raison d'être*. However, it did depend on this enemy-threat in 1948–50 for a more limited purpose: to provide an external stimulus and motivation for developing the internal energy to overcome the inertia of national sovereignty and finally achieve the institutionalization that was needed. This once done, there was no chance it was going to disappear when the Cold War was over. Nor was there any reason for it to disappear. Not a single one of its member countries wanted to dissolve it, in contrast to the Warsaw Pact which all members except the USSR wanted to dissolve. Russians would do well to stop dreaming of NATO dissolving like the Warsaw Pact or complaining about why it didn't happen. And Westerners would do well to stop fearing that it will dissolve at the drop of a hat, or lose its reason for existing if it adapts to new conditions.[17]

The longer perspective is more comprehensive than the perspective that starts in 1949. It is better for explanatory and predictive purposes. It is, in sum, more accurate. It contains less distortion, more truth. It provides a basis for a historical reconceptualization—an honest one, which happens also to be a convenient one. For, with the benefit of this honest re-conceptualization, Russians and Westerners alike would be able to recognize an expanding Atlantic Alliance as a central part of the history of the modern world. The re-conceptualization would look, in outline form, like this:

1) Roots of the Atlantic Alliance—the formation of a North Atlantic society in the centuries of trans-Atlantic colonization. The Northern part

represent a modernizing Protestant empire, locked in bitter struggle against the Catholics. The original enemies of the North Atlantic society: Spain and France. Growth of the North Atlantic society for 170 years after 1607. Division of this society into two halves in 1776, thanks to intervention by France, which inserted itself between the allies on the two sides of the Atlantic, drove a wedge between them, played upon their differences, and finally "divided and deceived" them. Nevertheless, the further expansion of this society in its American side in the 1800s, while its Western European side caught up with democratization in the same period.

2) Reconstitution of North Atlantic unity in a new form after 1890: diplomatic rapprochement of England and America, after a century of mutual enmity. This lays the foundation for the modern Atlantic alliance, which in greater or lesser degree has existed continuously ever since. Bismarck foretells that the commonality of language and heritage among the English and Americans would be the decisive accident of the twentieth century. This proves prescient, but also misses part of the matter; it ignores the fact that many of the common roots of political and social heritage are shared with others, not English-speaking, in Northwest Europe, making the grouping extensible.

3) Extension of the North Atlantic grouping in the next decade, with a reconciliation and alliance of England and France (incorporating the historic enemy of *les pouvoirs* Anglo-Saxons).

The Atlantic grouping thence proceeds onward cumulatively:

4) The first generation of the contemporary Atlantic alliance, with England, France, and America joining as allies on the battlefield in World War I.

5) The better-organized Anglo-American-French Alliance of World War II.

6) Peacetime institutionalization of the Alliance in 1949 with the North Atlantic Treaty and the consequent Organization, NATO. Alliance growth becomes permanent and uninterrupted.

7) Incorporation into the Alliance, 1949-54, of its World War I and II enemies, Germany, Italy, Turkey, and indirectly Japan. These were the

most terrible fighting enemies the alliance ever faced, far more terrible than the USSR.

8) Inclusion in 1982 of Spain (the original enemy of the North Atlantic society).

9) 1991-94 throwing the umbrella of NACC and PFP over its Cold War enemies and declaring all PFP participants eligible to be considered for membership in the Alliance.

10) 1997-2002, invitation of 10 former Cold War Communist enemy states to join.

There is no reason for the process to stop here. More than a dozen other former Communist states remain. One of them is Russia, which NATO has only begun to take seriously into its sights.

To be sure, the Alliance is caught in a half-way house on Russia. In NATO circles, many people still say the Alliance should welcome Russia as a special permanent partner but would lose its *raison d'être* if Russia became a member. There is a contradiction here: if the Alliance needs Russia as an implicit adversary to justify its own existence, then it cannot genuinely accept Russia as a permanent partner; if it welcomes Russia as a strategic partner, then its *raison d'être* cannot be anti-Russian and cannot be inherently damaged by Russian membership. The contradiction has endured for nearly a decade, but at a high cost and cannot go on forever. Either the fear of closeness to Russia will undermine the partnership, as has happened several times in the past decade, or else the need for the partnership will lead people to reconsider the fear and figure out how to work together in a less fear-ridden way in the future.

In overcoming this fear, NATO will need help from the larger history we have outlined above, the history of *la longue durée* Atlantic Alliance. It is evident that Russia was in no sense the original enemy of this Atlantic Alliance. The Cold War was just one of the later generations in the life of the Alliance, not its *raison d'être*. Inclusion of Russia, far from being an act of existential self-obliteration of the Alliance, would be a natural continuation of its historical development. In each stage it incorporated a former enemy and overcame a former existential division among the great powers, dramatically improving the global security of the Atlantic countries. Inclusion of Russia would do the same thing today. It would also confirm the continued relevance of the Alliance to the global security of the core Atlantic democracies—the only question that matters for the survival of the Alliance, and one on which expansion merely to the small Eastern European countries has been no help.

The American people have instinctively grasped the idea of inclusion of Russia in NATO. This may perhaps be attributed to the traditional American version of common sense, one that, in contrast to European common sense, tends to be more generous and broad-minded in its perspectives, more forward-looking, less backward-looking. It may also be attributed to America's relative objectivity about Russia, as a vast country that doesn't have to be afraid of Russia's size and is far removed from the Continent, in contrast to the Continental Europeans with their understandable fears and passions. It is much the same reason why America showed a more broad-minded and fair-minded approach than France when the issue was the admission of Germany into NATO.

The American people do not have a grasp, however, of the historical logic of their preference for including Russia or the institutional issues involved. Absent this grasp, the common sense of the people is readily susceptible to getting diverted among the elite, where the Cold War became an entrenched profession over a period of two generations, and a number of arguments have circulated against Russia-in-NATO, building on a perspective that goes back only to 1949. For a long time, it passed for realism to say that Russia could never be a part of NATO because the *raison d'etre* of the Alliance was based on having Russia as an enemy. This partly changed after September 11, which made evident the danger of a false realism, or of being backward-looking in one's conception as to who is the enemy.

Behind the loss of historical perspective on the Atlantic Alliance lies the fact that the Atlanticist movement faded out in the 1960s; it was almost completely displaced in elite thinking by other frameworks for understanding international affairs. It never recovered to provide an adequate perspective on past and future. In its absence, what remained was the Cold War framework of analysis (including the framework of the opponents of the Cold War effort), which understood NATO merely in terms of 1949, i.e. as one of the two mutually opposed subsystems of the Cold War. Lost was the appreciation of NATO's role as the core institution of the Atlantic system, and of the Atlantic system itself, in its generic aspects, as an organic subsystem of the world order ever since 1492. After 1989, the bulk of the scholarly world remained mired in this framework. It failed to provide adequate analysis, adequate memory, or adequate prognosis. The failure largely continues, despite corrections to accommodate the facts of Alliance survival and growth in the 1990s.

Nevertheless it is the business of the political elites and the scholarly world to fill in the necessary range of background, analysis and perspective for making possible a healthy dialogue in the general public. The evidence of the polls is that the public would be quite educable. It is the elites that remain the open question.

Notes

1   For poll data, see below and Ira Straus, "The American people want Russia included in NATO," *The Russia Journal*, 15 November 2002.
2   The use in the 1990s of the argument that there must be an enemy already extant against whom to unite—that it was not enough to have a basket of common risks and threats, against which to organize unity—was unfortunate. It cost America dearly. Logically, it was a slippage from the democratic realism of Hans Morgenthau into the darker form of realism associated with Carl Schmitt, the Weimar theorist of the "conservative revolution" and of the primacy of the enemy-relation in life and politics. Ever since the 1890s, with Alfred T. Mahan and Henry Adams, the argument for building up the Atlantic Alliance by forethought has been to head off wars and discourage enemies from even arising; organizing to win wars after they have started has always been viewed as a second-best purpose for the Alliance. NATO institutionalized the Alliance by forethought in 1949, in peacetime, as a deterrent to war, because people had learned from bitter experience that temporizing in the first half of the century had tempted potential aggressors and given space for world wars to get underway. The argument against Russia entering NATO in the 1990s was in this sense a regression to pre-NATO thinking.
3   For this, the reader may be referred to the Committee on Eastern Europe and Russia in NATO (CEERN) Report at www.fas.org/man/nato/ceern.
4   The relation between NATO expansion and the new "Great Game" was both direct and dialectical. Directly, each alienated Russia, and each argument with Russia on one front gave fuel to the proponents of a more anti-Russian posture on other fronts. Also directly, each strengthened the independence of former Soviet and Warsaw Pact countries from Russia, so both could be understood by American politicians as part of a national policy of promoting "freedom" and "democracy"; although in reality the equation of "independence" (from Russia) with "democracy" was accurate only in parts of Eastern Europe, and proved the opposite of the truth in Central Asia. Dialectically, the Clinton Administration's policy on NATO expansion was criticized, in the partisan American politics of the time, for being not too harsh but too soft on Russia, and the "Great Game" was pushed as a kind of compensation.
5   It might be called a policy of "mutual troublemaking" or "competitive Islamism." The main instances of it are, in the minds of Americans, the behavior of Russia in "playing" Iraq and Iran against the US; in the minds of Russian, the behavior of the US in "playing" Pakistan and the Taliban against Russia in the 1990s, and playing up to Chechnya and Saudi Arabia as well. The reality is that that this kind of mutually harmful behavior has occurred on both sides, although not always in the way it is perceived; in Chechnya, the US role has been almost exclusively rhetorical.

6   The literature on this starts with Hobbes' Leviathan and The Federalist Papers of 1788. In the 20th century the same point was affirmed in basic realist writings on international relations, on the one side, and on the other, in the federalist writings of the 1930s that motivated the initiators of the Marshall Plan, NATO, and EU. It was later developed in new forms by "integration theory" writers who reflected on the development of NATO and the EU. Karl W. Deutsch, Richard W. Van Wagenen, Sidney A. Burrell, Robert A. Kann, Maurice Lee, Jr., Martin Lichterman, Ramond E. Lindgren, and Francis L. Lowenheim, in *Political Community and the North Atlantic Area: International Organization in the Light of Historical Experience* (Princeton: Princeton University Press, 1957), indicated various senses in which mutual institutions and behaviors must be "adequate" in order to eliminate planning for mutual conflict, but did not attempt to specify substantive structures and agendas of institutions that might make for "adequacy," merely indicating that the requisite institutional needs might vary from case to case depending on the scope of interdependence. Deutsch personally favored a "minimalist" focus on multiplying communications channels; Van Wagenen took a more functionalist approach. (See Ira Straus, *Supranational Norms in International Affairs*, chapter 5, Charlottesville, VA, University of Virginia Department of Government and Foreign Affairs, 1992.) Ernst Haas, in *The Uniting of Europe* (Stanford: Stanford Univ. Press, 1958), did specify what institutional structures would be adequate, at least in the case of Europe, and arrived at conclusions not far from The Federalist Papers or from Jean Monnet's federalism, although implying that interim integrative processes might be "adequate" for sustaining mutual confidence during the transitional period to the goal. The stagnation of European and Atlantic integration after the early 1960s led to a replacement of integration theory with "regime theory" in the 1970s and a lowering of goals. Game-theorizing showed some capacity for learning of cooperation through iterative experiences, without necessarily requiring institutions. The minimalist trend was reinforced by a public relations preference in NATO for modesty about its own institutional strengths. The crisis of the EC in the early 1980s and the response—a resumption of integration by way of major institutional construction—led to a renewal of federalist thinking on the European level that continues to this day but has yet to be squared with the minimalist trends on the wider level.

7   "NATO chief hasn't ruled out Russia's membership," *The Associated Press*, Moscow, May 28, 2000.

8   This chapter was originally written in 2002 in the aftermath of the establishment of the NRC. At that time, the Russian government was projecting a posture of relative satisfaction and Western circles were treating the "Russia problem" as solved. As the issue of Iraq came to a head, however, disagreements reached a high pitch, bringing mutual recriminations, and a new rise of anti-American sentiment in Moscow to a level comparable to that reached during the war in Kosovo. Once again, Russia complained of insufficient political consultations in the NRC, expressing dissatisfaction that cooperation on the process level was being substituted for the basic work of reconciling differences on the policy level. This would seem to confirm the prognosis that the NRC, after its delays and whittling down, would not provide a sufficient foundation for cumulative progress in relations; and unless supplemented soon by more daring steps, the gradual achievements in its sheltered environment would be constantly vulnerable to disruption by the turbulence of international events.

A MAP for Russia 145

9   Calling it a "process" with defined "stages" should not be mistaken as reducing it to a routine procedure; rather, there is a lot of substantive creative work that would have to be done, particularly in stage two. Nevertheless, it is a fairly straightforward process.

10 In the aftermath of September 11, students in Russia, Italy, and the US, working through a ten-week simulation process, undertook to attempt the work of a reconciliation of the strategic concepts and interests of the two sides. For a summary of the procedures used and the results, including specific terms for reconciliation of interests in a number of strategic theaters around the world, see Ira Straus, "Students show the way for Russia, West," *The Russia Journal*, 23 August 2002.

11 The blunder appears to have been primarily the responsibility of the West. Russians made suggestions for closer communication and coordination as they were developing new doctrines; however, the West tended to brush them off with arguments such as that NATO did not have a "security doctrine" in the same sense and form as Russia did.

12 Proceeding with MAP implementation does not mean proceeding pedantically until every detail is fulfilled completely, but, as has been done with the smaller candidates, proceeding until enough progress has been made for them to be considered "within range" and a qualitative leap—membership—to be advisable while helping them to the finish line.

13 There is some evidence of learning better. A recent case: "Russia's goal is to establish efficacious cooperation with NATO rather than seek a transformation of that alliance into some kind of a political structure, Deputy Foreign Minister Vladimir Chizhov said in an exclusive interview with Itar-Tass Wednesday [1 January 2003]. 'There is every ground to believe that NATO will remain a union of countries with a strong military underpinning in the foreseeable future,' Chizhov said. 'Russia will make practical efforts to help it turn from a structure of the Cold War era to the one that is fighting with the global challenges of our time—a realistic plan that has become possible after the emergence of the Russia-NATO council,' Chizhov said." Ksenia Kaminskaya, "Official says Russia's goal to cooperate with NATO" Itar-Tass 1 January 2003. Sergei Karaganov, in another realistic formulation, told the present author that Russia would naturally be opposed to NATO's strength as long as Russia was outside NATO, but this would change if Russia was in NATO.

14 I must confess to having myself originally accepted these formulations on trust. Then one day in the early 1980s I was talking with Ambassador Theodore Achilles, who had done more than any other single person to write the NATO Treaty (he had been director of the Western European division of the State Department while the Treaty was being prepared, and as a believer in Atlantic integration he made a tremendous effort for the Treaty). I was saying that certain things couldn't be done since every country has a right of veto in NATO. He replied, to my amazement, that I was mistaken; there is no right of veto in NATO. Re-read against the NATO Treaty, the Council is left free to set its own rules. And this was deliberate, he assured me: we didn't want the alliance to be hamstrung as are most international organizations by a requirement of getting consensus among its members for all decisions.

15 In the actuality, when Congress ratified the protocols for the seven new members on May 7–8, 2003, it attached a resolution calling on NATO to reexamine its decision-making within eighteen months and reconsider the consensus procedure, and to consider possible procedures for expelling ill-behaving members. This makes the scenario outlined in the present chapter more "live" and less hypothetical than it was in previous years.

16 The American polls have been fairly precisely worded but not given frequently or with much experimentation with wording for distinguishing nuances. Russian polls have been less clear; a few polls, such as the ones cited, have provided a simple "for" or "against" choice on membership, but most have instead asked what kind of relationship Russians should have with NATO, with "membership" listed as one among multiple options including politically safer choices such as "cooperation," "partnership," and "no relation" for distinguishing nuances. For further details and references, see Ira Straus, "The American people want Russia included in NATO," *The Russia Journal*, 15 November 2002.

17 To be sure, the predictions could yet become a self-fulfilling prophecy—US could kill the alliance, if it persuades itself that it is senseless—but this would be an unnatural act and would require a considerable effort. The time when it seemed most likely to happen was in the immediate aftermath of the Cold War, when there was a genuine widespread sense of bafflement about why NATO was still there; yet no momentum ever developed to get rid of it. The current rhetoric about NATO's military irrelevance is in the decades-old tradition of posturing about burden sharing and pressuring the allies to make a better effort militarily.

PART III:
NATO, THE EU
AND THE "WAR ON TERRORISM"

Chapter 8

Toward New Euro-Atlantic Euro-Mediterranean Security Communities

Hall Gardner

Despite a number of high profile "internationally sponsored" attacks within the territory of most of the major advanced industrial powers since the late 1960s and prior to 11 September 2001 (such as Black September at the 1972 Munich Olympics, the 1993 attempt to blow up the World Trade Center, the failed effort of Algerian hijackers to ram a passenger plane into the Eiffel tower in 1994, the Sarin nerve gas attack on the Tokyo metro in 1995, among many others), such actions did not cause the US, Europe, and Japan to engage in strong and concerted counter-measures against the real threats of both nationally and internationally-based "terrorist" movements.

As terrorism was largely considered a secondary concern, the major focus of US policy throughout the 1990s was largely on Russia, and on the effort to prevent the latter from ever attempting to re-engage in imperialist expansion in eastern Europe. NATO enlargement into central Europe in 1999 and then into eastern Europe by 2004 was accordingly intended to provide a "buffer" around a newly unified Germany, and then gain advantages from a greater forward outreach into the region (and beyond). NATO enlargement was also intended as *preclusive* yet peaceful action designed to check the possibility of Russian imperial designs.

This perceived anti-Russian focus also manifested itself most directly in the US refusal to work with Moscow against the Taliban after Soviet withdrawal from Afghanistan (in part due to close US-Pakistani-Saudi ties and mutual oil pipeline interests) as well as in regard to the wars to block pan-Serbian expansion in Bosnia and Kosovo. (The US tended to regard Belgrade as a Russian surrogate in southeastern Europe, a viewpoint that tended to downplay Russian efforts to mediate the crisis.) From Moscow's perspective, it appeared that each round of NATO enlargement (in which NATO was urged to "go out of area or out of business") has coincided with "out of area" wars in Bosnia, Kosovo, and then Iraq—a correlation which has deeply disturbed Moscow.

In this regard, the war "over" Kosovo took precedence over the war with Bin Laden and Al-Qaida: The attacks on the US embassies in Kenya and Tanzania took place in 1998 roughly one year before the war "over" Kosovo in mid-1999.[1] In retrospect, one wonders if it would not have been wiser for the Clinton administration to focus on thoroughly eradicating Al-Qaeda then and consequently work with the Russians to negotiate a "deal" *against* both the Taliban and the Milosevic regime.

It was really only after September 11 that the US recognized that Russian diplomatic and military supports would be necessary in the "war on terrorism." Although there were previous signs of more positive US-Russian cooperation toward the end of the Clinton administration, it still took the horrors of 11 September 2001 for the United States and NATO to re-assess their positions vis-à-vis Russia and to recognize that Russia was not an immediate "threat" at least in the near future. In what actually helped to build both domestic and international support for President Bush (who had won the presidential election through a majority of votes of the electoral college, but who had lost the popular vote), the Bush administration, after 11 September, would seek to forge a new cooperative relationship between NATO and Russia and begin to bury Cold War antagonisms (but not altogether eliminate mutual suspicions).

In the initial phase of war with the Al-Qaeda and the Taliban in Afghanistan, the United States, Europe and Russia thus began to forge tighter relations; the policy appeared to be based on multilateralism; yet the more the Bush administration threatened *preclusive* war with Iraq, the more France and Germany questioned the point as to where one should draw the line between "terrorists" who engage in operations of *asymmetrical* warfare and states that are developing Weapons of Mass Destruction (WMD). See Introduction and Chapter 16.

Despite US-EU-Russian disagreements in regard to intervention in Iraq, a more effective "war on terrorism" will continue to require a closer multilateral effort. Dealing effectively with a whole range of new "threats" will ultimately require a far-reaching re-structuration of the NATO-EU relationship, and the development of a more concerted US-EU-Russian strategy in which the EU could play a greater and more proportional role in both "power" and "responsibility sharing" along side the United States and Russia. The formation of a *Transatlantic Political Economic and Strategic Council*, perhaps superceding the NATO-Russian Council, may represent one option.[2] At the same time, however, due to a large extent to the Franco-German opposition to US intervention against Iraq, US policy makers have generally opposed giving the EU a more proportional role. Washington has threatened to more actively attempt to check the formation of a Common European Foreign and Security Policy (CEFSP), in part by playing the UK, Spain, Italy, Poland against France and Germany.

It will consequently be argued that the US, EU and Russia must attempt to put aside their differences in the rebuilding and reconstructing Iraq, a process easier said than done. (See Hall Gardner, Chapter 16.) Here, it is essential that the US take steps toward mutual cooperation on a wide-ranging number of actual and potential conflicts that can help mend the deep fissure in the Atlantic Alliance caused by Iraq and other bones of contention. It is furthermore essential that the United States and the European Union both work to develop the defense, political economic, and institutional links necessary to guarantee that Russia remains in a long lasting entente or alliance relationship, so as to prevent its isolation and potential anti-American (if not anti-European) militarization.

NATO and Russia

After more than a decade of missed opportunities since the break-up of the Soviet Union, NATO and Russia belatedly declared a newfound friendship based upon a common "enemy"—the "scourge of terrorism." At the May 2002 North Atlantic Council meeting at Reykjavik, NATO opted to meet as "20" (19 NATO members plus Russia) in the new format of the NATO-Russia Council (NRC), a format originally proposed by former Russian Foreign Minister Kosyrev in 1991.[3] It was hoped that the new NRC would prove to be more effective than the previous NATO-Russia Permanent Joint Council—in that Russia will be more directly engaged in NATO decision-making.

At the same time, however, the NRC will ostensibly meet only on issues of concern to NATO: Russia will not be permitted to set the agenda or be able to veto NATO decisions.[4] Moreover, due in part to objections by the three new NATO members, Poland, the Czech Republic, and Hungary, plus concerns raised by Germany and the US Secretary of Defense, Donald Rumsfeld,[5] the initial agenda of the NRC was to be "fairly modest" in order to make certain that there will be "some quick successes in order to persuade skeptics that the NRC can work, and to avoid disillusionment at an early stage"[6]—such as cooperation on sea rescue missions.

The NRC has been confronted with some rather burdensome security and defense issues. In addition to the struggle against "terrorism," the NRC has to tackle the proliferation of weapons of mass destruction, problems surrounding civil defense—not to overlook the fundamental issue of NATO-Russian military cooperation.[7] The NRC will ultimately need to address military cooperation in regard to Kaliningrad and the Baltic region, and contemplate the necessity for more formal NATO-Russian accords in regard to force deployments in central and eastern Europe, the Caucasus (Azerbaijan) as well central Asia (Uzbekistan, Kyrgystan and Afghanistan), if not ultimately the Euro-Mediterranean and Persian Gulf.

Russia and the NATO-EU "Double Enlargement"

For the first time in its history, NATO invoked its Article V guarantee of mutual security in the aftermath of September 11, but in response to a direct attack on the US, and not on Europe, as had largely been expected during the Cold War. The "war on terrorism" has consequently resulted in largely unprecedented political, military and intelligence cooperation between the NATO allies (albeit largely on a bilateral basis), but also with many other states—with a number of the latter hoping to join on the bandwagon and obtain offers of NATO and/or EU membership. The US, backed primarily by the UK, may have taken the leading role in the actual combat against Al-Qaeda and the Taliban in Afghanistan, but the important logistical and intelligence support of other states cannot be ignored.

At the same time, however, despite the formation of a new post-September 11 coalition, many of the security issues that confronted NATO and the EU in the past have not entirely faded away. The issues raised by the "double enlargement" of NATO and the EU, as both regional blocs expand their membership but without necessarily coordinating their security strategies, remain on the back burner, not to overlook US-EU political-economic rivalries due to the rise of the EU's tremendous economic potential, the new role of the Euro as a reserve currency, and as the EU implements a presidential system and CEFSP in the next few years.

Following the November 2002 Prague summit—which was devoted to the issues of transformation, enlargement, and cementing NATO relationships with states the new eastern members—the new NATO is to incorporate seven of the ten states of the Vilnius group in a Big Bang, for a total of 26 states by the year 2004. The "Big Bang" enlargement of 2004 is expected to be followed by the "Big MAC" expansion of the three remaining states of the Vilnius group, Macedonia, Albania and Croatia.

The concern raised here is that enlargement could be an unwieldy process, which may prove difficult to manage, particularly as the United States has no substantial and direct political and historical experience with eastern Europe. New members in 2004 will include the three Baltic states (Lithuania, Estonia and Latvia); Slovenia and Slovakia (which possess direct lines of communication to Hungary); plus states deeper into eastern Europe and the Black Sea, Romania and Bulgaria, which possess direct lines of communication to Turkey (and then Iraq).

The irony of this expanded enlargement is that it brings in states that are largely "consumers," rather than "producers" of security and which are not entirely politically or economically stable. Their main strengths rest in their geostrategic position. The new enlargement furthermore leapfrogs key strategically positioned and democratic states of Sweden, Finland, and Austria, which are crucial for the defense of north eastern and south eastern Europe. If the latter states will not join NATO, this should imply the necessity for a closer NATO-EU-Russian cooperation through the formation of a new Transatlantic Council. (NATO expansion to eastern Europe has initially strengthened the hand of the US versus the EU, but bringing in Sweden, Finland and Austria into a new NATO-EU relationship could help restore the "balance," but not to the exclusion of Russia.)

The EU has likewise continued its own plans of enlargement with little consultation with the United States. In addition to the three states that have recently joined NATO (Poland, the Czech Republic and Hungary), EU applicants (which are expected to enter the EU in 2004) include the three Baltic states, Slovenia, Slovakia, Romania and Bulgaria as well as Malta and Cyprus. The possible entry of Romania and Bulgaria in 2007 would bring the EU to the Black Sea. The membership of Greek Cyprus (and ultimately the Turkey in some "new" form of EU membership?) would thus draw the EU's geopolitical and economic interests toward Israel and then the Middle East/Persian Gulf—and particularly if the problematic issue of Turkish membership was resolved.[8] (Post-Iraq war Turkish confrontation with the United States in regard to Iraqi Kurdistan may make the latter look closer to the EU; but *if* Ankara is continually rebuffed by the Europeans, it may find itself dangerously isolated.)

The dilemma is that each step of NATO-EU enlargement further risks disturbing the already delicate Euro-Atlantic geopolitical and political-economic equilibrium. As NATO and EU engage in their respective enlargements, it is not clear that either regime has the resources or political will to manage the security ramifications of such extensive commitments, and particularly as US attention has increasingly been drawn to Persian Gulf, Central and South Asia, the Far East, as well as Africa. In addition, both regimes appear to vying for the political allegiance of central and eastern European states. The EU insists that all its members support the International Criminal Court [ICC], for example, which was most strongly supported by Berlin. Washington, however, demands that both US soldiers and civilians be exempt from the ICC's jurisdiction. Here, the US voted with Iraq, Iran, Israel, and China—against the ICC![9] Moreover, in the clash between Germany and the US over the ICC, the US threatened to pull US forces out of Germany (an issue considered since the Clinton administration)—if Berlin continued to press for a broader base of jurisdiction than the consent of the national state of the accused.[10]

Both Washington and the Europeans competed intensely for eastern European allegiance in support for, or against, intervention in Iraq. Not only did new NATO members Poland, the Czech republic and Hungary support the US position, but the Vilnius Ten group also produced a letter on 5 February 2003 in support of the tough US stance in regard to Iraq, that Iraq was already in material breach of UN Resolution 1441. Their statement, updated from that of November 2002, not-so-ironically utilized Cold War ideological rhetoric: "The *clear and present danger posed by the Saddam Hussein regime requires a united response for the community of democracies*" (emphasis mine). The purpose of the statement was to make certain that the US would sustain its security commitments to all NATO members, and to prevent the possible break-up of NATO itself due to disputes between its most powerful members. At the same time, the question of whether Iraq truly represented a "clear and present danger" represented a bone of contention between Washington, Paris and Bonn.

France and Germany, however, have thus regarded the new eastern European state members in NATO as American surrogates, and began to question their loyalty to the EU. French President Jacques Chirac stated that east European states were "badly brought up" (*mal élevé*), and would need to learn when to be quiet, in March 2003 in that they did not consult EU members (meaning Germany and France in particular) before making their statement in support of US policy.

On the one hand, the Franco-German liaison with Russia has raised the fears of eastern Europeans. In part, this is due to threat perception: while western Europeans do not tend to see Russia as a potential threat; most eastern European states still fear the Russian bear. (This is true for the most part, except perhaps for Slovenia and Finland. The latter, interestingly, appeared more attracted to joining NATO—since NATO announced its new partnership with Russia in May 2002.) On the other, the US effort to play Spain and east European states (coupled with the significant sale of F-16 fighter jets to Poland, stronger supports to the Baltic states, coupled with efforts to foster a Polish-Ukrainian alliance in regard to peacekeeping in Iraq) may work to divide an expanding EU and simultaneously alienate a retrenching Russia, despite continued Russian cooperation in the "war on terrorism."

In many ways, France, Germany, and the EU as a whole will soon be forced out of its comfortable nest as the US begins to downsize some of its bases and 70,000 troops away from more expensive, and less strategically positioned bases in Germany (except Ramstein), and step toward Poland (5,000-10,000 troops), Romania and Bulgaria, as well as Azerbaijan (15,000 troops aimed primarily at Iran), and Djibouti (5,000-6,500 troops), closer to the "new threats."[11]

As US forces are downsized in Germany, as well as in Turkey (shifting to Azerbaijan), NATO itself may take a back seat in most military operations. The fact that the United States essentially overlooked NATO as a vehicle to deal with the conflict in Afghanistan, combined with the fact that the United States has appeared more interested in affairs in the Persian Gulf and Asia, raises eastern (as well as western) European fears that the United States will not back European interests in time of need.

At present, Europe as a whole seems far behind in developing an adequate military capability to handle some of the "new threats" (even more so if one ignores the possibility of a Russian backlash). The 2004 Prague NATO summit did discuss issues relating to the Allied defense burden. The United States spends 3.5% of its gross domestic product on defense and would prefer to see the Allies reach the 2% level. The Europeans counter that they make up some of the difference with aid and development assistance, which they regard as crucial to the long term prevention of terrorism, but they also realize that if they cannot pick up defense spending that they could be left out of the decision-making process. (In concession to EU demands, the US has promised to open its markets to "fair defense trade.")

The Prague NATO summit called for a 20,000 man NATO Response Force "able to deploy in- or out-of-area, ready for action within 7 to 30 days, and able to sustain itself in the field for up to a month." As US Ambassador to NATO Nicolas Burns put it: "A NATO Response Force, focused on combat missions, will complement and not compete with, the EU's proposed Rapid Reaction Force which will focus on peacekeeping duties of the Petersberg tasks. In fact, we see these two forces as mutually reinforcing, as we see the entire range of NATO-EU cooperation. We must now follow up to ensure that Allies participate in and contribute to the NATO response force, and get it ready to put planes in the air, ships under sail, and boots on the ground as soon as possible."

It is still not clear, however, that the Europeans will accept force specialization that could divide the alliance between American "war fighters" and European "peacekeepers." Issues of "duplication," in regard to key areas of intelligence reconnaissance, for example, will continue to plague the intra-Allied debate, as could issues of "decoupling" and "discrimination." (The 3-D's condemned by the Clinton, and then the Bush administrations.) The Europeans also insisted that Washington take state and society building more seriously in regard to Bosnia, Kosovo, Afghanistan, and now Iraq, in addition to other areas where the US has intervened, such as Nicaragua, Panama, and Haiti. Doing the dirty work in terms of peacekeeping, state and society building is, in fact, in the US interest, in that troops on the ground will help influence the course of political, social and economic development in the future.

Russia

NATO and EU Enlargement, as well as the deployment of Ballistic Missile Defenses, likewise remain issues that can upset the newfound NATO-Russian entente, in addition to widening the "war on terrorism" to new fronts in Central Asia and the Caucasus that affect Russian interests. Moscow has denounced what it calls a potential "blockade" of Kaliningrad once Poland and Lithuania join the EU (planned for 2004)—in that it has feared the implementation of overly strict visa requirements and a significant reduction of trade advantages for the enclave, which is seen by Europeans as transit point for drug smuggling and other illicit activities of organized crime. While Russia and the EU reached a general accord over Kaliningrad dealing with the immediate issue of "travel" rights through the creation of "facilitated travel documents" in late 2002, the larger geopolitical and geoeconomic questions have not yet been resolved. (See Arbatova, Chapter 6.)

On the one hand, Russia itself may fear the prospects of immigration from Central Asian states and the Transcaucasus, thus enacting a visa regime may set a precedent that actually suits Moscow's interests—and need to liberalize Russia's own hyper-bureaucratic visa regulations. On the other hand, Moscow may find itself increasingly unable to sustain the economy of the region: Moscow has argued the issue is not a "corridor" like that through East Germany to Berlin as during the Cold War as often stated in the American and European press, but rather the question that the EU needs to consider "an exception to the Schengen agreement" due to the uniqueness of the situation.[12] Despite plans for a ferry boat to St. Petersburg, among other proposals, the Russian enclave may increasingly feel itself "isolated" politically, economically and militarily from Russia—and surrounded by EU and NATO members by the year 2004. Such a prospect raises Russian fears that the enclave could demand greater autonomy—or potential secession. Concurrently, the fact that Baltic state borders with Russia have not yet been adequately defined could pose problems for both NATO and the EU, which would have to deal directly with the problem with Russia.

Although rhetoric in regard to Baltic state membership in NATO as representing a *casus belli* for Moscow has appeared to fade, the membership of the Baltic states in NATO remains problematic in that NATO must soon tackle the difficult question of permitting Russian military land and over-flight access to Kaliningrad through Lithuanian space. While Moscow seeks cooperation with NATO in matters of security (US and NATO forces have begun to help stabilize Central Asia, but also enter the Caucasus in Azerbaijan and Georgia, for example), Russian hardliners continue to see NATO as a military organization with potentially offensive capabilities, despite its claims to post-Cold War "transformation." Coupled with NATO enlargement into former Soviet/Russian spheres of influence and security, the fact that the US military intervention has been aimed at former Russian/Soviet allies (ex-Yugoslavia and Iraq) represents a bitter pill, one that could spark a backlash—if not compensated in some other way.

Arms Reduction Issues

As the Bush administration appears allergic to treaties and other inter-state formalities in general, having unilaterally scrapped the 1967 Anti-Ballistic Missile (ABM) treaty, in addition to the 1966 Comprehensive Test Ban treaty (CTBT) and the 1997 Kyoto Protocol on global warming, for example, there is absolutely no guarantee that Russia will necessarily continue—in the long term—to trust the formula that the US and Russian relationship is moving toward the day that "no arms control treaties will be necessary" in the words of US Secretary of Defense Donald Rumsfeld. US policy has accordingly tended to downplay the importance of engaging other states into formal cooperative engagements through binding international treaties, and the need to formulate new international accords.

The Bush administration's position appears to ignore the importance of a number of existing arms control treaties, such as the adapted 1999 Conventional Force in Europe (CFE) treaty and 1987 Intermediate Range Nuclear Forces (INF) treaty, if not the 1967 Outer Space Treaty. (Moscow has called for new treaties limiting the militarization of Outer Space.) The refusal to ratify the CTBT has worked to undermine the 1968 Non-Proliferation Treaty (NPT), while the decision to abrogate—rather than renegotiate the ABM—undermined efforts to complete a compliance protocol for the Biological Weapons Convention.[13]

One day after the US formally scrapped the ABM treaty in June 2002, Russia dropped out of the 1993 START II treaty. Although Moscow denied the linkage between the two events, this fact has meant that Moscow is no longer required to eliminate its heavy, potentially destabilizing, land-based SS-18 and rail-mobile SS-24 multiple warhead missiles. (Russia had previously stated, before the US scrapped the ABM treaty, that it would keep a number of multiple warhead SS-18 and SS-24s divisions until 2016, when their service life is to expire.) On the more positive side, in May 2002, Washington and Moscow did agree to the Moscow Treaty, which is to reduce the number of deployed strategic nuclear warheads from about 6,000 to between 1,750 and 2,200 over the next 10 years. The treaty was ratified by the US Senate in March 2003 but has been delayed by the Russian Duma in ostensible protest to US intervention in Iraq. Yet the latter treaty is to expire in the year 2012 and will need to be renewed—if not re-negotiated to implement even lower ceilings for warheads.

In this regard, Moscow has insisted that all new NATO members sign the adapted 1999 version of the 1990 CFE treaty (dating before Soviet collapse in 1991) enforcing conventional arms reductions and has threatened to break out of the latter if the Baltic States do not ratify the treaty prior to becoming NATO members.[14] Russia has argued that the adapted CFE treaty must be signed before the Baltic states join NATO in 2004 "in order to avoid any possible loophole and gap in Russian state borders."[15] Prior to its invitation to join NATO, Lithuania refused to link NATO membership to signing the adapted CFE treaty and argued that this issue should be discussed *after* the states join NATO.[16]

Likewise, the Bush administration's decision to unilaterally scrap the 1967 Anti-Ballistic Missile treaty (without sincere Russian agreement) resulted in Russian demands for a new formal "Treaty on Mutual Security" to replace the ABM treaty that would significantly eliminate large numbers of nuclear warheads and place possible limitations as to what extent both sides can develop ballistic missile defences.[17] Russian threats also include dropping out of the 1987 INF treaty. Such a threat (whereby Russia could sell Intermediate Range Ballistic Missiles (IRBMs) to third parties despite the risks of that strategy backfiring against Russia itself) could be revived if Russian military-industrial interests are not thoroughly incorporated into helping to develop new systems of theatre missile defence (TMD), for example, as proposed by the Bush administration itself.

As the new US-Russian interrelationship continues to possess elements of positive cooperation mixed with aspects of mutual suspicion, new waves of NATO (and EU) enlargement, plus threats of US military intervention in areas of former Soviet/Russian interests such as Iraq, still possess the risk of the permanent alienation of Russia with the concurrent threats, albeit less articulated under the Putin administration than under Yeltsin, to forge a Eurasian alliance with China, India, and Iran—if Russia is not fully on board for whatever reason. Russia does not see entirely eye to eye with the United States, particularly in regard to China, and continues to provide the latter with advanced military-technological supports. Russia sustains strong ties to India (70 percent of Russian arms sales go to China and India), but also to North Korea, Iran, and to a certain extent, Iraq, where Moscow opposed military intervention despite US efforts to buy it off. Sustained Russian ties with the latter three "axis of evil" states have strained the new-found post-September 11 US-Russian entente. (See Hall Gardner, Chapter 16.)

Initially, Moscow attempted to balance its position *vis-à-vis* the Europeans and Americans, but in February 2003 it signed a joint accord with France and Germany, later joined by China, in support of extended UN inspections of Iraqi WMD in February 2003 in opposition to the US position. Contrary to American expectations, Russia thus began to toughen its stance in the UNSC toward *preclusive* US intervention in Iraq. On the one hand, in addition to the fact that the Russian population was largely against war with Iraq, Russia sought to take advantage of the dispute between the US and EU in order to gain concessions from both sides, particularly since Germany is Russia's largest trading partner. Here, however, the EU has not yet made any major steps toward granting Russia some "new" form of EU membership, much like NATO's "19 plus 1" arrangement with Moscow, as Russia has requested.

Russian hardliners see the Putin leadership as giving too much ground (such as acquiescence to the US scrapping the ABM treaty and permitting the US to deploy troops in Central Asia and the Caucasus, inluding Azerbaijan and Georgia) but without getting much in return. The Bush administration rejected the Russian proposal that Iraqi disarmament be fully guaranteed by Moscow and pressed instead for "regime change." US-Russian tensions over Russian opposition to *preclusive* US-UK intervention in Iraq had been accompanied by hints that the US Congress might not forgive Russian debt, that it might fail to repeal the Jackson-Vanik amendment, and that Congress might not fully support Russian membership in the WTO, and that it might cut Russian (as well as French and Chinese) oil companies out of deals that had been finalized with the regime of Saddam Hussein.

But perhaps the most salient factor is that the Bush administration stated that it was considering the repositioning of US forces from Germany to Poland, Bulgaria and Romania, so as to better approach Iraq, but apparently did not inform Moscow. Romania permitted the US to fly transport planes from air bases near the Black sea ports; Bulgaria provided a training camp, as did Hungary. Furthermore, as there have been requests for a NATO HQ in the Baltic states, which can not really be defended without a forward NATO presence, there is a risk that the US could forward deploy more significant forces in eastern Europe. This kind of action could break the new-found NATO-Russian entente, and puts into question the NRC "19 plus 1" relationship, as NATO had promised (without any formal treaty) not to deploy troops in eastern Europe.[18]

Inter-Allied Issues

New waves of NATO and EU enlargement risk problems for the transatlantic relationship itself. Such problems could result from the inability to forge a concerted strategy and "power" and "responsibility" sharing arrangements with new NATO members as well as with EU members—and particularly with key strategically placed EU member states which are not NATO members, such as Sweden and Austria. In effect, NATO enlargement has, ironically, leapfrogged these two democratic states despite the new-found post-Cold War claims of both neo-liberals and neo-conservatives that NATO represents an alliance of democracies.

The fact that EU members Sweden, Finland and Austria possess such strategically positioned positions between new NATO/EU members and Russia has meant that the EU should play a more proactive role in forging overlapping NATO-EU-Russian security guarantees for the entire region. (Here, Austrian refusal to permit NATO over flight rights during the war "over" Kosovo in 1999 has represented one reason the US Congress has thus far opposed Austrian membership in NATO.)

The second crucial issue is the possible overextension of NATO political-economic capabilities and a consequent break down in its political consensus, which critics argue is already strained at a membership of nineteen. Here, the US push to expand NATO has tended to overlook two key questions: The first is how "Article V" security guarantees will be applied to a membership of twenty-six allies or more. The second is how NATO will make its decisions in an expanded alliance, problems already confronted in the "war by committee" in the war "over" Kosovo.

The third issue relates to new potential crises or conflicts caused by drug smuggling (which is often related to civil wars, terrorism and state supported terrorism), economic slump and unemployment, mass migration, ethnic or territorial disputes within the new Euro-Atlantic Euro-Mediterranean region or at its periphery (Belarus, Ukraine, Moldova, the

Caucasus). Such disputes, even if not of the magnitude of conflict in ex-Yugoslavia, could drag in NATO and/or the EU—and overstretch resources. Here, US focus on Iraq has already resulted in the US decision to withdraw its peacekeepers from Macedonia in the spring of 2003 and possibly those in Bosnia in 2004, and turn peacekeeping responsibilities over to the EU (while Russia pulled its peacekeepers from Bosnia and Kosovo largely for financial reasons, but out of lack of enthusiasm for US policy.) EU Peacekeepers may also be deployed in Moldova, under an OSCE banner, but only with Russian acceptance

In many ways, the second post-Cold War wave of NATO enlargement (not including that to include eastern Germany) possesses even greater risks than the first wave—but only if the NATO-Russia Council ultimately fails to address *legitimate* Russian security concerns and if Moscow consequently believes itself cut out of NATO decision-making that affects its perceived "vital" interests.

Likewise, should EU enlargement result in trade diversion, as opposed to trade creation, in regard to trade with Russia and with the other economies of the Commonwealth of Independent States (CIS), or if Moscow is ultimately unable to reform its economy substantially so as to enter the World Trade Organization (WTO)—as restructuring its oil industry remains one of the key issues of contention—Russia could likewise turn against its present, generally positive, acceptance of EU enlargement into former Soviet/Russian spheres of influence and security.[19]

Here, the EU has tried to assure Russia (and Ukraine) that its expansion to 25 members is not intended to isolate the Commonwealth of Independent States (CIS). Russia concurrently signed a draft agreement to create a "unified economic zone" encompassing Ukraine, Kazakhstan, Belarus, and Russia (with 219 million people), which it sees as a step to WTO status. Belarus then accused the US Congress of attempting to pass the Belarus Democracy Act as an action intended to break up the CIS.[20]

Regional Cooperative-Security Communities

What are the implications of President Bush's decision to engage in a robust NATO enlargement? Under what specific conditions or modalities should this new enlargement take place, given the fact that most of the new entrants are *consumers*, rather than *producers*, of security? Could a *new* form of NATO membership, that ultimately includes Russia and Ukraine, help stabilize Euro-Atlantic relations as a whole—and hence act as a true barrier against the spread of "terrorist" activities—be implemented throughout the region? It would appear that such a possibility would require a radical re-structuration of transatlantic NATO-EU-Russian relationship—and of Euro-Atlantic Euro-Mediterranean security in general due to the expanding nature of the NATO-EU "double enlargement."

Since the pre-Iraq war NATO-EU-Russian coalition was built upon a commonly perceived "threat" of "terrorism" it is absolutely essential, in the aftermath of the Iraq conflict, to build new structures of political-economic and military cooperation in the "gaps" or "weak links" between the coalition partners, and to engage in political-economic measures designed to prevent a resurgence of new "threats."

Although not a panacea, drawing Russia into a *new* form of NATO membership can help to mitigate the potentially destabilizing effects of NATO and EU enlargement and possible Russian counter-reaction. In addition to more intensive NATO-Russian cooperation through the NATO-Russian Council, a concrete way to bring Russia, Ukraine and the Vilnius Group as a whole into a deeper relationship with NATO and the EU will be to form a NATO-EU-Russian *Transatlantic Political-Economic and Strategic Council*.

Russian "membership" in the *Transatlantic Political-Economic and Strategic Council* would accordingly involve NATO-EU-Russian nuclear-strategic cooperation and NATO-EU-Russian military-technological participation in developing Ballistic Missile Defense systems for the entire Euro-Atlantic and Euro-Mediterranean community. It would also involve the formulation and implementation of *overlapping* NATO-EU-Russian security guarantees to states throughout eastern Europe. (These accords would need to be stronger than the overlapping security guarantees granted Ukraine by the UN Security Council members, the US, UK, France, Russia and China, granted at the time when Kiev gave up its nuclear weapons in 1994).

While NATO would nominally retain "Article V" security guarantees, the concept of "full" membership could be radically altered, particularly as *Article V is no longer regarded as the ultimate and automatically binding accord that it was during the Cold War, and as it would most likely be implemented under more ambiguous circumstances*.[21]

Three basic types of NATO states (and their "associate" EU and Russian partners) would be recognized within the *Transatlantic Political-Economic and Strategic Council*:

1) Those states (the US, UK, France and Russia) with nuclear capabilities willing to engage in strategic nuclear cooperation and provide security guarantees for other members or partners in coordination or association with the other nuclear states;

2) Those states willing to engage in "coalitions of the willing," preferably under general UN mandates as required by the North Atlantic Treaty (NAT) itself, and who would back up new NATO "members" or "partners" with conventional force security guarantees;
3) Those states willing to engage in regionally integrated *conflict prevention* deployments and peacekeeping missions under separate or joint commands, preferably under UN or OSCE mandates.

These concepts imply a fundamental re-structuration of NATO that could permit greater flexibility in regard to both EU members and Russia. As decisions could be made at each of the three levels it would appear that the decision-making process could be weighted in accord with the extent of the participation and financial contribution of each participant at each of the three levels. (Some states, of course, would be willing to play two or all three roles.) One way to *prevent* the rise of terrorism in the long term is thus for NATO, the EU, and Russia to work toward the development of "regional cooperative-security communities" as a means to fill the gaps of uncontrolled space between potentially conflicting powers.

Problems to Consider

In addition to the question as to whether or not to obtain a UN mandate (and whether the UNSC itself should be restructured), one problem with "coalitions of the willing" is what to do about those states who are *not* willing to act. NATO has dealt with this issue by calling for "constructive abstention" a situation in which states that do not support NATO activities provide over-flight rights, but do not fight directly, for example.

The second issue is that of states which adamantly oppose NATO intervention or proactive NATO policies—and thus do not agree to act in "consensus." Here, just before the March 2003 Iraq War, France and Germany sought to block the deployment of Patriot missiles and AWAC's to Turkey not only because Iraq might regard such deployments as offensive and thus refuse to disarm in accord with Franco-German efforts, but also because Turkey could use such deployments to cover its own essentially offensive and unilateral intervention into Iraqi Kurdistan. France and Germany, plus Russia, belatedly hoped that UN weapons inspections in Iraq could have been given greater credence if supported by multinational peacekeepers under a UN mandate. It is highly ironic that two of NATO's most loyal allies during the Cold War, Germany and Turkey, have become increasingly estranged from NATO (and the US) since the end of the Cold

War—while France was always the "reluctant ally." (See Hall Gardner, Chapter 16.)

The only real way to get around such problems (which will not entirely disappear) is to devolve power relationships within NATO, and permit the EU and Russia greater power-sharing, while at the same time thinking in terms of a greater peace keeping role for the new NATO-EU-Russian relationship. Rather than thinking in traditional terms of the expansion of large blocs of military power, NATO should think more in terms of *customizing* approaches of cooperative security to specific regions and situations and threats. Thus, instead of attempting to expand a system of security in which one size fits all, as NATO has tended to do thus far, NATO should consider creating a number of interlocking "regional cooperative-security communities" under separate commands that would be integrated with the armed forces of each of the states of a particular region and which, in turn, would receive development and state building and reconstruction assistance from the US, EU and Russia—under general UN or the OSCE mandates.

More intensive Russian political-military involvement in multinational peacekeeping and *conflict prevention* deployments through Combined Joint Task Force (CJTF) can ultimately help draw Russia closer to NATO (and the EU) at the same time that such forces guard against potential regional political instability and threats in central and eastern Europe and central Asia—and possibly the Transcaucasus, if the Russians ultimately accept. Potential socio-political tensions in non-NATO non EU states of Belarus, Moldova, and Ukraine, for example, could lead to problems of immigration or domestic violence that might require external diplomatic and "peace keeping" or "peacemaking" intervention.

Potential and actual tensions in these areas (as well as those now stirring in the Transcaucasus, Central Asia, the Middle East, Persian Gulf and Far East) will require greater policy coordination between NATO, the EU, and Russia so as to prevent major states from being drawn into potential conflict in support of opposing sides, and to assure the formation of concerted strategies and avoid overextension. Likewise, as a means to clamp down on terrorism, "out of area" conflicts may also require NATO-EU-Russian military intervention or else peacekeeping, under general UN mandates, if initial disputes cannot first be quelled by concerted and preventive diplomacy, assuming states can overcome the trauma caused by US preclusive intervention in Iraq.

The very process of forming a coalition against vaguely defined acts of "terrorism" will require a truly concerted NATO-EU-Russian coalition designed to:

1) Create as broad a coalition as possible to identify, isolate, and to either contain or else eradicate, the major mutually agreed upon "terrorist" or "partisan" threats.

2) Dampen conflict by utilizing new strategies of crisis management and dissuasion, utilizing a broad range of diplomatic, political, economic, and military tools intended to implement social and political reforms and resolve conflict—and seek political compromise where possible by serving as a trustworthy "honest broker."

3) Attempt to prevent conflict *before* it breaks out through concerted and sophisticated preventive diplomacy and by developing regionally integrated "cooperative-security communities" which will seek to prevent new and possibly unexpected threats from emerging, and indirectly help to coordinate development assistance.

Putting multinational peacekeepers under a NATO-EU-Russian command structure could provide the political-military means to help to stabilize states throughout the Euro-Atlantic and Euro-Mediterranean regions as these states continue to engage in potentially destabilizing socio-economic reforms intended to modernize their outmoded economies. Rather than deploying such forces *after* conflict breaks out, as has been the case in Bosnia, Kosovo, and now Macedonia, *conflict prevention* forces, which would form integrated systems of defence, could be deployed throughout the Euro-Atlantic and Euro-Mediterranean community with NATO, Russian and EU oversight—but *before* the potential for conflict breaks out.

EU peacekeepers would play a key role. Some EU states would deploy *conflict prevention* forces; others would participate in "coalitions of the willing" that would be ready to intervene in the case that conflicts do develop, once again under general UN or OSCE mandates. EU members Sweden and Austria in particular would be key to the building of cooperative-security communities in their respective regions. The deployment of PfP *conflict prevention* forces could be initiated in the Baltic States, as a means to concretize overlapping NATO-EU-Russian security guarantees. Making Kaliningrad a *Transatlantic Political-Economic and Strategic Council* headquarters could likewise help stabilize the Baltic region and would likewise help draw Russia closer to NATO.

In 1999-2000, Russia had offered to provide "security guarantees" to the Baltic states in a regional treaty or charter as an "alternative" to NATO membership, an offer similar to the 1998 US-Baltic charter. Latvia and Lithuania stated that Russia must accept the NATO membership of the

Baltic states before they accept Russian security guarantees. But here, it seems the United States and Russia, along with the EU, could offer *overlapping* guarantees—as part of a *new* form of NATO membership that brings the Baltic states and Russia "into" NATO simultaneously by May 2004. The Baltic states could also sign a *revised* 1990 CFE treaty at roughly the same time that they formally join NATO (assuming the CFE treaty can be updated by May 2004). Concurrently, if Russia should ultimately drop out of any accords, NATO and EU *conflict prevention* forces would already be there—with a physical military presence on the ground—to defend Baltic state sovereignty or that of other states backed by such overlapping accords.

If NATO-EU-Russian confidence can subsequently strengthen, then these regional systems of cooperative security can be expanded. These systems of regional cooperative security can ultimately be built out of NATO peacekeeping units in the Balkans—once and if the ex-Yugoslavia states can ultimately put aside their differences. Regional systems of security can likewise be built in central Asia and possibly the Transcaucasus—in the effort to prevent the spread of pan-Islamic movements in that region. A truly multilateral US strategy as formulated by a *Transatlantic Council* can furthermore implement a number of regional "contact groups" that permit each of the regional actors, in cooperation with the US and other major powers, to find appropriate policies of conflict resolution, peacekeeping and development for a number of significant regional conflicts and crises. Peacekeeping, by itself, will not necessarily keep the peace unless there are viable political accords, which may involve the changing of boundaries, economic aid and assistance and various forms of power sharing and confederal or autonomous arrangements.

Conclusions

NATO-EU-Russian cooperation in the "war on terrorism" will not necessarily eliminate all of the problems of the Euro-Atlantic Euro-Mediterranean communities; it may certainly deflect or postpone many of those problems, but it will not resolve them. It could also create a number of "new" disputes and conflicts. A clear and easily identifiable "enemy" or "threat" (such as Al Qaeda) can help forge a new coalition of states, but if that "common" enemy or threat ultimately disappears; or if the various partners in a coalition can no longer agree as to the nature of the "threat," or if they fundamentally disagree on strategy and tactics as to how to deal with that "threat" (as has been the case in regard to Iraq), then such a coalition, initially based on mutual immediate and concrete geopolitical interests, could begin to break down.

One major risk is to fall into the trap set by Al-Qaeda and other terrorist organizations such that the military actions by the United States and its allies indirectly or directly result in the spread of conflict to other states, either widening the potential for war (due in part to the failure to rebuild the societies of the states attacked) or else indirectly resulting in the destabilization of various regimes. An alternative yet realistic and concerted strategy will need to pick and choose precisely which state leaderships are to be appeased, which are to be contained, and which are to be assisted and/or reformed, and which to be undermined or overthrown and then rebuilt—at the same time that a broad coalition of states seeks to identify, locate and eradicate key "terrorist" cells.

As an integral part of the war on terrorism, NATO, the EU and Russia must begin to resolve their post-Iraq war differences within the entire Euro-Atlantic and Euro-Mediterranean communities in such a way as to guarantee the legitimate security concerns on all sides. There is a significant risk, however, that disputes over the war against Iraq and its aftermath may work to undermine collective efforts to establish new political, military and economic institutional frameworks that can sustain the new found NATO-EU-Russian coalition in the long term and ultimately transform it into a viable federation.

If the US, the EU and Russia are to ultimately "succeed" in this war against a rather amorphous "terrorist" threat (involving politically complex understandings and accusations of "double standards") that provides no clear and decisive "victory," they can only do so if NATO resurrects its broader and original mission that it possessed immediately after World War II. In this regard, NATO was created as a *conflict prevention* organization designed to prevent major power conflict in Europe (broadly speaking) by bringing together former enemies, and potentially conflicting states, into one broad alliance. (See Ira Straus, Chapter 7.)

By developing a large coalition of states, the US, the EU and Russia can then begin to lay the foundations for a wider peace in the Euro-Atlantic Euro-Mediterranean community and the world at large. The concept of "regional cooperative security communities" backed by overlapping NATO, EU and Russian security guarantees is as simple as placing air marshals on airplanes. It is a commonsense *on the ground* deterrent against all possible forms of threats. It is designed to create cooperative forms of regional security with the backing of the states and populations involved. Its political-military purpose is to negotiate between actual and potentially conflicting factions so that all sides can live side by side without fear. Although peacekeeping in general has thus far been downplayed by the Bush administration, this concept requires a strengthening of the US commitment to the Partnership for Peace, the Euro-Atlantic Partnership Council and the NATO-Russian Council—and not a retraction of that support. Yet, perhaps these structures can all be superseded through the formation of a *Transatlantic Political-Economic and Strategic Council*, combined with regional "Contact Groups" such as that designed to deal with the Bosnian crisis.

For the "war on terrorism" to ultimately be "successful," the US needs to move much faster on the political-military front, in the rebuilding of a broad and *sustainable* coalition of the major powers, in addition to winning the support of states in the region. The danger, however, is that temptations by any of the major parties (particularly the United States) to engage in unilateral actions could furthermore undermine the endeavor to create a truly multilateral barrier against the spread of "terrorist" activities through any form of regional "cooperative-collective security" communities or loose confederations.

An additional risk in the not-so-distant future is the emergence of significant disputes over trade relations (subsidized steel, aerospace, and agriculture), ecological issues (genetically modified organisms and global warming), socio-cultural differences and human rights (capital punishment and the International Criminal Court), among other significant disputes, not to overlook post-Iraq war haggling over oil concessions and reconstruction contracts. These issues may make the issues surrounding military spending and defense responsibility sharing even more difficult to heal; they represent only a few of the many issues that threaten to split the Alliance, if not an expanding EU as well.

Notes

1   See Hall Gardner, "The Genesis of NATO Enlargement and of War 'over' Kosovo" in *Central and Southeastern Europe in Transition*, ed. Hall Gardner (Westport, CT: Praeger, 2000).
2   See points made in the Conclusion, Hall Gardner and Radoslava Stefanova, eds., *The New Transatlantic Agenda* (Aldershot: Ashgate, 2001), 197. Such a Council could be made up of advisers to the US, UK, French, German and Russian governments (or to a new EU foreign minister).
3   Hall Gardner, *Dangerous Crossroads* (Westport: Praeger, 1997).
4   R. Nicholas Burns, US Permanent Representative to NATO, Speech, "New World, New Europe New Threats: NATO and the EU in the New Millennium," Paris: The American University of Paris, 8 December 2001.
5   See Ira Straus, this book.
6   US Ambassador Alexander Vershbow, "Russia, The United States and the Challenges of the 21st Century" *Johnson's Russia List* #6369 25 July 2002. www.cdi.org. Tasks of

the NRC are to include: Assessment of the terrorist threat; Crisis management; Non-proliferation; Arms Control and Confidence-Building Measures; Theater Missile Defense; Search and Rescue at Sea; Military-to-Military Cooperation; Defense Reform; Civil Emergencies; New Threats and Challenges (including scientific cooperation and airspace management).

7 The Polish national security council, for example, has "endorsed cooperation between Russia and NATO, on the condition NATO retains its identity and structure ... Three areas have been identified for cooperation: the fight against terrorism, against proliferation of weapons of mass destruction and ensuring civil defense. Poland additionally proposed "to add military cooperation, notably with the Kaliningrad region" as an additional issue to be discussed in the new NATO-Russian Council. While Russia's participation in the anti-terrorism coalition is a "new development," military cooperation between NATO and Russia "remains very limited." National Security Advisor, Marek Siwiec (Warsaw: Agence France Press, 11 January 2002).

8 In November, Giscard D'Estaing, head of the European Union Convention, an institution responsible for shaping the EU's future and its constitution, was quoted in Le Monde as saying that "Turkey's capital is not in Europe, 95 percent of its population lives outside Europe, it is not a European country," and that letting non-European countries join the 15-member club would be "the end of the European Union" as it would lead to a Moroccan demand for membership of the union. He added that "Those who have pushed enlargement most strongly in the direction of Turkey are the enemies of the European Union" with probable reference to the UK and USA. The official Turkish response: "Our attitude should emulate the French saying: Les chiens aboient, la caravane passé [The dogs bark, but the caravan moves on]. *Office of the Prime Minister, Directorate General of Press and Information.* Here it seems a possible solution might be to seek an integrated free trade association of states in North Africa and Turkey that is more closely linked to the EU.

9 Sarah Sewall and Carl Kaysen, "The United States and International Criminal Court: The Choices Ahead," *American Academy of Arts and Sciences.* www.amacad.org. An excellent critique of US rationale for not joining the ICC: US cannot reject the ICC and then expect to set up a separate war crimes tribunal for Iraq, for example.

10 See George Nolte "The United States and the International Criminal Court" in *Unilateralism and US Foreign Policy*, ed by David M. Malone and Yuen Foong Khong (Lynne Reiner 2003), 81. The US refused to accept the compromise proposition that the jurisdiction of the ICC require either the consent of either the national state of the accused or the territorial state of the crime. The US motion to accept the former, but not the latter, was rejected by the 1998 Rome Conference. Ibid 76-77.

11 Greg Jaffe, "In Massive Shift, US Is Planning to Cut Size of Military in Germany" *Wall Street Journal*, 10 June 2003. In addition, Semi-permanent bases are to be maintained in Algeria, Morocco, Tunisia, plus Senegal, Mali, Ghana (all former French colonies in addition to Djibouti) as well as Kenya. One of the primary goals is to protect Nigeria, expected to provide some 25% of US oil needs in the future.

12 Russian Foreign Minister, Igor Ivanov, cited in "Foreign Minister says Russia more accepted, respectable to Western Eyes" *BBC Monitoring Former Soviet Union* (July 10, 2002).

13 Steven E. Miller, "Gambling on War" in *War with Iraq: Costs, Consequences and Alternatives.* American Academy of Arts and Sciences http://www.amacad.org/publications/monographs/War_with_Iraq.pdf

14 Russia could radically reconsider its position towards the Treaty on Conventional Armed Forces in Europe (CFE) if Latvia, Lithuania, and Estonia enter NATO without first joining the CFE. New states will be able to join the CFE only after an agreement

on adapting the Treaty is ratified, for the acting CFE is a closed treaty, which makes it impossible for new states to enter it. See "Russia Might Reconsider its Position Towards CFE if Baltic States Join NATO" Moscow: *Interfax*, 11 Jan 02.

15 "Moscow Won't Take Military Steps in Response to Balt's Entry—Defense Minister *Baltic News Service*, 29 July 2002.

16 "Lithuania Won't Sign CFE Pact Before NATO Entry In Spite of Russia's Pressure" Baltic News Service 29 July 2002. See also, Arbatova, this book.

17 Michael Binyon, "Moscow Demands a New Arms treaty with US" *The Times* (UK) 14 January 2002.

18 "Russia's Shifting Allegiance Toward the European Union" www.stratfor.com (7 March 2003). This could be the third time the US has violated Russian trust by first moving NATO forces into eastern Germany and then bringing eastern European states in NATO as well, after promising verbally in both cases, not to do so. The "contract of the century," the $3.5 billion sale of 48 US F-16 fighters to Poland (for 2006-08), in direct rivalry with Swedish Gripin and French Mirage 2000-5 fighter jets, and which includes over $6 billion in a foreign military financing (FMF) loan package, 43 offsetting projects and direct US foreign investment, has upset French and Swedish arms producers, Germany (the major investor in Poland), as well as EU Commission President Romano Prodi, not to overlook Russia. *REF/RL* "Poland, Belarus, Ukraine" (Vol. 5, No. 15, 22 April 2003).

19 EU-standard trade regulations could substantially reduce or eliminate Russian economic privileges as the exclusive supplier of energy resources to eastern Europe, for example. Russia is concerned with the imposition of EU-standard import duties upon Russian goods, new restrictions on the transit of Russian cargo, and new visa requirements for Russian citizens. Russia will need to more carefully balance its relations between the US and EU. Russian efforts to enter the WTO, if successful, could, on the other hand, bolster Russian trade with the EU and US. See *RFE/RL Security and Foreign Policy in Russia and the Post-communist Region* (Vol. 4, No. 45, 12 November 2003).

20 Belarusian President Lukashenka also told legislators on 16 April that "it is necessary and possible to constructively resolve problems with America," but he added that "the US Congress is now trying to pass the notorious Belarus Democracy Act, which provides for appropriating nearly $50 million for compulsory democratization" of Belarus, Belapan reported. "The real target of attacks against our country is primarily Belarusian-Russian integration," he added. In this context, the Belarusian president said the "Russian and foreign press" has gotten used to asking the question, "Who will be the next one in the axis of evil?" See *RFE/RL Newsline* (Vol. 7, No. 74, Part I, 17 April 2003) and "RFE/RL Newsline," (24 February 2003).

21 Here, it is possible that NATO may well be in the process of relaxing its Article 5 guarantees while the EU may be in the process of tightening those alliances as based on the 1948 Brussels Pact, causing new concerns.

Chapter 9

Dealing with Terrorism: The EU and NATO

Karsten D. Voigt

I

In his speech in the Reichstag in May 2002, President Bush made it clear again what a dividing line September 11, 2001 had cut in the history of the United States. In order to be able to correctly appreciate the President's remarks, one has to remind oneself of the murderous attacks of that day: the attacks on New York and Washington claimed more victims than Pearl Harbor in 1941. Their shock waves also ran deeper: the American nation could watch on TV as the very heart of America was being attacked and symbols of America's power were being destroyed or damaged. The concern expressed by American politicians that the country could become the target of an asymmetric attack, a concern Europe had previously smiled at, proved well founded. Neither America's military supremacy nor its deterrent capability was able to prevent these attacks. The myth of American invulnerability to assault from outside was dispelled.

For the first year after 9/11 then, the top priority of American foreign policy has been to "wage war" against international terrorism. In this aim the US Administration is sure of the solidarity and support both of the political class and of the country as a whole. If, even before the attacks of 9/11, Americans already regarded themselves as representing good in the fight against evil, this feeling has become even stronger since. Americans are more determined than ever to stand up for "the American ideal," for the vision of America as the invincible stronghold of freedom and democracy, and to defend this "ideal" against international terrorism or threats by weapons of mass destruction. One consequence is America's desire to establish a deterrent capacity against asymmetric attacks as well. This is the background to the homeland security and missile defence projects as well as the preemptive strike doctrine.

For the US Administration, the obligation to fight international terrorism is on a par with earlier successful American missions in the face of other totalitarian challenges, for instance National Socialism or Marxism-Leninism. While the "house of freedom" is being built, President Bush said in his address in the German Reichstag, sources of danger must be removed if necessary using offensive—including *ultima ratio* military-means.

The mood swing in America becomes even clearer when compared with reactions in Europe to the events of 9/11. In Europe, the spontaneous solidarity of the people in the streets and the resolve of politicians to join the US in the fight against terrorism on the one hand testified to transatlantic solidarity. Chancellor Schröder immediately pledged unstinting solidarity with the US in the global fight against terrorism. Since then that support has acquired real political and military substance, backed up also by the police and intelligence services. When Chancellor Schröder decided in November 2001 to commit troops to Operation Enduring Freedom and the military campaign in Afghanistan, he even placed his political future on the line—and won the day. In November 2002 the Bundestag renewed Germany's commitment to Enduring Freedom. Ultimately the attacks were directed not only at the US, the most potent symbol of the democratic community of values, but also at Europeans, as part of that community.

On the other hand, Europe was not attacked directly. Europe itself can look back on its own experiences of terrorism, and the memories of the terrible destruction wrought by two World Wars are still vivid. Europe has had to get used to living with its vulnerability. It has been trying to counter the risk of future destruction primarily through political and economic means—for example with the project of European integration—and a multilateral approach—for example with NATO and the UN. Because of these different experiences and perceptions, it was difficult for Europe to comprehend how profoundly 9/11 had wounded the US and how America would react.

II

These differences provide an explanation for transatlantic disgruntlement surfacing in 2002. They are also first clues to the transatlantic discord which erupted in the Iraq-case.

Iraq was a major issue in the Bundestag elections in Germany and the mid-term elections in the United States in the fall of 2002. It was discussed in very different, even opposing terms on either side of the

Atlantic. President Bush sought to persuade an undecided nation that war might be necessary, while Federal Chancellor Schröder won support by insisting that German soldiers would on no account participate in any such war. As a result, a good many harsh words and accusations were traded across the Atlantic. Rather than grappling with arguments, the media for their part trotted out familiar stereotypes: American cowboys or Rambo figures on the one side, naive and wimpish Europeans or EU-nuchs on the other. I need not emphasize how much I personally regretted these verbal combats. Displays of anti-American prejudice in Europe or anti-European prejudice in America are just as unhelpful as the stereotypes themselves are false. What's more, they completely misrepresent the reality of German-American and European-American friendship. This special relationship was, is and will continue to be founded on shared values, interests and ultimately visions of what kind of world Americans and Europeans want to see.

Bearing in mind this bedrock, the obvious question is how did the debate on Iraq evolve into the current discord.

First of all, it should not be forgotten that on the fundamental issues in the case of Iraq Germany and the US are in full agreement. They agree that Saddam Hussein is a brutal and aggressive dictator who has flouted UN Security Council resolutions with presumably the worst of intentions. They agree that the weapons inspectors must be able to do their job without hindrance and that Iraq must not be allowed to possess either weapons of mass destruction or the relevant delivery systems. However, Germany and the US do not always agree about the best means to achieve these common goals. Germany welcomed the US decision to go to the UN in search of a multilateral solution. As a result of this step, the UN Security Council adopted Resolution 1441, which has paved the way for a political solution. Last November in Prague NATO heads of state and government pledged their full support for the implementation of Resolution 1441. What is needed now and over the weeks ahead is to proceed strictly in accordance with the steps set out in the Resolution. Germany is helping to do as much as lies in its power, by providing German experts for the UN team of inspectors, for example, and chairing the Security Council committee dealing with Iraq sanctions.

Secondly, although this whole controversy between the Europeans and the Americans is essentially about the best way to deal with Iraq, one reason for the current dissension is also the fact that Europe and the United States lack a common strategy towards the Greater Middle East. Despite what some people think, the American position on Iraq is not determined purely or indeed primarily by oil. Obviously no one can pursue any policy for the Gulf region without taking into account the possible consequences of such a policy for international oil supplies. However, the Administration's overriding aim is driven by foreign and security policy considerations: beyond disarming Iraq it wants a fundamental political shift in a number of major countries and actors in the region, with a corresponding increase in its long-term stability. The Administration believes greater stability in the region would also have a positive effect on the Middle East conflict.

Many people in Europe, however, fear US policies might lead not to greater stability but to greater instability. Germany is not alone in believing that non-military means are more effective in bringing about change for the better in this part of the world. The primary key to greater stability in the Near and Middle East is in Germany's view the resumption of the Middle East peace process under the auspices of the so-called Quartet (US, Russia, UN, and EU).

Thirdly, the current divisions over Iraq are essentially a matter between the German and the US Governments. Ordinary people on both sides of the Atlantic—whether in the US or in Europe—ask the same questions and voice similar concerns. While Americans seem relatively supportive of military action against Iraq, even people in Britain are deeply skeptical, despite their government's ardent support for the US Administration on the issue. In Germany military action against Iraq would be supported only by a minority and then only if the UN expressly authorized such action and there was no other way to prevent Iraq getting its hands on nuclear weapons.

The Iraq issue highlights the fact that as a nation Germans feel generally torn about matters of war and peace. Given their traumatic memories of World War II, most people are highly reluctant to see German troops sent to war. For people living in the eastern part of the country—formerly the GDR—the situation is even more complex. As a result of their own post-war history, they are deeply suspicious of any German role in defending global security or other interests. They are particularly averse to such a role leading to German military involvement on any significant scale.

A study by the Chicago Council on Foreign Relations and the German Marshall Fund makes clear, the prevailing mood in Germany is not one of anti-Americanism. The real issue is the way Germans feel about military power and how it should be used. On the one hand, people in Germany have fewer problems than the French or British with the Americans' superpower status and have just as many warm feelings towards them as the British. On the other hand, compared to the French and the British, Germans are less inclined to think the EU should become a superpower like the US, and they are less convinced their future is best served if Germany takes an active role in the world.

Fourthly, the study also shows that Germany has already come a long way since 1990. In the face of strong opposition, successive governments have gradually stepped up German participation in international military operations. Over the past decade Germany has seen its troops in action in Somalia, Bosnia, East Timor, Kosovo, the Caucasus, Macedonia and now Afghanistan. Currently, some 9,500 German troops—second only to the US—are serving with military missions abroad, either in the Balkans (KFOR 4,600, MAZ 220, SFOR 1,500) or with Operation Enduring Freedom. Some 100 German elite soldiers are fighting in Afghanistan, German NBC reconnaissance vehicles are stationed in Kuwait and the German Navy is patrolling off the Horn of Africa. Some 2,400 German troops are already serving with ISAF in Kabul, with an additional contingent due to arrive once Germany assumes lead-nation responsibility for the Force together with the Netherlands.

Ten years ago, such military engagement would not only have been impossible but also inconceivable. Thanks to sound political leadership, Germans are gradually getting used to a more robust policy that does not exclude the use of force as a last resort. It was not for nothing that Defense Minister Struck noted in December 2002 that Germany's defense in the 21st century begins at the Hindu Kush. Such general observations aside, I have to point out that until now the Federal Government has not been persuaded that there is at present any justification for German participation in a military campaign against Iraq. Looking to the future, however, and being a convinced optimist, I predict that over the next decade German public opinion will progressively shift in favor of a more robust security policy, bringing attitudes more into line with those of the French and the British, for instance.

III

Iraq is not the only issue generating transatlantic tension. Other well-known sources of friction are the Kyoto Protocol, the International Criminal Court and genetically modified products. Here, too, Europe and the US generally agree in principle on the objectives but differ about the means to achieve them. In the final analysis there is a cultural difference between the US and most European states on all these issues. As already pointed out Europe, in a realistic assessment of its own potential, has generally relied on multilateralism as a foreign-policy instrument with which to promote its interests. In contrast, the United States, given its military, political and cultural self-perceptions, can afford to practise selective multilateralism, meaning that multilateralism is but one foreign-policy tool among many. Unilateral action will in future remain one of the possible military options for the US, though not for Germany.

However, the United States has recognized that it does have partners in the fight against international terrorism as well as in the Iraq-debate and that these partners are useful. To that extent, its behaviour has in practice become more multilateral. Time and again surveys demonstrate that the American citizens have a considerably more multilateral view than is generally believed. The number of Americans in favour of military intervention abroad increases disproportionately if this policy is supported by America's partners. Iraq is a good case in point. At the same time the attacks on New York and Washington strengthened the United States' belief in the legitimacy of its values and interests; conscious of this legitimacy it will in an emergency also try to enforce its goals on its own if no partners are available.

Another cultural difference emerges in this context. As a result of European integration, the European states are prepared to cede more and more sovereign rights to the EU. Given the myth surrounding the foundation of the United States, Americans find it very difficult to understand this, never mind to consider the possibility of their own country doing the same. This goes some way to explaining America's hesitancy about transferring national sovereign rights to international organizations.

We will continue to see a gulf in American politics between those who favor a more multilateral approach and those who prefer to focus on the option of unilateral action. We will have to face up to this reality. The goal of Europeans can only be to encourage the United States to pursue the course of cooperative engagement.

However, the controversy over multilateralism and unilateralism is not just about ideologies and convictions. European criticisms of America and America's problems with Europe have always derived in no small measure from Europe's weakness. Anyone who seems weak is not regarded as relevant in the US. The stronger and better Europe is the more ground America's supporters of multilateralism will gain. Two examples to support this theory: back in the 19th century, when the US was still a young and, in comparison with Europe's world powers, weak state, the Americans were firm multilateralists who wanted to put an end to Europe's power politics. And as economic areas, the EU and the US are on a par; in this field the Americans appreciate the EU as an equal partner.

But it is not just a matter of being accepted by the US as a relevant player. The events of 9/11 made it more than clear to the European partners that after the end of the Cold War there are dangers outside Europe that directly or indirectly compromise their security. These dangers are not restricted to international terrorism, but emanate also from the worldwide proliferation of weapons of mass destruction and their delivery systems, from drugs, international crime, money laundering (which accounts for an estimated 2 to 5% of global income), from epidemics and attacks on computer systems and thus potentially on our supply systems. In many cases external risks pose a greater challenge to internal than to external security. Since the Second World War risks increasingly blur the dividing line between external and internal security. The asymmetric threat to some extent directly affects everyday life—the anthrax attacks in the US being a case in point.

The consequence of all this for Europeans is the need to improve their capacity for action, in other words they must have adequate diplomatic, police, intelligence and military capabilities. The European Security and Defence Policy has been created to give Europe capacities for action. In December last year the French and German Foreign Ministers, Dominique de Villepin and Joschka Fischer, went a step further, presenting to the EU Convention a number of proposals designed to turn the ESDP into a European Security and Defense Union (ESDU). On the occasion of the 40th anniversary of the Elysée Treaty, Franco-German initiatives demonstrated impressively the crucial role of this cooperation in fostering European integration. These proposals point the way forward to a EU capable of effective policy-making and coherent action in the wider world. In the field of security and foreign policy they touch on a number of sensitive issues such as the establishment of a European armaments agency and political commitments to strengthen Europe's military capabilities. The time has now come to act.

For of one thing there can be no doubt: Europe cannot satisfy the expectations of its citizens unless it succeeds in making decisive progress on the CFSP and ESDU and indeed across the whole spectrum of European foreign and security policy.

However, Germans do not see a more effective Europe as creating some kind of a counterweight to the United States. Germans believe a more effective Europe will in fact be a better partner for the US. Equipped with enhanced capabilities, Europe would become more relevant in the eyes of Washington.

The question of relevance is not merely about "hardware" but also "software." In a market of ideas Europeans and Americans are in tough competition in which it is not enough merely to criticize America's strength. Therefore Europeans need viable concepts for the tensions in the Middle East, for the global financial architecture and issues such as the scarcity of water. This list again shows that the framework for the transatlantic dialogue has become much broader. For instance, the "dialogue with Islam" presents a new challenge for the transatlantic community. In this framework as well the transatlantic partners must together take an intellectual and cultural look at the causes of terrorism and develop and implement joint positions. Europeans must introduce draft solutions into the transatlantic dialogue and ensure that they are given a hearing in America. They have in the past proved that they can hold their own in the competition of ideas—for example the Stability Pact for South-Eastern Europe, the establishment of the NATO-Russia Council, or the creation of the International Criminal Court (though the latter is rejected by the U.S in its current form). The more convincingly Europeans act here, the more we will become an equal partner for the United States.

IV

The key test for the transatlantic relationship is whether, with all the many things we have in common, we can also deal with our differences. The events of 9/11 and subsequent developments have permanently changed our view of the world and at the same time brought an end to the transatlantic routine. These views, our ways of thinking and the routine had until then still been firmly stuck in the Cold War era, even though the wall came down over ten years ago. US President Bush and Russia's President Putin both explicitly announced the definitive end of the Cold War in speeches in 2002 in the Reichstag here in Berlin, the place symbolic of that age. In future Europeans must pay more attention to questions relating to stability on the edge of and outside Europe rather than to stability at the heart of Europe.

The United States and a strong Europe can only meet the global challenges if they act together. President Bush expressed his commitment to close transatlantic cooperation to this end in his speech in the Reichstag. The new flexible coalitions pulled together by the US in the fight against international terrorism do not mean a rejection of Europe: transatlantic relations will remain the backbone of American foreign policy.

Security issues will continue to play an important role in the Euro-Atlantic community. In future it will still be NATO that will focus on these issues. On 12 September 2001 NATO invoked Article 5 of the Washington Treaty in a situation utterly different from that intended by the founders of

NATO 50 years ago. The application of the mutual defence clause also demonstrated that it is a long time since NATO was targeted against Russia. On the contrary, the first invocation of Article 5 in the Alliance's history brought NATO and Russia closer together. At the joint summit in Rome end of May 2002, both sides set the seal on a new partnership. This helped ease the way to the admission of seven new members to NATO and the Prague Summit in November 2002. Europeans and Americans all know that Europe will become more secure if Russia cooperates closely with NATO and the EU. Constructive cooperation with a country as big and as important as Russia is indispensable for the solution of global problems, be it the threat of terrorism, problems with disarmament, control of weapons of mass destruction or global climate protection.

This development impressively demonstrates that the Alliance lives! Besides enlarging the alliance NATO at the Prague Summit also made it ready to tackle the security threats of the 21st century. It remains to be an alliance of nations of largely coinciding values and interests, an alliance not only of tactical but also of strategic partners. This is the forum for the most trusting multilateral dialogue; this is the forum for the multilateral integration of national defence and security policies. American politicians, above all President Bush, have repeatedly given a firm commitment to NATO and reaffirmed its vital importance.

The attacks of 9/11 made clear the importance and necessity of deepening and enlarging the EU. True, the military decisions in the crisis were taken in the national capitals, but at the same time decisions taken by the European Councils on 21 September and 19 October, 2001 on combating terrorism gave strong impetus towards the deepening of the EU, particularly in the field of the so-called third pillar, i.e. justice and home affairs, but also with regard to the Common Foreign and Security Policy. This will not fail to affect the discussions in the run-up to the EU Intergovernmental Conference in 2004. We must take advantage of the momentum towards reform. In Copenhagen last December the EU agreed to accept ten new members.

In the transatlantic domestic relationship, 9/11 widened the field of cooperation for the EU and the US to include inner security (homeland defence) and justice. Within this relationship we must also find ways to ease internal frictions, particularly in trade policy. For this we do not have at our disposal the traditional mechanisms with which the societies of the Euro-Atlantic community resolve internal conflicts, for example elections. The answer must therefore be firstly to constantly enhance the transatlantic dialogue at all levels of society. At the political level the Transatlantic Legislators' Dialogue between the US Congress and the European

Parliament is an important approach. There must be further work on the fora that emerged from the New Transatlantic Agenda (NTA). The Transatlantic Business Dialogue, like the Canada-European Roundtable, is already a great success; other NTA fora must be strengthened.

Even though the percentage of transatlantic trade disputes is low in relation to the total volume of trade—less than 5% with daily trade of 1.25 billion euro—these disputes invariably get great attention. This is due not least to the fact that their quality has changed over the years. Increasingly such disputes stem from matters that used to belong to the domestic sphere, for example: the merger of the two American companies General Electric and Honeywell, which was blocked by the EU. The coordination and dispute settlement mechanisms in this area must be improved. One idea is to coordinate the various cartel law procedures for company merger approval, including in terms of time. In this context administrative and technical obstacles to smooth trade and service transactions must be removed.

Contrary to what the prophets of doom have been predicting, the Atlantic has not grown wider in recent years. Quite the opposite: the differences we are seeing now are signs of constantly increasing closeness, of a quasi-domestic relationship across the Atlantic. This is due not least to the expanding economic ties across the Atlantic. Numerous global corporations today are basically Euro-Atlantic companies.

V

Despite the current disagreements, Europeans, Canadians and Americans alike have to keep the big picture in mind. As pointed out North America and Europe are linked by shared values, interests and ultimately visions of the world they want to see in this 21st century: a world founded on freedom, human rights and the rule of law. Not a single problem in the world can be solved if Europe and the United States are at odds. The transatlantic partnership is a key factor for stability and security throughout the world.

That is something everybody would do well to remember when from time to time they feel compelled to differ in assessment and strategy. Yet, transatlantic friendship and solidarity are built on extremely sound foundations that cannot be shaken by differing views on individual issues.

Chapter 10

German Perceptions on the "War Against Terrorism" in a Historical Perspective

Norbert Baas*

To combat terrorism effectively it will be crucial in the German view to preserve the broad international coalition established in the wake of 11 September. Fighting terrorism should not be equated with countering the proliferation of weapons of mass destruction unless clear evidence demonstrates the involvement of states in question. In this case, the United Nations will have to play a crucial role in the findings and in the decision-making. Germany's commitment to multilateralism will remain a central guiding line of its foreign policy.

When thousands of Germans lit candles for the victims of September 11, the pictures were particularly moving in Berlin. Spontaneous solidarity with the Americans merged with memories of their defending the West of the divided city for fifty years and unequivocal American support for German re-unification a decade ago. Chancellor Schröder, backed by his Green coalition partner and a consenting Christian-democratic and liberal opposition in the German Bundestag, declared unrestricted solidarity with the United States. The Europeans for the first time in post-war history were to assist their most powerful ally. Never before had it been conceivable to invoke Article 5 of the North Atlantic Treaty in defence of the United States. A reversal of traditional roles thus for a short time appeared to mark a paradigm change after President Bush said that Washington needed its allies. The United States seemed vulnerable as never before.

Given the long-standing friendship with the United States and the brutality of the attack, Germany's public showed strong support to the concerted efforts under American leadership to combat terrorism. However,

---

* The author is expressing his personal opinion.

this determination to assume responsibility in the coalition against terrorism is clearly seen as an alliance to preventing states from acquiring weapons of mass destruction. As long as terrorism, and the efforts by some states to procure weapons of mass destruction, do not interlink or merge into a combined threat, the responses should be tailored to the specificity of the threat they each represent. With regard to Iraq, evidence available so far does not indicate that Baghdad supported the attack of 11 September.

The German government commended and backed up the U.S. decision to forge a broad international coalition against terrorism. Such unity remains a fundamental prerequisite to eradicate terrorism effectively and in the long run. In the German and European Union's view, the fight against terrorism requires a comprehensive and multifaceted international approach comprising political, legal, economic, diplomatic, and if necessary, military means. Alongside the political dialogue focus should also be on the need for technical assistance to those countries not capable of implementing counter-terrorism measures effectively. Military means should only be used as a last resort and, like coercive measures, have to be in accordance with the UN Charter.

In the current debate about Iraq, Germany expressed a clear preference for involving the United Nations Security Council. The German government welcomed the decision by President Bush to seize the Council and adopt a Security Council Resolution allowing the inspection teams to begin their investigations. This does not only reflect an undisputed German position after the Second World War to support the United Nations Security Council as the organ possessing the primary responsibility for the maintenance of peace and security and holding a monopoly for the organization of peace. It also expresses a continuing conviction in the benefits of multilateralism and the need for comprehensive security with growing emphasis given to conflict prevention.

Germany's post-war policy of military abstention in conflict situations indeed underwent a marked change in 1999 through its military participation in the Kosovo operation. However, this was an urgent humanitarian intervention. A "culture of restraint" (*Kultur der Zurückhaltung*) in combat missions is not be discarded. At the same time, Germany's participation in peace operations has increased considerably and will continue to rise in 2003 after Berlin and The Hague decided to take over the lead of ISAF jointly for six months.

Political analysts have long associated West Germany's political identity with a deeply rooted caution about military operations as a result of German aggression in World War II. The horrifying death toll and destructions speak for themselves. Reluctance in the German population against the use of air power is also due to the suffering of the German population under the allied bombing of their cities, which is still vividly remembered by the older generation. Politically, it stood for defeat and punishment. Sympathy with innocent civilian victims plays a prominent role. In the Kosovo crisis, the government argued that avoiding the ongoing massive human rights violations and a humanitarian catastrophe was a German obligation just because of World War II and the Nazis' concentration camps. Foreign Minister Fischer, taking on his reluctant Green Party, explained that the pacifist credo "never again war" for him was to be complemented by "never again Auschwitz." So Germany made a significant step ahead to becoming a more "normal" European power recognizing its broader responsibilities in extreme cases for humanitarian intervention similar to France, the United Kingdom, Italy and others. Its participation in the NATO operation against Belgrade, though small in comparison to allies, was confronted with some harsh domestic criticism, in particular from intellectuals. Eventually, following a heated debate, a comfortable rate of public approval emerged. As a result, Germany returned to the international scene for the first time in a military operation. The ensuing peace efforts based on Foreign Minister Fischer's initiative resulting in Security Council Resolution 1144 were soon to heal some of the domestic wounds and re-state Germany's image as a "civilian power" giving priority to non-military means to resolve conflicts. However, Germany was no longer the same. Military responsibilities, if limited and clear in scope, are generally more accepted than prior to the Kosovo crisis and German participation in peace-operations increased considerably. Parliamentary approval, stipulated by the German Constitution, will remain a central precondition.

When the legitimacy of the Kosovo operation was discussed in Germany, some criticised the Auschwitz argument as morally inadequate and exaggerated. To others, it seemed to be an undue prolongation of Germany's image of a "nation of perpetrators."[1] The political preference for military abstention, including in peacekeeping missions, was so solidly enshrined in Germany's society – in the West as well as the East – and fears by its neighbours about German "dominance" at the time of re-unification not so distant that it is difficult to imagine German military participation without Fischer's strongly worded moral wake-up call to his green party majority. Fischer's appeal stirred up a much larger part of the German public because silent escapism was abundant. Almost a much cherished icon, Germany's post-war arguments for military abstention were loosing credibility. Hans-Peter Schwarz in 1994 pointedly accused the Germans of being "rich in thoughts and poor in action."[2] An enlarged military role seemed even further away after re-unification since common German assessments centred on the argument that Germany could take a more relaxed view of its future since from now on it was only surrounded by friends and allies. An inclination to isolationism, hesitation, *Ängstlichkeit* and the idea of becoming a somewhat "larger Switzerland," as Schwarz argued,[3] went hand in hand with a new optimism over the rise of the new economy, a growing enthusiasm for globalisation and Germany's apparently happy role as a "civilian power" gradually abandoning national interests and acting within a strengthened European Union. The Chancellor and Foreign Minister, confronted early in 1999 with the Balkan crisis, therefore could hardly resort to well-defined German "national interests." Moral legitimacy as a criterion in the debate on whether the Kosovo operation was rightful therefore became the much stronger reasoning to challenge the credo of military reservation. Somewhat paradoxically, consenting to the use of military force could only emanate from both the Green party itself and the Social-Democrats in order to become acceptable for Germany as a whole. With the support of the conservative and liberal opposition, Germany's first steps in 1999 to act militarily in accordance with the other allies was thus backed by an impressive majority in parliament.

The steadfastness of the Chancellor and the Foreign Minister in the aftermath of 11 September equally met with broad agreement of the other German parties. The government remained committed to its enhanced international role. However, some lingering moods of German *Friedens- und Angstmetaphorik*[4] and deficiencies in the *Bundeswehr* to conduct larger operations at the same time – an almost unthinkable possibility for almost fifty years – suggested a stronger parliamentary signal in favour of the government. Chancellor Schröder decided to put his policy of support for the U.S.-led coalition in the anti-terrorism campaign "Enduring Freedom" to a confidence vote in the Bundestag 16 November. Parliamentary agreement to lend military assistance in this case, he explained, would mark a turning-point in German post-war history. For the first time the Bundestag was asked to give its green light to an operation out of Europe. It won him the necessary support from his own coalition ranks and adding the consent in substance by the opposition, Germany's political class could claim a broadly-backed determination to stand side by side with the U.S and other allies. The readiness to shoulder military responsibility since then has grown significantly even though it went almost unnoticed. Today, an unprecedented 9,000 German troops, second in number after the U.S., are serving worldwide in peace operations. Germany also supported the concept of a NATO Response force to be launched at the Prague NATO summit in November 2002 as complementary to the European Security and Defence Policy, which in the German view could not be decoupled from NATO but should rather strengthen, through the EU, its European pillar. Equally, the new capabilities commitment adopted in Prague will be elaborated and implemented with active German participation. Thus, Germany's interest and participation in NATO with its integrated defence structure remains undisputed. This is not just lip-service. Berlin would loose substantially by distancing its own defence interests and European security from NATO.

The major German cross-party consensus on NATO's enlargement and its need to adapt to the new security environment confirmed readiness to an enhanced global German role in the framework of allied defence. However, the distinction between operations in accordance with the Washington Treaty and the Charter of the United Nations as a matter of legitimate self-defence and military operations as a more active counter-proliferation strategy remains crucial. The debate is being conducted with great seriousness. German commitment to multilateralism with binding international law as a solid yardstick continues to be strong and unequivocal. And it is this multilateral set of rules, which in the German view should be developed further and can secure a more comprehensive and effective non-proliferation policy.

Turning now to Germany's recent own experiences with terrorism, an extremely complex historical record emerges.

Generally, the notion of terrorism is associated with violent actions by forces operating in the underground and targeting the "symbols" of the ruling political order. It is not "from above" but "from below." Often, terrorists invoke an alleged state terror to legitimise their actions.[5] In an almost "classic" justification of terrorism, the Russian group *Narodnaya volya*, responsible for the murder of Tsar Alexander II in 1881, claimed that the goal of their activities was to destroy the prestige of the government and to prove that it would be possible to fight them so that the revolutionary spirit of the people could be strengthened.[6]

Terrorism in the nineteenth century, as Daniel Bell maintains,[7] was different for its Utopian revolutionary zeal from the terrorism of 11 September. For the latter did not aim at changing the American system "from within." But the terrifying scope was to mark dangerously false frontlines between civilisations. The enormous spectre of asymmetrical warfare in combination with suicide attacks[8] and the increased possibilities of access by terrorists to high-tech devices will pose an even greater threat if underpinned by greater acceptance in the Islamic world. On the other hand, terrorists have always used the availabilities in the market. The first

Minister President of the German Weimar Republic, the Social Democrat Philipp Scheidemann, was almost killed in 1922 by an attack through a chemical device. The widespread use of gas during the First World War, first used by the German Army, had set an example. Scheidemann only survived because the unexpected wind direction dispelled the lethal substance.

One of the most disturbing effects of terrorism on German history was the murder of Archduke Franz Ferdinand in Sarajevo 28 June 1914, which lead to the outbreak of the First World War. The July crisis had quickly gone beyond a mere revenge policy for Franz Ferdinand.[9] His murder acted more as a catalyst for imperial expansionism, not for the fight against the core and motives of radical political dissent. Both the Habsburg Empire and Imperial Germany were guided by the antagonizing systems of alliances in Europe. Instead of uniting all states affected by terrorism the government in Vienna preferred unilateral advantages with the German government ready to act as the most important and encouraging ally. European Monarchs and Republican Heads of State were deliberately not invited to attend the funeral of the Archduke.[10] Rather, the gate was pushed open for the competing cabinet and military machineries to prepare for war. Given the comparatively easy German victory over France in 1870/71 and inspired by the light-handed patriotism both of the Emperor and the ruling political class in Berlin with their conspicuous lack of political measurement, the Germans went to war in a strikingly confident mood. The dramatic unfolding of diplomatic and military pressures went undisturbed and William II himself, in a faint last-minute effort to avoid war, could no longer stop it.

In spite of the devastating and horrifying experiences of the First World War, the Nazi terror and the Second World War, West Germany was by no means immune against terrorism. Comparable in Europe only to Italy,[11] it arose as a combative strategy and alternative to the student revolt's growing dedication to reform the system (*Marsch durch die Institutionen*) rather than to change it by force. The German terrorists declared that they fought the authoritarian state structures as remnants of fascism. At the same time they took a "global" approach with the United States' war in Vietnam as the centrepiece of criticism. The German Red Army Faction 1977 described as the dialectics of the "anti-imperialist struggle" that the "system" by escalating the counter-revolution and by transforming the political state of emergency into a military one would reveal itself as the enemy and, "through its own terror,"[12] would bring up the masses against itself, sharpen the contradictions, and thereby make the revolutionary fight a constraint. It has been argued that part of the terrorist strategy consisted of sparing the German public from the difficult debate over the German guilt for the Holocaust and to make it feel comfortable with some of the prevailing opinions in the 1950s and 1960s, which were reluctant to accept German responsibility. Ulrike Meinhof, one of the leading German terrorists, wrote in prison 1972 that "... national socialism was only the political and military anticipation of the imperialist system of the multinational trusts"[13] thereby implying that only by questioning the assumption of a specifically German disposition to the Nazi rule and a collective German guilt could the terrorists of the Red Army Faction hope to win support by public opinion in the Federal Republic.[14] In another publication the Red Army Faction, after the Black September's terrorist attack against Israeli participants at the Munich Olympic Games 1972, went as far as to compare Moshe Dayan with Himmler.[15]

Terrorism, it has been argued, contains a manipulative hope by the perpetrators. The belief is that attitudes of the masses will change under the shock of the terrorist attack in their favour and by an intended change of roles.[16] Here lies one of the fundamental differences with genocide such as the Third Reich's elimination of the Jewish population in Germany and in the occupied States. In other words, "state terror" or acts of atrocity conducted "from above" may become limitless in violence like the concentration camp death machineries of the Third Reich, whereas terrorism "from below" and "against above" is working with the intended elevation of murder into heroism or martyrdom, based on identifiable actors and a limited number of victims. Terrorism in Germany during the seventies followed this pattern. Similar to the United States today, German society was once described by the editor Henri Nannen as "being in war" at that time. To many Germans, this was a bewildering view since terrorism was, of course, far from reaching the burdens of the last two memorable wars. But his statement was characteristic of the domestic tension.

In the current transatlantic debate, the U.S. Administration's growing preference for "coalitions of the willing" is often confronted with Europe's traditional attachment to multilateralism. Indeed, the widespread comfort with the multilateral rules of the post-war era can be explained by its powerful integrating and unifying impact on the war-ridden European continent and by the bonds it created between Europeans and Americans. The multilateral network including the disarmament and arms control treaties also greatly helped ease the tensions and build confidence on a more global scale. For Germany in particular, it was most welcome as a means to overcome the divisions of Europe and allow re-unification.

An important German multilateral ambition was the coupling of military defence and deterrence with active diplomacy for arms control and disarmament. In the late 1970s, Chancellor Schmidt had argued that strategic parity, as codified by SALT, would neutralize the strategic nuclear capabilities of the two superpowers, which, in turn, magnified the disparities between East and West in tactical nuclear and conventional weapons.[17] Schmidt's observations gave momentum to NATO's review of its nuclear forces leading to the LRTNF modernisation. After growing political pressure especially from Germany, the 1979 "double-track" decision was taken and détente seemed to be reconciled with defence. However, opposition to the deployment of the Pershing II and cruise missiles grew with the perception that the negotiating track was underemphasized by the new U.S. administration with its anti-Soviet rhetoric. After the ruling coalition in September 1982 had split over a number of predominantly economic issues and the new Christian-Democratic-Liberal government under Chancellor Kohl confirmed the previous government's stand on LRTNF, the debate became even more emotional and culminated in the "hot autumn" 1983 with demonstrations rallying an estimated 1 million people in Germany[18] alone and flanked by sizeable rallies in France, Britain and the United States.

The German peace movement expressed growing concerns that the two Germanys could fall victim to a limited nuclear war. It was argued that Germany was not allowed to take part in a war of aggression forbidden by Article 26 of the Federal Republic's Basic Law. This was connected to the new weapons since they were said to have "first strike quality."[19] The popular slogan by the *Aktion Sühnezeichen* to "create peace without arms" was linked to the post-war claim *Nie wieder Krieg*,[20] which was seen as a historic and lasting German obligation. A recurrent theme became apparent in the feeling of exposure to the two superpowers' confrontation. The Federal Republic of Germany could hardly be expected to define its interests with the same confident rationality as France and Britain who enjoy an uninterrupted and more natural balance in their foreign political assertiveness and, in addition, dispose of their own nuclear deterrents and hold permanent seats in the U.N. Security Council. Hence a stronger German "emotionalism" and sensitivity, a more philosophical and even religious approach to the peace debate by pacifists. Gradually, the notion of a responsibility for peace emerged in the German society as a lesson learnt from history. It went far beyond the peace movement and became more or less enshrined in the established parties.[21] Pierre Hassner at that period observed that the French inclination to neutralism was at least as deep and persistent as the Scandinavians' and even more decided than the German and British. But it was based in France on the country's *sacro egoismo*, not on moralism, and its roots were power politics, not its rejection.[22] In June

1984, after the crucial November 1983 Bundestag decision to go ahead with deployment, fear of war in Germany had dropped to 15 percent coming down from 42 percent a year earlier.[23]

Only five years later, with the advent of Soviet *perestroika*, popular unrest in Leipzig, Dresden and Berlin lead to the fall of the Berlin wall. The quest for peaceful and democratic change went hand in hand with the perspective of German unification embedded into a "unified Europe." Concerns arose that despite some reassuring signs from President Gorbatchev and encouragement by President Bush Sr. outbreaks of violence in the GDR could trigger off military suppression by the Soviet Union with severe consequences for Germany, the U.S.-Soviet relationship and the European future. Maintaining the peaceful character of change in the German Democratic Republic was therefore imperative.[24] In the following years, Foreign Minister Genscher's notion of *Verantwortungspolitik* (politics of responsibility), as opposed to obsolete *Machtpolitik* (power politics), expressed commitment to peaceful change, the need for an underlying European consensus and it gave rise to a debate on a more active participation in UN peacekeeping forces.

The impressive handling by Chancellor Kohl and Foreign Minister Genscher of the German re-unification process reinvigorated the belief in multilateralism even more. German policy had never before been more successfully engaged on the winning side in hammering out a lasting and constructive peace settlement in harmony with allies and neighbours. Together with the crucial part played by the four allied powers, it almost appeared a cure to Germany's skeptical self-assessment about its own political abilities dating back as far as the thirty years war.[25] European integration, a strong transatlantic link with the United States and membership in NATO as well as a continuing dialogue with Moscow and an active policy in Eastern Central Europe greatly favoured German goals and paid off well. Germany could take pride in steering responsibly through difficult waters. Indeed, it became part of a highly respected *Staatskunst*[26] raising the standards for political action and success considerably. Multilateralism – including the CSCE process – proved to be an extremely valuable tool for peaceful change of authoritarian rule in Central and Eastern Europe and it favoured the cause of human rights and democracy. As we have seen above, the German foreign political direction almost a decade long after unification was cautiously oriented to act as a "civilian power" until it was confronted with charges of escapism and the avoidance of new responsibilities. But it was decidedly only in 1999, when Chancellor Schröder and Foreign Minister Fischer advanced Germany's international role in the Kosovo conflict. This step, historically, undoubtedly complemented the range of *Verantwortungspolitik* and enhanced Germany's international credibility.

In the light of the stunning transatlantic achievements it is difficult to believe only a decade later that Americans today could be "from Mars" and Europeans "from Venus." Interestingly, recent opinion polls demonstrate that the transatlantic differences are far less pronounced than Kagan assumes. But differences in Europe cannot be dismissed. To be sure, Germans and French share many world views and want to see a more active European Union, but the German public is more at ease than France with the United States as the remaining only superpower. There is no ground to assume that a new anti-Americanism is gaining ground in Germany. Criticism in Germany of the Bush Administration's policy towards Iraq appears less emotional than previously during the LRTNF debate and should not be equated with growing anti-American sentiment.

Where then are the differences?

In the light of Germany's and Europe's positive experiences with the multilateral system, the American terminology of a "war against terrorism," when focused around a new unilateral assertiveness of American strength, is being questioned in Europe. The European Union prefers to speak of the "fight against terrorism." Waging a war implies a larger armed conflict, more damage and war-like consequences as a possible reaction. The American terminology evokes the prospect of prolonged armed conflict. Also, the notion of an "axis of evil" poses difficulties for its subjectivity since it does neither lend itself to present legal standards of justice nor to accountability and criteria for punishment.[27] It suggests that the borderlines between terrorists and uncomfortable regimes are not drawn accurately enough.

In Germany, a more or less rational reasoning is prevalent today in the political class. The mood is not against Americans but in search for a sensible international strategy to combat terrorism and to give new impetus to non-proliferation, arms control and disarmament. German criticism of the United States policy towards Iraq must not be interpreted as an expression of anti-American feelings. Many Germans believe that as good friends of America and in the light of their own bitter errors they should warn against what is perceived as too much risk-taking and patriotism in the U.S. This is almost the contrary to the gloomy heritage of German political romanticism or the distortions of Germany's idealism. It reflects an emancipated political thinking and risk assessment rather than an alleged typical German irrationalism, even though in the media reflections about a persistent German emotionalism and an inclination to *Weltfremdheit* are still making headlines. According to opinion polls, Americans, Germans and other Europeans do not seem that much separated. They agree on the urgency to fight international terrorism. The European comprehensive understanding of security, in which conflict prevention through dialogue and development cooperation are considered important ingredients, is also demonstrated by the new American National Security Strategy. Even if European and American disagreement over pre-emptive actions have been expressed and may reveal even fundamental differences, substantial parts of the American Security Strategy largely reflect German and European thinking. Also the U.S. quest for a more distinct American influence on world affairs[28] could be reconciled with European ambitions for an effective multilateral system, which can act as a unifying force.

With regard to Iraq, most German analysts do not see a short-term risk for the production or use of nuclear weapons by Saddam's regime. To them, American geopolitical and oil interest are mingled with the aim to gain more influence over the Middle East. It is still unclear and somewhat confusing that the claims for disarmament are being superseded by a new American agenda for regime change. Germany is not against democracy in Iraq but there are strong doubts whether this could be achieved by military means and without the United Nations. New agendas worldwide with unforeseen risks for the stability of the international system could be developed. The German analysts are also critical of applying different political standards to North Korea and Iraq. In addition, reservations in Europe against a new "doctrine" reserving the right to unilateral pre-emptive actions, as hinted at first by President Bush in his Westpoint speech 1 June 2002, are gaining ground. They spring *inter alia* from the potential precedents they may set for some less benevolent states. It is also unclear how the information base is to be determined to judge whether or not a threat is imminent and anticipatory action in accordance with Article 51 of the United Nations Charter is required. On this issue, a closer understanding between the U.S. and Europeans is highly desirable.

Both German Chancellor Schröder and his challenger in the electoral campaign 2002, Bavarian Minister President Stoiber, made clear that Germany's role in a military operation against Iraq would not be active military participation. Here, the traditional "bi-partisan" consensual approach to fundamental issues concerning security and foreign policy orientations worked well again. Notwithstanding a highly controversial domestic debate about the state of German-American relations, apprehensions were expressed prominently in all parties about the prospect of war with unforeseeable consequences including a conspicuous rise in terrorist activities and a radicalisation of the Islamic world with serious consequences for the Arab-Israeli conflict. The German government and the opposition therefore welcomed the United Nations Resolution 1441 to send the inspection team back to Iraq with the full authority of the international community. Eventually the European Council in Copenhagen 12 and 13 December 2002 underlined its full and unequivocal support for Resolution 1441 stressing that the goal of the EU remained the disarmament of Iraq's weapons of mass destruction in accordance with the relevant UN Security Council Resolutions.

The recent opinion poll conducted by the Chicago Council on Foreign Relations and the German Marshall Fund clearly demonstrates that Europeans and Americans are largely in line on sensitive international strategic orientations. The picture by Robert Kagan about fundamental differences[29] can hardly be based on empirical evidence in the broader societal sphere. This holds more or less also true for attitudes towards Iraq. Only 20 % of the Americans feel that the United States should intervene in Iraq alone vs. 10 % of the Europeans questioned.[30] And 28 % of the Germans – quite in agreement with the 27 % French – in difference to only 20 % of the British and 13 % of Americans respondents believe that the U.S. should not invade Iraq. The recent PEW Global Attitude Project, on the other hand, shows that Germans among Europeans are – together with the British – the strongest advocates of removing Saddam Hussein, so there is no sympathy for the dictator.[31] Germans are probably more inclined to remove Saddam by other means than by a military offensive. On the U.S. in general, the almost identical views of the French and Germans are striking. Both are equally sceptical of unilateral U.S. action. It is also noteworthy that 65 % of Americans and 60 % of Europeans – Germany: only 56 % – would favour intervention with UN approval and the support of allies.[32] There is one striking difference: According to the PEW findings, 53 % of the Germans, compared to only 21 % of the French, believe that U.S. foreign policy makes an effort to take the interests of their country into account.[33] In the light of these results, it is difficult to accept Robert Kagan's view[34] of a growing rift between "Europeans" and "Americans" in general. Differences between Europeans can not be overlooked. The British respondents generally show more understanding for American views. Both Germans and French want a stronger EU, but the French would go further than the Germans in defining it as a "puissance" in its own rights. Undoubtedly, Kagan's reflections about the rise of different strategic cultures will deserve further attention and indeed the gap between the American and European defence expenditures and military capabilities will require more decided European – and especially German – priorities. It should equally encourage more American cooperation efforts for keeping the transatlantic link and integrated defence intact.

According to the polls, Germans show a comparatively relaxed attitude to the American role as a superpower. Only 48 % of the Germans against 91 % of the French and 56 % of the British believe that the European Union should become a superpower like the U.S. and a large majority believe that the EU as a superpower should closely cooperate with the U.S. But 22 % of the Germans compared to 3 % of the French and 20 % of the British believe that the U.S. should remain the only superpower.[35] All the data available reflecting the current mood in Germany demonstrate that there are no serious indications for a kind of anti-Americanism, as Kissinger maintains, that "... may have become a permanent temptation of German politics."[36]

To sum up, the debate in Germany after September 11 showed that Berlin will remain committed to an effective functioning of multilateralism and to an adequate combination of diplomacy and military strength. It will also accept growing responsibilities in peace operations worldwide. Public acceptance of peace operations by the *Bundeswehr* has increased over the last decade,[37] though to a lesser degree in East Germany. As to improvements for the multilateral system, additional efforts by more united groups of states or ad-hoc coalitions may indeed be required. But to preserve and advance its legitimacy and its backbone in human rights, democratic standards and legal norms it must not be undermined by setting new rules without a credible consent of the international community. This is not to satisfy "German idealism" and it should not be equated with post-modern European Kantian dreams born out of sheer weakness[38] thus offering excuses for inaction rather than convictions. For Germany, it is a political challenge tied to its European, transatlantic and global interests with the future cohesion and effectiveness of the enlarged European Union as well as NATO at the political centre. Between the two, a strategic partnership would best serve the interests on both sides of the Atlantic. Russia would become a close partner inseparably linked to it.

Both the United States and Germany should use the continuing public interest in each other as an asset for confidence-building. It would also help the US – European dialogue. Clearly, a Franco-German political revival is in the making and can have a stimulating impact on the EU's adaptation to the new threat environment and on stronger joint European efforts for security, defence and a more commonly agreed strategic orientation. The suggestions by the German and French foreign ministers of 21st November 2002 for strengthening the EU are following these lines. Clearly, the currently biggest challenge with EU enlargement ahead is a more concerted common foreign and security policy of the EU. In addition, a more common positioning in the UN context is urgent.

Germany's foreign policy direction, contrary to some of the traditional judgments, appears today more shaped by rational circumspection than by the less "Cartesian" thinking in preceding decades. In spite of a broadly-felt discomfort or rejection of war across the political party spectre, emotions and moral arguments at the time of the Pershing and Kosovo debates were clearly ranking higher than in the current debate about Iraq, terrorism and counter-proliferation. Neither the political class in Germany nor the media are indulging in moralism, idealism or pacifism. Both the common interests of the international community and the political rationality not to turn the Middle East into a powder-keg are the currently well-accepted lines of argument in Germany. The list of questions concerning the impact of military action against Iraq on regional stability, Islam, terrorism and a post-Saddam strategy, raised by the German government,[39] demonstrated clarity and balanced risk assessment. In substance, the German reasoning is in line with the arguments put forward in most of the European capitals though not by all European cabinets. The German conservative opposition, even more after Pope John Paul's public messages, is sceptical about a premature military operation against Iraq but is challenging the government by a more pronounced support for the military build-up as a means to exert pressure on Saddam Hussein. But in general, the arguments in the CDU/CSU are equally centred around weighing the pros and cons.[40] As for the German public, the ongoing debate demonstrates that it can hardly be singularised for its views in Europe On the contrary, support for the German position in the United Nations seems to be growing.

On the whole, German assessments differing from Washington's views do by no means signal a decline in interest or in positive feelings towards America. Rather, the enduring German commitment to the transatlantic community and its values – so deeply intertwined with the United States' support for Europe - is distinctive for German foreign policy and firmly tied to its European momentum. The EU will need the transatlantic link to grow. And the U.S., for its own part, should encourage a stronger European cohesion.

Notes

1   Martin Walser's highly controversial statement that Auschwitz does not lend itself to be instrumentalized marked the extreme end of the debate. It was also argued that it would be responsible to explain the criminal regime in Yugoslavia as the real reason to fight it by military means. See Frank Schirrmacher: Luftkampf Deutschlands Anteil am Krieg, Frankfurter Allgemeine Zeitung, 17. April 1999, Nr. 89, 41; critically also Sonja Margolina, who sees the "Berlin Republik" resort to mythological elevation: "Während aber Amerikaner (wie zum Beispiel Henry Kissinger) es sich leisten können,

die geopolitischen Schäden und Gefährdungen durch den Nato-Krieg für amerikanische Interessen klar zu benennen und den Begriff der Menschenrechte gar nicht in den Mund zu nehmen brauchen, um überzeugend zu argumentieren, inszeniert die deutsche Politik eine moralische Orgie, einen wahren Wertekarneval." See Sonja Margolina, Geschichte im Fluß, Merkur, Deutsche Zeitschrift für europäisches Denken, Sonderdruck aus Heft 004, Stuttgart 1999, 680.
2   Hans-Peter Schwarz, Die Zentralmacht Europas, Deutschlands Rückkehr auf die Weltbühne, Berlin, 1. Auflage, 1994, 15; also Adrian Hyde-Price, Germany and the Kosovo War: Still a Civilian Power? In: German Politics, Volume 10, Number 1, April 2001, Special Issue; New Europe, New Germany, Old Foreign Policy? Editor Douglas Webber, Sothgate. London, 20, 22.
3   Ibid., 20.
4   Karl Heinz Bohrer, Editorial, Merkur, Deutsche Zeitschrift für europäisches Denken, Heft 11, 55. Jahrgang, November 2001, 955: "Mit der...Politik der deutschen Regierung kündigt sich ein epochaler Wechsel der politischen Moral und Mentalitäten an. Die Sozialhelfermentalität und die utopische Flucht aus der Weltpolitik in die soziale Idylle zwischen multikulturellem Miteinander und machtfernem Gespräch werden nicht verschwinden, aber sie werden im seriösen politischen Diskurs nicht mehr die alte Rolle spielen. Ihren Aposteln wird weniger geglaubt werden, und der politische Provinzialismus der Deutschen, der seit den frühen achtziger Jahren eklatant erkennbar wurde und bis heute in allen Schichten grassiert, wird sich nicht mehr lohnen, sondern sie teuer zu stehen kommen."
5   Peter Waldmann: Terrorismus Provokation der Macht, München 1998, 2nd edition 2001, 11.
6   In 1879, two attempts at the life of the respected German Emperor William I failed. Plans were later discovered to kill William I together with the Crown Prince, Bismarck and general field-marshall von Moltke. By such an act of violence, the very heart of the Prussian-German power centre in Berlin after the establishment of the Empire in 1871 would have been hit. ibid., 27.
7   Daniel Bell: Revolutionärer Terrorismus: vier Rechtfertigungen, Merkur, Heft 5, 56 Jahrgang, Mai 2002, 433.
8   It is worth remembering that the culture of martyrdom and suicide attacks had precedents albeit in distant centuries. Quite spectacularly, the Syrian Assasins at the end of the 12th century succeeded in isolating young men from their families. Spiritual promises on paradise lured them to destruction and to subsequent suicide. Cf. Heinz Halm, "Die Assasinen 1092–1273," in *Das Attentat in der Geschichte*, ibid., 62–63.
9   Bernd Sösemann: Die Bereitschaft zum Krieg, Sarajevo 1914, in: Das Attentat in der Geschichte, ibid., 313.
10 Ibid.
11 Waldmann, ibid., p. 83 and ibid., 27; leaving aside Turkey and Northern Ireland as special cases with a distinct historical background, Germany and Italy in the 1970s and 1980s showed the highest number of terrorist actions in Europe with Italy leading in the death toll; cf. ibid, 23.
12 Ibid.
13 Quoted from: Oliver Tolmein, Vom Deutschen Herbst zum 11. September, Die RAF, der Terrorismus und der Staat, Hamburg 2002, 34.
14 Ibid.: Tolmein describes them in this sense as a "sehr deutsch geprägte Stadtguerilla-Gruppe" rather than "Hitler's children" as some argued at that time.
15 Ibid., 37; it should also be remembered that RAF terrorists received logistical and training help from the PLO.

16 Waldmann also mentions the change of roles intended by terrorism: those who attack and provoke want to be depicted as the "real" victims, ibid., 34: "Terrorismus ist, auch wenn dies zynisch klingen mag, eine politische Strategie, der eine gewisse Gewaltökonomie zugrunde liegt. Terroristen, und das nämliche gilt für Terrorregime, wählen eine begrenzte Zahl von Opfern aus, um den Rest im Sinne ihrer Zielvorstellungen manipulieren zu können." Ibid., 30.

17 For a summary of the LRTNF debate cf.: Nuclear Weapons in Europe, by John Cartwright, Julian Critchley, Co-Rapporteurs, Special Committe on Nuclear Weapons in Europe, North Atlantic Assembly, November 1984, 7.

18 Ibid., p. 97, see also: Pierre Hassner, Rüstungskontrolle und die Politik des Pazifismus im protestantischen Europa, in: Uwe Nerlich (Hrsg.), Sowjetische Macht und westliche Verhandlungspolitik im Wandel militärischer Kräfteverhältnisse, Baden-Baden, 1. Auflage 1982, S. 451.

19 Alfred Mechtersheimer (Hg.), *Nachrüsten?* Dokumente und Positionen zum NATO-Doppelbeschluß, Herausgegeben von Freimut Duve, Reinbek bei Hamburg 1981, 202.

20 Ibid. "Wie leben in einem Land, das sich einst schwor: "Nie wieder Krieg!," einem Land mit den dritthöchsten Militärausgaben, einer schnell.wachsenden Zuwachsrate an Rüstungsexporten und der größten Atomwaffendichte der Erde, einem Land, das – so Helmut Schmidt – nur um den Preis seiner Zerstörung zu verteidigen ist" ibid., 227.

21 Even Franz-Josef Strauß, in a polemic speech against "red pacificism" ("lieber rot als tot") at a CSU party rally in 1981, described himself as a pacifist, however with the different connotation of belonging to the category of "...Verantwortungspazifisten, die nicht idealistisch schwärmerisch sagen, Gewaltanwendung auf keinen Fall und damit dem, der Gewalt anwenden will, die Risikofreiheit geradezu notariell garantieren." The very fact that Strauß for himself accepted the notion of a "responsibility pacifist" – of course in clear contrast to the general understanding – demonstrates its weight in the debate in Germany and in Europe Rede des CSU-Vorsitzenden Franz-Josef Strauß auf dem CSU-Parteitag am 12. Juli 1981 in München (Auszüge), in: Alfred Mechtersheimer, ibid., 196.

22 Pierre Hassner, ibid., 460.

23 John Cartwright, Julian Critchley, ibid., 103.

24 Hans-Dietrich Genscher, Erinnerungen, Berlin 1995, p. 688: "Sowohl Gorbatschow als auch Schewardnadse gegenüber wies ich darauf hin, daß wir für die Entwicklung in der DDR keine Verantwortung trügen.... Wir empfänden wirklich kein Gefühl des Triumphes, doch die Probleme könnten nicht von uns gelöst werden. Ausdrücklich erinnerte ich daran, daß die Deutschen in der DDR mit außerordentlicher Verantwortung handelten. Sie hätten alles vermieden, was Anlaß zur Beunruhigung gebe. Jede Gewaltanwendung sei unterblieben."

25 Heinrich August Winkler: Der lange Weg nach Westen, Erster Band, München, Dritte Auflage 2001, S. 22.
It is worth remembering that the States forming the "Holy Roman Empire" and their peoples were suffering from the worst and traumatic violence ever. The war was "total" in a modern sense. Nobody was spared by the heavy burdens arising from forced fund-raising, by famine, oppression, looting, destructions and the resulting enormous death toll with a reduction of the population from 17 to 10 million. Friedrich Schiller in his history of the thirty-years war bemoaned the moral decay of the population and its uncontrolled revenge as a consequence of the warriors' reigning despotism, which in the view of the German idealistic and freedom-loving classical period was prolonged and became even more painful and difficult to accept since it was supported by foreign, namely French und Swedish intervention. The repercussions of the thirty-years war on

the further course of German history were far-reaching. Even though the Empire survived, a "state in imagination" in Hegel's words, it was too weak and multinational to act as a focal point for political and democratic nation-building. Winkler concludes that the thirty-years-war strengthened absolutism in the many small states of the Empire at the cost of its central powers and contributed to a typically German inward-looking policy that lacked the grand stage for articulating political dissent. See also: Friedrichs von Schiller sämtliche Werke, Fünfzehntes Bändchen, Stuttgart und Tübingen, Cotta'sche Buchhandlung 1828, 256–57.

26   Philip Zelikow, Condoleezza Rice, Sternstunde der Diplomatie, Die deutsche Einheit und das Ende der Spaltung Europas, 2. Auflage, München 2001, 491.
27   Hannah Arendt used the term "radical evil" in her early writings to describe the atrocities of the Nazi concentration camps and after the Eichmann trial introduced the term "banality of the evil," Hannah Arendt, Elemente und Ursprünge totaler Herrschaft, Frankfurt/M, 1955, 651 and Douglas Klusmeyer and Astri Suhrke, Comprehending "Evil": Challenges for Law and Policy, in: *Ethics and International Affairs 2002*, Volume 16, Number 1, 37–39.
28   *The National Security Strategy of the United States of America*, September 2002.
29   Robert Kagan, "Power and Weakness," Policy Review, No. 113, June/July 2002: "The United States and Europe are fundamentally different today ... American military strength has created a propensity to use that strength. Europe's military weakness has produced a perfectly understandable aversion to the exercise of military power."
30   The Chicago Council on Foreign Relations, The German Marshall Fund, Worldviews 2002, released September 4, 2002 (www.worldviews.org), 3
31   The Pew Global Attitudes Project, *What the World Thinks in 2002*, Washington, 2002.
32   Ibid., 58.
33   Ibid.
34   Kagan, op.cit.
35   The Chicago Council, op. cit.
36   Henry A. Kissinger, *The 'Made in Berlin' Generation*, 2002 Media Services International.
37   This was the result of a round table discussion in the Deutsche Gesellschaft für Auswärtige Politik in Berlin 14 January 2003, chaired by Karl Kaiser, with the presentation by the Institut für Demoskopie in Allensbach with a recent opinion poll.
38   Kagan, op.cit.; Kenneth Adelman, in contrast, argues that opposite to American foreign policy "Europeans schooled by their history on "realpolitik," often disdain the moral plain." Cf. Keneth Adelman, "The Case against Saddam," *The Wall Street Journal*, 28 August 2002.
39   cf. Address by Joschka Fischer, Minister of Foreign Affairs of the Federal Republic of Germany, at the Fifty-seventh Session of the United Nations General Assembly, New York, 14 September 2002; see also interview with Foreign Minister Joschka Fischer in the Frankfurter Allgemeine Zeitung, 17 Januar 2003, 6.
40   "Alle Gründe der Vernunft sprechen gegen einen Krieg im Irak, und sie tragen den Protest, der sich im übrigen auch von Anfang an in den USA selber entwickelt hat." See Heiner Geißler, "Immanuel Kant und der Irak-Krieg," Süddeutsche Zeitung, 20. Januar 2003.

Chapter 11

Six Dimensions of the Growing Transatlantic Divide: Are the US and Europe Definitively Driving Themselves Apart?

Marcel Van Herpen[*]

France does not realize it, but we are at war with America.
Yes, permanent war, vital – an economic war ...
They are hard, those Americans. They are voracious.
They want undivided power over the world.
(Former French President François Mitterrand,
International Herald Tribune, 18–19 January 1997)

Introduction

Recently there has been much debate about a growing divide between the United States and its European allies after September 11. The question I want to answer here is if there exists, indeed, such a divide, and, if so, what will be the consequences for the transatlantic partnership. The second question I will try to answer is if this gap has a *temporal* or a *structural* character. If it is *temporal*, this means that the divide is the result of specific historical circumstances which may change over time. Since 1945 the transatlantic relationship has known many ebbs (Suez, Vietnam, NATO's "double track" decision) and flows (Berlin crisis, Vietnam, Kosovo) and there seems, at first sight, no reason that this will be different now. Would, on the contrary, the growing transatlantic divide have a *structural* character, then this would mean that the estrangement between

---

[*] © Marcel Van Herpen, Paris, 2003. Marcel Van Herpen is director of the Cicero Foundation – a pro-EU think tank.

the US and Europe is not a temporary event, but that it is the expression of deeper underlying forces that irresistibly tear America and Europe apart. To analyse what is the case I have divided the transatlantic drift into six different components, which are:

1. a transatlantic *perception* gap
2. a transatlantic *capabilities* gap
3. a transatlantic *attitude* gap
4. a transatlantic *value* gap
5. a transatlantic *religion* gap
6. a transatlantic *strategy* gap.

The "perception gap" affects the different ways in which Americans and Europeans perceive the terrorist threat, as well as their respective vulnerability to this threat. The "capabilities gap" has to do with the growing disparity of the military capabilities of the US on the one hand and Europe on the other. The "attitude gap"—that is the result both from the perception gap and the capabilities gap—concerns US unilateralism and its enhanced readiness to use its (overwhelming) military power to reach its political objectives. Underlying, more basic divides, are the growing transatlantic "value gap" concerning the role of international law and a "religion gap" which has to do with the growing influence of fundamentalist Christian groups on US policy that strongly contrasts with a negligible role of religion in politics in a mostly dechristianized and secularized Europe. All this leads to a "strategy gap": the fact that the US strategy of "regime change" and active intervention to remake the Arab world are met in Europe with scepticism, if not open hostility. I will argue that some of these divides have a temporal character and may be bridged over time. Other divides, however, seem to show a more structural character, as is the case with the value gap and the religion gap. One may expect, therefore, that despite some possible mutual ad hoc realignments in the field of threat perception and strategy, transatlantic misunderstandings will not disappear, and that the existing divide might eventually even become deeper in the future.

The Six Dimensions of the Growing US-European Divide

Let us now look at some of the major changes in the US, many of which—but not all—were brought about by the events of September 11:

1. a. The US considers itself to be *at war*.
   b. At the same time it considers itself to be extremely *vulnerable* to terrorist attacks.
2. After September 11 and the Afghan campaign the US has taken full consciousness of its position as a *global hegemon* that disposes of an overwhelming military power that is unique in human history.
3. This new, unchallenged power position enables the US not only to opt for a growing *unilateralist* approach in the way it conducts its foreign policy. It also gives it a clear preference for *military* solutions to cope with adversaries in the international arena.
4. This new US unilateralism is not the product of a cynical, value-free, foreign policy realism, based on a narrowly defined concept of the "national interest," as one might think, but it is backed by conservative values and a solid moralism. This moralism, however, is quite different from its European equivalent. The clash between Americans and Europeans over foreign policy issues can, therefore, not be reduced to a debate between US "realism" versus European "moralism." It is a clash between two different kinds of moralism, which makes consensus building much harder.
5. Behind this "value divide" there is a religious divide: the fact that in the US fundamentalist Christian groups recently have become increasingly politically influential and have begun to shape the way in which important members of its political class, President George W. Bush included, view the outside world.
6. The US has adopted a new strategy of "regime change," that is primarily focused on Iraq, but that has wider implications as a strategy to get rid of "rogue states" and to "remake" the Arab world.

How did Europeans react to these changes?

1a. The US is at war, Europe is not

Since September 11, 2001, the United States is at war. This fact is evident for all Americans. This is, or was, however, not evident for many Europeans. Those Europeans who visited the United States in early 2002 were often surprised, and sometimes shocked, by the war fervor they found in America. Accustomed to the fact that US foreign policy makers tend to use a more aggressive manner of verbal expression than their European counterparts, they might have thought that the "war on terrorism"—that was proclaimed by the US—was a variant of earlier proclaimed "wars," as, for instance, the "war on drugs" which was perceived in Europe as some kind of an enhanced, sustained police effort. For Americans, however, there was no doubt from the beginning: The war on terrorism was a *real war*.

For Europeans it was *not*. After the successful campaign in Afghanistan a general feeling in Europe emerged that an enhanced vigilance and international police cooperation might be enough to contain the terrorist threat. Europeans were inclined to think that Al Qaeda's terrorism had *peaked* on September 11. Americans, on the contrary, considered the September 11 attack as *a first great strike* in an escalating series of ever more massive and murderous attacks. Only a sustained, total war against this invisible and omnipresent enemy could avoid the worst from happening.

1b. The new vulnerability of the US versus the old vulnerability of Europe

The September 11 attacks were a huge psychological shock for the US. They combined the effects of the surprise attack on Pearl Harbour with the sudden sense of vulnerability caused by the successful launch of the first Soviet Sputnik in 1957. The fact that this was the first attack on the American homeland since the British burnt the White House in the War of 1812, was, however, not the only reason for this new, deep sense of vulnerability. It was also caused by the totally different nature of the new enemy. In the case of Pearl Harbour and the launch of the Sputnik there were foreign governments involved that could clearly be identified and attacked, respectively deterred. The new terrorist threat that the US was facing in 2001 could, on the contrary, *not* be reduced to inter-state relations (although the terrorists had the open or hidden support of some foreign governments and a handful of warlords in failed states).

The fact that Al Qaeda was a non-governmental actor consequently meant that it was not possible to deter this group from using weapons of mass destruction. Deterrence is based on a strategy of mutual assured destruction, which is guaranteed by a second strike capability that can eventually be launched "from the grave." Having no national territory, nor a national population that can function as a hostage, attacks conducted by this new kind of "hyperterrorists" could not be deterred. A second element that made deterrence obsolete was the *irrational, suicidal character of the terrorists*. Deterrence can only work when actors on both sides behave rationally and prefer survival to a certain death. The only way to defend oneself in such a *post-deterrence situation* is to prevent the enemy from hitting. This led the US administration to adopt a strategy of pre-emptive attacks.[1] This represented a change of strategy that was criticized by some European governments, who called it a *Pandora's box*, which, once it was opened, made unlimited intervention possible, thereby endangering the existing world order based on the principles of national self-determination and the inviolability of national frontiers.[2]

As a matter of fact, the European phlegm may reflect a different historical experience. Having never lived with the unique protection of an insular continent, Europeans are more accustomed to vulnerability. The Cold War, which divided their continent in two hostile blocs, ended only twelve years ago. Terrorism is not new here: many countries have their own "home-made" terrorists. Add to this the recent ethnic wars in the Balkans, the geographical proximity of the unstable Middle East region, the large immigrant populations from Islamic and Arab origin and it will be clear that Europeans possess a sense of vulnerability that Americans never have experienced.

Europeans might, therefore, be tempted to consider themselves as being psychologically better equipped to cope with this vulnerability. Considering it a fact of life, they seem to be more detached. But an American could easily criticise the European *Gelassenheit* as a "wait-and-see" attitude, and even as an irresponsible fatalism and he could accuse the Europeans of "undercommitment" in the fight against a common enemy. He could, rightly, ask if they would still react in the same detached way if Paris, London, or Berlin became the theatre of the same kind of massive terrorist attack that hit the US on September 11.

2. The growing power gap between the US and Europe

It is, strange enough, only recently that the US has become fully conscious of the fact that it is the most powerful nation that has ever existed in human history. This *prise de conscience* is, in a certain sense, the product of the unexpected quick military successes in Kosovo and in the Afghan campaign against the Taliban. Until very recently there was a debate going on in the United States about the question as to whether the collapse of the Soviet Union would result in a unipolar world or not.[3] Many leading American analysts, including Samuel Huntington, expressed their doubts, considering the US as only one of several leading powers.

As a matter of fact, nations and their respective governments need ten to fifteen years, sometimes even more, to adapt to new geostrategic realities. This process of psychological adaptation to geostrategic change can also be seen elsewhere. The reunified Germany needed it and is still in the process of psychologically adapting itself to the change from the Bonn republic with sixty million inhabitants into the Berlin republic with eighty million. Russia needed it and is—like Germany—still in the process of adaptation in digesting its transformation from an empire with 285 million inhabitants into a country with only 147 million. It is true: In contrast with an expanding Germany and a contracting Russia, the territory of the United States did *not* change.[4] However, the United States also went through a similar process of psychological adaptation. More than a decade after the collapse of the Soviet Union, the US only started to realise its new and unique position in a unipolar world in which it is the only remaining hegemon. This new position is based on *external* developments, especially the demise of the Soviet Union, but equally so on *internal* developments. The economic and technological boom of the1990s has led to a rapid increase of US military power, which is not only facilitated by a sustained high defence budget, but also by the high proportion of this budget that has been devoted to defence R&D.[5] This fact has translated into a steadily growing technological advance of the US vis-à-vis Europe, especially in the field of intelligence, power projection, and precision-guided missiles.

All this has happened in a decade in which European integration has made tremendous progress. The Europeans not only launched, with great success, their own common currency that could rival the dollar, but they also started an ambitious European Security and Defence Policy and prepared for a historical enlargement of the Union with ten and more members, most former communist countries. It was, indeed, a rude awakening for Europe. Instead of becoming more equal vis-à-vis the United States, Europe is lagging behind economically, politically, and militarily. The first decade of the twenty-first century seems to have brought Europe back to the 1950s, a period in which the US was an equally overwhelming power. But the difference is that in the 1950s the Europeans were very satisfied to have such a powerful ally vis-à-vis the Soviet threat. Fifty years later the sustained, and even enhanced American superiority, has, for many Europeans, become a source of frustration, if not a deep malaise. It is as if the great and never ending effort of the Europeans to unify and integrate their continent has all been in vain.

3. Europe's Angst *in regard to the increased US preference for military solutions*

It is not so long ago that Europeans referred with a certain disdain to the so-called "Vietnam syndrome" to explain the American reluctance to engage in wars abroad, especially in the Balkans. Europeans expressed their fear that the US might more and more be tempted to conduct a policy of retreat, which might, over time, lead to a new period of "splendid isolation." The European defence projects: first the European Security and Defense Identity (ESDI) in NATO, and later the European Security and Defense Policy (ESDP) in the EU, were partly born from the fear of US disengagement. Today, ironically, Europeans seem almost to have nostalgia for this period. Things, indeed, have changed. September 11 represented a shock therapy and has suppressed in one stroke all US isolationist temptations. It has, all of a sudden, put an end to the Vietnam syndrome. Instead of retreating from the international arena, the US is turning itself more and more toward the external world. But it does so in a unilateralist spirit. The apparent contradiction between its perceived new vulnerability and its massive military superiority leads the US to seek primarily military solutions. Europeans get more and more uneasy, as has become clear from the diplomatic conflict between Germany and the US over an eventual attack on Iraq. Most Europeans favor diplomatic means over military means to resolve international conflicts. Germans tend to speak about the EU as *Zivilmacht Europa*, a "civil" Europe that instead of military power prefers to use its huge economic power as a means to influence, and eventually change, the behavior of foreign governments

4. American versus European values: a growing divide?

This brings us directly to the next point : the question of values. Recently there has been a debate about the diverging value-systems on both sides of the Atlantic. In an article in *Policy Review* the American analyst Robert Kagan argued that the fact that Americans preferred military action and Europeans preferred a multilateral approach based on international law could be explained from the fact that Europeans were militarily weak and Americans strong : "Europe is turning away from power, or to put it a little differently, it is moving beyond power into a self-contained world of laws and rules and transnational negotiation and cooperation (...) The United States, meanwhile, remains mired in history, exercising power in the anarchic Hobbesian world where international laws and rules are unreliable (...)."[6] Fukuyama added to Kagan's argument that the US-European divergence should also be explained from the European experience with integration and supra-national institutions: "Americans tend not to see any source of democratic legitimacy higher than the constitutional democratic nation-state. (...) Europeans, by contrast, tend to believe that democratic legitimacy flows from the will of an international community much larger than any individual nation-state."[7] And elsewhere, he comments, ironically: "Like former smokers, they want everyone else to experience their painful withdrawal symptoms from sovereignty."[8]

Fukuyama adds another, *third* reason for the divergence between Americans and Europeans: the American "sense of exceptionalism": "Americans believe in the special legitimacy of their democratic institutions and indeed believe that they are the embodiment of universal values that have a significance for all of mankind. This leads to an idealistic involvement in world affairs, but also to a tendency for Americans to confuse their national interests with universal ones."[9] Fukuyama seems here to neglect completely *European* messianism and universalism. Not only the traditional messianism and universalism of a country like France—expressed in the famous universalist triad: *liberté, égalité, fraternité*—but also the messianism and universalism of the smaller European countries. The Netherlands, for instance, considers itself—and this without any irony—as a *gidsland* (a "guiding country"), because it spends 0.7 percent of GDP for development aid. The country of Hugo Grotius equally considers itself as a promoter of international law and the Dutch think, therefore, that it is not by accident that the International Court of Justice, the Yugoslav War Crimes Tribunal and the International Criminal Court are located in The Hague. For the Scandinavian countries this is equally true. They spend also 0.7 percent of GDP for development aid and consider themselves key promoters of international peace. The role played during the last decade in international peace mediation by a small country as Norway, for instance, is exemplary.

5. The religious divide: God or human rights?

The difference, therefore, is not US messianism and universalism versus the absence of messianism and universalism in Europe. It is a difference between *two specific kinds* of messianism and universalism. European messianism is based on *secular, inner worldly values* as democracy, human rights, social equality, and the rule of law.[10] This is logical for a secularized, dechristianized continent in which the majority of the population considers itself as non-believers. The American universalism, on the contrary, has clear religious overtones. Many Americans are convinced of the unique providential role the US has to play in the world. Much as has been the case in Israel, many people in the US consider their country as a *chosen nation* that has a special vocation in the world. President Reagan described the Soviet Union in biblical terms as an "evil empire." By doing this he went beyond the normal diplomatic jargon to give the conflict with the Soviet Union a quasi-metaphysical character: a fight of the forces of good against the forces of evil. George W. Bush did the same in his "axis of evil" speech.

Europeans are extremely sensitive for this kind of rhetoric (which the former French Minister of Foreign Affairs, Hubert Védrine, immediately qualified as "simplistic"). For Europeans this jargon is as repulsive as when Iranian ayatollahs qualify the US government as "the Great Satan." The point is that these differences between Europeans and Americans cannot be reduced to mere differences of expression.[11] Behind it, we can discern different conceptual frames of reference. More than a hundred and fifty years ago, De Tocqeville had already observed an "exalted and almost wild spiritualism" in American society, the presence of "bizarre sects" and "religious follies."[12] The fact is that in the past few decades evangelical and charismatic Christian movements have flourished in the US as never before. What is new, however, is that former apolitical and isolated "born again" sects have started organising themselves into political movements, such as the Christian Right and the Christian Coalition, with the purpose of winning state power.[13] They were an important electorate for Ronald Reagan and were already represented in his administration.[14] Both the presidents George Bush and George W. Bush were elected with the votes of the evangelical voters.[15] And the *direct* political influence exerted by these groups is growing. The chief speechwriter of George W. Bush, Michael Gerson, is a fundamentalist Christian. John Ashcroft, who heads the Department of Justice, is a Pentecostalist, who holds a daily prayer meeting in the offices of his department. Bush himself considers himself as a reborn Christian.[16] The impact of this fundamentalist religious revival must not be underestimated. It is quite clear that it reinforces the American administration's tendency to see the "war on terrorism" through the prism of a Manichaean struggle. One is for or against. Between the forces of good and the forces of evil no compromise is possible. Only a total destruction of the enemy can bring solace. In this simplistic black-and-white vision there is no place for an analysis of deeper geostrategic, social, economic, and psychological factors that play a role.[17] A sign of the deep concern in Europe about this development is the fact that even a moderate diplomat as Javier Solana, the EU's foreign policy chief, recently declared to be "surprised at how religion has permeated the White House's thinking."[18] "It is a kind of binary model (...) It is all or nothing. For us, Europeans, it is difficult to deal with because we are secular. We do not see the world in such black and white terms."[19]

6. Regime change: new imperialism or noble idealism?

When President George W. Bush took office everybody expected the new US administration to be less internationally involved than the precedent Clinton administration. Bush seemed, indeed, inclined to give more importance to the Western hemisphere than to the rest of the world when he went not to Europe for his first official visit as a president, but to Mexico. Europeans even feared that the Bush presidency would be the beginning of a period of new US isolationism. September 11 changed all this. The September events not only obliged the US to go to war with the Taliban regime in Afghanistan, but also to radically rethink its international priorities. The Arab world had particularly become a special source of preoccupation. Many of these countries shared the same characteristics: they had corrupt, authoritarian regimes, backward economies, and lacked an independent civil society. Together with high birth-rates, high unemployment, and a radical, mostly young population that often openly sympathised with the Al Qaeda terrorists, this made for an explosive mixture. The Arab countries—not only a "rogue" state as Iraq, but also allied countries, such as Saudi Arabia and Egypt—were black holes, a breeding ground *par excellence* for Islamist terrorists.

Some members of the Bush administration favoured a *pro-active approach*. The US should not restrict its policy to a purely defensive stance—even if this took the form of a pre-emptive action—but it should use its new status as the only remaining superpower to actively *reorder the world* as it had done after World War II when the US nuclear monopoly gave it a similar position of unchallenged power. The US—so was the argument—had in the next ten to fifteen years a unique window of opportunity to change the world for the better. After 1945 it had brought democracy to Japan and restored democracy in Germany, giving the latter in the process a US inspired federal constitution and a US inspired Supreme Court (*Bundesverfassungsgericht*). Germany's and Japan's populations were still grateful. Would it not be possible, so was the argument, to do the same in the Arab world? *Regime change* became a keyword. Regime change did, however, not mean that it would be enough to topple the autocrats. Regime change would be part of an overall reform programme that would also include economic reforms and the build-up of democratic institutions in order to bring these countries in line with the rest of the developed world.

It is interesting that European reactions to these plans did not so much evoke the post World War II as the *pre World War I* situation. An article in the French daily newspaper *Le Monde* got, for instance, the title "The American Neo-Imperialist School"[20] And if in this context a reference was made to other American presidents, it was not to Franklin Delano Roosevelt or Harry Truman, but to Theodore Roosevelt, a representative of the imperialist era, known for his "Roosevelt corollary" to the Monroe Doctrine, proclaiming a US right to intervene in the Western Hemisphere to defend its national interests.[21] A columnist of the *Financial Times*, who wanted to give the US the benefit of the doubt and was ready to accept noble US intentions, nevertheless qualified these plans as outright "foolish."[22] In fact there are at least *five* problems Europeans have with this strategy. These problems concern first its *legitimacy*, second its *consistency*, third its *feasability*, fourth the *involved risks*, and fifth a barely hidden *distrust of US motives*.

Legitimacy

After World War II the legitimacy of reshaping Germany and Japan was for everyone clear and evident. Both countries had started a war against the United States and were defeated. A comparable case for a legitimate regime change in the Middle East would have been Saddam Hussein's Iraq *immediately after his defeat in the Gulf War*. But the US then decided not to remove Saddam to avoid the potential dismemberment of Iraq. Twelve years later the case for regime change in Iraq is less clear. The only legitimate way is a flagrant breach by Iraq of UN resolution 1441. If, however, the US would want to extend its strategy for regime change to other Arab countries or "rogue states," the legitimacy would still be harder to find. What would be the legitimacy, for instance, for a regime change in Iran, Syria, or Libya?

Feasibility

The feasibility of regime change is an other issue. Europeans—the UK government included—consider a war as a solution of the last resort. It should only be considered if there are clear proofs that Saddam Hussein is cheating on his obligations to declare and destroy his weapons of mass destruction. Regime change *as such* is for them not a valid reason to go to war. Containment of Saddam Hussein through a strictly applied international control regime is for them a viable alternative option.

Consistency

Europeans doubt the consistency of the US strategy. An armed intervention in Iraq, far from being considered by the Iraqi and Arab populations as an act of liberation, could easily be interpreted as a new step of US-European imperialism in the region—as long as the Israeli-Palestine conflict has not been solved. If the US really wants to rebuild the Middle East into a region of peace, democracy and prosperity, Europeans argue, it should start to take away this greatest obstacle for peace in the region. The first condition for this is that it must give up its pro-Israel bias and take a genuine impartial position vis-à-vis both parties in the conflict.

Risks

Europeans fear also the risks of an armed conflict in this turbulent part of the world. Their fears are threefold and concern *intra-war risks*, *extra-war risks*, and *post-war risks*. The intra-war risks concern the risks inherent in the war itself. Every war, how well prepared it may be, has its miscalculations and imponderabilia—as the accidental bombing of the Chinese embassy in Belgrade during the Kosovo war has shown. There could, for instance, be an escalation of the conflict when Iraq would attack the invading armies or Israel with weapons of mass destruction. Both the US and Israel have declared not to exclude nuclear retaliation in case of such a WMD attack. And even if one does not think of an escalation of the conflict, there is the possibility that a conventional war could be much longer and protracted than was foreseen. There could be heavy street fighting in Baghdad, leading to a great number of casualties among the civil population, what would cause a general uproar in the region that could menace the moderate Arab regimes.

Extra-war risks are also not to be excluded. These are risks that during the war other armed conflicts will erupt that are not necessarily connected with the war in Iraq. An example of this is the Suez crisis in 1956, when the Soviet Union took advantage of the war in the Middle East to invade Hungary with the other Warsaw Pact members in order to repress the Hungarian revolt. One could think of a new confrontation between Pakistan and India, military adventurism by North Korea, or a stand off between China and Taiwan. Such risks would become greater when the war in Iraq will take longer than was planned for, so that the US will not be capable of giving its full attention to other trouble spots in the world.

Post-war risks concern the situation after the war. These risks will not only be dependent on how the US has won the war (a great number of killed Iraqi civilians will certainly lead to an anti-American backlash in the region), but also on how the US handles the post-war situation. If the US thinks that no generous financial help is necessary and that the rebuilding of Iraq can totally be paid from the latter's oil revenues, or if it thinks that a UN-led peace force does not need a strong US component, this will be a recipe for failure. An other post-war risk is connected with the introduction of a democratic system in Iraq. Jack Snyder has rightly stressed the fact that introducing a western-style democracy and free press in a multi-ethnic country without democratic traditions can easily lead to heightened ethnic tensions.[23] The democratization of Iraq should therefore be a prudent and cautious process.

Distrust of US motives

Last but not least there is a European distrust of American motives. How far can one be certain that the great American design for the Middle East is not really a concealed way to expand US interests? There is the fact that Iraq has the second largest oil reserves in the world. US control of these reserves would make it more independent vis-à-vis its greatest provider, Saudi Arabia, with which its relations have been strained since September 11—due to the Saudi origin of many terrorists. If a friendly regime would replace Saddam Hussein and *a forteriori* if Iraq would thereupon leave OPEC, US oil imports could become much more independent from OPEC, taking also into account the growing role of non-OPEC member Russia as a main provider of the US oil market.[24]

Conclusion

The question is what will happen in the coming years. Will the transatlantic divide further deepen—in the end even threatening the cohesion (and existence) of NATO—or is this divide only the product of specific historical circumstances (September 11) and will many of the disparities and misunderstandings disappear as was so often the case before in transatlantic relations? To answer this question we should differentiate between the various dimensions of this divide. This will teach us that developments do not go everywhere in the same direction. Some of the divisions can be expected to diminish, other divisions, on the contrary, will remain and could even become still deeper.

The Perception Gap: Towards a US-European Convergence?

As concerns US and European divergent perceptions on the nature of the war on terrorism and their vulnerability to the terrorist threat, we may expect a *convergence* to take place. This for two reasons:

1. As times passes by in the US the great trauma of the September 11 attacks will—slowly—heal. The US war fervor will, therefore, loose some of its strength.
2. At the same time Europeans, who might in the beginning have been tempted to underestimate the dangers, are becoming more conscious of the imminent terrorist threat since they dismantled several networks that were preparing attacks in Europe.

The Capabilities Gap and the Growing Political Will in Europe to Bridge this Gap

The transatlantic capabilities gap will certainly remain for at least a decade and a half. Changes can only be expected in the longer run. Two factors should here be taken into consideration:

1. US defense spending has received a supplementary boost after September 11. This extraordinary defense effort is not sustainable in the long run against the background of the growing US budget deficit. The risk of an "imperial overstretch" can even not be excluded—certainly when the cost of a war in Iraq is not paid by the allies or financed from Iraq oil revenues, but has to be paid by the US itself.
2. In recent years Europeans have become increasingly aware of the capabilities gap and are prepared to take action. They took already the initiative for a European Security and Defense Policy. European defense cooperation will get a new boost in the Convention on the Future of Europe that prepares a European Constitution. Plans are on the table to create a Europeans Armaments Agency and a European Defence Research Agency that might attract a part of the € 4.4 bn annual EU research budget (until now defence research is excluded from direct EU funding). The Convention is also expected to remove article 27b of the Nice Treaty that forbids enhanced cooperation of a group of member states in the field of

defense.[25] We may, therefore, soon after EU enlargement see the emergence of a vanguard group or "core Europe"[26] that will work closely together in the field of defense. Americans have often underestimated the European project. They did so when the euro was introduced. They should not make the same mistake today. The European drive to create their own defense and diminish their dependence on the US should be taken serious.

The Attitude Gap: Will the US Stick to its "Multilateralism à la carte"?

What will happen with the "attitude gap" between Europeans and Americans? Will the disposition of the US toward unilateral action and its predilection for military solutions grow or, on the contrary, will it diminish and come closer to the multilateral approach and the search for diplomatic solutions that are so dear to the Europeans? In fact there are here two opposed tendencies:

1. Its military supremacy will quite naturally push the US administration to prefer unilateral positions and military solutions
2. At the same time there are pressures inside the administration, especially from the State Department, and from the European allies to take a more multilateral approach.

Until now both tendencies seemed to be kept in a delicate balance. The US went to the Security Council before launching an attack on Iraq. At the same time it did not exclude to attack Iraq without a second resolution. The Bush administration will certainly stick to this policy and act multilaterally only in those cases that enable it to achieve its objectives. If US objectives run the risk to be thwarted by a multilateral approach, the temptation will be great to act unilaterally. This *multilateralism à la carte* will certainly not satisfy the European allies and it is also a far cry from the genuine multilateralism that is advocated by Joseph S. Nye Jr., former Assistant Secretary of Defense in the Clinton administration.[27]

The Value Gap

The same can be said on the value gap. "Multilateralism à la carte" will only give an *opportunistic* respect for international law. Europeans and Americans will, therefore, continue to disagree on core values.

The Religion Gap

The religious fervor in the United States has strong societal roots and needs therefore a sociological explanation. The presence of many sects and the simultaneous absence of a monopolistic religion in the US have prevented a power conflict between the state and the church from emerging, as was the case in France or Germany (*Kulturkampf*). In the US the separation of state and religion is therefore less strict than in Europe. Religion will continue to play an important role in America—also in politics. According to some authors the influence of the Christian Right has reached its apogee in the Bush administration and the movement would be already in decline.[28] This is, however, an optimist estimation. One thing is certain: the religious influence on politics will continue during the presidency of George W. Bush, and equally so during an eventual second term. For Europeans this is a worrying situation. They would welcome the moment when the inhabitant of the White House will be more inspired by pragmatist statesmanship than by fundamentalist Christian zeal. It would make US policy in their eyes more predictable and reliable.

The Strategy Gap

Will "regime change" and an interventionist "remake" of the Arab world remains a US objective in the coming years? If so, the "strategy gap" between the US and its European allies will not disappear because of the European reluctance to support this strategy. In the case of a successful regime change in Iraq, there are several options open for the US. A successful removal of Saddam Hussein could enhance its appetite for regime changes elsewhere. It could, on the other hand, also lead the US to refrain from further interventions if the task of rebuilding Iraq would prove much more difficult and complicated than foreseen, necessitating an American military and financial engagement for many years. In this case, a second term of George W. Bush—if there is such a second term—could be a quieter and less interventionist period than his first term.

Notes

1   The proposal for the new strategy had been transmitted to Congress on September 20, 2002. Francis Fukuyama was one of the first to mention this option in an article in the *Financial Times*, four days after the attacks: "A war against terrorism means defeating your enemy militarily, which may require striking pre-emptively against those who threaten you (...)." Francis Fukuyama, "The United State," *The Financial Times*, September 15–16, 2001.

2   Cf. Richard Wolffe, "The Bush Doctrine," *The Financial Times*, June 21, 2002. Wolffe makes the point that "if other nations, such as India and Pakistan, adopted pre-emption, the risk of nuclear war would rise sharply (...)." Fukuyama, therefore, writes, one year later: "Washington owes the rest of the world an elucidation not just of its new doctrine of preemption, but of what the limits of that doctrine will be." (Francis Fukuyama, "U.S. vs. Them," *The Washington Post*, September 11, 2002).

3   Cf. Stephen G. Brooks and William C. Wohlforth, "American Primacy in Perspective," in *Foreign Affairs*, Vol. 81, No. 4, July/August 2002, pp. 20-33. Cf. also John Mearsheimer, *The Tragedy of Great Power Politics*, New York-London (W.W. Norton & Company, 2001), 381: "But the international system is not unipolar. Although the United States is a hegemon in the Western Hemisphere, it is not a global hegemon. Certainly, the United States is the preponderant economic and military power in the world, but there are two other great powers in the international system: China and Russia."

4   But the US has the fastest growing population of all developed countries, due to the combined effects of immigration and a high birth rate. Fred Halliday expects that the 275 million US population will more than double in this century: "By 2100 there will, it is estimated, be 571 million Americans." *The World at 2000* (Palgrave: Basingstoke and New York, 2001), 92.

5   SIPRI puts US defence spending in 2001 at US$ 281.4bn. This roughly equals the defence spending of the next big nine spenders. (SIPRI Yearbook 2002, Appendix 6A.)

6   Robert Kagan, "Power and Weakness," in: *Policy Review*, No. 113, June 2002. See also Robert Kagan, "The US-Europe Divide," *The Washington Post*, May 16, 2002.

7   Francis Fukuyama, "The West may be Cracking," *International Herald Tribune*, August 9, 2002.

8   Francis Fukuyama, "The US-Europe Divide," op. cit.

9   Francis Fukuyama, "U.S. vs. Them," op. cit.

10   Saskia Sassen, for instance, stresses the fact that human rights law plays a greater role in Europe than in the United States: "This growing authority of human rights law is particularly evident in Europe. It was not until the 1980s that such law began to exert significant influence in the United States, where it still does not carry the weight it has in Europe." (Saskia Sassen, *Losing Control – Sovereignty in an Age of Globalization*, Columbia University Press: New York/Chichester, 2001, 98.)

11   We have, of course, to differentiate between Democratic and Republican governments. Where the former tend to defend progressive values (democracy, human rights, and economic, racial and gender equality), the latter tend to concentrate on conservative values ("family values," "law and order," "the nation").

12   "On trouve çà et là, au sein de la société américaine, des âmes toutes remplies d'un spiritualisme exalté et presque farouche, qu'on ne rencontre guère en Europe. Il s'élève de temps à autre des sectes bizarres qui s'efforcent de s'ouvrir des chemins extraordinaires vers le bonheur éternel. Les folies religieuses y sont fort communes." Alexis de Tocqueville, *De la Démocratie en Amérique*, Tome 2, Paris 1981, chapter XII, 169.

13   Cf. Sara Diamond, "*The Christian Right Seeks Dominion—On the Road to Political Power & Theocracy*," www.publiceye.org/eyes/sd_theo.html.

14   "The election of Ronald Reagan brought "Christian Zionism" deeper into the White House: Lindsey (an evangelical writer, M.H.v.H.) served as a consultant on Middle East affairs to the Pentagon and the Israeli government. Interior Secretary James Watt, a Pentecostalist, in discussing environmental concerns, observed: "I don't know how

many future generations we can count on until the Lord returns." Secretary of Defence Caspar Weinberger affirmed, "I have read the Book of Revelation, and, yes, I believe the world is going to end—by an act of God, I hope—but every day I think time is running out." It was no accident that Reagan made his "evil empire" speech at a meeting of the National Association of Evangelicals." (Nancy Gibbs, "And Finally: The Bible and the Apocalypse," in: *Time Magazine*, June 23, 2002.)

15 Sara Diamand, ibid. p.1: "In 1980, when Reagan won with only 26 percent of the eligible electorate, white evangelical voters accounted for two-thirds of Reagan's ten-pont lead over Jimmy Carter." "In 1992, despite Bush's defeat, exit poll data showed that there were only two constituencies consistently loyal to the Republican Party: people with incomes over USD 200,000 a year, who are few in number, and the Christian Right." With Bush in the White House, God is as much as ever at the heart of the American political project. The president starts each day kneeling in prayer, he has told Christian friends. His earliest executive orders called for a national day of prayer and a faith-based war on want. He says he reads a passage of the bible each day and mentioned last year that he was also reading daily devotionals of Oswald Chambers, the Scottish-born Christian thinker, and Billy Graham, the favourite evangelical of modern American presidents." (James Harding, "Preaching to the converted," in: *The Financial Times*, January 4–5, 2003).

16 "The line between church and state grows fuzzier each year—from the creation of George W. Bush's Office of Faith-Based Organisations last year to a recently defeated congressional bill that would have allowed religious leaders to discuss politics in public without endangering the tax-exempt status of their organisations" (Betty Lu, "US politicians getting wary of playing the religious card," in: *The Financial Times*, October 30, 2002).

17 Cf. Johan Galtung, *USAs utenrikspolitikk—En fortsettelse av teologi med andre midler (USA's Foreign Policy—The Continuation of Theology with other Means)*, Oslo, 2000.

18 Judy Dempsey, "Solana laments rift between Europe and "religious" US," in: *The Financial Times*, January 8, 2003.

19 Ibid.

20 Cf. Alain Frachon and Daniel Vernet, "L'école néo-impérialiste américaine," in: *Le Monde*, 19 September 2002.

21 "During Roosevelt's presidency, the United States intervened in Haiti, fostered a revolution in Panama that led to its secession from Colombia and laid the basis for the completion of the Panama Canal, established a financial protectorate over the Dominican Republic, and, in 1906, sent American troops to occupy Cuba." (Henry Kissinger, *Does America Need a Foreign Policy? Toward a Diplomacy for the 21st Century*, Simon& Schuster: New York/London, 2001, 241).

22 Cf. Philip Stephens, "America's noble but foolish designs for the Middle East," in: *The Financial Times*, November 22, 2002.

23 According to Snyder "…there are strong indications that nascent democratisation and its close cousin, press liberalization, heighten the risk of nationalist and ethnic conflict in our own time, just as they have historically" (Jack Snyder, *From Voting to Violence – Democratization and Nationalist Conflict*, W.W. Norton & Company, New York/London, 2000, 31.)

24 Cf. Edward L. Morse and James Richard, "The Battle for Energy Dominance," in: *Foreign Affairs*, Vol. 81, No. 2, March/April 2002, 16–31.

25 This article was added on the initiative of the British government that feared that Britain would be excluded from an avantgarde of eurozone countries, led by France and Germany, that would take an initiative on defense.
26 The first proposal for such a European avantgarde or "core Europe" (Kerneuropa) was made by a group of German Christian Democrats in 1994. Cf. Schäuble/Lamers, *Überlegungen zur europäischen Politik (Reflections on European Policy)*, Bonn, 1 September 1994.
27 Cf. Joseph S. Nye Jr., *The Paradox of American Power—Why the World's Only Superpower Can't Go It Alone*, Oxford University Press, 2002, 158: "Multilateralism involves costs, but in the larger picture, they are outweighed by the benefits. International rules bind the United States and limit our freedom of action in the short term, but they also serve our interest by binding others as well. Americans should use our power now to shape institutions that will serve our long-term national interest in promoting international order."
28 Cf. Betty Lu, "US politicians getting wary of playing the religious card," op. cit.: "The Christian Coalition with 1.5m members, is still the most powerful religious grassroots organisation, representing the equally powerful electorate of Americans who call themselves Christian conservatives. And yet observers note the coalition is no longer the force it once was."

PART IV:
"WAR ON TERRORISM": REGIONAL AND GLOBAL RAMIFICATIONS

Chapter 12

Central Asia and the West After September 11

Robert M. Cutler[1]

To see Central Asia in perspective, it is useful to bear in mind no fewer than seven scales of analysis, even if one focuses on only a few of them at a time. This chapter does not address all of them, but still a comprehensive point of departure is the best. The first and finest scale of analysis is the national scale—i.e., state level—of analysis where each of the Central Asian countries may be taken separately. (This scale of analysis may also be considered to subsume a yet finer scale, that which analyzes sub-national differentiations such as the contrast between northern and southern Kazakhstan.) Second, more broadly, there is the regional scale of Central Asia itself, which takes the five former Soviet republics together as a whole and also considers their transnational cultural and demographic interrelationships. Third, the "macro-region" we may call Greater Central Asia includes "political" Central Asia (i.e., the five former Soviet republics) plus their cultural and increasing economic connections with such neighboring regions as western China, southern Russia (including southern Siberia), northern Afghanistan, and northeastern Iran.

Fourth is the "meta-regional" scale of Central Eurasia, a still broader construct. Although "Central Eurasia" is sometimes used as a shorthand-designation of the former Soviet territory, it is more apposite to define that it "include[s] Turkic, Mongolian, Iranian, Caucasian, Tibetan and other peoples [, and] extends from the Black Sea region, the Crimea, and the Caucasus in the west, through the Middle Volga region, Central Asia and Afghanistan, and on to Siberia, Mongolia and Tibet in the east."[2] Conceived thus in a broader historical and cultural sense, Central Eurasia (like Greater Central Asia) includes swathes of Russia and China but not necessarily the whole of both countries. However, these latter are fully integrated at a fifth, "mega-regional" scale of analysis, including not only all of Russia and China but also the whole of South and Southwest Asia from India and Pakistan through Iraq and Turkey, and to which we may refer simply as Eurasia. A sixth scale of analysis is Greater Eurasia, which includes the whole of geographic Eurasia proper, from Spain to Sakhalin and Spitzbergen to Singapore, including the European Union and its family of institutions. Finally, the seventh scale of analysis is the global scale, which adds the United States, transnational corporations with a global reach, and worldwide international organizations having especially an economic, industrial or financial vocation.

It is hardly necessary to treat all these scales of analysis together, although it is useful to employ the first and the seventh together so as to anchor any discussion. The present chapter, for example, uses reference to the first and the seventh so as to anchor a discussion focusing on the fourth, fifth, and sixth.[3] These "scales" of analysis differ, both in conception and in application, from what are traditionally "levels" of analysis in international relations. These differences means that they are not in reality stacked upon each other in a mechanistic manner, even though it is convenient to discuss them sequentially for expository purposes. Because they are not strictly hierarchical, it also means that they are not "nested."[4] Rather, as in any "complex system," these scales of analysis overlap; and what one sees depends upon where one stands.[5] The first three sections of this chapter look at Central Asia respectively in the context of the Central Eurasian, Greater Eurasian, and global scales. On that basis, the fourth section examines Central Asia and international order after the Cold War; and the fifth section concludes with a practical discussion of prospective relations between Central Asia and the West in the twenty-first century.

Central Asia seen at the Central Eurasian Scale

In 1995 Uzbekistan, as part of its recurrent diplomatic competition with Kazakhstan, had won official designation as a "strategic partner" of the United States. After Kazakhstan was granted the same honor a few years later, Uzbekistan replied by joining the GUAM (Georgia–Uzbekistan–Azerbaijan–Moldova) entente, turning it into GUUAM. In line with this turn away from Russia, Uzbekistan left the CIS Collective Security Treaty in May 1999. However, after the February 1999 Tashkent bombings were followed in summer by incursions from the Taliban-backed Islamic Movement of Uzbekistan (IMU), Russia's profile increased. At the time, Russia appeared to be the only great power that would send troops to Central Asia to fight militants who might threaten the regimes in power there, and Uzbekistan in the first instance. Thus during President Vladimir Putin's December 1999 visit to Tashkent, Uzbekistan's President Islam Karimov publicly declared his recognition of "Russia's interests in

Uzbekistan," and anti-Russian propaganda in the country's mass media was subsequently toned down.[6] U.S. Secretary of State Madeleine Albright visited Tashkent in April 2000 during a whirlwind tour of Central Asian capitals, but when Putin followed her a month later, Karimov went still further than his already strong December 1999 statement and declared that there was no discrepancy whatsoever between Uzbekistan's strategic view of Central Asia and Russia's.[7]

Uzbekistan did not participate in the "Shanghai-5," as it was then called, when this group was set up in 1996 among China, Russia, Kazakhstan, Kyrgyzstan, and Tajikistan. This was because the group focused at the time on delimiting and demilitarizing the China-CIS border, and Uzbekistan has no border with China. In the late 1990s, the Shanghai-5 shifted its focus to address Islamic militancy. Its August 1999 Bishkek summit reached an agreement on fighting terrorism. Part of that agreement involved setting up an anti-terrorist center in Bishkek itself, eventually to host a joint Sino-Russian rapid deployment force. This center, which the CIS decided would serve to coordinate its own activities in the field as well, has not yet been established. Although Karimov did not attend the August 1999 summit of the Shanghai-5, he let his interest in cooperation be known in early 2000.[8]

In June 2001, with Uzbekistan in attendance as a new member, the Shanghai grouping institutionalized itself as Shanghai Cooperation Organization (SCO), a self-standing international organization with an autonomous secretariat first planned for Shanghai but in June 2002 established in Beijing.[9] For Uzbekistan to join SCO looked in mid-2001 like part of the ongoing consolidation of regional international systems, in the context of the emergence of a networked global international system following the end of the post-Cold War transition. It seemed that Central Asia would be divided between competing Russian and Chinese spheres of influence, the latter seeking to expand westward from Xinjiang but also potentially threatening Russia interests through illegal immigration to Siberia in addition to Central Asia. At the SCO's founding meeting, China's deputy foreign minister responsible for SCO affairs emphasized to the gathered international press and diplomats that Beijing intended to use the organization to promote trade and investment in its search for influence over Central Asia. Indeed, although Afghanistan was not an SCO member, a Chinese delegation was in Kabul on 11 September 2001 to sign a long-term economic and technical cooperation agreement with the Taliban regime.

These changes in great-power politics in Central Asia are not set in concrete. But by unfreezing the earlier-emergent Sino-Russian joint hegemony over Central Asia, the U.S. has also opened up the reconnections between Central Asia on the one hand, and, on the other hand, South and Southwest Asia. Consequently, Uzbekistan is confirmed as the geopolitical pivot, and Central Asia as the shatterbelt, of the broad Eurasian landmass. Demographic and economic realities would have led to this development in about two decades, regardless of Afghanistan. Now, however, its criticality is being made manifest earlier than one might have anticipated, and therefore under different circumstances. This offers the countries concerned a respite from the earlier emerging Sino-Russian vise-grip, and chance in the early twenty-first century finally to implement serious moves towards economic reform and democratization.

Central Asia seen at the Greater Eurasian Scale

On 11 September 2001, all indicators were that Russia and China were reaching an understanding that would have set the framework for geopolitical realities in Central Asia for the next several decades. Two indicators of understanding, which has not necessarily fully been sundered, are salient. First is the bilateral treaty signed in summer 2000; second is the two countries' cooperation in the Shanghai Cooperation Organization (SCO).

The new Sino-Russian treaty only codifies bilateral relations that have been developing for over five years. It includes provisions not only for combating Islamic militancy in Central Asia, but also for increasing Russian arms sales to China, including advanced technology transfers, and the exchange of military training (up to two thousand Chinese officers to attend Russian military schools yearly). In fact, before the treaty in the early 1990s, Russian arms sales to China averaged one billion dollars per year. This figure more than doubled before the decade ended. China is following the old Soviet strategy of importing (or stealing) foreign technology to create "pockets of excellence" in its own weapons development programs. This has important consequences for China's ability to impose its own political will on Asia.[10]

Indeed, China's strategic weapons development and deployment program uncannily resembles the Soviet strategy in the late 1970s that led to the dangerous tactic of putting medium-range SS–20 missiles in Eastern Europe. These were not able to reach the U.S. but they were capable of striking West European capitals in a matter of minutes. The purpose was to sow fear among West European elites and terror among their publics, paralyzing the political will to Moscow's political, diplomatic and military move in Europe. Both the June 2000 founding of the SCO and the July

2000 bilateral treaty allowed Russia and China to demonstrate their agreement on fundamental issues of international politics, particularly the question of relations with United States.

In the SCO, Russia's interest was originally to represent itself as Asia's interlocutor with the United States. Indeed, the first Bush-Putin meeting, in Ljubljana in summer 2000, took place only two days after the end of the SCO's founding conference as an international institution (transforming itself from having been a loose grouping). The SCO also intended to create of a joint rapid deployment force at an "anti-terrorism center" in Bishkek, Kyrgyzstan. Such an anti-terrorist center was planned to function as a joint coordinating center for the SCO and the CIS, raising the specter, in some minds, of Chinese and Russian troops eventually stationed together in Central Asia at the core of a military and political bloc. That joint center has yet to be established, although Russian troops recently were stationed at an airfield near Bishkek.[11]

Central Asia seen at the Global Scale

Russia and China were deep in the process of establishing a strategic condominium ("joint rule") over Central Asian affairs, when the sudden and perhaps long-term U.S. military presence in the region interfered, in the wake of the attack on the World Trade Center. But to grasp the full significance of this unexpected development, a look back to the 1990s is necessary. The decade of the 1990s was a transitional period from the late Cold War system of international relations to a new system being born before our eyes. The first half of the decade witnessed the breakdown of old structures, especially in Central Eurasia and Central Asia in particular, not least of which was the final disintegration of the Soviet Union. The second half of the decade saw the incipient consolidation of certain trends that had begun to emerge already in the first half of the decade.

However, this is 2003. Not only would no one argue that the disappearance of the USSR reestablishes the *status quo ante*. The U.S.–Soviet bipolarity was not even the only significant characteristic of the international system during the last half of the twentieth century. Of equal if not greater importance in the long run was the dissolution of the British and French Empires. Without this development, regional systems of international relations would have been unable proliferate in Eurasia after 1991. In fact, such regional systems of international relations, with increasing relative autonomy of the dominant bipolar system, began to appear in evidence in other parts of the world in the 1980s.

This is no surprise to people familiar with complex systems. (This term is used in its technical-scientific, not its ordinary-language or even social-science academic sense.) New complex systems may be formed from the recombination of parts or aspects of other complex systems. Indeed, such composites permit rapid evolution. The "system-dominant" bipolarity of the late Cold War era, and its exclusive focus on military capabilities, obscures such developments in retrospect even though they were widely commented and analyzed at the time. From the early 1970s and throughout the 1980s, a system we might call Multipolar Interdependence (most notable in the economic and increasingly in the financial realms of international affairs) came to be adjoined to the bipolar Cold War system inherited from the 1950s and 1960s.[12]

Only the decolonization of the British and French Empires made possible the explosion of variety in international affairs that occurred in the 1990s. The increased worldwide levels of literacy, education, economic well-being, communication, and political participation make it much more difficult even for the new American dominance to succeed in neutralizing such mobilization, much less in reducing it to its 1948 level. The greatest danger, as we have seen, is that it this mobilization acquires a hostile profile. Such a consolidation of anti-American sentiment will not distinguish between the United States and Europe, but instead lump them together. Such a view is in fact hard to dispute from the standpoint of the *longue durée*. Looking back at the second half of the second millennium, it is entirely justified to regard North and South America together with Europe from the Atlantic to the Urals as a socio-cultural Renaissance/ Enlightenment bloc in world history.

The terrorist attack in New York on 11 September 2001 did not change the world. However, it did accentuate and intensify a trend in U.S. domestic and foreign affairs whose advocates had been struggling for influence over national policy throughout the 1990s. The terrorist attack presented an "opportunity" for the U.S. to attempt to constrain the complexity of the emerging international system as a whole by shifting international focus to the relatively narrow, but no less significant, issue-area of "anti-terrorism." Since then, the U.S. has made consistent and persuasive, indeed unremitting, attempts to reduce many other items on the international political and economic agenda to an anti-terrorist essence. In this way, current American international behavior represents a return to Cold War styles of thinking and acting, even if developments in technology and communications have radically changed their implementation. The "Son of Star Wars" program is an epitome of the continuity.[13]

Central Asia and the International Order after the Cold War

The events of 11 September 2001 motivated a realignment of Russia's foreign policy towards the West, meaning not only Europe but also the U.S. (which had been in doubt). As such, they clarify an important ambiguity arising out of the disintegration of the Soviet bloc and the Soviet Union. Indeed, it is necessary to distinguish analytically between the disintegration of the Soviet bloc and that of the Soviet Union: we may refer to them in shorthand, respectively, as "1989" and "1991." The ambiguity arises from the fact that 1989 would mark the years 1989-2001 as a transition to a normatively new international order characterized by a succession of international systems, themselves animated by the tension between unipolarity and multipolarity. The year 1991, on the other hand, would mark the hiatus 1991-2001 as a transition to another bipolar system within a "Long Twentieth Century" international order.[14]

What events suggested that the international transition of the 1990s was a transition to another bipolar international system rather than to a new international order (the "1991" interpretation)? Trends in Russian foreign policy the mid- and late 1990s suggested a new emergent bipolarity, coming from a disaffection of Russian public opinion with the West in general and the United States in particular, and a turning of Russian elite opinion towards Asia. Indeed, Russian diplomacy seemed to replicate patterns in its decline from great power status after defeat in the Crimean War. After losing Crimea in the mid-nineteenth century, Russia turned its attention to Poland, the Pacific coast (now meaning and including China as well as Japan) plus south and southwest Asia, and the Balkans. That was the same pattern that Russian diplomacy was following before Putin, with minor emendations: Poland had become Poland/Lithuania/Baltics, and the Pacific coast now included China and Japan. The orientations were regionalized but the pattern was remarkably similar. Such a revision to an old pattern had created the basis for continued bipolarity in Europe, providing a foothold on the Continent for a Russocentric geopolitical pole opposing the Euro-Atlantic community on a global scale.

To take the year 1989 as a cutpoint, on the other hand, makes it a marker of the end of bipolarity, a specifically Cold War bipolarity moreover not European in origin but rather projected into Europe (and the developing world) by the ideological and great-power confrontation between the U.S. and the Soviet Union as superpowers in the second half of the twentieth century. In fact, the bipolar structure of the Cold War began to evaporate before 1991, with Gorbachev's 1988-89 doctrinal innovations already dissipating ideological conflict. In this view the post-1989 unification of Europe under NATO/EU then becomes, on the global level, analogous to the unification of Germany under Bismarck on the European level. Following Bismarck's exit from European diplomacy, tension arose from his successor's failure to respect a balance of interests with Austria, and in particular from their projection of German interests into the eastern Mediterranean and southwest Asia. The structural analogue to this development in the contemporary era is the disregard, if not sometimes scorn, with which American diplomacy increasingly dismisses European interests in that very same region, superposing its own upon them. The American projection of interests yet further into Central and Southwest Asia is the early twenty-first century analogue to the German projection of economic and geo-strategic interests into the Balkans and Asia Minor towards the end of the nineteenth century.

Just as the rebirth of the Holy Alliance (in the form of the Three Emperor's League) followed Bismarck's passage from the scene in 1890, so we now have a reversion to NATO in the form of enlarged-NATO-plus-PFP. Indeed, just as an ineffectual Quadruple Alliance was as like a superstructure to the Holy Alliance, so an ineffectual OSCE is superstructure to the new NATO/EU. If one follows this reasoning, then, the years 1989-2001 were a transition not just to a new international system but indeed to a new international order, an order that will be animated by the tension between unipolarity and multipolarity just as the European system was so animated from 1890 to 1914, and like it resolving into a bipolarity.

What then should we expect from such a perspective? The Concert of Europe hid an ideological (i.e., normative) opposition—republicanism *vs.* autocracy—that later came to the fore as the principal structural basis for the geopolitical bipolarization (the Triple Alliance versus the Triple Entente) that led to the First World War. If we project into the future a pattern similar to the bipolarization of the European alliance system that followed Bismarck's disappearance from the diplomatic scene in the late nineteenth century, then we should anticipate: (1) that the contemporary "postmodernization" of the Enlightenment (i.e., its end as an era) will become the basis for a system-wide ideological bipolarization as was evident between England and Russia but covered over by the Concert of Europe; (2) that this bipolarization will become increasingly evident towards the middle of the twenty-first century as a now-emerging multipolarity, seeking to counter American unipolarity, disintegrates; and (3) that the unipolarity-*vs.*-multipolarity tension now characterizing international affairs will be replaced by a new bipolarity such as emerged in the 1890s and led to the First World War.[15]

What none of those projections suggests, is who the contending parties will be. However, let us try to guess. It is possible, without endorsing Huntington's "clash of civilizations" thesis, to uphold the idea that one geopolitical (or geo-cultural) bloc now consolidating itself is clearly Euro-Atlantic. Any emergent Asiatic geo-cultural unification could be the catalyst for a system-wide restructuring in the middle of the twenty-first century, reducing into a more bipolar framework the now-emerging multipolarity. In fact, this unification need not even be political like Bismarck's of Germany; it may be transnational and social. Will Central (and Southwest) Asia lean to the "East" or to the "West"? If the major blocs in the twenty-first century will be geo-cultural (which is not the same as their being civilizational), then the centrality of Central and Southwest Asia becomes evident.

Thus Central and Southwest Asia together represent a potentially emergent entity, where cultural evolution may later influence the normative bases of any future international order and play a critical role in determining the identities of the actors (including alliances and coalitions) in any future international system. In this context, the conflict with Iraq represents an American attempt to pre-empt hegemony over a strategic part of Eurasia, not just to motivate a political transformation of autocratic Muslim regimes, but moreover thereby to socialize their next political generation and so deny their populations, as a geopolitical resource, to Chinese influence later in the twenty-first century.

Conclusion: Central Asia and the West in the Twenty-First Century

Tautological as it sounds, the geopolitical significance for Central Asia, of the strong U.S. military presence in southwest Asia, is the on-the-ground foothold that it gives the American military in the region. Certainly China views the U.S. presence as a hindrance to its strategic objectives of dominating the region. Beijing and a number of European capitals believe that the U.S. does not have the staying power or dedication or focus to remain in the region for a long time. It is quite possible that such a view is wrong. But it is indisputable that even the current, relatively short-term presence has monkey-wrenched the impending closure of Sino-Russian hegemony over Central Asia and, still more significantly, motivated the beginning of a rapprochement between Moscow and Washington. Moscow tacitly recognizes, if no one else does, that Washington has basically solved, at least for the time being, the problem of Islamism and the CIS's porous southern border.[16]

It is not unusual to find references to Central Asia as the "backyard" of, variously, Russia or the United States, or even China. However, the seemingly neutral analogy of a "backyard" carries cultural and spatio-temporal baggage. To speak of Central Asia as a "backyard" evokes the neatly mown lawns of early twentieth-century small-town America or its post-World War Two suburban orderliness and middleclass conformity. But Central Asia is not a backyard; vast reaches of it will remain forever a hinterland: the difference is significant. A hinterland—literally a "behind-land"—is neither so well defined nor well manicured. It extends indefinitely beyond an ill-defined boundary. A more Anglo-American equivalent of "hinterland" is "back country": think rather of a settlement along a riverbank, behind which there is wooded land where flourish other forms of life having the effrontery to consider the domain their own. The more one seeks to domesticate a hinterland and transform it into a backyard, the more acute and inevitable becomes the confrontation with the increasingly agitated autochthones. Such an extended metaphor is not a useless reflection of the rise of Islamic fundamentalism. Accreted as it is around the conceptual nucleus of Lockean appropriation, it is all the more apposite as an image of Western ingress into what was once called Inner Asia. But that does not mean that it is a model to be emulated.[17]

So has the global anti-terrorist coalition formed by American diplomacy in the wake of September 11 rendered obsolete and meaningless the Sino-Russian rapprochement marked by the creation of the SCO and the bilateral treaty signed earlier this year? Hardly. Rather, it is necessary to recognize that this rapprochement is oriented not only against Washington's best intentions (not to speak of its "interests") but also against the interests of people living in Asia. It favors only the interests of the Russian and Chinese military-industrial elites and their representatives in the national political executives. No U.S.-sponsored "war on terrorism" will change this hard fact, which, after the overthrow of the Taliban regime, is perhaps today the greatest long-term threat to Central Asian stability from outside the region.

The greatest long-term threat to Central Asian stability from within the region as a whole is to be found in Uzbekistan. The increasing destitution of Uzbekistan's larger population and their lack of either political or economic freedoms, combined with the country's situation as a geopolitical key to both Central Asia and the broader international environment, becomes a cauldron of discontent. The appearance of the Islamic Movement of Uzbekistan in the late 1990s was a symptom of this syndrome. Uzbekistan is also key to a growing security schism within Central Asia itself, separating itself and Turkmenistan (which may be grouped together geopolitically despite their recent bilateral diplomatic conflicts) from Kazakhstan and Kyrgyzstan, with Tajikistan falling in between.

The presence of ethnic Uzbeks in Kyrgyzstan and Taijikistan in particular, together with a regional foreign-policy profile that is hard to describe as conflict-averse, makes Uzbekistan a security problem externally as well as internally.[18] Uzbekistan does not fall easily in to any local sphere of influence—be this Russian, Chinese, Turkish, or Iranian—but it does have a special relationship with the United States. Indeed, the U.S. recognizes the acuteness of the domestic situation in Uzbekistan and has for years been pushing President Karimov to marketize and democratize, yet without much success. The entrenched elite gains too much from the status quo and fears to lose too much from significant change.[19]

The formation of a U.S.-sponsored "global anti-terrorist coalition" has not undercut the basis for the Sino-Russian rapprochement signaled by the signature of their bilateral friendship treaty and the institutionalization of the SCO. These developments favor the interests of the Russian and Chinese military-industrial elites and their representatives in the national political executives. As such, they are oriented against the interests of the peoples of Central Asia. Insofar as NATO intends or decides to enhance its profile in Central Asia, maintaining a long-term and increasingly influential presence in the region, the challenge before it is to do more than promote the "war on terrorism" in the region.[20]

As the same, time the current marginalization, indeed exclusion, of the publics in Central Asia from influence upon their own fates will not last forever. Although indigenous North American peoples were eliminated as political contenders in the nineteenth century, nevertheless they have in South America emerged since 1991—in alliance with the economically disadvantaged strata in Brazil, Venezuela, and Argentina—as among the most important actors determining their countries' political course not only domestically but moreover internationally. This development should stand as a warning against the myopia of any view that seeks to minimize the significance of the Central Asian citizenries in their national political life. The continual acceleration of history in our era means that they will become important within the professional lifetimes of current observers of the scene.

It is perhaps therefore proper that the existing doctrine and practice of "cooperative security" receives renewed emphasis. With the United States fixated upon the military and strategic instruments for executing the "war on terrorism," NATO might organize itself and the international community—and its European members should lobby the EU—so to offer specific, well-considered assistance in realms that go well beyond purely military issues. This is the only way to persuade the citizenries and future elites of the Central Asian countries that NATO's relations with the region can be to common long-term advantage. The explicit declaration and pursuit of such a focus will be the only and most persuasive evidence that the West's interests in the region differ at all qualitatively from Russia's and especially China's focus on cajoling the elites currently in power through constant psychological pressure so as to appropriate choice sectors of their national economies.

Notes

1   Dr. Robert M. Cutler <rmc@alum.mit.edu> <http://www.robertcutler.org> is Research Fellow, Institute of European and Russian Studies, Carleton University, Canada. All URLs (web addresses) are verified to be correct as of 25 February 2003.
2   Central Eurasian Studies Society, "About CESS," <http://cess.fas.harvard.edu/CESSpg_org_info.html>.
3   For a complementary analysis, which uses the first and the seventh scales to anchor a more extended discussion of the second, third, and fourth, see Robert M. Cutler, "Energy Networks, Economic Development, and Political Sustainability in Central Asia," Journal of International Affairs 56 (Winter 2003): in press.
4   For a discussion of what does and does not make games nested, see George Tsebelis, *Nested Games: Rational Choice in Comparative Politics* (Berkeley and Los Angeles: University of California Press, 1990).
5   Robert M. Cutler, "Complexity Science and Knowledge-Creation in International Relations Theory," in *Institutional and Infrastructural Resources*, in *Encyclopedia of Life Support Systems* (Oxford: EOLSS Publishers for UNESCO, 2002), <http://www.eolss.net>.
6   "Uzbek–Russian Positions Coincide, Uzbek Head Tells Russian Premier," *Uzland News*, 18 December 1999, <http://www.uzland.uz/news/12_18_99.htm#putin5>.
7   "Uzbek–Russian Presidents Hold News Conference in Uzbek Capital," *Uzland News*, 20 May 2000, <http://www.uzland.uz/2000/05_20.htm#putin13>.
8   Gregory Gleason, "Inter-State Cooperation in Central Asia from the CIS to the Shanghai Forum," *Europe–Asia Studies* 53 (November 2001): 1077–95.
9   See "Declaration of Shanghai Cooperation Organization," *People's Daily*, 15 June 2001, <http://english.peopledaily.com.cn/200106/15/print20010615_72738.html>.
10 Stephen J. Blank, "Military Capabilities of the People's Republic of China," Testimony to the Armed Services Committee, U.S. House of Representatives, 19 July 2000.
11 L[iz] F[uller], "Russia Deploys Fighters at Airbase in Kyrgyzstan," *RFE/RL Newsline*, 3 December 2002.
12 For fuller discussion of these and subsequent points, see Robert M. Cutler, "The Complex Evolution of International Orders and the Current International Transition," *InterJournal*, Article 255 (1999), <http://www.interjournal.org/cgi-bin/manuscript_abstract.cgi?38855>. Compare Hedley Bull and Adam Watson (eds.), *The Expansion of International Society* (London: Oxford University Press, 1984).
13 John Lewis Gaddis, *Strategies of Containment: A Critical Appraisal of Postwar American National Security Policy* (London: Oxford University Press, 1982); for

interesting afterthoughts, see Gaddis, "Strategies of Containment, Past and Future," *Hoover Digest*, 2001, No. 2, <http://wwwhoover.stanford.edu/ publications/ digest/ 012/gaddis.html>.

14   Compare Ian Clark, *Reform and Resistance in the International Order* (Cambridge: Cambridge University Press, 1980); Cutler, "The Complex Evolution of International Orders and the Current International Transition"; James G. March and Johan P. Olsen, "The Institutional Dynamics of International Orders," *International Organization*, 52 (Autumn 1998): 943–69; Hendryk Spruyt, "Institutional Selection in International Relations," *International Organization*, 48 (Autumn 1994); 527–57.

15   Compare Michael Mastanduno, "Preserving the Unipolar Moment: Realist Theories and U.S. Grand Strategy after the Cold War," *International Security*, 21:4 (Spring 1997), 49–88.

16   Compare Lincoln Bloomfield, "Competing 21st Century Threats: Scenarios and Realities," in Willem J.M. van Genugten *et al.* (eds.), *Realism and Moralism in International Relations* (The Hague: Kluwer International, 1998), chap. 14.

17   See Cyril E. Black *et al.*, *The Modernization of Inner Asia* (Armonk, N.Y.: M.E. Sharpe, 1991).

18   For a good summary of some of the contemporary complications, see International Crisis Group, *Central Asia: Fault Lines in the New Security Map*, Asia Report No. 20 (Osh and Brussels: International Crisis Group, 4 July 2001), pp. 3–9; those seeking authoritative and exhaustive detail should consult International Crisis Group, *Central Asia: Border Disputes and Conflict Potential*, Asia Report No. 33 (Osh and Brussels: International Crisis Group, 4 April 2002), pp. 2–17.

19   See, for example: Shahram Akbarzadeh, "How the Elite Survives in Uzbekistan," *Political Expressions* 2 (No. 1, 1998): 31–45; International Crisis Group, *Uzbekistan's Reform Program: Illusion or Reality?*, Asia Report No. 46 (Osh and Brussels: International Crisis Group, 18 February 2003), pp. 22–25.

20   For a prescriptive policy analysis in the field of military cooperation, see Stephen J. Blank, *The Future of Transcaspian Security* (Carlisle Barracks, Penna.: U.S. Army War College, Strategic Studies Institute, August 2002) <http://www.carlisle .army. mil/ ssi/pubs/2002/trnscasp/trnscasp.pdf>.

Chapter 13

Russia and the US in the New Balance of Power in Central Asia

Anton Koslov

The events of September 11th have changed the world as perhaps no other event since the Pearl Harbor attack. The United States had to face a new and elusive enemy which it never seriously considered as threat. The newly declared war on terror brought to the forefront of military and political strategic planning a new type of conflict—the asymmetrical war on global scale. The threat once again comes from the East, yet this time the targets are no longer clearly defined. The United States may now face its biggest challenge in modern history as a guerrilla war defies any rapid military solution and is the hardest to contain. As Henry Kissinger once put it, "the guerrilla wins if it does not lose." The challenge is not only structural, but also cultural—the United States has no experience in fighting wars in continental Asia. The new conflict brought a new geometry to the US-Russian relations, propelling Russia to the first rang of US allies in the war on terror. This chapter will try to sketch the new US-Russian 'rapport de force' in the light of the last 25 years of often conflicting US-Russian relations in Central Asia.

Russia is the biggest continental power in the world: its borders stretch from the Gulf of Finland to the hills of Manchuria. The dual nature of Russia's Eurasian geographic position and its complex ethno-cultural composition determine its strategic interests, its borders and its foreign policy. For the past two hundred years, Russia used its position in Central Asia to compensate for its foreign policy failures in the West. Russia's main goal in Central Asia, besides securing Russian borders, was to exercise pressure on Western adversaries, first England, and later the United States by threatening its colonies, allies, communication routes and strategic zones, like the Persian Golf. This was done through the combination of economic assistance, military and ideological expansion.

During the Soviet period Russia gave at least de jure statehood to the Central Asian people and incorporated them into the Communist superstate. The newly created Asian socialist republics were meant to serve as a show-case the rest of Asia. In its struggle with the West, Russia needed allies and friends in the East. In this game, Afghanistan meant to play the role of Russia's buffer state and a spring board for continuous Soviet expansion in the region. The culmination of this policy was the Soviet-backed military coup in Afghanistan in 1978 and the ensuing military intervention in 1979.

Following the Soviet retreat in 1989 and the dissolution of the Soviet Union in 1991, the Central Asian security paradigm changed due to the fragmentation of the political forces in the region. This change meant that Russia was no longer the master of the region and had to recognize and adopt itself to the new geopolitical reality, while considering Russia's security zone extending as far as the borders of the former Soviet Union. Russia loss of preeminence enjoyed by the Soviets created a power vacuum gradually filled by the forces hostile to its interests.

Central Asia and Russian Security

Throughout the 1990s, Russia had a number of security concerns in the Central Asian region. The first post-Communist Russian military doctrine clearly stated that one of Russia's strategic objectives was protecting the 25 million Russians living in the "near-abroad" (euphemism designating former Soviet republics other than Russia) defined regional stability as the foremost political goal. Russia claimed to have vital interests in the former Soviet republics—access to communication lines, strategic resources, and protection of its borders.

Post-Soviet economic dislocation hit hard all Central Asian republics and created a climate of instability, which in turn posed serious security problems. One was the spread of Muslim fundamentalism and separatism, which heartened both the stability of Russia's bordering regions and the integrity of the Russian Federation itself (as Russian federation has a large Muslim separatist-prone minority in Tatarstan and Bashkorstan). The other was the threat of losing access to the gas and oil fields in the Caspian basin region. Inter-regional infighting in Tadjikistan and the rise of Muslim fundamentalism in Uzbekistan had forced Uzbekistan and Tadjikistan to work with Russia on ensuring security in the region. Tadjikistan in particular was military weak and politically vulnerable to threats, and was openly dependent on Russian military presence in its capital Dushanbe and on its borders.

The rise of inter-regional fighting in Tajikistan and radical religious revivalism in Uzbekistan and later—in Kirghizstan[1]—were not isolated developments, but had been closely linked to the conflict in Afghanistan. Throughout the 1990s, Afghanistan was a growing source of instability in the region due to the ongoing civil war, the flow of weapons, drugs and religious propaganda to the neighboring Tadjikistan and Uzbekistan. The situation was further complicated by the rise of the Pakistan-backed Taliban movement, openly hostile to Russia and friendly to its enemies. The Taliban government, backed by Pakistan and Saudi Arabia, was the only one to recognize the independent state of Chechnya. It also assisted the Islamic Movement of Uzbekistan and the Islamic insurgents in Tadjikistan and Kyrghizstan.

Given these circumstances, the Russian strategy in the region in the mid-1990s was determined by at least three objectives. The first was to check the spread of Islamic fundamentalism and ethno-regional strife in Central Asia in particular in Tadjikistan and Uzbekistan. By late 1990s the spread of Sunni fundamentalism throughout the region was taken were seriously by Russia and its allies in the region. In the summer of 2000, Sergei Yastrzhembsky, Russian speaker on Chechnya made an official statement announcing Moscow's intention to launch preventive air strikes against the training camps of Osama bin Laden in Afghanistan. Uzbekistan openly supported the idea and declared Russia to be its "defender." In the fall of 2000 Kirghiz President Askar Akaev declared that six former Soviet republics Armenia, Belarus, Kazakhstan, Kyrgyzstan, Russia and Tajikistan would form a unified combat unit "to stop the Islamists in case of a major aggression."[2] This development would certainly need a major backing from Russia and would coincide with the Russian desire to consolidate control over the former Soviet Central Asian republics and create a zone of stability on its south-eastern boarders. This objective was also linked to the struggle in Chechnya and the necessity to neutralize Chechen separatists and their allies who have been using Afghanistan as the training ground. The Chechen rebel leaders like Shamil Basaev and Habib Abd al-Rahman Al Khattab received financial, military and personnel backing from the Sunni fundamentalist groups, and openly declared the creation of the Muslim khalifat in the region as their goal, thus clearly linking their struggle with Russia to a general plan of redrawing the map of Asia.

The second objective was to counter the expanding role of Pakistan and indirectly, of Saudi Arabia, both of which Russia viewed as threatening its interests; both Pakistan and Saudi Arabia were seen as the beneficiaries of the instability in the region.

The third objective was to slow Western politico-economic penetration into the traditional Russian sphere of influence, in particular giving the context of oil and gas resources in the region.

These objectives were guiding Russian security strategy on the CIS southern borders. Throughout the second half of the 1990s the implementation of this strategy had mixed results due to the breakdown of traditional economic and political ties in the region, Russian economic and military meltdown and the centrifugal forces in the corrupt and authoritarian Central Asian regimes. Nevertheless, despite its dwindling influence in the region, Russia had mastered a number of instruments that were conducive to the promotion of its interests in the Asian "near abroad." Among these instruments were the following:

a) interdependent industrial and energy infrastructure—legacy of the Soviet industrial era. For many years Russia was the source of capital investment in Central Asia and until today remains the source of employment, a significant market for local products, and, the principal energy supplier. Russian control over Eurasian energy routes allowed Russia to use the pipelines as an instrument of pressure. In 1997 Gazprom denied Turkmenistan pipeline access over a payment dispute, thus blocking the Turkmen gas export routes to Europe.[3]
b) common threats to the regional stability in the form of Islamic fundamentalism and separatism;
c) Russian-speaking minorities which constitute an important bond between Russia and central Asian states. Defense of the Russians living in the near abroad makes up an important element of the Russian military
d) political culture common to Russian and Central Asian political elites. Russian, Chinese and Central Asian elites share a common political culture as the nations that gradually emerge from the period of totalitarian communist rule. The common characteristics they all share are preponderance towards authoritarian rule and corruptibility.
e) Russia's consolidation of its relations with the Chinese through economic and military cooperation. Despite vast geo-strategic differences and a number of unresolved territorial disputes, Russia and China have common strategic objectives: 1) containing Muslim separatism and extremism in the region, and 2) maintaining an anti-American, anti-NATO axis. In the 1990s Russia became and remains China's biggest arm supplier, while China acquired access to Russian and Central Asian consumer markets.

One outcome of the Russian political maneuvering in the region was the creation the Shanghai Cooperation Organization (SCO), also known as the Shanghai Six. The SCO was formally established in June 2000, when Uzbekistan joined the existing "Shanghai Five" group, which has been meeting annually since 1996. Today the SCO includes Russia, China, Kazakhstan, Kyrgyzstan, Tajikistan and Uzbekistan.[4] Russia, along with China, is the major beneficiary of the SCO treaty, as the organization is aimed to serve as an instrument of its foreign policy designs in the region. The SCO may also be used as an effective instrument to counter US interference in what is viewed as traditional Russian sphere of influence.

Russia and Challenges to the US Foreign Policy

Despite all the past and present antagonisms and conflictual interests of Russia and the United States, the creation of the SCO and Russia's return to Central Asia may actually benefit the United States strategic position in the region. The US-Russian relations in Afghanistan in particular and in Central Asia in general should be considered in the larger context of American position in the Middle East and in Central Asia. The anti-American forces in the Middle East and in Afghanistan may be roughly sub-divided into three groups: 1) Shi'ite extremism linked to Iran, but not confined to it; 2) Arab nationalism of which Saddam Hussein is the most vilified figure; 3) Saudi Arabia and Pakistan—sponsored Sunni extremism which often identified with Wahabbism. These different elements are antagonistic and locked in the merciless struggle with one another. The only unifying factor of all these forces is their virulent hatred of the state of Israel in particular and the West, broadly designated as "international Zionism"—in general. The analysis of these different elements makes clear that all three are present a challenge to the US, including those who are viewed as American allies. The anti-American nature of Iran-backed Shi'ite extremism and Iraq's nationalism is a rather simple case to make. The case of Saudi Arabia and Pakistan is more complex.

Both Saudi Arabia and Pakistan are traditional American allies. Saudi Arabia is one of the biggest US weapons buyers and oil suppliers. US backed Saudi Arabia because of their opposition to pro-Soviet Arab regimes (Syria, Nasser's Egypt, North Yemen, and Iraq) and Pakistan's opposition to India. Later on two more factors added up: a) Saudi and Pakistani potential to assist anti-Communist Muslim forces in Afghanistan and b) their opposition to the Revolution in Iran. Beginning with the PDPA coup in Afghanistan in April 1978 the US embarked on assisting Muslim radicals in their struggle with the Soviet-backed regime in Kabul. After the Soviet invasion of Afghanistan, this assistance became part of the US foreign policy strategy defined by the Carter Doctrine. Saudi Arabia and Pakistan became US proxies in its war with the Soviet Union.

Both, however, had their own agenda in this conflict: Saudi's policy was in great extent guided by the presence of wealthy religious-minded donors like Osama bin Laden who had close links to the Saudi governing establishment and whose goal was to advance the cause of Sunni revivalism dominated by the Wahabbism—the official religion of the ruling House of Saud.[5] Pakistan, on the other hand, was aiming at increasing its influence in the region to the position of domination, as a part of an overall strategy in its conflict with India. This strategy was in part based on supporting radical Muslim movements in and outside Pakistan. In the early 1980s revivalist radicals received backing of the general Zia-ul Haq.[6] During the rule of Zia, Muslim militants were organized in such radical groups as Sipah-e-Sahaba and Lashkar-e-Jhangvi. Both the Saudi-backed Wahabbis and the Pakistan and Saudi-backed Deobandis were instrumental in rendering Afghan mujaheddins operational in their struggle with the Soviets, just as later they made the Taliban operational against the Afghan war lords. US, Saudi Arabia and Pakistan, as well as numerous private Muslim donors provided between 2 and 3 billion dollars of assistance to the anti-Russian resistance, including advance weaponry systems like the Stinger anti-aircraft missiles.[7]

The war in Afghanistan lasted for nine years and transformed rag tag gang of Muslim radicals into a fighting force to reckon with. It also contributed to the development of jihaddism—a radical trend within the Muslim revivalism, with the central tenet being the holy war against the infidels. US strategy of backing Muslim guerrillas against the pro-Soviet Kabul government was victorious—but the victory was pyrrhic: The Afghan state and social institutions were destroyed and the country plunged into the state of permanent civil war and distraction. As the United States lost interest in Afghanistan, the true beneficiary of the Afghan chaos was Pakistan.

The rise of Pakistani activities in war-torn Afghanistan coincided with the dissolution of the Soviet Union: as the Soviet influence in the region dwindled, Pakistan attempted to fill the power vacuum. It is at this time that the issue of Central Asian oil and gas reserves became of paramount importance. The Pakistani secret service—the ISI—after helping to drive the Soviets out of Afghanistan, had moved its operations closer to the Russian borders. It was behind the major escalation of the Islamist movement in Tadjikistan; the ISI-directed operations against Tadjikistan date as early as the spring of 1990.[8] The ISI was also behind the rise of the Taliban in 1994. So was Saudi Arabia that financed the Taliban and the Al-Qaeda network.[9]

In Russia, the rise of the Taliban in 1994-96 and proclamation of the Islamic Emirate of Afghanistan was seen as a part of a larger US strategy to gain access to the natural resources of Central Asia. American policy in the region was viewed by many as the continuity of containment strategy based on supporting Russia's regional foes. The role assigned by the Russian press to the US in assisting the Taliban was certainly exaggerated, but the United States did demonstrate the complacency if not the incompetence towards the Taliban. In the context of Afghan chaos, the Taliban appeared as the source of stability that could guarantee development of the energy related sectors in the region. Between 1995-98, US support of the Taliban was driven by the joint American-Saudi UNOCAL/Delta pipeline project, linking Turkmenistan and Pakistan.[10] UNOCAL withdrew from the project only after the US navy attacked Bin Laden training camps in the summer of 1998.

New Security Paradigm

Given these elements, the states that did indirectly contribute to the September 11th attacks were Saudi Arabia and Pakistan. Without their assistance the Al-Qaeda network would never have become operational. The United States overestimated the reliability of their allies and underestimated the potential of their enemies. Ironically, those who benefited the most from the consequent US invasion of Afghanistan were Russia and other members of the Shanghai Six, in particular Uzbekistan and Kirghizstan. The Russian and Uzbek-backed Northern Alliance, from a marginalized force of Tadjik and Uzbek insurgents controlling less than 5 percent of the Afghan territory, turned into the leading military force in Afghanistan. Moscow has maintained its assistance to the Northern Alliance since the late 1990s, and significantly expanded it after the US. attacked the Taliban. By October 2001, Russia committed a $70 million arms package to the Northern Alliance, including tanks, military helicopters, and anti-aircraft missiles. Vladimir Putin signaled high strategic priority of the anti-Taliban war, assigning the Chief of the General Staff Victor Kvashnin to oversee Russian military strategy in Afghanistan. Kvashnin was one of the few senior Russian military officers to assist the NA military planning. These developments underscored Moscow's determination to play a major role in the struggle for power in Afghan post-war politics by backing the Northern Alliance's bid for power. Russia pledged almost half a billion dollars in humanitarian assistance program to northern Afghanistan.[11] Russia was also instrumental in pulling through the Bonn Agreement in November 2001 which installed Hamid Karzai at the head of new Afghan government.

The success of the American intervention in the region, in Afghanistan and elsewhere, will depend on the cooperation of Russia and other former Soviet republics. The United States needs Russia just as Russia needs the United States. Russian and Western interests in the region converge: both desire a stable and secure environment through economic development and suppression of Islamic extremism. Russian foreign policy in Central Asia is going to take on its traditional course: Central Asia was always Russia's strong card in its relations with the West. Current political situation will certainly reinforce Putin's positions on other issues.[12]

The circumstances of the September 11th led the Bush administration to recognize that the Caucasus and Central Asia are a major factor in US-Russian bilateral relations. Russia's southern borders are now its most sensitive frontier and the Caucasus and Central Asia are its top security priority.[13] The United States and France—Russia's most staunch critic over the war in Chechnya—recognized Russia's right to intervene in the Caucasus. The terrorism issue presents Russia with a new opportunity to achieve its objective of dominating the CIS and using the organization as an instrument of its foreign policy.

Further benefits may follow. Stability in Central Asia depends on the regional economic development. In April 2002 the President of the World Bank James Wolfensohn visited Kazakhstan, Kyrgyzstan, Tajikistan, Turkmenistan and Uzbekistan. The World Bank clearly indicated the importance of the region in maintaining global stability and pledged its willingness "to partner with governments in the region to speed the reform process and provide support for institutional building."[14] Three months later in July 2002 Treasury Secretary of the United States, Paul O'Neill visited Central Asian states and discussed economic assistance. Any Western investment in Central Asian economies will also indirectly benefit Russia, without posing any strategic threat to it. Developed infrastructure and economic growth will reinforce democratic institutions and contribute to the strengthening of civil society in Central Asian states. This in turn will weaken inter-regional, inter-ethnic and religious divisions. At the same time, Russia maintains enough options in Central Asia to counter any US attempt to increase its influence, if any potential conflict of interests between US and Russia will manifest itself.

As the US-led invasion of Iraq demonstrated, the Middle East and the Central Asian region needs a new collective security system that would bring all parties in line with the norms of international law. The United States must not act unilaterally, but build a reliable network of regional strategic partners if it wants to bring stability to the region. The first step in that direction would be to recognize the future partners' economic and political interests in the region. The new security system must not be unilateral; it must involve both US and Russia. In fact, Russia must be allowed to play a crucial role in this emerging equation. The creation of the

NATO-Russia Council in May 2002 indicated Western desire to cooperate with Russia in Europe. A similar structure is needed in Asia and the Middle East. The US and Russia need to work together towards creating a durable institution that would be effective in the times of peace as an instrument of economic development, and in the times of war—as an instrument of collective defense.

Notes

1   Martha Brill Olcott, *Central Asia's New States*, US Institute of Peace Press, Washington, D.C., 1996, 165 The fundamentalist group Hizb al-Tahrir al-Islami, founded by Palestinians, which operates in southern Kyrghizstan, is influenced by the Wahabbism, but advocates creation of Islamic khalifate through peaceful means. AFP dispatch from October 21, 2000.
2   AFP dispatch from October 21, 2000.
3   The government of Turkmenistan has been considering the construction of a 1,630-kilometer Trans-Caspian Gas Pipeline. The pipeline, supported by the Royal Dutch/Shell, would run from Turkmenistan under the Caspian Sea to Azerbaijan, through Georgia and terminate in Turkey.
4   The Moscow Times, January 7, 2002. In January 2002 the SCO decided to set up a regional counter-terrorism agency and a "mechanism for emergency response." The SCO declared role is the maintenance of stability in Central Asia. During the same summit the SCO foreign ministers signed a joint declaration which formally laid out the similarities with the war in Afghanistan to the presences of "terrorism, separatism and extremism" in their own countries. The ministers agreed that terrorism in all forms must be "hit hard," but that the scope of counter-terrorism should not be indefinitely expanded and "that the United Nations should play a leading role in the campaign." Uighur separatists were among groups to be targeted. The SCO member states also recognized Russia's fighting in Chechnya as part of the international fight against terrorism, but expressed caution in expanding the US-led action in response to the September 11 terror attacks beyond measures agreed by the United Nations.
5   The modern Saudi state was founded on the 18th-century alliance between the Wahabi religious movement and the House of Saud. Muhammed bin'Abd al-Wahab's alliance with Muhammad Ibn al Saud dates back to 1745. Ibn Sa'ud relied on the influence of Abdl al-Wahab to regain power over the Arabian Peninsula. The alliance rested upon the agreement that the political sovereignty should rest with Ibn al-Sa'ud, whereas religious authority should belong to Muhammad bin 'Abd al Wahab. The alliance was short-lived. Today the Wahabbi who are are opposed to the House of Saud (like bin Laden) dispute the authenticity of Saud's wahabbism.
6   Zia was a fervent admirer of Sayyid Abu'l-A'la Mawdudi, one of the founders of the Deobandis related groups like Jama'at al-Islami and advocate of the global Muslim state.
7   Women's Health and Human Rights in Afghanistan. A Population-Based Assessment. A Report by Physicians for Human Rights Boston, Washington DC, 2001, 18.
8   Yossef Bodansky, The Task Force on Terrorism and Unconventional Warfare of the US Congress, http://www.americanfriends.org/nuclear/islam_war3N32.html.
9   Just in one instance, according to the papers filed in a $3,000 billion US lawsuit by lawyers representing the families of Sept. 11 victims, senior members of the Saudi royal family paid "protection money" totaling at least $300 million to Osama bin-

Laden and the Taliban to prevent them from attacking targets in Saudi Arabia. *Jerusalem Post*, 25 August 2002.
10 For more details see Rashid, Ahmed, *Taliban: Militant Islam, Oil, and Fundamentalism in Central Asia*. Yale University Press, 2000.
11 *The Analyst*, Central Asia-Caucasus Institute, John Hopkins University, November 21, 2001.
12 The current US-Russia cooperation in Central Asia is far from being smooth. The rift within the Russia's military and foreign policy makers in regard to Russia's relationship with the United States and the NATO alliance, as well as traditional Western animosity towards Russia may complicate close bi-lateral cooperation. The last issue was recently raised Colonel-General Leonid Ivashov, vice-president of the Russian geopolitical Academy, (former Chief of the Defense Ministry's Directorate for International Military Cooperation) who following the 9/11 attack, expressed a view that even without the tragic events of Sept. 11, the Americans would still have found a pretext for entering Afghanistan – in order to establish control over the oil-and gas rich regions including the Caspian. Interview in *The Russia Journal*, Dec. 14, 2001.
13 The Brookings Institution, Policy Brief No. 80, May 2001.
14 Central Asian news, Bulletin of the Uzbekistan National News Agency, 4 April, 2002.

Chapter 14

Kashmir and a New Cold War

Sten Widmalm*

It is not only the conflict between India and Pakistan that is shaping the future of South Asia. Obviously the situation is still critical, with over a million troops being mobilized along the border around and south of Kashmir throughout most of 2002. A war here could nullify the entire American effort in Afghanistan. A nuclear exchange as a consequence of an extended conflict cannot be ruled out. But beneath this surface of scattered skirmishes, sometimes escalating into war, and continual terror attacks, there are even larger processes determining the appearance of the political map in the future. It is China, the US and India that are together pursuing the overall political process. Within another decade we should be seeing the most concrete results of the fall of the Wall—in all probability a new cold war between China and the US, in which India has found itself on the side of the West. In this cold war the border between the blocs runs straight through Kashmir.

Conflicts between Pakistan and India

The Kashmir conflict claimed more than 30,000 lives in the 1990s and a bigger war may be triggered off at any time. As long ago as 1990 the risk of a nuclear war was considered relatively serious by the US government. There is information to suggest that the Pakistani military was preparing missile attacks with nuclear weapons on India during the Kargil conflict of 1999, but without the knowledge of the then prime minister, Nawaz Sharif. During the crisis that has existed between India and Pakistan in 2002 both countries have kept their nuclear forces in combat readiness.

---

* This article is based on two articles previously published in Sweden: "Gränsen i ett nytt kallt krig skär genom Kashmir," published in *Axess*, October 2002; "USA - en bricka i spelet om Kashmir," published in *Svenska Dagbladet* 9 July 2002.

The Kashmir conflict is one of the main reasons for India's inability to develop more rapidly, both socially and economically, and the reason for the fact that Pakistan is one of the few countries in the world whose economic development has gone into reverse. And since the nuclear weapons tests in India and Pakistan in 1998 the military expenditure of both countries has risen. The relative strengths appear to remain uneven, however. India's defence budget is roughly four times that of Pakistan, which was between three and four billion dollars in 2000. India has risen to eleventh position in the world in terms of military spending. India's armed forces have 1.3 million men—more than twice as many as its neighbour to the west can call on. India's air force is almost four times the size of Pakistan's, and the Indian navy and army are twice the size. The trend is equally uneven if we look at the countries' missile defence systems.

The Ghauri missile has the longest range in the Pakistani arsenal: this is a ballistic missile built with the assistance of China and North Korea. It is said to be capable of carrying nuclear warheads. The air force's American F-16 fighter is regarded as an important means of dropping atom bombs. The Ghauri and the F-16 each have a range that covers most of India.

The Indian programme is greater in scope, more sophisticated and incorporates more of its own technology. The short-distance *Prithvi* missile can carry nuclear weapons and has high precision using the global positioning system (GPS). The Prithvi has a range of between 150 and 350 kilometres and has been developed primarily for use against Pakistan. India's medium-range *Agni* missile, which can strike over more than 2000 kilometres, suggests however that India has considerably greater ambitions. At least one version of the Agni can carry nuclear weapons that would be able to reach Beijing.[1] In the longer term, India would also be able to convert parts of its advanced space programme to produce intercontinental ballistic missiles for nuclear warheads.

As far as number of ready nuclear weapons is concerned, India has, according to the latest calculations of the American Centre for Defence Information (CDI), around sixty available, compared with Pakistan's figure of between twenty and forty warheads. It is clear that, whatever the basis for comparison, India has a military lead over Pakistan which will remain unassailable for the foreseeable future. The question that arises is naturally what use can India envisage for what appears to be an overcapacity?

One explanation might be that India wants the superiority that is required not only in order to defend itself against Pakistan, but also to *attack* its western neighbour. However, the more reasonable explanation is that in the long term India is arming primarily against the east—namely

China—an arming process which began back in the mid-1960s. But is it reasonable to depict China as India's real number one enemy in the middle of disturbances between India and Pakistan? To examine this question we may begin by looking more closely at an interesting manoeuvre by the Indian defence minister George Fernandes a few years ago when the new Hindu nationalist government was only a month or so old.

Just before the nuclear weapons tests of May 1998 Fernandes said quite frankly that it is China that is India's main enemy. A few weeks earlier Fernandes had openly accused China of having violated the border of the state of Arunachal Pradesh. Despite this, the chief of staff of the Chinese Army paid a visit to India at the end of April in that year and there was a temporary improvement in relations between the countries. Then came Fernandes' dramatic pronouncement on 6 May and only five days later the Indian nuclear weapons tests began. This strengthened the impression that India was issuing a warning to China with its tests. However, China took a fairly restrained line. Fernandes was of course known for his spontaneity or unpredictability. But there are still strong indications that his statement had a deeper message. There is after all a very deeply rooted antagonism between India and China that goes back to events in the 1960s.

China's Relationship with India

There is a somewhat conventional picture of conflicts and security cooperation in South Asia since independence. We often hear it said that India and Pakistan have fought a number of wars over the territory of Kashmir. Independence in 1947 led immediately to the first war between the states and the ceasefire line which was drawn up then has largely been preserved and since come to function as a *de facto* border between India and Pakistan in Kashmir. In 1965 and 1971, and again in 1999, Pakistan and India fought further wars which concerned or greatly affected Kashmir. Another stereotypical view is that during the Cold War the US and China supported Pakistan while India's strongest ally was the Soviet Union. But these pictures need to be filled out with some important details. In the early 1960s, for example, India's and Pakistan's respective alignments with the great powers could not be taken for granted.

India's first prime minister, Jawaharlal Nehru, tried to launch an alternative movement for Third World states outside the great power blocs - the non-aligned movement (NAM).[2] The idea was that China and India together would assume a leading role, but the NAM never became a serious reality. India was quick to oppose China's interests in the Tibet question.

During the 1950s India received Tibetan refugees and in 1959 the Dalai Lama was granted asylum in India. The conflict in Tibet quickly spread to the borders of India and China. In order to grip Tibetan resistance forces more effectively, China upgraded an old caravan trade route running from North-East China down to Tibet, straight through the eastern portion of Kashmir that is known as Aksai Chin. India protested against this development and signalled with a certain amount of military mobilization that the territory would be defended. This led to minor confrontations in 1959-1961 and a final offensive by China against India in October-November 1962. Before the war China had made sure that neither the US nor the Soviet Union would intervene in the matter—the Soviet support was "traded" for China's support of the Soviet Union in the Cuba question that was brewing up.[3] China was therefore able to launch its offensive relatively safely on 20 October, right in the middle of the Cuba crisis. The Indian army suffered a comprehensive defeat and Chinese troops were soon posted along the southern slopes of the Himalayas; it is said that China could have continued its march towards New Delhi without very much resistance. However China withdrew and has since contented itself with retaining control of Aksai Chin.

China's attack and superiority were a deadly blow to India. The NAM project withered at the same rate as Nehru's health. He took the defeat hard. One of his biggest political visions had been crushed and he died in May 1964. Only a few months later China carried out its first nuclear weapons test, which further increased tension between China and India. In this world dominated by the great powers India finally found itself forced to seek alliances with a stronger party.

For a while the Americans had tried to support both India and Pakistan in order to counter the influence of the Soviet Union and China. There are indications that for a period in 1964-65 the US was on the point of giving India direct support in building nuclear weapons.[4] But the Vietnam War forced the US to move its forces eastwards and with the Indo-Pakistan war in 1965 the military support of the Americans to both Pakistan and India stopped.[5] However the Soviet Union showed a growing interest in supporting India, especially against China.[6] When the US later drew closer to China in 1971, and China in turn drew closer to Pakistan, the great power alignment became increasingly distinct.

The reason for India's strong investment in its nuclear weapons programme was primarily the threat from China. The first tests took place in 1974. It was only after the war between India and Pakistan in 1971 that Pakistan decided to launch a nuclear weapons programme of its own.[7] At first, the US had reservations about the Pakistani programme and it therefore halted its financial support to Pakistan towards the end of the 1970s to limit the spread of nuclear weapons. However, the US withdrew its sanctions as soon as Pakistan was needed in the campaign against the Soviet invasion of Afghanistan. During the Reagan years the Americans chose to look the other way when Zia ul-Haq started a new phase in the build-up of the Pakistani nuclear arms programme. It was also then that Pakistan acquired its F-16 fighters from the US. During this period India cooperated closely with the Soviet Union and, for example, voted against the UN's condemnation of the invasion of Afghanistan. In the 1980s, the positions in South Asia became more rigid and were controlled by superpower policies. But after the end of the Afghan war and the fall of the Wall, the US withdrew from Pakistan, which then had to keep in step with China. The American government resumed its criticism of the Pakistani nuclear arms programme and reimposed sanctions.[8]

The end of the 1990s is a period which is a "formative moment" as strong as the period in the sixties. China and India have now become more and more interesting to American business. The growth in China is regarded increasingly as a pointer to what will happen in India. One advantage of India which is increasingly appreciated by all those who are willing to invest risk capital is that the country is also democratic and open. This is something which in the long run may favour investment more than the volatile situation in China.

New Pattern of Alliances in South Asia

During the nineties India gradually came to be seen as an expanding trading nation, rather than as a developing country. Even if the growth curves and the trade figures do not always show a definite plus, it is clear that growth continues and trade is increasing in the long term and that India is being integrated more and more into the world economy. The US is now India's biggest trading partner. These economic changes have definitely given rise to a new role division. For India's part, the US has taken the place of the former Soviet Union—and not only as a trading partner.

After the nuclear weapons tests of 1998 the US imposed sanctions on both Pakistan and India. The effects of these were not particularly great in India's case, whereas it was the sanctions that helped to crush such little fragile democratic structure as remained in Pakistan. But before Prime Minister Sharif was deposed, India and Pakistan managed to fight a war limited to the Kargil area of Kashmir. Then it became clear that Pakistan was behind the attacks. The US came down firmly on the side of India and urged Sharif to make sure that the Pakistani insurgents withdrew. Pakistan obeyed, the war came to an end, and a long honeymoon, without previous parallel, began between the US and India. Only a few months after the Kargil conflict the US and India found that they had a common enemy in the Taliban regime and Al Qaida, when an India airliner was hijacked by "Kashmir sympathizers" from Afghanistan and elsewhere. In the spring of 2000 Clinton paid a highly successful visit to India and in the autumn the Indian prime minister was able to go to the US and address Congress. During this period the military and security cooperation between the countries, in particular, was strengthened.

So far the division appears clear. The US is lining up more and more strongly behind India while Pakistan is being forced out into the cold and having to rely increasingly on uncertain support from China. But the attack on the US on 11 September 2001 put the cat among the pigeons. The US was obliged to mend its fences with Pakistan and the financial sanctions were quickly replaced with promises of economic aid.

At first the Indians were quite concerned at the American change of course. Then they became annoyed when the US urged restraint on India with regard to Pakistan after Kashmiri separatists, allegedly with the support of Pakistan, attacked the Indian parliament in December 2001. At the time India was considering applying the part of the Bush doctrine which says that a state attacked by "terrorists" has the right to strike back with much greater force against the terrorists and also against the state giving them protection. A war between India and Pakistan might however have threatened American interests in Afghanistan and Pakistan, so India was exhorted by the US not to start any military offensive. Naturally many Indians recalled what was seen as the treachery of the Americans in the sixties and seventies when the US first gave India military support to counter the influence of communist states, and then pulled out, only to pop up again in direct negotiations and cooperation with China. But on the other hand India soon discovered that the American presence in Pakistan gave India a good means of bringing pressure to bear on Pakistan.

The Americans were obliged to mollify India and the outside world by demanding that General Musharraf dissociate himself from the Kashmiri separatists who had established bases in Pakistan. Musharraf gave way and for a while even imprisoned some leaders of Taliban-friendly organizations and groups that had been identified as separatists in the Kashmir conflict— groups to which Musharraf had previously given support.

The paradox here is that even if India watched the cooperation of the US and Pakistan with disquiet, a kind of political victory was achieved over the Pakistani leadership on the Kashmir question, such as it had not been possible to achieve at any time in the nineties when Kashmir was such a burning issue. No doubt the Indian government quickly realized that this situation was something to be exploited. The only problem was that the Americans could not exert unlimited pressure on Musharraf. If the general acted too harshly towards the religiously mobilized political groupings he risked being deposed in a coup. And when the most extensive operations in Afghanistan had been concluded as far as the US was concerned, i.e. when the Taliban government had fallen, Musharraf released several of the "radical elements" that he had previously kept behind bars. The Indians protested, but the US was satisfied with the fact that Musharraf had succeeded in preserving stability in the country. But then came the attack on the Indian parliament on 13 December. Kashmiri separatists based in Pakistan were accused of being behind the deed. India probably realized that there was a good deal to be gained here by demonstrating a distinct reaction—primarily to get the US to put pressure on Pakistan. And thus began a game of brinkmanship for very high stakes.

The peace researcher Richard Ned Lebow has written about "brinkmanship" in a comprehensive analysis of wars around the world and the most striking definition of the concept he uses comes originally from Yehosephat Harkabi, who describes it as "the art of deliberately precipitating crises to the verge of war in order to prevail upon the opponent to retreat." The intention is, in other words, not to start a war, but to achieve specific political goals. And the Kashmir crisis of 2002 may be seen in these terms. It is true that India mobilized because sectors of domestic opinion demanded it, but a more important reason was that it gave the opportunity to force Pakistan to cut off its support for the separatists once and for all.

The Americans gave India important tools in this process. India could invoke the new Bush doctrine and increase its effort in the conflict and mobilize on a large scale without risking criticism from important countries elsewhere. And as a war would have such a devastating effect on the whole American project in Afghanistan, India succeeded in putting pressure on Musharraf, through the US, once again positively to dissociate himself from the separatists.

However, Pakistan also understood how it could exploit this situation. When during the winter/spring the sabre-rattling from India became too loud, Pakistan threatened to move troops who were guarding the border between Pakistan and Afghanistan to the border with India. And if the border between Pakistan and Afghanistan was not guarded, the American Afghanistan project could suffer. Thus Pakistan, too, managed to put pressure on the US to induce India to moderate its demands that

Pakistan extradite suspected terrorists. In other words the US became an important piece in the Kashmir conflict for both India and Pakistan.

A good example of how India and Pakistan tried to make use of their relationship with America came in May 2002 when the American minister of defence Donald Rumsfeld stated that Al Qaida supporters were active among the separatists in Kashmir. Rumsfeld was visiting South Asia to try to take the heat out of relations between India and Pakistan and he had recently had an important meeting with the Indian prime minister. The Indian government was pleased with the statement but the Pakistani leaders were extremely displeased and at a press conference in Pakistan journalists demanded to know what evidence there was for the assertion. Rumsfeld was forced to retreat and admitted that there just was no evidence available. The most important thing here is not whether the rumours about Al Qaida are true or not. What is interesting is that it so clearly shows that the US has difficulty in maintaining a consistent policy and at the same time maintaining relations with both India and Pakistan. This has undoubtedly led to a heightened risk of war in South Asia because both India and Pakistan believe that they can gain from a game of brinkmanship and both countries will try to continue to play the American card as and when they can.

Lebow studies in detail thirteen historical examples of brinkmanship crises. Half of these were preceded by one party considering that the balance of power was being radically changed and that it was compelled to act to prevent a serious loss in the power relationship. The Kashmir situation could also be described in this way. The revived alliance between the US and Pakistan has evidently encouraged India to play for high stakes with war as a threat. A third of the cases of brinkmanship studied by Lebow resulted in war. The most dangerous and best known brinkmanship crisis where the parties managed to avoid war was the Cuba crisis. Now we have another brinkmanship crisis, and, as in 1962, two nuclear powers are involved. That is where we are today.

The Indians still hope that it is the relationship between India and the US that will prove the more durable. The relationship between the US and Pakistan will probably only last as long as the US wants to solve more pressing problems in Afghanistan. That is how it has been in the past, of course. And the new relationship is regarded by many in India as worth cultivating if the US can offer protection against China. For India's relationship with China today is reminiscent of the relationship between Pakistan and India. For example, China's armed forces consist of two and a half million men, and its military budget is between two and three times the size of India's. For this reason more and more Indians see cooperation with the US as a necessity. The biggest incentive probably lies in the promise of coming under the "missile umbrella." India's purchase of the "Green Pine" radar system from Israel may be seen as a step towards integration in the US plans for a missile defence system. However, in June 2002 China opposed India's decision to buy the "Phalcon Airborne Warning and Control System" (AWACS), which can detect up to 60 targets within a radius of 800 kilometres. If India comes under what is today available of the US umbrella, says China, the current "balance" in power relations will be threatened—a reaction that shows that there is a serious downside to an alliance between the US and India.

Naturally the new developments could lead to stability and peace. If China and the US are able to agree, it is these two countries that will together be able to bring peace between Pakistan and India. But as yet there is much to suggest that new crises may equally well ensue. India has unresolved conflicts, not only with Pakistan. The border with China is strongly disputed and if we consider how in recent years India has expanded its missile defence there is much to indicate that serious hostility persists here. In a scenario where the US and India have entered into some sort of alliance, and China and Pakistan are cooperating more closely, the great powers and their front-line states have aligned themselves in a manner that had no counterpart in the previous cold war. In those days the US and the Soviet Union were fighting their wars in territory beyond their own borders. But now a dividing line between a new east and west would run between India and Pakistan, two neighbours who themselves possess nuclear weapons and who are in turn supported by other nuclear powers. The most critical border between the new blocs would run straight through Kashmir – one of the world's most troubled and war-torn areas. The Kashmir conflict escalated from being primarily a regional conflict in the early 1980s to being an inter-state conflict towards the end of the 1990s. With new alliances it is possible that the conflict will spread further and to higher levels in world politics.

Notes

1 There are in fact several versions of the Agni. The one with a range of between 2000 and 2500 kilometers is called the Agni II and was tested in January 2002.
2 This is despite the fact that John Foster Dulles described India's wish to remain neutral between the great powers as "immoral." Cohen 2002: 271.
3 Garver 1993.
4 Perkovich 1999.
5 See Cohen 2001. India also saw an American decision in the same year to withdraw its agricultural support to India in the middle of a famine as a hostile act (even if the American decision did not affect current aid deliveries in the short term).

6   Garver 1993.
7   Perkovich 1999: 165.
8   This occurred under the "Pressler amendment," which implied a reduction/withdrawal of military and financial support to Pakistan throughout the nineties. See Cohen 2001.

References

Abraham, Itty. 1998. *The Making of the Indian Atomic Bomb – Science, Secrecy, and the Postcolonial State*. Zed Books: London.
Centre for Defence Information (www.cdi.org).
Cohen, Stephen, P. 2002. *Emerging Power – India*. Brookings: Washington, D.C.
Faust, John R. and Judith F. Kornberg. 1995. *China in World Politics*. Lynne Rienner, Publishers: Boulder.
Federation of American Scientists (www.fas.org).
Garver, John, W. 1993. *Foreign Relations of the People's Republic of China*. Prentice Hall, New Jersey.
Lebow, Ned. 1981. *Between Peace and War – The Nature of International Crisis*. The Johns Hopkins University Press: Baltimore.
Perkovich, George. 1999. *India's Nuclear Bomb*. University of California Press.
The SIPRI military expenditure database 2002 (www.sipri.org).
Wolpert, Stanley. 1996. *Nehru – Tryst with Destiny*. Oxford University Press: Oxford.

Chapter 15

Iran and the New Threats in the Persian Gulf and Middle East Since 9/11

Steven Ekovich

For more than half a century, threats in the Persian Gulf have had impacts beyond instability and conflict in the region itself and have increasingly implicated the entire Middle East, as well as becoming a geopolitical and geo-economic epicenter for much of the rest of the world. This is, of course, mainly due to the voracious appetite for energy of the industrialized economies, energy that has required vast quantities of oil. Interruption of stable and regular access to the region's enormous oil reserves has been a constant, long-term threat. For example, President Jimmy Carter's declaration that the Persian Gulf constituted a vital interest to the United States, and the implication that military force could be used to protect the interest, was dignified with the appellation of the "Carter Doctrine." However, the specific configuration of instability that has threatened access has changed over the years and often led to crises with global repercussions. The foreign policy choices of regional as well as global actors have, therefore, been frequently put to the challenge. So, even though threat to the access of Gulf oil is relatively long-term, its specific nature has frequently changed, so that we may speak of new threats to oil access.

The proliferation of nuclear, biological and chemical weapons' technologies, as well as improved means to deliver them, has added a new dimension to the global threat emanating from of the region. Whereas previously the reach of weapon technologies was limited mainly to the parties in direct conflict, we have already witnessed the use of improved ballistic missiles to implicate those outside the immediate conflict, for example, Israel during the "First Gulf War" (the term used here to define the coalition intervention after the invasion by Iraq of Kuwait and not the previous Iraq-Iran War). And if a regional power like Iran manages to develop even longer range missiles the entire Near East, South Asia and all of Europe could be threatened. The use of anthrax against Americans in the wake of September 11, even though the source remains unknown, has also resoundingly demonstrated that biological weapons of mass terror may be easily deployed without missiles by a very distant adversary with malicious intent. September 11 also demonstrated that actors from the Gulf and Middle East could also cleverly use the openness of democratic societies to inflict horrible damage without any military technology or weaponized biological and chemical agents. The threat of terrorism has existed for quite some time in the Gulf and the Middle East, so it is not really a new threat, although it has been given salience since 9/11 because of its unprecedented reach and magnitude. Furthermore, what also may be seen as new, and therefore surprising and even shocking, is that effective terrorism has not come from states, but from non-state actors, albeit sometimes protected by governments or benignly tolerated by them. The most unsettling innovation is that instigators of terror attacks may hide their tracks and remain unknown, undermining the classic responses of defense and deterrence.

An analysis of new threats in the region must take into consideration, then, the new forms of the "old" threat to Gulf oil access, as well as the new reach of terrorism far outside the region. The new forms of existing threats, which have given them renewed intensity, and the qualitatively new threats, should be analyzed not only in terms of the capacities of actors to inflict harm or engage in military action, but also in terms of the evolving strategic context – which necessarily will include a consideration of the intentions of states and non-state actors. For the purposes of this analysis the strategic context will be viewed in several layers, with the Persian Gulf serving as the foundation and with frequent focus on Iran and, secondarily, on Iraq because of the volatility of its situation. But a fuller understanding of the influence of 9/11 will have to take into consideration to some extent the rest of the region, as well as South Asia and the current nature of the interminable Israeli-Palestinian conflict, Europe (including Turkey), and of the interests of outside powers like Russia, China and, of course, the paramount importance of the United States.

The Continuing Importance of the Region's Oil

According to the most recent report published by the US Department of Energy, *Annual Energy Outlook 2003*, net US oil imports could, depending on price, account for as much as 65-70 per cent of total domestic demand by 2025, up from 55 per cent in 2001. It is forecast that in 2025, 51 per cent of world oil production will come from OPEC, up from the current 38 per cent. About two-thirds of OPEC production comes from the Gulf. The report predicts higher long-term oil prices because of rising world demand, which is expected to increase from 76 million barrels a day in 2001 to 123 by 2025. The American report mirrors the conclusions of the Paris-based International Energy Agency's recent report *World Energy Outlook*. For example, it is projected the US economy is likely to grow at a rate of 2.5-3.25 per cent between 2001 and 2025. Other economies, notably that of China, are expected to grow at an even higher rate. And at present almost half of Chinese oil supplies come from the Middle East. So, energy consumption will rise as economies grow, although the energy may be used more efficiently than in the past – partly due to transitions to lower energy consumption in post-modern production and partly from new energy technologies. A related security concern is the threat to the biosphere of increased global warning as a result of higher levels of carbon dioxide emissions, which are projected to increase at an average annual rate of 1.25 per cent up to 2025. Nevertheless, it is possible that dependency on Middle East oil could actually decline in the near future as new sources and means of delivery are developed in the Atlantic basin as well as Russia and the Caspian Sea. Nevertheless, the basic geological fact is that 70 per cent of proven oil reserves are in the Middle East – so the geostrategy of oil is likely to remain pretty much the same for the next two decades.

The Evolution of Gulf Geostrategy: Changing Shapes of the Old Threat

Recent security strategies applied in the Gulf, but now abandoned, must be taken into consideration when searching for future continuities and discontinuities in security threats. In the early 1970s Iran was to ensure Gulf stability alongside Saudi Arabia. This became known as the "Two Pillars" strategy. For the US this strategy was designed to maintain stability in the Gulf while at the same time impeding Soviet expansionism in the region. This policy was particularly attractive to the Americans since it avoided the need for a large-scale US presence in the Persian Gulf. The two pillars also proved to be, at least through the 1970s, an effective way of ensuring that insurgencies in Iraq did not threaten the rest of the region. However, territorial claims and internal instabilities in both Iran and Iraq flared up and ignited a political conflagration that undermined the solidity of the two pillars for the next two decades. This turbulence was gravely compounded by the Iranian revolution in 1979. The opposition led by Ruhallah Khomeini ousted Shah Mohammad Reza Pahlevi and Iran's foreign policy fanned virulent anti-American sentiment while arousing animosity toward regimes in the region.

Overnight, Iranian support for American interests crumbled, while relations with Iraq took a new turn difficult to control. With the support of moderate Arab states, the United States and Europe, and heavily financed by Gulf states, Saddam Hussein had become the defender of Gulf Arabs against a fundamentalist Iran and the agent of realpolitik for those who needed Gulf oil. Thus, Iraq received economic and military support from its allies who, faced with no good immediate choices, cynically overlooked Saddam's violation of an international border, his use of chemical warfare, and his efforts to develop nuclear weapons, military technology provided by the Soviet Union, Germany and France.[1] The United States was desperately seeking some stability, even if in the short term it entailed opportunistically "switching sides" between Iran and Iraq in the 1980s in the midst of the Iran-Iraq War. The US did not want either power to gain a decisive position. Therefore, it oscillated its support to each side merely to ensure that neither fell to the other.

In 1991, with the Iraqi invasion and annexation of Kuwait, the balancing of the previous decade came to an end. The US faced a new, potentially hegemonic threat from Iraq that needed to be opposed. With the end of the First Gulf War Iraq now became an object of US containment. At this point containment policy was no longer aimed at communism because the Soviet Union was falling apart. Furthermore, with US relations to Iran breaking up containment was extended there as well, leading to the policy of "dual containment."

Changed Strategy for a Changed Situation

The new doctrine of dual containment drew heavily on the strategy applied by the US during the Cold War. Some proponents of dual containment even see it as a replication of the Cold War policy. One, for example, has touted this policy as "an excellent way for the West to deter external aggression until rogue regimes no longer pose a threat, at which point the US security presence can be dramatically reduced." Drawing on the historic parallel, the argument was made that "Long-term prospects are much the same as those when George Kennan recommended containment for the Soviet Union in 1947, and for the same reason: these regimes will eventually change because they cannot meet their people's needs."[2] The new policy focused its efforts on containing Saddam Hussein's threats to his neighbors and his own people, while at the same time pursuing multilateral efforts to prevent Iran from acquiring and developing weapons of mass destruction and the ballistic missiles needed to deliver them. The containment of Iran was also meant to seek change in the Iranian policies of support for terrorism, subversion of friendly governments, and violent opposition to the Middle East peace process. Besides political and diplomatic isolation, economic pressure has been applied, aimed mainly at Iran's oil industry.[3] This pressure originally consisted of threatening sanctions and opposing World Bank and IMF loans, as well as trying to persuade allies to maintain pressure on Iran so it could not pursue normal commercial relations. As well as Europe, it also sought to convince China, Japan and Russia to refuse Iranian attempts to buy weapons of mass destruction (and the precursors of WMD) and advanced conventional weapons that might augment a regional threat.[4]

The dilemma in containment, the dilemma in future security decisions in the Gulf and the Middle East, is to decide at what point sufficient change has taken place in the targeted state to warrant the first steps toward re-engagement, and what those steps should be. In the case of Iraq, containment remained implacable and even hardened because the US was convinced that Saddam Hussein would never submit to UN Security Council resolutions. So containment of Iraq took as its goal regime change, and this starting with President Clinton.

In regard to Iran, the changes would have to come in several areas. Its conventional military capabilities would have to be limited so that an upward-spiraling arms race in the region, rooted in the security dilemma, would not be unleashed. Change would also have to come in verified non-proliferation of weapons of mass destruction, whose dangers could reach beyond the region. And it would have to come from a halt in Iranian support of terrorism that, in many alarming cases, has attained global reach. Of course, all of this would be shaped by positive changes in Iranian intentions within the region and beyond. The extent to which this requires regime change is not easy to evaluate. If a non-democratic (even reformed) Iranian regime that accepts the outside world and reasons according to national interest rather than by religious ideology (Iran before Islam) is not possible, then some measure of democratization may be necessary, leading to the well-known instability endemic to the initial stages of democratic transition. There has been a notable, and perhaps fragile, recent trend in the Gulf toward countries attempting to resolve their disputes through negotiation, arbitration and judicial settlement rather than force or the threat of force. Of course, the Iraq of Saddam Hussein was most outside this trend.[5] Even so, it is not clear to what extent political reform in Iran will modify its WMD efforts since national security and defense policies are fervently controlled by a few hardliners, above all Supreme Leader Ali

Khamenei, and are infrequently subject to wider discussion. Furthermore, it is not certain that reform President Khatami would really want to curb Iran's WMD programs, even if he could gain more control of national security decisions. It appears, however, that some Iranian officials, particularly those in the foreign ministry, argue that Iran's security will be better served through cooperation with international non-proliferation regimes and efforts to attenuate regional arms races.[6]

Iran and Conventional Military Weapons

Iran's conventional military capability is fairly extensive but for the moment a serious threat only to its immediate neighbors, and therefore peace and stability in the Gulf. When Iran reaches beyond the region it is by employing and supporting terrorism via proxies. The Iranian armed forces are comprised of the regular defense forces (the army, air force, and navy), and the Iranian Revolutionary Guard Corps (IRGC). The latter was created as an ideologically driven force of elite status. The Guard Corps, however, lacks the professionalism and skills of the regular forces, which nevertheless are also considered to fall short of high levels of effectiveness. Iran's land power is significant even though forty to sixty percent of its equipment was lost in the Iran-Iraq War. However, it still lacks power projection capability. So, Iran cannot truly engage in decisive warfare with the GCC, especially since the US Navy is in the Persian Gulf. Iranian forces could, nevertheless, easily defeat Iranian Kurds or any other internal opposition force. Iranian rearmament has been a slow process. Although quantity has declined, quality has improved despite a lack of standardization largely due to frequent Iranian changes in arms suppliers.[7] Iran has imported large amounts of weapons from Russia, including T-72 tanks.

The Iranian navy poses a nuisance, perhaps a relatively significant one. Iran has attempted to overcome the limitations of its surface forces by relying on other forms of naval warfare. Besides obtaining midget submarines from North Korea, the navy has three Russian Kilo class diesel submarines.[8] These subs would probably not last long against the US fleet, but could still sink a few ships and cause a great deal of consternation and outrage. Iran's navy may also lay mines in the Gulf as a means of sinking shipping and restricting maritime movement. The Iranian Navy also possesses smaller vessels that can serve as platforms for anti-ship missiles.

Iran has a fairly large air force. From 1990 to 1994, Iran acquired MiG-29 and Su-24 aircraft from Russia. But the Iranian Air Force lacks major strike capability and would probably be effective only against its neighbors, including to some extent GCC countries, if they were not protected by others. It cannot challenge Pakistani, Turkish, US, Saudi, and British air power with any hope of telling effectiveness.

Iran's missiles are a far greater threat than the Iranian Air Force. In fact, Iran's most worrisome conventional military assets are its missiles, whose capabilities the regime has undertaken to develop, above all by extending their range. The Iranian missile force attempts to make up for an air force that has not been able to modernize or even to keep up its operational capacity. An air force must also be foreign-supplied and is dependent on foreign sources for training, maintenance, and upgrading. Missile technologies do not require the same level of foreign dependence and may even be manufactured by an indigenous national defense industry, providing a relative autonomy in security planning. Tehran has acquired nearly a hundred C-801 and C-802 anti-ship missiles from the Chinese that could be launched from surface vessels and shore-based facilities. Both missile types are roughly the equivalent of the French Exocet, and can be launched from ships, land, and aircraft. Iran has sought more advanced missiles from Russia, North Korea, and China. The IRGC operates Chinese Silkworm surface-to-ship missiles from land; by 1995 there were fifty to sixty of these missiles under their control. Some of these units were deployed near the Straits of Hormuz to cover the entrance to the Gulf. Also in 1995 Tehran announced the production of an indigenous cruise missile.[9] Iran possesses the 300-km range Scud-B and the 500-km range Scud-C missiles and is thus able to strike targets in Iraq, Saudi Arabia, and elsewhere in the immediate region. Iran is also seeking to acquire the 1,000-km range Nodong missile from North Korea, which would enable it to target Israel for the first time. In addition, Iran is working on a missile with a 1,300-1,500 km range with assistance from Russian firms, and seeking to develop the Shahab-3 and Shahab-4 ballistic missiles with ranges up to 2,000 km.[10] In March 2002 an intelligence community official upgraded the missile threat from Iran by testifying before Congress that the U.S. would "most likely" face an intercontinental ballistic missile threat from Iran by 2015.[11] These increasing ranges raise disquieting uncertainty over whether Tehran means their use as strictly defensive, or even as a regional deterrent, or as something more – perhaps as providing an extended deterrent to the Islamic and Arab world, at least for propaganda purposes. The worry that they may also be used offensively cannot be comfortably set aside. It is easy for analysts to conclude that Iran's missile program does not lend itself to benign interpretations of its motives. As one analysis of Iranian national security policy asserts, "The onus is on Iran to make its missiles appear less threatening to its neighbours. To do this, it will have to speak with one voice and avoid resorting to boasting for (domestic) political effect."[12]

Regional Geostrategy of Conventional Weapons

There are three possible methods of warfare for the use of Iranian force: strikes with ballistic missiles and WMD; a war of attrition against the US Navy and trade in the Persian Gulf; and terrorism. It may be assumed that a lack of power projection and the presence of the US Navy will prevent Iran, if only from a strictly military perspective, from engaging in a significant land war in the region. Iran's only possible use of conventional force would be a war of attrition meant to limit US influence in the Gulf. Such a war would involve strikes by Iran against the US Navy, oil installations, and trade vessels by means of cruise missiles, anti-ship missiles, mine warfare, and submarines. Iran also has significant defensive strength. Only a ground force of a substantial number of divisions could completely defeat Iran. Therefore, any US war against Iran would necessarily have recourse to the method of a war of limited aim. However, Iran could make this costly by conducting a war of attrition with little worry of being completely destroyed or even facing heavy casualties or a serious disruption of its national infrastructure. Anti-ship missiles could be launched from the coast of Iran and would be difficult to locate and destroy. Furthermore, naval surface vessels are constrained by enclosed and shallow waters like the Persian Gulf. Such maritime action could cut off, or more likely limit, the international oil trade from the Persian Gulf since Iran's ability to directly block the Straits of Hormuz is viewed as a "technologically defunct argument."[13]

The US would be severely limited in its retaliatory options to nearly airpower alone. Air and missile strikes would be unlikely to destroy Iranian missile sites entirely, giving Iran a crucial advantage in the relative cost of the war. Even if all Iranian missile sites were destroyed, the cost of damage done to shipping and the US Navy would probably far exceed the cost to Iran in engaging in the war. The only remaining US option would be a limited amphibious landing. The purpose would be to seize Iranian territory, like the Straits of Hormuz, making the war more costly for Iran and providing the US with a bargaining chip to end the conflict. A landing would be a major threat to Iran, but could also be very costly for the US, at least in monetary terms. Otherwise, the only option to significantly damage Iran would be nuclear weapons, which is not a plausible option except in the most extreme, even unrealistic scenario. Besides the obvious moral stigma attached to using nuclear weapons, their use would run the risk of retaliation from Iranian WMD, even though this capability might be marginal.[14]

Another method of warfare that Iran could adopt is strikes with its ballistic missiles, possibly loaded with WMD. Iran could use its ballistic missiles against the Gulf States or other regional targets, such as Turkey. In the Iran-Iraq War ballistic missiles played an important role in the 1988 "war of cities." Because of limited accuracy, these missiles would only be useful as countervalue weapons. Furthermore, a large number of missiles would need to be launched or carry warheads of mass destruction in order to cause significant damage. In either case, Iran would be risking severe US retaliation. A theatre missile defense system, for example protecting the GCC, could render Iranian strikes ineffective, undermining Iranian missiles as a deterrent. The greatest benefit of WMD and ballistic missile programs for Iran is raising the costs of an attack or a riposte against it. But more reassuringly, if Iran lacks a substantial second-strike capability its ballistic missile and WMD capabilities provide only a minimal deterrent. However, these scenarios appear rather far-fetched. Iran would be foolish to engage in a massive military engagement with the United States. If necessary, the US could easily launch a blow that would cripple Iran, making any gains nowhere near commensurate to the cost of the war. Without a great power ally Iran would only be able to respond minimally, if at all. Therefore, any Iranian offensive action would rely entirely on US reluctance to use its full strike capability. The US would surely withhold use of nuclear weapons unless Iran used WMD against the GCC or other vital US assets.[15]

United together the GCC (Saudi Arabia, Bahrain, Kuwait, Qatar, Oman, and the United Arab Emirates) could deter Iran from military aggression. Although their total population is only about 23 million (excluding non-nationals) to Iran's 67 million (with the combined military manpower fit for military service in about the same ratio),[16] the military might of these states could rival Iran's air strength and also stop an amphibious attack. The US has, thus, supported greater GCC coordination. However, the small steps already taken to put together a coordinated defense still leaves the GCC as relatively fragmented and vulnerable. It has been pointed out that "The fundamental defence policy on which the Gulf states have relied since the formation of the GCC (and before) has been a holding strategy of initial self-defence until the Western cavalry arrives from over the horizon."[17] Still, the build-up of armaments in the Gulf has blunted the effectiveness of the Iranian military to engage in a regional war. The quality of Saudi weapons, for example, counters Iranian numerical superiority. Saudi Arabia has combat aircraft that are more modern than

Iran's. Nevertheless, Iran has the military capability to make credible threats and use intimidation for diplomatic ends.[18]

Iran and Weapons of Mass Destruction

Even though Iranian WMD programs have not advanced as quickly as Iraq's, let alone Pakistan's, Iran is acquiring technology and know-how. In terms of nuclear weapons it should be recalled that Iran remains a member of the NPT and the IAEA. To date, no violations of the NPT have been found by inspections, although IAEA inspections remain an imperfect mechanism for monitoring clandestine weapons programs and experts are divided as to the effectiveness of such visits.[19] Early in the 1980s, the Ayatollah Khomeini abandoned the Shah's nuclear weapons programs, but Iran subsequently resuscitated its dormant program later in the decade, fully reviving it by 1991.[20] Iran has significant deposits of uranium, and facilities have been constructed to process it. China and Russia have been willing to help Iran develop nuclear facilities, perhaps even nuclear weapons. For example, in 1994 Iran signed a deal with China for a nuclear reactor near Tehran and expressed interest in more reactors. Russia is involved in building a 1,000-megawatt light-water reactor at Bushehr. It is currently unclear if the Iranians are intent on using these facilities to help them develop nuclear weapons. The United States has argued that Iran has sufficient oil and gas reserves for power generation, and that nuclear reactors are expensive, unnecessary, and could be used for military purposes. The United States strongly opposes the project (which must be said is permitted under the NPT) and has in the past provided Russia with intelligence information pointing to the existence of an Iranian nuclear weapons program. Despite this, the Russians are proceeding with work on Bushehr. The intriguing question is to what extent the Russian government is encouraging, or at least tolerating, the transfer and development of nuclear weapons' technology. The Putin government acknowledges that there is indeed Russian nuclear assistance to Iran, but that it is "private proliferation" by Russian "entities" that are contravening Russian policies and laws. This still troubles Washington. Moscow has a strategic interest in cultivating good relations with Tehran, even though Iranian missiles (eventually loaded with WMD) could also threaten Russia. Russian aid in nuclear development may also be seen as opening doors to future commercial relations in other sectors, and not only military.[21]

In 1992, CIA Director Robert Gates told Congress that Iran was indeed building nuclear weapons and estimated that Iran could have them by the year 2000. The Secretary of Defense William Perry, believed it would take much longer.[22] In testimony before the Senate in September 2000, the Deputy Director of the DCI Nonproliferation Center stated that Iran was actively attempting to acquire from a variety of foreign sources, but especially Russia, the fissile material and the experience and technology necessary to transform it into nuclear weapons. The Israeli Defense Ministry believes Iran could have nuclear weapons capability by 2005.[23] However, to date, Iran's WMD programs are not patently threatening and are seemingly pursued in a haphazard manner and perhaps in disarray. Even though there are some in the Iranian government who oppose the acquisition and development of WMD, and even though Iran has repeatedly called for the Middle East Nuclear Weapons Free Zone, and even though President Mohammed Khatami tried to reassure the world as recently as 23 December 2002 that his country had no ambition for nuclear weapons, there nevertheless remains significant skepticism in the rest of the world. In short, despite official pronouncements such as these, few seem to doubt Iran's *intention* to develop a covert nuclear weapons program. These doubts were recently reinforced when commercial satellite photos made in December 2002 revealed at least two new sites, Arak and Natanz, which US experts believe could be another part of a nuclear weapons program.[24]

But the more ominous evaluation of Iran's nuclear capacity, which was described to *The New York Times* by American officials, is apparently not based on evidence that Iran's indigenous efforts to build a bomb have achieved a breakthrough. Rather, it seems to be based on the fact that the United States cannot track with great certainty increased efforts by Iran to acquire nuclear materials and technology on the international black market, mainly from the former Soviet Union. In effect, CIA analysts have warned that given Iran's intensive efforts to steal or buy highly enriched uranium and plutonium, it is possible that it may have more bomb-grade material than previously believed.[25]

Iran and Chemical and Biological Weapons

The Iranian chemical weapons production program dates to early in the Iran-Iraq war. Iran used chemical agents to respond to Iraqi chemical attacks on several occasions during that war. Since the early 1990s it has put a high priority on its chemical weapons program because of its inability to respond in kind to Iraq's chemical attacks and the discovery of substantial Iraqi efforts with advanced agents, such as the highly persistent nerve agent VX, a drop of which kills in minutes. The CIA claimed in February 1996 that Iran was continuing to expand and diversify its chemical weapons program, considered among the largest in the Third

World. In 1996 the U.S. Defense Department estimated that Iran might have a minimum of several hundred tons of blister, blood and choking agents. In the same year the Arms Control and Disarmament Agency believed that the Iranians might have as much as 2,000 tons of chemical agent. Even though these chemical agents are World War I era weapons, the step to producing more advanced and more lethal nerve agents may have already been taken.[26] China is an important supplier of technologies and equipment for Iran's chemical warfare program. Therefore, Chinese supply policies will be key to whether Tehran attains its long-term goal of independent production of these weapons. In the future, as Iran becomes more self-sufficient at producing chemical agents, there is a potential that it will become a supplier to other states trying to develop CW capabilities. For example, it is reported that Iran supplied Libya with chemical agents in 1987.[27]

Even though it has ratified the Biological Weapons Convention, Iran is believed to have begun offensive biological warfare research during the Iran-Iraq War. The intensity of these efforts has probably increased because of the 1995 revelations about the scale of Iraqi efforts prior to the Gulf War. The relative low cost of developing these weapons may be another motivating factor. Iran's biological warfare program is now generally believed to be in the advanced research and development phase. Iran is judged to be able to support an independent BW program with little foreign assistance (although some foreign BW expertise, especially from Russia, is flowing to Iran). While only small quantities of usable agent may exist now, within 10 years Iran's military forces may be able to deliver biological agents effectively.[28]

Regional Geostrategy of WMD

Why would Iran want to possess nuclear weapons? The first, classic, motivation would be to defend Iranian independence and security by establishing a deterrent against the use by adversaries of their nuclear weapons, or even against a conventional attack. Perceived threats come from Israel and the United States. A nuclear-armed Pakistan is also not reassuring, especially when it manifests good relations with Saudi Arabia.[29] There must be added to this the fear that neighboring Iraq under Saddam Hussein would attain nuclear weapons capability, a fear supposedly now dissipated. The fall of Saddam's regime could contribute to persuading Tehran that nuclear weapons may not be needed for immediate regional stability. There remains, however, Israel's nuclear arsenal. Israel's nuclear weapons program dates back to the late 1950s and the construction of its nuclear facility at Dimona, in the Negev desert. Here, at first with French and later South African assistance, the Israelis undertook a nuclear weapons program that, according to U.S. Intelligence estimates, is thought to have built by now between 75 and 130 devices. The Israeli government does not admit to possessing nuclear weapons and is not a member of the NPT (Dimona remains a closed site not subject to international inspections or safeguards) and prefers that only conjecture, albeit strong conjecture about nuclear weapons in its hands, serve as its deterrent – a sort of overt covert arsenal. Therefore, there is no official mention of how nuclear weapons fit into Israeli strategic thinking. Their role in the Israeli Defense Force's doctrine is thus also a matter of conjecture. However, the states arrayed against Israel avert that it is their right to develop nuclear weapons as a deterrent to the Israeli arsenal, even though it has not been publicly avowed. They believe that Washington maintains a double standard by ignoring Israel's acquisition of weapons of mass destruction while opposing the transfer of even peaceful nuclear technologies to others. They could also claim a parallel right to secretly develop, as did the Israelis, their nuclear deterrents. This, of course, ignores the fundamental role of the importance of overall intentions in the pursuit of these weapons.

Besides the legitimate concern for defense and deterrence, a desire for hegemony in the Gulf could also explain Iran's quest for nuclear weapons, especially in the absence of an Iraqi nuclear threat. In such a scenario only a nuclear threat from outside the Gulf, for example American nuclear weapons, could maintain deterrence in the region against Iran. An additional problem with an Iranian nuclear capability would be an intensification of Israel's sense of vulnerability, especially since the current Iranian regime is hostile to even the existence of the Jewish state. Israel's nuclear weapons are an outgrowth of this sense of being under siege. This could tempt Israel to engage once again in pre-emptive action in the Gulf – as it did against the Iraqi Osiraq reactor in 1981. Since Israel lacks strategic depth, its military doctrine has privileged pre-emptive conventional capabilities as well as the ability to carry the battle away from Israeli territory and its population centers. Also, given the delays inherent in mobilizing a largely reservist army, the country relies heavily upon its air force to give its army time to take the field. Thus, any threat that undermines this role of the air force also calls into question the Israeli concept of defense and deterrence.[30] Arab advances in missile technology, air defenses, and chemical weapons seem to offer just such a threat.[31]

The prestige that comes with the possession of nuclear weapons can also not be excluded as a motivation. Shahram Chubin says that the pursuit of nuclear weapons and missile technology is viewed in Tehran as an expression of Iran's entry into the modern world of scientific achievement and consequently a source of national pride. All restrictions on transfer to Iran of dual use technologies (which may also be used in weapon development) is perceived as a policy to slow down Iranian science.[32] Of course nuclear weapons may also serve to make up for conventional military weaknesses. Chemical and biological weapons could also serve this purpose, however. Since Iran lacks a nuclear umbrella, the development of missiles and WMD can be perceived as Iran giving itself security, but it could also be viewed as destabilizing and even provoke pre-emption.

Terrorism

Terrorism emanating from the Gulf until recently has been mostly aimed against the region's regimes allied with the United States and the West, or against sites of U.S. presence, especially military presence. The Islamist groups are the most active and their main source of support has been Iran, even though five other of the seven states currently on the U.S. terrorism list are in the region (besides Iran there are Iraq, Syria, Libya and Sudan). But especially since the inauguration of President Mohammad Khatami in 1997 (and somewhat before), these attacks against regional powers have ceased and Iran has even made conciliatory gestures towards the United States – including public condemnations of terrorist attacks by Algerian and Egyptian groups. Also, in general, before September 11 a decline in state sponsorship of terrorism was noticeable. After September 11, Iran and Sudan even cooperated to some extent with the war against Al Qaeda. Nevertheless, Iran is still considered to be the most important state sponsor of radical Islamic groups that engage in terrorism, particularly against Israel. The Iranian attempt to deliver weapons aboard the Karine A to the Palestinian Authority is the most recent and striking example. For many years Iran has helped support Hezbollah, Hamas and the Palestinian Islamic Jihad.

Even if there is a decrease in terrorist attacks in the region, other than against Israel, the announced goals of Islamic terrorism remain the overthrow of pro-Western governments, the expulsion of non-Muslim control or influence from Muslim-inhabited land, and the derailment of the Arab-Israeli peace process. The main goal outside of the region continues to be the vast project of doing away with secular democratic government as well as other religions. Most terrorist attacks now take place against Israel or outside of the region. For example, worldwide casualties caused by terrorism increased to 405 in the year 2000 from 233 the previous year.

However, the number of attacks increased only slightly in the same period – from 392 to 423. Of the 423 attacks in 2000, only 16 occurred in the Middle East and only 19 of the 405 casualties.[33] The suicide attacks against Israel of the second Intifada is bringing the balance of attacks and casualties back to the Middle East. However, the global reach of terrorism emanating from the region remains the major new characteristic. Al Qaeda is obviously the pre-eminent example.

The network of Osama bin Laden has evolved from a regional threat to US troops in the Persian Gulf, to a global threat. However, Al Qaeda activists are still linked to opposition movements in the Persian Gulf. In Yemen, for example, the government is aware of Al Qaeda presence, but is either ill-equipped, and perhaps still reluctant to take action against the network. The network's ideology has led it to support Islamic fighters or terrorists against Serb forces in Bosnia, against Soviet forces in Afghanistan (and now Russian forces in Chechnya) against Indian control over part of Kashmir, and has a presence more or less identifiable elsewhere in the world. This presence is often in alliance with affiliate or subordinate groups – from Latin America, to Indonesia, to the Philippines.[34]

Nevertheless, Iran could once again employ terrorism in the Gulf region. Terrorism would be a more indirect and therefore safer method of wearing down the United States. Iran has conducted terrorist attacks in the past to show the West the costliness of being involved in the region. Thus, terrorism might be viewed as a simple means of thwarting Western influence.[35] By killing civilians and US military personnel Iran would hope to shake US resolve to remain in the Persian Gulf. Terrorism used in this manner is not based on the classic outcome of military engagements, but pursued with the aim of demoralizing an adversary. However, Iran could restrict its use of terrorism since any large-scale attack, especially using WMD, would undoubtedly be met with a robust American retaliation. So, Hezbollah, Hamas, Islamic Jihad, and other terrorist organizations could act as proxies to harm the US. Iran could, as in the past, extend subversive activities in Bahrain and Saudi Arabia. Terrorists could repeat attacks on US facilities like Al-Khobar. However, it should not be forgotten that in the recent past the unintended result of Iran's use of terrorism was to increase its isolation and make it a pariah state. "More recently," says Chubin, "partly as a result of changes in its politics (and society), Iran has substantially repudiated this tactic, which has been morally discredited. For Iran today, terrorism is confined to the assistance extended to Palestinian groupings in support of their 'liberation struggle'." This use of terrorism is seen as a manifestation of the hardliners' perceived revolutionary mission as leader of the Islamic world.³⁶ It is not clear to what extent this use of terrorism is being challenged within Iran as hurting Iranian national interests.

The Poppy Crop and the Geostrategy of Opium

Perhaps up to 90 per cent of heroin consumed in Europe comes from Afghanistan's poppy crop. Opium has been grown in Afghanistan for many years, but the scale of cultivation increased dramatically during the Afghan-Soviet War. After the Soviet withdrawal and the cessation of military aid to the mujahedeen in 1991, there was a further increase in poppy cultivation as the combatants in the Afghan civil war had to find new means to finance their conflict. It became, of course, a very lucrative cash crop for desperately poor farmers. By the turn of the century it was estimated that perhaps 30 to 50 per cent of the Afghan population, and as much as 80 per cent of its economy, was involved in some aspect of cultivation, production or trafficking. Drugs cross the permeable border with Iran on their way to Turkey and Europe despite Iran's efforts to stem the flow.

A 1995 United Nations report affirmed that "annual turnover in the drug trade could be as high as $500bn."³⁷ The profits are huge. Afghan growers sell opium for the equivalent of $30 a kilo in food. Smugglers earn $15-30 a day. By the time a kilo of opium arrives in Teheran it sells for $600. After getting into Turkey it goes for $2,400. Once refined it yields 100 grams of heroin. In Europe the street price for a gram of heroin, from 20-35 per cent pure, runs from $25-35. It must not be overlooked that Iran is on the shortest route from the producers in Afghanistan to European consumers. The Iranian route is all the more attractive since the Central Asian states of the former Soviet Union have split into separate countries, putting in place many new borders to cross. Via Iran there are only two.³⁸ Not only Europe suffers the health and social consequences of opium and heroin consumption, the entire Central Asia region is experiencing a sharp rise in drug addiction and the appearance of HIV, with Pakistan and Iran suffering the strongest impact. For example, Iran is reported to have at least 1.2 million addicts and 800,000 casual users, but some estimates put the figures even higher – to 6.2 million consuming drugs to some extent. Seventy per cent of Iranian HIV and AIDS cases are believed to have resulted from shared needles. Officially there are 2,721 AIDS cases. While the Iranian government admits that there may be an estimated additional 10,000 cases not in the official statistics, it is believed by non-government observers that this is no doubt much higher.³⁹

But opium also poses a geo-strategic problem. Not only does it breed government corruption, but it may also pave the way to an increased number of possible narco-states in the region, with their related violence. Clashes on the borders with traffickers have become a daily occurrence, resulting in the death of some 3,000 security officials in recent years.[40] And, of course, the drug trade is potentially, and perhaps even currently, an important source of revenue for terrorist groups. For example, the Taliban regime in Afghanistan had an ambiguous policy toward poppy cultivation, at least until July 2000 when Mullah Omar decreed that the Koran forbids cultivation and trade in the crop. By the time the ban went into effect, however, it was estimated that 250 tons of heroin had already been stockpiled in Afghanistan – which amounts to a two-year supply for Western Europe. It is reported that poppy production has skyrocketed from 185 tons in 2001 to 3,400 tons in 2002. The Afghan Interim Administration of Hamid Karzai has not yet been able to get a handle on controlling the production.[41]

Beyond Double Containment?

The goal of double containment, like the historic goal of the containment of the Soviet Union, is to prevent the spread of threats while awaiting, and when possible provoking, regime change. The difference in Gulf containment, which can be seen as a significant difference, is that the containment of the communist bloc was consistently supported by a strong and unceasing commitment from America's allies. The US has had difficulty bringing others to perceive threats in the Gulf the way Americans see them. In particular, after the end of the Gulf War the international anti-Iraqi consensus that had emerged during the war underwent substantial weakening. To neighboring Arab governments, Turkey, Western European states and Russia, Saddam Hussein was perceived as less of a threat, and the Iraqi 'problem' as less pressing an issue. Outside great powers, like Russia and China, have even found opportunities to insert themselves further into an American-created vacuum – as demonstrated by their support of Iranian projects that could lead to Teheran's attainment of WMD. The staunchest ally of containment has been Israel, but this has not helped promote the doctrine in the Arab world.

History has shown that successful containment requires steadfast allies to a common cause willing to impose isolation and sanctions and bear their costs. One consequence of a lack of shared commitment in the Gulf, or at least of the same intensity, is that the US has come to be viewed as defending only its interests, which since the election of George Bush Jr. has reinforced the perception of unilateralism. Moreover, double containment has not provided the US with sufficient coercion or incentives to change the behavior of the targeted regimes – at least in Iran. The strategy of containment has not lead Iran to completely abandon terrorism, its WMD programs, or its missile capabilities. Sanctions have caused only relatively mild economic difficulties, like increasing prices. Former National Security Advisors Zbigniew Brzezinski and Brent Scowcroft see no reason to believe that containment will stop terrorism. In a study they co-chaired for the Council on Foreign Relations they call for "differentiated containment." This would focus the economic embargo only on a narrow range of specific items such as WMD components, missiles and dual-use technology, and even allow US companies to negotiate deals with Iran. It would also cool down the rhetorical war and explore the potential for dialogue.[42] Yale researcher Ray Takeyh advocates a similar policy of simultaneous cooperation and competition, continuing the containment of terrorism, proliferation and adamant hostility to an Israeli-Palestinian settlement while engaging Iran economically and reassuring it strategically.[43] Is it not time to conclude that a policy that proposes gains to Iran has a greater chance of success than containment? In more general terms it might be questioned whether the proliferation of WMD and ballistic missiles can ever be completely stopped. Eventually more and more states will get hold of these weapons, changing the nature of warfare. Non-proliferation may only be a delaying action and not an ultimate attainable goal. Modifying the intentions of those possessing these weapons, and at best gaining them as allies, will be better than fighting them in the future. Without changed intentions, it could be said, as the most recent Iraqi crisis has demonstrated, that containment will not end WMD programs. Only war will.

The policy of containment has not allowed the US to capitalize on opportunities to improve its position. This has not been a problem for other powers, who have not hesitated to exploit openings in Iran. For example, China, Russia and France signed contracts with Iraq to develop oil in view of the lifting of sanctions. French, Russian, and Malaysian contractors have agreed to develop Iranian oil fields despite US sanctions. European and Asian products are replacing US products in Iran.[44] Russia also has political as well as economic interests closer to home in the Caspian, the Caucasus and Central Asia. Saudi Arabia sees containment as inhibiting its attempts to improve relations with Iran.[45] Containment, then, may be seen as surrendering Iran to others. Containment has also required a large military presence in the Gulf. This presence makes populations in the region feel dominated by the United States. The feeling of domination weakens stability and reinforces opposition to the US. Of course, elements inherently hostile to the US fan the sense of domination in order to gain support for radical actions like terrorism and the overthrow of GCC regimes.[46] It may be asked if the containment of Iran is isolating not only Tehran, but also Washington.

What, concretely and realistically does the US expect from Iran? At a very minimum, in the realm of arms, the US would want Iran to limit its cruise and ballistic missile production. It would also be imperative for Iran to stop supporting terrorism. It would be untenable to engage in détente with Iran while it was promoting, or suspected of promoting, terrorism. Short of a full rapprochement with Iran, the US could continue to maintain deterrence in the Gulf, but with fewer ground forces in the GCC countries. This would require greater GCC coordination and a concomitant consolidation of their ground and air forces. If an American military presence is still required for deterrence it would have to depend more on a naval presence — so the Fifth Fleet would stay in the Gulf, but would have to patently display a minimal defensive posture. This, of course, might still not avoid an Iranian sense of being aggressively boxed in and lead to the classic upward cycle of the security dilemma. Deterrence would also need at least to repose on stable neighboring regimes that have the support of their populations. This would in turn probably require further movement toward democracy and most certainly require a renewed and serious effort to diffuse the Israeli-Palestinian conflict. But even a changed and improved deterrent context in the Gulf may still not bring about the minimum changes hoped for in Iranian behavior. Only a renewed commitment to peace and peaceful coexistence by Tehran can bring this about.

Rapprochement?

Iran can potentially gain more benefits from peace than from war. Despite sanctions Iran's economic performance has improved, providing an opportunity to reduce Iran's debt. Debt reduction will increase the level of long-term growth. Richard Herrmann and R. William Ayres claim that in the 1990s Iran has been more interested in pursuing power through commercial rather than military means.[47] For Takeyh, "Economic imperatives are finally leading Iran to subordinate its revolutionary zeal to pragmatic considerations, and to deal constructively with a state [the US] that it has long demonised."[48] Iran had a 2001 GDP of purchasing power parity (ppp) of $426 billion, which was a per capita GDP of $6,400, and a growth rate of 5 per cent with 13 per cent inflation. By contrast, Saudi Arabia for the same year had a GDP (ppp) of $241 billion, and per capita GDP of $10,600. Its 2001 growth rate was 1.6 per cent but with inflation at

1.7 per cent. The statistics for Iraq (admittedly of questionable reliability) are catastrophic in comparison, with estimated per capita at $2,500, a negative growth rate of 5.7 per cent and 2001 inflation running at 60 per cent.[49] Iran is now just recovering from the Iran-Iraq War. Engaging in another war would mean a return to economic hardship and probably push to the brink a population sick of war. These are the fundamental factors working against an Iranian temptation to aggression. Iran is doing better without war. The economy is healthier and an indigenous industrial capacity has even developed because of Iran's isolation. However, the economy has still not attained the performance it experienced before the fall of the Shah when Iran was inundated with petrodollars, especially after oil prices quadrupled in 1973. Although almost everyone benefited to some extent from the new riches, which provided roads, electric plants, schools, hospitals and other infrastructure, a visible minority gained far more than most of the population. As a former US diplomat and scholar of Iran puts it: "There was a surplus of luxury villas and apartments and a shortage of affordable housing for middle- and lower-class families; students in government schools sat in overcrowded classrooms, whereas students from newly wealthy families flocked to booming private schools; some Iranians made monthly shopping trips to Europe, whereas others stood in line for onions and milk."[50] Nevertheless, Iran has paid an enormous economic price for its Islamic revolution and the subsequent war with Iraq. A former finance minister in Iran's pre-1979 government, Jahangir Amuzegar, says that "Despite a 100 per cent rise in average annual oil income since the revolution, most indicators of economic welfare have steadily deteriorated." Inflation and unemployment remain high and growth and productivity low. "As a result, continues Amuzegar, "Iran's per capita income has declined by at least 30 per cent since 1979. By official admission, more than 15 per cent of the population now lives below the poverty line, and private estimates run as high as 40 per cent."[51]

The regime in Tehran may still conclude it can get definite gains through military means in the Persian Gulf without exorbitant cost to itself. Iran must be convinced that the economic losses of war are not worth it. Nevertheless, Iran has a strong bargaining position because of its military capability. Will the lure of free trade and normal relations be sufficient to convince Iran to compromise on reducing, or at least control with verification, these capabilities? Obviously and ideally the US should take measures to reinforce the option of normalization and peace. Even though Iran's per capita GDP is less than Saudi Arabia's, it must be obvious to Tehran that it is far better off than worn-torn Iraq. It is reported that there is a new sense of self-reliance as indigenous products have been forced to replace imports. The share of Iran's economy from exports has decreased and investment into oilfields is inadequate. However many foreign companies are seeking to invest in Iranian oil. Iran, for its part, is interested in US oil and gas technology in order to further develop its oil industry.[52] In short, if containment is not doing that much harm, the US cannot expect proposing its termination as a powerful bargaining chip, albeit a chip of some value. Instead the US will need to rely on other concessions and demarches in order to achieve its goals with Iran. The most significant boost to Iran's economy would come after extensive political and economic reform, even democratization, which would create an investment climate favorable and reassuring to foreign capital.

An Insolvable Dilemma?

Without an anti-regime revolution from below rapprochement and an eventual renewed partnership can only get under way after taking the first, small steps toward détente – perhaps by opening a genuine direct and official dialogue, if possible. A recent opinion survey done by an Iranian polling agency in conjunction with Gallup revealed that three quarters of Iranians favor resuming dialogue with the United States. The directors of the Iranian polling agency were promptly arrested. One of them, Abbas Abdi, played a leading role as a young student in the takeover of the US embassy in Tehran in 1979. The poll also revealed that public support for Supreme Leader Khamenei stood at 1.2 per cent.[53] So, with whom in Iran is dialogue possible?

Since Washington has no trust in the ardent fundamentalist hardliners of the current regime, and seems to have given up on President Khatami's ability to provoke reform, it has, at least for the moment, limited its options, at least publicly, to supporting change from below, from the Iranian people themselves. Of course a successful popular movement would introduce a risky period of instability, with consequences difficult to anticipate. It is not even certain that a new regime would be democratic. This is the worry of Jahangir Amuzegar. "The West's hope," he says, "and the opposition's claim, is that it will be a pluralistic, and participatory democracy with all its prerequisites – civil liberties, a transparent and accountable government, free elections, and thriving civil societies. But given the absence of a democratic tradition in Iran's paternalistic and patrimonial culture, and its historic rule by a monarchic/Islamic accommodation, such hopes and claims may still remain just that – hopes and claims."[54] Amuzegar's hope is that history will not repeat itself. It may be reassuring, however, as one sociological study points out, that the generation coming to political consciousness in Iran is "more educated, and certainly less dependent on traditional household structure." There is also evolution in gender roles and the economic and social expectations of a very young population.[55] In any case, viable and enduring democracy does not come overnight. It is a project that takes years, and even generations.[56]

Another dimension of the conundrum is that obvious open US support of a liberal democratic revolution in Iran would undoubtedly provoke the current hardliners in power to engage in a violent crackdown on its population and tempt them to reconsider the costs of military action and renewed terrorism in the Gulf, and even beyond. Short of rapid and drastic political change in Iran, the US will have to continue to muddle through in its diplomacy with the current regime – or to put it more positively, to use creatively any diplomatic openings based on shared interests, a policy of "managed tensions."[57] In the immediate future this will probably require discreet contacts if open dialogue is not possible. Pragmatic and discreet rapprochement based on shared national interests has already been seen in the limited informal cooperation from Tehran following 9/11 and the American military intervention in Afghanistan. Tehran and Washington may very probably have shared intelligence, for example, and the regime authorized the use of its air space for rescue missions.[58] This cooperation was rooted in a shared interest to get rid of the Taliban regime and showed that each side could be sensitive to the legitimate security concerns of the other. Such an approach would reinforce the pragmatic directions in Iranian foreign policy that place national interest ahead of Islamic solidarity. In the numerous conflicts around its borders, including in the new states that emerged from the breakup of the Soviet Union, Tehran has not supported the obvious Islamic candidates for diplomatic support. For example, the only former Soviet republic to enter into an alliance with Iran has been Christian Armenia, in order to serve as a counterweight to Azerbaijan's alliance with Muslim Turkey. Iran has also cultivated ties to India to balance against Muslim Pakistan, but has refused to become involved in the Kashmir dispute.[59] Outside reinforcement of pragmatic Iranian national tendencies might help to lead to some measure of détente by cultivating a perception in Tehran of being less embattled. It has been suggested that "By embarking on a dialogue with Tehran on important regional security interests Washington can indicate to Tehran that its concerns will be taken into account on issues ranging from the reconstruction of post-war Afghanistan to the future of Iraq."[60]

A modified US military posture in the region might also play a role in attenuating a sense of being under siege. This is all the more important because of the changed political-military situation around Iran's borders.

The elimination of the Taliban in Afghanistan is a relief to Tehran, but the military presence there of outsiders cannot be viewed with equanimity. The fact that the presence in Afghanistan is not only American, but also UN and multilateral, may provide only meager reassurance. Recently Tehran has been sowing mischief in Afghanistan so as to make it difficult for the US and others to perpetuate their presence there. Iran would certainly not want to see Pakistan rebuild its influence in Afghanistan on a new basis.[61] The composition of a post-Saddam regime in Iraq will also have vital consequences for Tehran's sense of encirclement. In the Gulf itself, it would probably be wise for the US to reconfigure its military presence in order to demonstrate as much as possible its strictly defensive nature, as merely containment of the Iranian military. It would also mean shoring up GCC defenses by relying more on indigenous forces. Putting more emphasis on a naval presence and less on ground and regional air forces could help. Of course a less menacing post-Saddam regime in Iraq should lift significant pressure off of the GCC, modifying the calculation of an order of battle necessary for containing Iran. It would also allow the US to redistribute some of its military assets to an eventual friendly regime in Baghdad, probably in conjunction with others.

All military, diplomatic and political measures adopted to reassure the Iranian regime could, however, be exploited by the hardliners as resounding successes in the teeth of threats to the Islamic revolution, an attempt to legitimate the current regime. Tehran may also interpret positive demarches as eagerness on the part of Washington to improve ties and lead the current foreign policy establishment of Iranian hardliners to demand an increase in the cost of their cooperation. So, the future crucial strategic decision by the US will entail an evaluation of how far reform has gone in attaining an acceptable reduction of threat and a sufficient threshold of political and economic liberalism to warrant significant re-engagement that is mutually beneficial to both Iran and the US. The narrow options available vis-à-vis Iran are, for the present, the major source of new threats in the Persian Gulf – and not only since 9/11.

Notes

1   See for example John L. Esposito, "Political Islam and Gulf Security," in John L. Esposito, ed. *Political Islam: Revolution, Radicalism, or Reform?* (Lynne Rienner Publisher, 1997), especially pp. 56–7.
2   Patrick Clawson, "The Continuing Logic of Dual Containment" in *Survival*, vol. 40, no. 1 (Spring 1998), 33.
3   Martin Indyk, "Remarks at the Council on Foreign Relations," (New York, 22 April 1999).

4   Gary Sick, "Rethinking Dual Containment" in *Survival* vol. 40, no 1 (Spring 1998) p. 8. For the most recent summary of sanctions see Kenneth Katzman, "Iran: Current Developments in U.S. Policy," *Issue Brief for Congress* (Congressional Research Service: updated December 26, 2002).
5   This trend is noted in several of the articles in Lawrence G. Potter and Gary Sick, eds., *Security in the Persian Gulf: Origins, Obstacles, and the Search for Consensus* (Palgrave, 2002).
6   Kenneth Katzman, "Iran: Arms and Weapons of Mass Destruction Suppliers," *Report for Congress* (Congressional Research Service, updated January 3, 2003), 2–3. Shahram Chubin, *Whither Iran? Reform, Domestic Politics and National Security* (Oxford University Press for The International Institute for Strategic Studies, Adelphi Paper 342, 2002), p. 37. Chubin also points out that security and defense decisions are limited to hardliners.
7   *The Military Balance 1999-2000* (Oxford University Press for the IISS, October 1999; *SIPRI Yearbook: Armaments, Disarmament and International Security* (Oxford University Press for SIPRI, 2000); Anthony Cordesman, "Iranian Military Capabilities" in Gary Sick and Lawrence Potter, eds., *The Persian Gulf at the Millennium: Essays in Politics, Economy, Security, and Religion* (London: Macmillan, 1997).
8   Data from sources cited above.
9   Ibid. Some naval and missile figures also in Clawson.
10   In "Non-Proliferation: Iran," Carnegie Endowment for International Peace at http://www.ceip. org/programs/npp/iran.html.
11   Cited in Kenneth Katzman, "Iran: Arms and Weapons of Mass Destruction Suppliers," 2.
12   Chubin, *Whither Iran?*, p. 69.
13   Richard Schofield, "Border Disputes: Past, Present, and Future" in Sick and Potter, *The Persian Gulf at the Millennium*, p.153. See discussion of methods of warfare in Newton Howard, *Seeking Peace in Our Time: Toward Global Defense Policy Laws* (1st Books Library: 2002), Chapter 3.
14   Howard.
15   Extended analysis in Howard.
16   CIA, *The World Factbook 2002*. A useful summary of the size of Gulf armed forces, defense spending and orders of battle may be found in Saideh Lotfian, "A Regional Security System in the Persian Gulf," in Potter and Sick, *Security in the Persian Gulf*.
17   J.E. Peterson, *Saudi Arabia and the Illusion of Security* (Oxford University Press for The International Institute for Strategic Studies, Adelphi Paper 348, 2002), 40.
18   Cordesman, p.195
19   Michael Donovan, "Iran, Israel and Nuclear Weapons in the Middle East," Center for Defense Information (February 14, 2002), available at www.cdi.org/terrorism/ menukes.cfm.
20   Sick, "Rethinking Dual Containment," p. 16.
21   Robert J. Einhorn and Gary Samore, "Ending Russian Assistance to Iran's Nuclear Bomb," *Survival*, vol. 44, no. 2, Summer 2002, esp. pp. 60–61.
22   Cordesman pp. 212–14.
23   Statement by Deputy Director, DCI Nonproliferation Center A. Norman Schindler on Iran's Weapons of Mass Destruction Programs to the International Security, Proliferation and Federal Services Subcommittee of the Senate Governmental Affairs Committee, As Prepared for Delivery on 21 September 2000. Available at www.cia.gov/cia/public_affairs/s.../archives/2000/schindler_WMD. See also Donovan.
24   Kenneth Katzman, "The Persian Gulf: Issues for U.S. Policy, 2003," p. 9.

25. James Risen and Judith Miller, "C.I.A. Tells Clinton an Iranian A-Bomb Can't Be Ruled Out," *The New York Times*, January 17, 2000.
26. "Adherence to and Compliance with Arms Control," Arms Control and Disarmament Agency, May 1996; "Proliferation: Threat and Response," Office of the Secretary of Defense (Washington: Government Printing Office), April 1996. Cited in W. Seth Carus, "Iranian Nuclear, Biological and chemical Weapons: Implications and Responses," *Middle East Review of International Affairs*, Vol. 2, no. 1 (March 1998).
27. "Iran Special Weapons Guide," Global Security.org http://www.globalsecurity.org/wmd/world/iran/index.html.
28. Carnegie Endowment for International Peace, "Non-Proliferation: Iran."
29. See J.E. Peterson on the complicity of Saudi and Pakistani ruling elites, pp. 18–20.
30. Geoffrey Kemp with Shelley A. Stahl, *The Control of the Middle East Arms Race* (Carnegie Endowment, 1992), pp. 104–5. See also Eliot A. Cohen, Michael J. Eisenstadt and Andrew J. Bacevich, "Israel's Revolution in Security Affairs," *Survival*, vol. 40, no. 1 (Spring 1998).
31. See both Carus and Donovan.
32. Chubin makes this argument at several points in *Whither Iran?*
33. Based on recent U.S. State Department annual reports *Patterns of Global Terrorism* (especially 2000 and 2001). See also Rensselaer Lee and Raphael Perl, "Terrorism, the future, and U.S. Foreign Policy," *Issue Brief for Congress* (Congressional Research Service, updated January 8, 2003).
34. Kenneth Katzman,"Terrorism: Near Eastern Groups and States Sponsors, 2002," *CRS Report for Congress* (Congressional Research Service, updated February 13, 2002).
35. Ibrahim A. Karawan, *The Islamist Impasse* (Oxford University Press, Adelphi Paper 314, 1997), p. 42.
36. Chubin, *Whither Iran?*, p. 87.
37. UN International Drug Control Programme, "Drugs and Development: Discussion prepared for the World Summit for Social Development," June 1994, p. 1.
38. Reported in the English version of *Le Monde Diplomatique* (March 2002), "The Heroin Route from Afghanistan to Europe: Iran Loses Its Drugs War," by Cédric Gouverneur.
39. Statistics cited in "Central Asia: Drugs and Conflict," International Crisis Group Asia Report N° 25 (26 November 2001), p. 10 and p. 14.
40. Claim made by Chubin, *Whither Iran?*, p. 45.
41. Pierre-Arnaud Chouvy, "La récolte d'opium a explosé en Afghanistan en 2002!," Monday, December 2, 2002, 20 Minutes France SAS. Also reported in *L'Hebdo* (December 5, 2002). Both available on the web. See also the web site of www.geopium.org.
42. Zbigniew Brzezinski, Brent Scowcroft, and Richard Murphy, "Differentiated Containment," *Foreign Affairs*, Vol. 76, No. 3 (May/June 1997), p. 27; Brzezinski, Scowcroft, and Murphy, *Differentiated Containment: U.S. Policy toward Iran and Iraq* (Council on Foreign Relations Press, 1997), 23–25.
43. Ray Takeyh, "Re-imagining US-Iranian Relations," *Survival*, vol. 44, no. 3, Autumn 2002.
44. Sick, "Rethinking Dual Containment," p. 12; and Richard Herrmann and R. William Ayres, "The New Geo-Politics of the Gulf: Forces for Change and Stability" in Sick and Potter, *The Persian Gulf at the Millennium*, p. 42.
45. See J.E. Peterson for an analysis of Saudi frustration with US containment of Iran, p. 34 and p. 72.
46. A point underlined by Brzezinski, Scowcroft and Murphy, p. 20.
47. Herrmann and Ayres, pp. 41–42.
48. Takeyh, p. 27.

49 CIA, *The World Factbook 2002*.
50 John W. Limbert, "Islamic Republic of Iran," in David E. Long and Bernard Reich, *The Government and Politics of the Middle East and North Africa* (Westview Press, 1995, 3rd ed.), p. 48. Limbert also summarizes the ramifications of Iranian economic decline.
51 Jahangir Amuzegar, "Iran's Crumbling Revolution," *Foreign Affairs*, January/February 2003.
52 Sick, "Rethinking Dual Containment," p. 23 and Shahran Chubin and Jerrold Green, "Engaging Iran: A U.S. Strategy," *Survival*, vol. 40, no. 3 (Autumn 1998), p. 154.
53 Poll results reported widely, even by the Iranian news service INRA, but among other places see the Agence France Press story "Reformist Blasts Judiciary over 'Political' Pollster Trial," December 26, 2002. See also "Gauging Oppostion," by Nader Sadighi in *Iran va Jahan*, November 11, 2002. These reports and many other relevant articles can be found at the website http//www.iranvajahan.net. Abbas Abdi was arrested on the 23rd anniversary of the storming of the U.S. embassy. President Khatami's brother condemned the charges against Abdi as a "pompous political address."
54 Jahangir Amuzegar, "Iran's Theocracy Under Siege," *Middle East Policy*, vol. 10, no. 1 (Spring 2003), conclusion.
55 Mohammad Hadi Semati, "The Coming Generation in Iran: Challenges and Opportunities," in Potter and Sick, *Security in the Persian Gulf*, p. 212.
56 For a brief, useful discussion of the possibilities of democratic transition in the Middle East see Marina Ottaway, Thomas Carothers, Amy Hawthorne and Daniel Brumberg, "Democratic Mirage in the Middle East," *Policy Brief* (Carnegie Endowment, 20 October 2002). As a comparison, the effort to rebuild democracy in post-World War II Germany took a couple of decades. See Steven Ekovich, "Relations between The United States and Germany: Deep and Troubled Waters," *Geostrategics*, March 2001, no. 2, pp. 41–51.
57 The term is Takeyh's.
58 Chubin, *Whither Iran?* p. 98.
59 See Fred Halliday, "Iran and the Middle East: Foreign Policy and Domestic Change," *Middle East Report*, Fall 2001, p. 45.
60 Takeyh, p. 28.
61 Ibid. See also Shaheen Fatemi, "IRI Attempts to Derail 'Iraqi Freedom'," *Iran va Jahan*, April 15, 2003. Available at http://iranvajahan.net.

Chapter 16

Preclusive War with Iraq: Regional and Global Ramifications

Hall Gardner

Al-Qaeda attacks on the World Trade Center and Pentagon have unleashed additional anti-systemic social, political and economic forces that could possibly result in US overextension and divide its major allies.

After having worked with other "freedom fighters" to force Soviet withdrawal from Afghanistan with American, Pakistani and Saudi assistance, Al-Qaeda has hoped to overthrow "corrupt" Arab/Islamic leaderships and forge a pan-Islamic alliance that will restore a pious Caliphate and establish an Arab-Moslem Ummah somewhat similar to that of the Ottoman Empire, and thus unify the oil-producing countries of the Middle East, as well as the Islamic peoples of Central Asia and Africa.

To accomplish these far-reaching goals, Al-Qaeda (along with other groups) have hoped to impel US forces to leave Saudi Arabia (and the Persian Gulf and Middle East in general) not only by means of sabotage and terrorism, but also by drawing the United States (or other powers) into over-reaction and over-extension. Much as a Hezbollah suicide truck bomber thwarted the deployment of US marines in Lebanon in 1983, and led to US withdrawal from the region, the groups linked to Al-Qaeda have hoped that that terrorist activities will weaken American resolve, overextend US resources, and divide US Allies.

In regard to the war with Iraq in 2003, pan-Islamic propaganda initially opposed both the secular pan-Arab leadership of Saddam Hussein, as well as an Anglo-American "occupation"; it also denounced "corrupt" leaderships in Islamic states and propagandized against Israeli and US actions in the region.[1] While the official US discourse focused on the evils of the Saddam Hussein dictatorship, pan-Islamic propaganda focused on the suffering of the Iraqi people in regard to both Hussein and the twelve years of sanctions imposed by the US/UN on the general population, as well as the effects of the bombing campaign, followed by the March 2003 US-UK military intervention.

This pan-Islamic strategy is based on the belief that forceful American pressures and military actions (intervention against Iraq, political pressure on Syria, Iran and other Arab or Islamic states, "occupation" of both Sunni and Shi'ite holy sites) will cause a backlash within states with predominantly Islamic populations, and, in effect, create new enemies and antagonisms. US overreaction would thus work indirectly to destabilize leaderships in countries such as Yemen, Jordan, Egypt, Morocco, Nigeria, Pakistan and Saudi Arabia, not to overlook the effects of Islamic movements in Indonesia, Malaysia, Philippines, as well as in Sudan, Kenya, Bosnia, Chechnya, Uzbekistan (and other post-Soviet republics) as well as in Xinjiang, China.

Ultimately, it is believed, a number of these states (or others) may be impelled to shift sides against the United States, or else their weak leaderships will simply lose control over their increasingly radicalized pro-Islamic populations.[2] The conflict has indirectly sparked rioting in Northern Nigeria, for example. New alliances of pan-Islamic forces (the Majlis-e-Amal MMA), for example, have hoped to overturn the pro-US government of General Pervez Musharraf (through electoral support as well as assassination) in order to forge an Islamic theocratic state with nuclear weapons. Fearing for the stability of his own regime, Egyptian president Hosni Mubarak had warned, prior to the fact, that US intervention in Iraq could create "a hundred Bin Ladens."

In the immediate aftermath of the 11 September 2001 attacks, President Bush had declared on 20 September 2001 that "Every nation in every region now has a decision to make: Either you are with us, or you are with the terrorists." Yet the black or white nature of this declaration appears to be precisely the response desired by the perpetrators of this heinous crime. By October 2001, the United States had engaged forces against Al-Qaeda and its Taliban supporters in Afghanistan; it then set its sights on Iraq. After intervention in Iraq, the US then threatened possible military intervention against Syria, Iran, and North Korea, among other states deemed to support terrorism or possess WMD.

This final chapter will argue that despite the fact that US-UK military intervention in Iraq has risked the further destabilization of key states in the Arab-Islamic world in the not-so-long term, the US must now work to help resolve the Israeli-Palestinian conflict, as well as defuse India-Pakistan tensions, if the war on terrorism is ever going to come to a semblance of an "end." In particular, by working through a strategy of *multilateral dissuasion* (see Chapter 2) to resolve these two central conflicts (Israel and Palestine; India and Pakistan), coupled with support for reforms in the Arab-Islamic world, the US and Europeans can, hopefully, help set the stage for a general political-diplomatic settlement to the general global crisis emanating from the Middle East/Persian Gulf/South Asia, and help prevent the construction of new "Berlin-like walls" between Israelis and Palestinians or Indians and Pakistanis in Kashmir, as argued by Marwan Bishara and Sten Widmalm respectively in this book, and prevent as well the formation of a new countervailing system of alliances.

One risk of preclusive US intervention in Iraq is that such as action may have encouraged both Iran and North Korea (among others) to speed up the development of the nuclear option, while states such as India, China and Israel might all use preclusive US actions as an excuse to "resolve" issues by unilateral force and not engage in diplomacy. In essence, unilateral and preclusive US-UK military intervention in Iraq, coupled with the failure to seriously address both the Arab-Israeli and Indo-Pakistani conflicts (not to overlook North and South Korea and China and Taiwan) has threatened to undercut the potential effectiveness of the most significant multilateral regimes, including the UN, EU, not to overlook NATO.

US credibility is also at stake in that the US justified the war on the basis of Iraqi possession of WMD, but had not found sufficient evidence. Should the US fail in its efforts to find WMD in Iraq, it will further delegitimize US-UK preclusive intervention in the eyes of the world. The US may well suffer from "the little boy who cried wolf" too many times before the actual wolf shows up. If, however, Iraq did indeed possess such weapons as the Bush administration claimed, then it raises questions as to what states or groups might have obtained those weapons, assuming they were not destroyed or well hidden.

Although the war was won rapidly (Secretary of Defense Donald Rumsfeld correctly predicted "between six days and six weeks but not six months"), US forces have had difficulties establishing daily security), and stood watching the widespread looting of hospitals, most public buildings, including some of the most ancient treasures and archeological sites of mankind as well as the most modern nuclear facilities. This is true despite the fact that many of these problems were clearly foreseen by American analysts prior to the war.[3] *The failure to deploy adequate troops and trained police for post-conflict roles reflects a technocratic and instrumentalist cost-cutting approach that ignores the political role of military deployments, for peacekeeping, but also for deterrence and reassurance. US intervention has, in effect, replaced the repressive "security" of a totalitarian regime with the chaotic "insecurity" of political, religious, ethnic and mafia-type rivalries, at least in the medium term. The failure reflects a new form of "short war illusion" in which the high tech nature of warfare creates the illusion of short wars, but in which the aftermath may involve long-term peacekeeping (and counterinsurgency).*

The US also promised to establish "democratic federalism" in Iraq, after years of warfare, sanctions, and "state terrorism," and to take steps to end the Palestinian-Israeli conflict through the Road Map for Peace, in what UK Prime Minister Tony Blair dubbed "even handedness." Both promises may prove very difficult to fulfill. In order to regain world confidence, and help to rebuild international consensus, the US will consequently need to demonstrate to the Iraqi people as well as to the region and to the world, that it can help rebuild Iraq; but this prospect will require a long term commitment in regard to state and society building in Iraq at a time when the US track record has not been stellar in regard to post-war Haiti, Bosnia, Kosovo, Afghanistan, and in regard to the developing world in general.[4]

US and European Approaches to Iraq

The Bush administration had begun an internal re-assessment of Clinton administration policy once it came to office in January 2001, and had raised the question of Iraq at that time. President Clinton had expected a number of "breakthroughs" following his efforts to achieve diplomatic settlements to a number of crises and conflicts in his last term of office, Northern Ireland, North Korea, Israel-Palestine. President Clinton likewise began to open relations with both India and Pakistan. In particular, he expected a "breakthrough" in regard to both North Korea and Israel-Palestine, but failed in both efforts. In effect, the Clinton administration left the Bush team with a number of crucial yet unresolved issues, including a failure to "change" the regime of Saddam Hussein.

The US policy of "regime change," while strongly supported by neo-conservatives (best described as "vultures" but not "hawks" as often depicted in the media) in the Bush administration, was largely a hangover from a Congressional mandate, passed during the Clinton Administration. In October 1998 Congress signed into law the Iraq Liberation Act (Public Law 105-338). The latter had stated "It should be the policy of the United States to support efforts to remove the regime headed by Saddam Hussein from power in Iraq and to promote the emergence of a democratic government to replace that regime." This Act raised two questions: The first was how to achieve "regime change;" the second was how to promote the "emergence of a democratic government."

In late 1998, the tactical concept was to engage in bombing of Iraqi military facilities and weaken the regime, and to support Iraqi resistance groups or engage in a *coup d'etat*; it was not to engage in direct military intervention. As the debate within US National Security circles (with the Pentagon largely in dispute with the State Department) continued, it was argued that the US and UK must "deal" with the perceived "threat" posed by Saddam Hussein—if not that posed by other states—by the *preclusive* use of military force.

In general, US neo-conservatives (in support of the Pentagon position) argued that forceful US diplomacy in Iraq would provide credibility to US policy. Furthermore, the establishment of a "democratic" Iraq in the heart of the Middle East would provide a demonstration model for other states to follow and begin "democratic" reforms. Neo-conservatives argued that a US bridgehead in Iraq would additionally provide pressure throughout the entire region which would, in turn, convince Syria, Iran, and Saudi Arabia not to support terrorism and provide a platform from which to wage war against both terrorism and states that were ostensibly developing weapons of mass destruction. It was argued that political instability in Saudi Arabia, and demands that the US remove its forces from Saudi territory (a tacit concession to Bin Laden), meant that the US would need to find an alternative site for its military bases in this region, so as to secure long-term access to oil, given increasing demand for oil from the region. (See Ekovich, Chapter 15.)

According to this argument, having eliminated Iraq, one of Israel's major enemies (and the pan-Arab spoiler of peace talks), it would be easier to press Israel to accept a Palestinian state, so as to finally end the Arab-Israeli crisis. Arab moderates could then be strengthened against hardliners. Once the US then dealt with the threat from Iraq (a major rival of Israel), it could then deal with Israeli and Palestinian question. Neo-conservative strategist Robert D. Kaplan dubbed this a question of "sequencing."[5] The concept later became transmuted into a question of "even handedness" in the words of UK Prime Minister Tony Blair in March 2003.

The United States thus began to take steps toward direct military action as its 1996 efforts to stage a *coup d'etat* had failed and later as UN inspections did not appear to make any progress.[6] Prior to 11 September 2001, the Bush administration's first major foreign policy initiative literally started off with a blast following the US-UK bombing of Iraqi military installations in southern Baghdad outside the no-fly zones established after the 1991 Persian Gulf war, a step-up from previous attacks taken in late 1998 under President Clinton.[7] Air strikes were justified on the grounds that Saddam Hussein's new defense capabilities appeared to give Iraq the capability to shoot down US-UK aircraft, and to keep its military in a state of total disrepair. Iraq was alleged to have built up new military capabilities, using the UN "oil for food" policy to buy weapons and gain assistance purportedly from Russia, China, Germany and North Korea, among others. (Here, it should be noted that the largest purchaser of Iraqi oil under the UN oil for food program was the United States itself, with $5.72 billion imports from Iraq, mostly oil.)

In addition to the fact George Bush Jr. had a chip on its shoulder for the decision of his father (George Bush, Sr.) not to go to Baghdad and to eliminate Saddam Hussein once and for all, plus an alleged 1993 Iraqi attempt to assassinate Bush Sr., an additional unspoken rationale for the new Bush administration's decision to target Iraq was also to prevent Israel from acting unilaterally. In 1981 Israel had acted preemptively to bomb the Osirak nuclear reactor (a factor that might have worked to accelerate Iraq's efforts to acquire nuclear weapons, rather than slow it down as often argued). Concurrently, the Iraqi effort to obtain nuclear weapons in the 1980s may have been obtained Saudi financing; Saudi Arabia may have sought to use Iraq as a strategic buffer against Iran.[8]

As the Bush administration pressured Iraq, it also entered into confrontation with China (after a collision with a Chinese fighter jet knocked a US spy plane onto Hainan island). Moreover, relations with Russia took a downspin as well, once the Bush administration took the controversial decision to unilaterally withdraw from the ABM treaty, and to develop Ballistic Missile Defenses. Relations with North Korea also deteriorated as the Bush administration took a more confrontational stance than did the Clinton administration, particularly after identifying North Korea, along with Iran and Iraq, as members of the "axis of evil."

President Bush generally sustained strong international support in the first phase of the "war on terrorism," in regard to attempting to root Al-Qaeda forces out of Afghanistan and then in overthrowing the Taliban regime in October 2001, yet he began to lose that support once he began to focus more sharply, if not obsessively, on Iraq. France and Germany, backed by Russia and China, began to oppose US policy once it became clear by late August 2002-January 2003 that the US was more concerned with "regime change" than with "disarmament."

In August–September 2002, German Chancellor Gerhard Schroeder, for example, stated in reaction to an August 2002 speech made by US Vice President Dick Cheney, that "it would be a mistake to intervene militarily in Iraq."[9] Schroeder then immediately ruled out the use of German forces whether under UN mandate or not. This statement set the stage for German-French opposition to intervention, although the French were more favorable to the possible use of force, but only with a clear UNSC mandate; otherwise, war was to be the means of last resort.

At their meeting in the Azores in March 2003, just prior to US-UK military intervention in Iraq, US President George Bush and UK Prime Minister Tony Blair called for a resolution of the Israel-Palestinian conflict. Tony Blair, in particular, argued that efforts to resolve the regional and symbolic crisis posed by Israel-Palestinian conflict would prove Anglo-American "even handedness"[10] in regard to Arab, Islamic and international perceptions. France, Germany, Russia, China, and most Arab/Islamic states including Saudi Arabia (but excluding Kuwait), however, questioned whether this was the appropriate "sequence" in which to address these issues, and whether it was truly "even handed." They also questioned whether preclusive war with Iraq would actually help "resolve" the conflict, or lead to even greater regional, if not global, destabilization.

The Iraqi question thus began to pit the US, UK, Spain and Italy, plus Poland and most eastern European states, against France, Germany, plus Russia and China. The latter differed significantly with Washington as to how to approach Iraqi violations of UN resolutions and in regard to Iraqi crimes against humanity, war crimes and WMD. Concurrently, Iraq itself counter-accused the US and UK of "lying" and of ignoring Israeli possession of nuclear weapons. In essence, France, Germany, Russia and China argued that the problem stemmed from US arrogance and unilateralism; it was Washington who was unwilling to listen to alternative points of view. From the US perspective, however, it was France and Germany who were unwilling to work as "team players" in the effort to thoroughly pressure Iraq upon the threat of war.

While France and Germany, whom Secretary of Defense Donald Rumsfeld dubbed the "old Europe," did recognize that only credible American military threats had impelled Saddam Hussein to accept tougher UN inspections, they still argued that military intervention designed to overthrow the regime should only be pursued as "last resort." Both France and Germany also argued that it would be premature to take on Iraq despite the apparently quick "victory" over the Taliban due to the fact that Al-Qaeda had not been thoroughly eradicated. (See Norbert Bass, Chapter 10.) France and Germany also warned that the political and economic costs of reconstruction may be too great.[11] (By July 2003, Secretary of Defense Rumsfeld stated that the occupation was costing $3.9 billion a month.)

French Foreign Minister Dominique de Villepin was in agreement with US Secretary of State Colin Powell, at least up until November 2002 in support of UN resolution 1441, which was unanimously supported by the UNSC; by January 2003, however, France turned against the hard line positions of US Secretary of Defense Donald Rumsfeld, and deputy Secretary of Defense Paul Wolfowitz, who had finally won out the internal inter-bureaucratic dispute with Colin Powell and the State Department. At this point, the US had definitely resolved that that the goal was regime change by military intervention, and not long term and "vigilant containment,"[12] combined with "smart sanctions." (Parenthetically, the latter option would not necessarily preclude the possibility of a *coup d'etat* or else a UN-mandated military intervention at a later date.)

The US had consistently argued that should Iraq fail to assist UN inspectors to do their job or refuse to disarm in accord with UN demands,[13] Washington (with or without the United Nations) could then decide to launch a second major military offensive against Iraq, and thus finish the job it started in 1991, based on the failure of Iraq to comply with agreements in regard to WMD reached in 1991 with Iraq after the first Persian Gulf war. The decision to make the motions to go through the UN to obtain a clear UN mandate had been urged upon President Bush Jr. by Colin Powell as well as UK Prime Minister Tony Blair, who hoped to rally the European allies to the cause. Blair argued that President Bush should follow the footsteps of his father in order to gain greater legitimacy for military intervention. The US and UK thus jointly pressed for UN Resolution 1441 in November 2002. US strategy in regard to Iraq appeared to represent a double-edged sword in that the Bush administration had not entirely foresworn multilateral action through the UN Security Council, but nevertheless continued to threaten unilateral military intervention—if UN measures did not appear sufficient.

Washington argued that Saddam Hussein had engaged in elaborate pattern of deception, and thus, as long as he was in power, he would strive for revenge and build his military arsenal as rapidly as he could. He would become a "nuclear Saladin." Europeans, however, countered that no substantial effort had been made to truly strengthen the sanctions regime, particularly as UNSCOM had made Iraq destroy significant quantities of weaponry, thus making Iraq effectively impotent. Rather than becoming a nuclear threat, the Iraqi regime was more likely to dissipate or break up.

Yet by February 2003, Tony Blair largely failed in his efforts to obtain UNSC support for military intervention against Iraq if the latter failed to destroy its WMD. This was true as UNSC members France and Russia aligned to press for more vigilant sanctions, also supported by China, and non-permanent UNSC member Germany. France and Germany, followed by Russia, proposed more muscular weapons inspections involving U-2 over-flights and multinational peacekeepers; the US argued this would repeat the mistakes of UN involvement in Bosnia when UN forces were taken hostage. France (with Russia and China in support) threatened to veto any US-UK resolution that would support military intervention. In all, the fifteen member UN Security Council had only four members in support of the US-UK proposal to engage in military intervention (the US, the UK, Spain and Bulgaria argued that enough time had been wasted) and eleven UNSC members were in support of a continuation of stricter inspections.

For the French and Germans, the crucial questions were: Where does one draw the appropriate boundary line between the "war on terrorism" and the possibility of *pre-emptive*—or really *preclusive* or *precautionary*—wars against states that may be engaged in the actual or potential development of WMD? And, what will be the domestic and regional consequences of overthrowing such regimes by force? How would these states and societies then be rebuilt, by what financing? What will be the new socio-political basis for the new governments? How will the new states be regarded in the region? What are the international legal ramifications of *preclusive* or *precautionary* action? What would be the appropriate balance between the rights of traditional Westphalian conceptions of state sovereignty and the goals of *humanitarian*, and now *preclusive*, intervention? European analysts generally argued that the consequences of war with Iraq would prove far more negative than positive and thus preferred a more vigilant inspection system and a continuation of containment policy in the long-term.

While the US would have preferred UNSC support (to gain international legitimacy and help pay for the overall costs), Washington believed that it could prosecute the war against Iraq "successfully." Moreover, as it ostensibly wanted Saddam to quit the country entirely, Washington ignored back channel proposals to avert war in which Hussein purportedly offered oil concessions to the US, acceptance of the US plan for the Middle East, and free elections in two years, as well as permission of 2000 US agents (FBI and scientists) to engage in weapons inspections.[14]

The key issue, however, as deputy Secretary of Defense Paul Wolfowitz argued, was to balance "the costs of action versus the costs of inaction and the costs of action now versus the costs of action later."[15] Yet the question of the eventual political, social and economic "costs" for Iraq, the region and the world, after *preclusive* intervention, still remains.

Diplomacy and Terror in the Middle East

Since 11 September 2001, Israel has tried to convince Washington that it is the central player in the "war on terrorism" in regard to the new wave of "suicide bombings" backed by Palestinian movements who have been seen as being supported by Iraq, Iran, Syria and Saudi Arabia. Palestinians, in turn, have denounced Israeli strong arm tactics as "terroristic," in that they have included the use of heavy weaponry such as tanks and aircraft, snipers against demonstrators, and the assassination of Palestinians charged with organizing the *Intifada*, or who have been accused of sponsoring suicidal "terrorist" actions against civilians or else assassinations of Israeli leaders.

It was evident the Oslo accords were failing prior to General Ariel Sharon's visit to the Haram-al Sharif (Temple Mount) on 28 September 2000, which then set off the Second Palestinian *Al-Aqsa Intifada*, prior to his becoming the Israeli Prime Minister in February 2001. The failure of the Oslo Accords (as well as the last minute Taba Accords of January 2001, which appeared to indicate a deeper compromise was, in fact, possible than that previously sought by President Clinton at Camp David in mid-2000) was, from the Palestinian perspective, largely due to the refusal of the government of Prime Minister Ehud Barak to stop the expansion of Israeli settlements on the West Bank. This failure was combined with closure policies designed to permit Palestinians from entering Israeli held territories without a special Israeli permit, a situation that was regarded as setting back the Palestinian economy. In many ways, rather than engaging in a more extensive "ethnic cleansing" as in 1948 or 1967, Israel has, since the end of the Cold War, engaged in more selective actions, such as closure of the West Bank and Gaza, that have been intended to impel Palestinians to leave the area. In effect, the Israeli government has generally attempted to move "cautiously" so as not to face sanctions from the international community.[16] The installation of a wall dividing Israelis and Palestinians may, however, draw international sanctions.

From the Israeli perspective, one of the major issues that blocked compromise was that of Palestinian "right of return." The latter, in effect, mirrored Israeli claims that the Jewish *Diaspora* had the right to return to a "greater" Israel (largely at Palestinian expense). As events unfolded, Bush administration foreign policy at least *initially* adopted the hard line Israeli approach, placing its priority on the effort to overthrow the Iraqi Ba'ath regime through the strategy of "sequencing,"[17] as discussed above.

The Sharon government thus attempted to deflect world attention from Israeli actions to the "threat" posed by Iraqi WMD at the same time that Israeli negotiations with Syria (a supporter of *Hizbollah* and *Hamas* among other groups) were put on hold. Iraq consequently called for Arab states to unify to support the Palestinian *intifada* in an effort to influence the March 2001 summit of the Arab League. Iraqi militancy represented, in part, an effort to drive a further wedge between the new Israeli Prime Minister Ariel Sharon and PLO leader Yasser Arafat. But here it appeared that military pressures on Iraq, coupled with Israeli military actions against

Palestinian "terrorism," tended to splinter Yassir Arafat's *Al Fatah* and augment the influence of *Hamas*, if not *Hizbullah*. Pressure on both Saddam Hussein and Yasir Arafat brought more, not less, "terrorism."

In November 2001, after a visit to the World Trade Center, President Bush used the word "Palestine" (President Clinton had first spoken of a "viable Palestinian state" on 7 January 2001); yet he did not engage in a very effective diplomatic demarche to reduce tensions in the region. An opportunity to open the door to diplomacy was then presented by the March 2002 Arab summit in Beirut that promised Arab state recognition of the state of Israel in exchange for the latter to return to its 1967 borders. Although a return to 1967 borders was not acceptable to Israel in that particular formula, the March 2002 Arab peace proposal at least indicated the possibility of historic compromise that could open the doors to a general settlement of the Arab-Israeli crisis. Bringing the key Arab states on board to recognize Israel could then raise the pressure on Iraq, and possibly on Iran as well, to finally accept a "two-state" settlement. The failure on the part of the US and EU to engage in regional diplomacy in late March 2002 was due in part in deference to Israeli domestic concerns and in response to "suicide" bombings, as well as Israeli efforts to undermine, if not eliminate, Yassir Arafat's position as the legitimate leader of the Palestinians.

The Israeli siege of Arafat's headquarters took place after a suicide bombing just 24 hours after the Arab Beirut Summit of 28 March 2002. It appeared that both Arab and Israeli hardliners sought to block steps toward compromise. Violent Israeli actions, however, ironically served to strengthen rather than weaken Arafat's position despite Israeli allegations that seized PLO documents linked Arafat himself to acts of terrorism. The Sharon government thus pressed upon the Bush administration the view that Tel Aviv represented its strongest ally in the "war on terrorism" and that the only way to deal with the PLO and other Palestinian movements was by force, combined with pressure to "democratize" the newly established Palestinian Authority (PA). By contrast, the EU angered Sharon by supporting Arafat and by trying to prevent the destruction of the PA. (The US and EU also disagreed as to whether groups such as Hamas represent "terrorist" factions.)

Consequently, the US began to argue for no negotiations and fundamental compromise with the Palestinians until such time as the latter undergo "democratization." On June 24, President Bush announced that the US would support an independent Palestinian state that would live side-by-side the state of Israel, but that the PA must first "democratize" to eliminate corruption, clientelism and abuse of funding. In practical terms, the US argued that the PA must create a position of prime minister who could, in effect, serve as a mediator or buffer between Ariel Sharon and Yassir Arafat. (Here, however, it appears dubious that true "democratization" of the PA can take place before the Israeli territorial occupation is over.)

In accordance with the so-called strategy of "sequencing," the Bush Administration linked the Middle East crisis with that concerning Iraq, but continued to give the Iraq issue priority. President Bush's 12 September 2002 demand at the UN that Iraq accept all UN resolutions, and that it truly begin the process of disarmament—or risk major US military intervention—had been accompanied by renewed multilateral UN-US-EU-Russian (the Quartet) efforts to engage in the Middle East peace process. Here, as the EU had been present at Taba in January 2001, as well as at Sharm el-Sheik, and as it had participated in the Mitchell Commission, the EU meeting at Elsinore on 30 August 2002 was regarded as crucial in helping to develop a three-phase "road map."[18]

On the one hand, President Bush emphasized the Iraqi threat and Iraqi violations of UN resolutions but mentioned at the outset the need to establish an "independent and democratic Palestine, living side by side with Israel in peace and security." The address of UN Secretary General Kofi Annan, on the other hand, while mentioning the need for Iraq to accept UN inspectors and eliminate weapons of mass destruction, tended to give primacy to the Israeli-Palestinian conflict. Hence the two speeches tended to counter-balance Arab/Islamic and Israeli perspectives, and perhaps the American and French/European viewpoints as well—but without really moving the issue forward.

In January 2003, as Washington continued to threaten military intervention in Iraq, US Secretary of State Colin Powell stated at the World Economic Forum in Davos, Switzerland, that Washington was committed to the goal of a Palestinian state by 2005. A promise of Palestinian statehood was to be part of a multilateral "road map" for peace that was to be unveiled after the January 28 general election in Israel. But the road map was once again postponed. Essentially three issues stood in the way: (1) Israel needed to set up its new cabinet; (2) the Palestinians needed to set up a new office of Prime Minister; (3) Israel would not budge until after the impending war with Iraq.

By March 2003, both President Bush and Prime Minister Blair, just prior to military intervention in Iraq, emphasized the need to engage in the Road Map for Peace as a question of "even handedness" in the words of Tony Blair. It was clear that the United States wanted Israel and the Palestinians to engage in a ceasefire once the United States intervened in Iraq; yet neither side accepted. Militant Palestinians preferred to escalate the conflict; Israel threatened to intervene in Iraq "if provoked" as it simultaneously expanded settlements in the West Bank and cracked down in Gaza. Israeli Prime Minister Sharon likewise stated his disagreement with fifteen key points of the Road Map.

By June 2003, following intervention in Iraq (and after the Bush administration threatened military intervention against both Syria and Iran), Sharon spoke of dismantling the "un-authorized settlements" and of ending the "occupation" despite the opposition of Israeli hardliners. Yet it was still unclear how far Sharon would go toward meeting the demands of the first Palestinian Prime Minister, Mahmoud Abbas, which would permit the latter to obtain a voice of authority over hardliners in Al-Fatah, Hamas and Hizbollah.

Contrary to his previous hands off approach prior to the Iraq war, President Bush became personally involved in the Road Map for Peace after the Iraq war; yet plans to establish a "contiguous" Palestinian state by the year 2005 appeared utopian. Critics of the road map argued that it is designed (whether intentionally or unintentionally) in such a way that it was doomed to failure: Acts of terrorism by any faction could jeopardize its implementation. By June 2003, it appeared that land mines had blown up the entire Road, as Israel vowed to revenge itself upon *Hamas* for supporting acts of terrorism. The October 2003 Geneva Accords, however, offered a glimmer of hope for peace, as a supplement to the Road Map,[19] although they were denounced by the Sharon government, and not given full support by Arafat.

NATO, the UN and Turkey

The prospects of war with Iraq began to further alienate Turkey, which feared the possible negative effects of a potentially independent Iraqi Kurdistan upon its own Kurdish populations in eastern Anatolia. Turkey also kept its eye on oil fields in Iraqi cities of Kirkuk and Mosul, which, it feared, might be seized by Kurdish forces, who could then obtain a financial basis for an independent Kurdistan. Ankara had claimed oversight of the region through the 1920 Treaty of Sevres and through irredentist ties to ethnic Turkmen who likewise opposed Kurdish control of the region.

The Turkish refusal to permit roughly 50,000 US forces through its territory risked prolonging the war by handicapping US efforts to take Kirkuk, Mosul, as well as Baghdad. Turkey opposed US policy despite US and Kurdish promises to maintain Iraqi territorial integrity. In February 2003, Turkish politicians suggested that the oil-rich areas of northern Iraq—including the Kurdish region—should be annexed to Turkey. The

Kurdistan Democratic Party (KDP), which controlled half of the autonomous Kurdish enclave in northern Iraq, then cautioned that it would resist Turkish intervention. Concurrently, Iraqi Turkmen (backed by Ankara) also claimed oil rich Kirkuk and opposed an independent Kurdistan.

As war with Iraq approached, tensions within NATO intensified. The Turkish question provoked a major crisis in NATO in February 2003. France, Germany, and Belgium refused to supply Turkey with "defensive" AWACs and Patriot missiles, plus anti-chemical and biological warfare capabilities intended defend Turkey, and then staged a filibuster in NATO against the deployment of AWACs and Patriot Missile systems in Turkey in part in the fear that Ankara might use such weapons to shield an offensive into Iraqi Kurdistan. It was considered one of the major crises in over 50 years of NATO history, but was largely overblown.

First was the question of timing: The three dissenters believed that deployment of such forces would disrupt negotiations intended to extend UN weapons inspections, including U-2 over-flights agreed to by Iraq; they also believed that Iraq did not represent a threat to Turkey. Behind the scenes, however, the problem was the fact that Turkish intentions were not at all clear. On the one hand, Turkish demands for NATO protection were in effect generated by US *preclusive* threats, and thus not truly "defensive." On the other, Turkey itself sent signals that it would intervene. Would Turkey work with NATO and US, permitting the US to deploy its forces on Turkish territory? Or was the real Turkish intent to use the refugee crisis in an effort to stamp out Kurdish independence movements in northern Iraq? Would Turkey attempt to seize oil rich Kirkuk and Mosul? How would Iran see Turkish actions?

Here, the crisis escalated as the French, Germans and Russians, later joined by the Chinese, argued that 10 to 12 of the fifteen members of the UN security council supported an extension of UN inspections beyond the date proposed by the US, while the US claimed that 16 out of NATO's 19 members supported US pressures and eventual military intervention (with France, Germany and Belgium opposing). It was assumed that further weapons inspections would only play into the hands of Saddam Hussein. The US, in effect, threatened to circumvent its "nay saying" members, by claiming that such defenses were needed for the overall security of NATO members, and not for Turkey alone. This crisis was "resolved" as NATO shifted the decision into the nearly defunct Defense Committee in which France, not being a member, had no right to participate in the vote, and as Germany and Belgium backed off.[20] In fact, however, even after Germany had reluctantly gone along with the decision to deploy four AWACs aircraft, German Foreign Minister Joschka Fischer threatened to bring back all AWAC's German personnel (one-quarter to one-third of the staff)—if Turkey acted unilaterally against the Kurds.[21]

Thus NATO was able to claim that a "consensus" existed—even though Turkey still refused to accept US forces and permit the US to use its airbases. (Here, one cannot argue that France, who had generally frustrated Turkish efforts to enter the EU, was root of this problem!) In part to make up for economic losses from the lack of cross-border trade since the first Gulf War with Iraq (Ankara claimed $40 billion in losses since 1991), Ankara demanded up to $35 billion in reimbursement for financial losses expected from renewed war with Iraq. At the end of February 2003, the Turkish parliament then voted by a slim majority of three votes against the deployment of US forces. The Turkish parliament initially rejected the US aid package, which meant that the US was forced to intervene from the south; Washington then engaged special forces, working along side the Kurds, to seize Kirkuk and Mosul. (The US did not bring the Turks, the Northern Iraqi Kurds, and Iraqi Turkmen into concrete agreements prior to the onset of war—truly an example of failed US diplomacy. Moreover, Turkey could not support the US intervention: Ankara did not expect US coalition peacekeepers to sustain a long enough presence that would prevent the Kurds struggling for their independence.)

Henry Kissinger found the situation incredulous: "(What)... I find difficult to understand is, as the possibility of war is approaching, that... France and Germany, are actually organizing the United Nations against the United States. That is unprecedented. That has never happened before. ... In regard to Turkey, sixteen other nations supported us. France, Germany and Belgium opposed planning."[22] On the one hand, Kissinger's statements indicate a blindness to changes in the NATO-EU-UN relationship that have taken place since the end of the Cold War and the advent of "out of area" wars in Bosnia, Kosovo, and now Iraq. On the other, Kissinger failed to understand the significance of the Turkish threat to intervene unilaterally, or the fact that US intervention was *preclusive*, not *pre-emptive*.

In the previous case of Bosnia, NATO and the UN had worked out an unsatisfactory power sharing arrangement involving a "dual key" decision-making process in which "enforcement" actions could be taken only once both NATO and the UN agreed. Contrary to Kissinger's assertions that the situation was unprecedented, the Europeans (in the Bosnian case, the French and British) sought to block US-NATO actions through the UN in Bosnia. Similarly, the Europeans then sought an alternative to US aerial intervention "over" Kosovo. These facts had already left a bitter taste in NATO *prior* to the crisis over Iraq.[23] *The only real difference is that Iraq represented a much more significant crisis in geostrategic and geo-economic terms than that of Bosnia and Kosovo.*

Changes in NATO-UN relationship have occurred precisely as NATO has moved out of a largely *defensive* stance, as traditionally defined by Article V of the North Atlantic Treaty (NAT), and toward a largely *proactive enforcement* stance (Article IV of the NAT) in regard to conflicts that are essentially "out of area." The changes in NATO, EU, UN politics are also due to the fact that the North Atlantic Treaty itself envisions appeal to the UNSC in the case of out of area enforcement operations (while defensive actions do not *initially* need to be taken to the UNSC).[24] The "old NATO" feared a "European caucus" inside NATO; yet the "new NATO"—in its drive to "go out of area or out of business"—will need to develop a more truly concerted approach.

In the effort to mediate between conflicting Turkish, Iraqi and Kurdish claims, US war plans called for American control of oil fields in Kirkuk and Mosul; Washington claimed that it supported the territorial integrity of Iraq and the establishment of a "democratic-federal" state, but it may still have difficulties supporting that concept vis-à-vis Turkish and Iranian pressures, as well as the dissent of internal Iraqi, Turkoman and Kurdish factions. American policy makers likewise complain that "democratic" Turkey is not following US directives in regard to the region as a whole, as Ankara itself appears unable to reform its own relations with the Kurds within Turkey.

Russia, China, Iraq and North Korea

Prior to September 11, it was largely only Russia and China that had combined against perceived pan-Islamic "terrorist" threats in the aftermath of the Cold War. The two had forged the Shanghai accords in 1996, along with Kazakhstan, Kyrgyztan and Tajikistan (and later Uzbekistan in 2001) against the alleged "terrorist" activities of partisan pan-Islamic movements that these states perceived as stemming from central Asia and the Transcaucasus. In addition, Beijing opposed Uighur and Tibetan "separatism" arising from Xinjiang and Tibet. Initially this Sino-Russian collaboration appeared to raise the threat of a Sino-Russian alliance. Concurrently, there had also been an effort by the United States to tighten its diplomatic and military relations with the "Shanghai Six" in part in the context of NATO's Partnership for Peace. The US military presence worked to establish links with countries such as Kyrgystan and Uzbekistan. The latter have routinely defined "extremism" as the "domestic opposition." Uzbekistan, a key central Asian ally in the US "war on terrorism," has defined all of its domestic opposition as Islamic "terrorists" in order to provide justification to arrest and imprison its opposition groups.[25] (See Cutler and Koslov, Chapters 12–13.)

And although the Bush Administration attempted to distance itself (somewhat) from Russian policies in Chechnya, as well as from Chinese actions in Tibet, Washington did add the Eastern Turkestan Islamic Movement (ETIM), an ethnic Uighur group, to its list of terrorist organizations in late 2002 in part to gain Chinese support in the UN Security Council for its own war against Iraq. Beijing argued the latter is fighting for an independent Islamic state in Xinjiang province. China has attempted to use the war on terrorism to rationalize its repression of Tibetan autonomists (who are seen as supported by India and the US) and of Uighur Moslems who are seen as supported by pan-Islamic movements. The Chinese definition of "terrorists" includes "underground gangs," "unstable social elements," and "separatists." Beijing considers the religious group Falun Gong a "terrorist" organization, which, in turn, considers itself repressed by Beijing; some of its members have been involved in hijackings, among other actions.

In an effort partly intended to gain Russian support for military intervention in Iraq, the United States promised to repeal the Cold War Jackson-Vanik act which continued to limit trade with, and investment in, Russia. Washington additionally promised greater backing for Russian entry into the World Trade Organization (WTO). Washington also added several Chechen groups to its list of terrorist factions in 2003 to "appease" Russia. The latter argued that Chechen secessionist movements, regarded as supported by Saudi Arabia and pan-Islamic movements, however, represent an internal affair, and that its actions (involving summary executions, "disappearances," looting, rape, and the indiscriminate bombing of civilian areas, mass graves) are intended to sustain Russian territorial integrity. Moscow has countered accusations of its brutal actions in Chechnya by criticizing the "collateral damage" caused by indiscriminate US actions in the wars in Iraq, Kosovo and Afghanistan. Moscow has thus far refused the possibility of US-EU mediation in Chechnya.

Despite Bush administration overtures, Russia, largely followed by China, began to more strongly and publicly back the Franco-German position in regard to Iraq in 2003 against military intervention and in support of giving UN weapons inspectors more time and resources. Russian and Chinese opposition to US "unilateralism" and "hegemony" can be explained primarily by the American refusal to heed the voice of other UNSC members and to opt for so-called *pre-emptive*, or really *preclusive*, military intervention that has begun to undermine traditional post-

Westphalian conceptions of sovereignty *without a conceptual replacement*. In essence, the French-Russian-Chinese (and German) opposition in the UNSC represented a protest vote against US determination to wield its supreme military capabilities without the sincere participation of all of the other UNSC members.

Although China opposed American actions out of principle against US "hegemony" and ultimately sided with France, Germany and Russia, it tried to do it in such a way as to not entirely alienate the United States. China saw itself as letting "barbarians fight barbarians" and letting France do the "lifting." On the one hand, China, like Russia, may have wanted to guarantee that its investments in Iraqi oil would be sustained in a post-Saddam Hussein regime; Beijing was thus reluctant to oppose the US in the UNSC. On the other, China (as well as Russian Eur-Asianists) may have been looking to strengthen relations with a stronger Iran, following Iraqi defeat, and thus take advantage of the situation at a later date. At first, Beijing may have also seen an opportunity in US conflict with Iraq as a means to draw US attention away from Asia. It had believed that war with Iraq would draw US forces away from Afghanistan; the latter would be replaced with European peacekeepers, for example, hence reducing pressures of "encirclement" upon Beijing.[26] Yet, instead, it was proposed that NATO take over the peacekeeping (formally accepted in April 2003); China had sought a rapprochement with NATO in late 2002.

Despite Chinese opposition to US hegemony, Beijing has also needed the US to help resolve the problem of North Korea. Here, the Bush administration's military threats to Iraq were being used by Pyongyang to fuel North Korean propaganda and to justify its own nuclear build-up. North Korea thus began to manipulate the US focus on Iraq by breaking out of NPT treaty in 2003 much as it once threatened a decade earlier in 1993. (This gambit had been hedged on the continuation of its oil supply, ultimately a ploy to gain official US recognition.)

The Bush administration's threats against the "axis of evil" thus appeared to be backfiring, raising tensions throughout the region. A nuclear North Korea could then impel Japan to develop its own nuclear arsenal (in that Tokyo would not necessarily trust the US to defend it—if US attention were diverted to the Persian Gulf or elsewhere). A nuclear Japan in turn would threaten China. Beijing consequently offered to host direct US-DPRK talks in which Beijing could play an important "facilitating" role.

Both Russia and China seek a resolution to the crisis in North Korea through a multilateral approach. Russia offered to guarantee North Korea's security in exchange for Pyongyang's renunciation of its nuclear ambitions, and proposed a multilateral security accord involving the US, Russia, South

Korea and China, with Beijing as a "facilitator." The Bush administration tried a dual approach of sanctions and military threats accompanied by promises to guarantee North Korea security, if Pyongyang renounced nuclear weapons.[27] The Bush administration then promised that Japan and South Korea could join the talks; North Korea would also like to include the EU. What is needed is a two track approach: North Korea can be granted multilateral UNSC security guarantees similar to those granted Ukraine in 1994 once Kiev destroyed its nuclear weapons capability, *combined with a strong bilateral US accord with North Korea that would guarantee the latter's political and economic security in exchange for not developing nuclear weapons, at the same time that North and South Korea begin to cooperate more closely and over time work to improve North Korea's socio-economic crisis.*

In dealing with China over North Korea, the US and EU will still need to pay careful attention to an increasingly powerful China—if relations with Beijing are not to sour over trade issues, human rights, the "war on terrorism," as well as Taiwan and Ballistic Missile Defenses, among other problematic concerns. China is willing to negotiate with the US in regard to North Korea (and does not support a nuclear Korea), yet it is more intractable in regard to the question of Taiwan. Here, one possibility is for the US and EU to press for a confederal approach, involving "two states, but one China."

Iran-Iraq

With the new external policy focus on Iraq since 1998, efforts to forge a rapprochement with a "reformist" Iran, that would reduce Iranian support for acts of terrorism, failed miserably. At first, the US attempted a rapprochement with Iran, which, along with India and Russia, had opposed the Taliban regime and supported the Northern Alliance. Support for the Northern Alliance, however, meant overlooking previous "terrorist" acts of members of that alliance in Kabul; a rapprochement with Teheran's "moderate" factions still meant ignoring the Iranian-backed Hizbollah based in Lebanon, for example.

Initially, US efforts to forge a rapprochement with Iran began to reverse themselves prior to President Bush's January 2002 "axis of evil" State of the Union speech in which Iraq, Iran and then North Korea were all lumped in the same basket as regional, if not potential global, "threats." US military pressure to prevent Iraq from acquiring nuclear weapons had been regarded as a symbolic threat by Iran, North Korea, in addition to other "states of concern," such as Syria or Libya. (The latter, however, has been trying to break out of its isolation.) Although North Korea (purportedly assisted by China and Pakistan) may well have sold advanced dual use and military technologies to both Iran and Iraq, no common foreign policy exists. Certainly Iran and Iraq have not resolved their bitter differences that initially helped spark the horrific 1980–87 Iraq-Iran war, a conflict Teheran claims was started by Saddam Hussein—with American backing. At the same time, each of these states may still seek to use various degrees of strategic leveraging to assert their own interests against the United States.

Alleged assistance to Al-Qaeda leaders by Iran's Revolutionary Guards (actions denied by Teheran), plus arms sales and support to Hizbollah and Al-Fatah, combined with opposition to US policies in Afghanistan, helped worked to place Iran back on the list of terrorist states.[28] In March 2002, the discovery of Iranian-supplied arms shipments to Palestinian Al–Fatah "partisans"[29] seemed staged to disrupt the compromise proposed by the March 2002 Arab summit in Beirut that promised recognition of Israel, if the latter returned to its 1967 borders.[30] It is possible that the "moderate" reformist leadership led by elected President Mohammed Khatami cannot control the hard-liners and revolutionary guards led by the Ayatollah Ali Khamenei, and thus the regime may well speak with two voices, somewhat mediated by former president Ali Rafsanjani.

Washington soon abandoned the policy of "double containment" of Iran and Iraq following US-UK military intervention versus the latter. (See Steven Ekovich, Chapter 15.) The Bush administration hoped that regime change and the future example of a "democratic" Iraq would help bring about real reforms in Iran. In large part due to skepticism about the real prospects for reform, the Iranian regime has faced a significant legitimacy crisis, revealed by significant abstention in voting in the March 2003 elections, and student protest in June. Iranian opponents believe the days of the Islamic Republic are coming to an end; but the regime (based on Islamic theology) may still have more staying power than generally believed. A Tiananmen Square style crackdown and repression (followed by co-optation) cannot ruled out. The question is, however, can the US really give the "democratic" movement appropriate direct or indirect assistance? Threats to use force could backfire, resulting in a hardening of the regime, rather than "democratization."

From a pan-Islamic Shi'ite perspective, in addition to the Israeli "occupation" of Jerusalem and US "occupation" of Saudi Arabia and its backing for the House of Saud, US intervention in Iraq can be interpreted as a US "occupation" of the Shi'ite holy cities of Karbala and an-Najaf. This interpretation may provide the Iranian regime with a new lease on life.

The continued US military presence in Saudi Arabia after the 1990–91 Persian Gulf War provoked Bin Laden; US intervention and "occupation" has divided both Iraqi and Iranian societies between those who see the US as a "liberator" versus those who see it as an "occupier." This fact may bring violent tensions to the streets of Teheran, in addition to outbursts of resistance in Baghdad, which may take some time to snuff out.

On the one hand, the US has continued to pressure Iran to stop its support of acts of terrorism; on the other, it has also opened the door to a potential appeasement of Iranian interests (that could inadvertently permit the self-determination of Shi'ite Marsh Arabs in Iraq). The deployment of US forces in Azerbaijan in 2003 may represent an ominous warning for Iran, as a means to pressure it against developing WMD and supporting terrorism, but it is unclear that such deployments will necessarily help foster "democratization" or ultimately prevent Teheran from accelerating its own nuclear program despite promises to permit international inspections. Here the US will need to more thoroughly coordinate policy with Russia and the EU to dampen Iranian nuclear options. Concurrently, the US, EU and Russia may need to consider Iranian and Syrian calls for a nuclear free zone in the Middle East that would include efforts to place the Israeli nuclear program under international safeguards on the basis of overlapping NATO, EU and Russian security guarantees.

Following the Iraq war, US "occupation" (and the subsequent removal of 450,000–500,000 Ba'ath party members from of positions of authority) has already sparked reprisals by the Ba'ath party loyalists, in addition to lesser resistance from Shi'ite factions.[31] The US immediately appointed an Iraqi Governing Council, but this group has been highly divided and largely unable to countermand US directives; it has also possessed little legitimacy inside or outside the country itself. As the Iraqi Governing Council has been regarded as discriminating against ex-Ba'ath party members (the former elites), radical pan-Islamic groups, as well as communist factions who resisted the rule of Saddam Hussein, a number of these groups have attempted to interfere in domestic power structures in order to make the US "occupation" as difficult and expensive as possible. These groups may seek external support. By November 2003, it was announced that the US was preparing to establish a provisional government by June 2004, but that US-led coalition forces would remain for the foreseeable future.

Regional Interference

Before the 1990–91 Persian Gulf War, the US built a US-led UN coalition against Iraq, which included Arab states but excluded Israel as it was feared that the involvement of the latter would undermine the coalition against Iraq. Unilateral US-UK attacks have risked enflaming Arab/Islamic opinion, particularly in those states not immediately threatened by Saddam Hussein, but also without resolution of the Israeli-Palestinian crisis. Certainly, eliminating pan-Arab regime of Saddam Hussein has not ended the threat of terrorism, and may have strengthened pan-Islamic fanaticism.

The intervention in Iraq divided Arab/Islamic states. The leaderships (but not the populations) of Kuwait, Saudi Arabia and Qatar (and behind the militant anti-American ideology, Iran) were generally supportive of removing Saddam Hussein; the leaderships of Egypt, Pakistan, Jordan and Morocco were much more hesitant and feared a popular domestic backlash. (In general, the Arab elite, however, would have preferably sent Hussein into exile, if he could not be overthrown by *coup d'etat*; Iran, by contrast, has hoped to take advantage of Iraqi state collapse.) The states of the region also hope that the US will withdraw as soon as possible in order to minimize the possibility of popular backlash, but this appears dubious given continued instability in both Iraq and Iran. The question then becomes: What kind of regime will be left to pick up the pieces? And how will the region and the world adjust to a new equilibrium now imposed by force?

Any Iraqi leadership will be scrutinized by both competing domestic pressures and regional interests. Turkey will tend to support the Turkomen versus the Kurds. If US coalition forces ultimately leave Iraq, or no adequate UN or NATO forces replace these troops, for example, it is possible that parts of Iraqi Kurdistan may demand independence, resulting in civil war and struggle over the control of oil in Mosul and Kirkuk. The Kurds may also clash among themselves: Kurdish Democratic Party (KDP), and the Patriotic Union of Kurdistan (PUK) may fight with the Kurdistan Workers Party (PKK), if not with each other. The possibility that Turkey and/or Iran might absorb Kurdish regions inside Iraq cannot be ruled out.

Teheran appears to be cynically supporting US actions now in order to take advantage of a weaker Iraq at a later date. Iran may well have secretly supported Shi'ite movements within Iraq *before* and *during* the war so as to be in better position to control local grassroots political movements *after* the war. The majority Shi'ite population is split between Iraqi secular nationalist and pro-Iranian factions; but even secular Shi'ite groups are not necessarily pro-American. Sunni groups (and minority Christians), generally oppose theocratic tendencies in Shi'ite movements.

Other external powers will also want to influence the nature and policies of the new government. Saudi Arabia, Egypt and Bahrain would prefer a Sunni-oriented government; yet Kuwait may push to put Sunni leaders accused of war crimes on trial, thus further weakening the Sunnis hold on power. Concurrently Iran, Syria and Saudi Arabia will compete for influence over the Sunni minority in the center around Baghdad. The majority Shi'ite populations in the southern region could increasingly come under the sway of radical Shi'ism, or else fission off into a separate state.

A "democratic-federal" government as proposed by the US may prove disquieting for Sunni-led countries in the region. Here, the US has had little to no experience dealing with social engineering in the region, and what may turn out to be an essentially "confessional" or "communitarian" approach to state and society building in Iraq, based on differing religious and ethnic groups, which in turn have had little historical experience with non-dictatorial rule.[32] The problem (not even taking into consideration the *utopian* dimensions of such a vast project of social engineering) raised here is that one cannot, by definition, *impose* "democracy"—which can be best defined as a historical process of developing a "culture of compromise"— by force *from outside* a society.

The Bush administration approach also risks diverting the focus away from the development of Iraq *in itself* and toward goals external to Iraqi society in the efforts to pressure the entire region to "democratize" in accord with neo-conservative or "conservative internationalist" goals. The process of establishing a new government may require long-term counter-insurgency operations and military presence, *particularly since the initial US military intervention was not based upon thorough dialogue and true "compromise" with a significant number of external international and regional actors as well as internal opposition factions.*

Moreover, and perhaps even more problematic, the collapse of the regime of Saddam Hussein may not bring with it "market liberalism," but instead, "black market libertarianism," much has been the case with former Communist states, thus resulting in the ascension of rival underground mafias beneath the "superstructure" of a political-economy highly dependent upon oil production. The fact that Iraq does not possess a well-established middle class may also forestall efforts to achieve "democratic federalism" or "collective" leadership.

Precisely who will control that oil wealth and how will it be distributed, and to what extent any new government will be chosen by Americans or by Iraqis, will likewise open up contention and dissent. Here,

US Congressmen have proposed, for example, an Alaska Permanent Fund style yearly re-distribution of oil dividends, at the same time, the high costs of the war may mean that profits cannot soon be redistributed. Ironically, contrary to the predictions of critics, the US may well support Iraqi membership in OPEC, precisely to keep oil prices as high as possible so as to pay the costs of the war and reconstruction!

The long-term ramifications of the intervention could result in the weakening or further destabilization of a number of pro-Western regimes in the region, such as Jordan (with its large Palestinian population) and Yemen. Syria has feared being next on the neo-conservative hit list, in that it has supported both Hamas and Hizbullah. The situation in Iraq could generally strengthen the hand of pan-Shi'ite Moslem factions against Sunni Moslem leaderships in a number of states, such as Bahrain. It could also strengthen the hands of pan-Islamic factions in Egypt and in Pakistan. It could spark a further radicalization of Saudi Arabia, whereby the House of Saud would have even greater difficulty controlling the rebellion of pan-Islamic elites opposed to extreme division of wealth and political corruption. In particular, Saudi Arabia fears the rise of radical Islamic influence in that its eastern province, which possesses the bulk of Saudi oil reserves, is largely Shi'ite.[33] The disaggregation of Saudi Arabia cannot be ruled out, if the society cannot begin to implement significant reforms.

India-Pakistan

The issue of potential Indian-Pakistani-Chinese conflict over Kashmir, and indirectly Afghanistan, still looms in the background of the "war on terrorism." Pakistan sees Indian repression of Kashmiri's as "state supported terrorism," yet India has tried to convince the US that it should represent the bastion of anti-terrorism in South Asia. New Delhi has argued that the US has become so obsessed with Al-Qaeda that it has ignored terrorist groups supported by the Pakistani regime. Ironically, however, Pakistan has used the events of September 11 to break out of its largely self-imposed international isolation and regain US diplomatic supports.

Just a week into the Iraq war, both India and Pakistan test fired nuclear capable weaponry (while North Korea refused to halt its nuclear program). The threat to use "tactical" nuclear weapons has been very real since the May 1998 nuclear testing by both sides that set back US nuclear nonproliferation efforts. President Clinton then imposed economic and military sanctions as mandated by section 102 of the Arms Export Control Act. A major clash—that marked the worst outbreak of fighting between India and Pakistan since the 1971 Indo-Pakistani war—then occurred in

May 1999 near the town of Kargil along the Line of Control (LOC) in Kashmir. Since conflict in Kargil, tensions over Kashmir have remained high, particularly following the 13 December 2001 terrorist attack on the Indian parliament. In the latter case, India alleged that pan-Islamic militants had been supported by Pakistan. India and Pakistan consequently placed sanctions against each other and mobilized their armies and nuclear forces.

As US pressure mounted to gain Pakistan's support in the war against Iraq, Islamabad argued that US pressures weakened its ability to contain terrorism and arrest Al-Qaeda leaders. Millions of Pakistanis demonstrated against the Iraq war and demanded the end of pro-American military rule and its support for Federal Bureau of Investigation (FBI) efforts to find Al-Qaeda operatives, among other issues. From the governmental perspective, Islamabad is concerned that US military intervention in Iraq will encourage India to act unilaterally in Kashmir. Even after September 11, Pakistani General Pervez Musharraf continued to support pro-Pakistani separatist groups in India-controlled Kashmir. In 2002, in reference to Kashmir, Musharraf argued that "a distinction be maintained between acts of legitimate resistance and freedom struggles, on the one hand, and acts of terrorism on the other."[34]

Just after 11 September 2001, the Bush administration lifted separate sets of sanctions imposed in 1978, 1990 and 1998 on both India and Pakistan related to their testing of nuclear weapons. The lifting of sanctions upon Pakistan did not apply to those imposed after Musharraf's bloodless 1999 coup. Pakistan was thus ineligible for loans from the United States and remained prohibited from sending its soldiers to the US for training. However, the lifting of the other sanctions removed the restrictions placed on military sales to Pakistan and made the country eligible for new economic aid. In March 2003, the US then ended all sanctions imposed upon Pakistan after the 1999 coup; US Secretary of State Colin Powell announced that the US would focus on reconciling India and Pakistan, in addition to Israel and Palestine through the Road Map to Peace.

While sending mixed signals involving the possibilities of "preemption" or "reconciliation," New Delhi argued that the government of General Musharraf has not been strong enough in repressing Kashmiri separatist and other terrorist movements. In March 2003, the Indian Foreign Minister stated that India had a "fitter case" for "pre-emptive" action against Pakistan than did the USA against Iraq due to Pakistan's support for Jihadi groups against India; but in April, the Prime Minister Atal Biharia Vajpayee at least appeared to offer an olive branch of reconciliation in a speech in Kashmir.[35] Much as Richard Haass, director of the US State Department's Policy Planning Staff has pointed out, India will not be able to obtain its fullest potential in world affairs if its conflict with Pakistan draws away finance, resources, and scares away foreign investments. In a tit for tat, Pakistan also claimed it could pre-empt India, but also began to consider the option of reconciliation. It appears dubious that Pakistan can sustain *parity* in an arms race with India (whose military spending is four times that of Pakistan).

Having defeated Iraq, the US could ultimately "lose" nuclear Pakistan to an alliance of radical Islamic factions that make up the Pakistan Muslim League (PML-Q) and the Muttahida Majlis-e-Amal (MMA), after winning the October 10, 2002 elections the Northwest Frontier Province and Baluchistan.[36] These radical Islamic parties (who supported the Taliban and Bin Laden) have gained greater support since September 11 and in opposition to the Iraq war. Pakistani support for the Taliban (prior to 11 September 2001) had been intended to provide Pakistan with "strategic depth" through an Islamic confederation in case of war with India and in support of Kashmiri independence—but instead, it largely led to Pakistan's international isolation. US intervention in Afghanistan (and now Iraq) has consequently re-inforced the convictions of an anti-American *jihadi* backlash, particularly in Pakistan's northern Pathan provinces that are historically related to Afghan tribes. The US/NATO military presence in Afghanistan may, to a certain extent, control Kabul, but it has not addressed the control of the countryside, nor has it dealt thoroughly with the key political, economic and strategic questions. General Musharraf has attempted to co-opt these radical forces, yet failure could result in a break-up of the country, or else a further militarization.

The United States has strongly urged India and Pakistan to respect the Line of Control through a ceasefire and return to the Lahore peace process. Thus far, the US has offered to be a behind the scenes *facilitator* of the peace process, but not help to negotiate. (Nelson Mandella, for example, has been proposed as a possible facilitator.) In February 2001, the Indian government repeated its earlier offer of joint patrols of the border; Pakistan, however, expressed doubts about its feasibility. Pakistani officials feared that this would represent a *de facto* endorsement of the LOC as the international boundary. Pakistan reportedly would prefer to have an international force monitoring the LOC, since such a force would be easier to implement and it would help internationalize the Kashmir issue.

India, however, is unlikely, at least officially, to welcome a multinational force because New Delhi sees itself committed by the 1972 Simla Agreement to bilaterally resolve all disputes with Pakistan. New Delhi is also concerned that a multinational force would put pressure on India to resolve the Kashmir dispute to Pakistan's advantage. New Delhi refused a referendum over Kashmiri independence as it feared that demands for Kashmiri independence might set off other secessionist demands within India. New Delhi also fears that an independent Kashmir could end up as a safe haven for Islamic *jihadi* groups. Ironically, India wants to draw international attention to the situation in Kashmir without "internationalizing" the situation—by bringing in the UN or other multilateral diplomatic efforts.[37]

If the line of control in Kashmir is not to become the new "wall" between rival blocs as argued by Sten Widmalm in Chapter 14 this book, it is clear that India and Pakistan need to take major steps toward reconciliation. It is possible that India might allow US special forces into Indian Kashmir ostensibly to hunt for Al-Qaeda forces but actually to monitor the border; the United States has purportedly agreed to give India sensors to monitor the border. Another option might be to deploy NATO-EU-PfP forces, under a general UN mandate. To accomplish the latter, the US, EU and UN may need to take more active steps to bring the two to the negotiating table and toward reconciliation.

Looking South

As NATO begins to expand its membership further into the eastern Europe, providing strategic lines of communication through Romania and Bulgaria across the Black Sea to Turkey (or now Azerbaijan), and as the EU may ultimately bring in Cyprus (and possibly Turkey) as members, it appears that the new Euro-Atlantic community must also begin to examine more closely the security of its southern periphery in the Euro-Mediterranean and Middle East/Persian Gulf. The fact that NATO has decided to provide peacekeepers in Afghanistan, and could possibly (but dubiously) provide them for Iraq, has meant a significant "out of area" expansion of duties. While both NATO and the EU have traditionally looked east, it is time, with Russian supports, to look south. It will only be by bringing the conflicts between Israel and Palestinians and that between India and Pakistan—that most directly affect the interests of the diverse Islamic world—to a general settlement that it might be possible to stem the cycle of terrorism and state-terrorism.

Immediately following the Iraq war, the US belatedly begun to more seriously press for Middle East peace, and thus has begun to institute the "road map" process as an integral aspect of the long-term strategy of "war on terrorism." Such a strategy was intended to attract "moderate" Arab leaderships and their populations away from the support for pan-Islamic extremists, and to work toward Arab state recognition of Israel; yet, in many ways, however, intervention in Iraq tended to widen, rather restrict, the scope of the "war on terror." The US, the EU and Russia will soon need to take more decisive diplomatic and peacekeeping action in an effort to truly play "honest broker" between both sides so as to prevent the acts of blind terrorism that have been escalating between Israelis and Palestinians and that could result in wider regional instability.

A political settlement could be based on a modified version of the Saudi/Arab peace plan that was proposed at the March 2002 Beirut Summit. The Arab states would formally recognize the state of Israel if the latter would accept a formula based upon a return to something approximating its 1967 borders, in "an exchange of land for peace." The firm promise of multinational force deployments backed by NATO, the European Union and Russia, under a general UN mandate, to protect both sides against indiscriminate acts of "terrorism" could hopefully help both sides to reach a political settlement, and should be conceived as an integral part of the Quartet process and Road Map for Peace.[38]

Such an agreement would also look toward the formation of a viable "democratic" Palestinian state that cooperates peacefully with its neighbor, on what, in actuality, would be on an unspoken *confederal* basis. This proposal is, of course, based upon the assumption that the non-compromising Israeli and Palestinian factions on *both* sides can ultimately be sidelined and that both sides can ultimately recognize the need for mutual cooperation (in regard to trade, water, exchange of labor, policing, joint controls over Jerusalem, among other issues). In addition to compromising over the question of 1967 borders, both sides would also need to accept compromise over the controversial issues of east Jerusalem and the number of Palestinian refugees to return, as discussed in the October 2003 Geneva Accords.

From the perspective of Israeli security, the major Israeli settlements in the West Bank should be merged into about three zones; the lesser settlements should be then dissolved entirely in both the West Bank and Gaza. This would make these areas easier to protect. These three major Israeli settlements in the West Bank, plus Palestinian-controlled territories in the West Bank and Gaza, would then be protected by the deployment of multinational peacekeeping forces backed by United States (NATO), the EU and Russia. Areas of Palestine taken by Israeli settlements would need to be compensated by areas within Israel in order to form a contiguous Palestinian state. These bold steps should ultimately lead toward the formation of a Palestinian state once both Israel and Palestine can recognize each other's legitimate right to co-exist as neighboring states, in a new form of "confederation."

Previous peace plans had proposed that the UN play the key role as peacekeeper; while Palestinians have pleaded for the deployment of international peacekeepers, the Israelis have tended to distrust the UN, seeing it as incapable of protecting it from its Arab neighbors. Israel has additionally been historically reluctant to permit foreign forces upon its territory, or even upon the "occupied" territories (despite the fact that the US protected Israel during the two Gulf wars with Iraq). The US, EU and Russia will accordingly need to convince Israel that it is in its own interests to finally permit the deployment of multinational peacekeeping forces, primarily upon the occupied territories. As Martin Indyk put it: "Without some form of effective international intervention, Israelis and Palestinians will continue to die and their circumstances will continue to deteriorate, fueling vast discontent and anger at the United States in the Muslim world and placing Israel's future well-being in jeopardy."[39]

Rather than using UN blue helmets, however, multinational peacekeeping forces, which have been trained by NATO and the Partnership for Peace, can be deployed under a general UN mandate so as to provide a more rigorous force, with substantial peacekeeping experience in former Yugoslavia, and now in Afghanistan. Both Israelis and Palestinians may find these forces more reliable, as they work to disarm militant Palestinian factions, at the same time protect against Israeli incursions. In this respect, Israelis could claim that NATO is providing security; Palestinians could claim that it is the UN.

Working with the Israeli and Palestinian leaderships, the US, EU and Russia could negotiate the nature, number and nationality of the troops to be deployed in the regions to be protected from acts of revenge. These troops could include American, Russian, European, or other peacekeepers from states such as Moslem Turkey that are acceptable to both Israelis and Palestinians. The United States, European Union and Russia could then provide overlapping security guarantees to both Israel and the new Palestinian state, under the general blessing of the UN. Beyond that, the US, EU and Russia can help guarantee Israel's security, as well as that of the new Palestine, vis-à-vis Iran, Syria, Egypt, or from terrorist groups, at the same time that they attempt to resolve other critical regional disputes. A determined and concerted US-EU-Russian diplomatic effort can also serve to deflect the pan-Islamic propaganda waged against Arab regimes throughout the Middle East and Persian Gulf who have been accused of acting in complicity with the United States and Israel.

The dilemma is that intervention in Iraq has only deflected the issue, not resolved it, as Israeli-Arab-Iranian tensions have, in some ways, become more fractious after the defeat of Saddam Hussein's regime. The daily acts of Palestinian vengeance were certainly not manipulated by Iraq alone—acts of retaliation and counter-retaliation appear to be escalating rather than receding. Whether Israeli PM Ariel Sharon (or another Israeli leader) possesses the far reaching vision of the conservative leader of South Africa, F.W. De Klerk[40]—and thus make peace with the Palestinians and with its neighbors, perhaps on the basis of the October 2003 Geneva Accords —remains to be seen. Much as De Klerk opted to make peace with Nelson Mandella and the ANC, as well as with other states in the region, putting an end to both South Africa's nuclear program and Apartheid, a similar Israeli leadership could likewise make amends with the Palestinians and possibly place its nuclear program under international safeguards, with Israeli security backed by NATO, EU and Russian security guarantees.

Here, it seems that NATO-EU-Russian security guarantees and peacekeepers can help prevent those driving on the Road Map to Peace from getting totally lost.

Policy Conclusions

If the United States, the European Union and Russia are to ultimately "succeed" in this war against a nomadic, amorphous if not virtual, "terrorist" threat that provides no clear and decisive "victory," they can only do so if the US resurrects NATO's broader and original mission that it possessed immediately after World War II. In this regard, NATO was created as a *conflict prevention* organization designed to prevent major power conflict in Europe (broadly speaking) by bringing together former enemies, and potentially conflicting states, into one broad alliance. Such a prospect, however, still requires significant reforms in today's circumstances. (See Hall Gardner, Chapter 8, this book.)

By developing a large coalition of states, the US, the EU and Russia together can then begin to lay the foundations for a wider peace in the Euro-Atlantic Euro-Mediterranean community and the world at large. The concept of "regional cooperative security communities" with separate commands backed by overlapping NATO, EU and Russian security guarantees represents a commonsense *on the ground deterrent* against all possible forms of threats. This proposal is designed to create cooperative forms of regional security and confederations with the backing of the states and populations involved. Its political-military purpose is to negotiate between actual and potentially conflicting factions so that all sides can live side by side without fear, and thus fostering political-economic development against the destabilizing forces of "globalization."

For the "war on terrorism" to be "successful," the US needs to move much faster on the political-military front, following the war in Iraq, in the creation of a broad and sustainable coalition of the major powers, in addition to winning the support of states in each region of conflict. Although multinational peacekeeping in general has thus far been downplayed by the Bush administration and the Pentagon, this concept requires strengthening. It also requires close cooperation with EU and Russian peacekeepers, and as many states as possible. This is particularly true as the number of regions requiring multinational peace keeping may continue to expand, from ex-Yugoslavia, to Afghanistan, Iraq, and to Palestine and perhaps the Kashmir Line of Control.

The clash over policy toward Iraq raised additional issues for the transatlantic relationship. Due to US efforts to impress its reluctant allies into service, those allies may not be as willing to cooperate with the US in a number of areas. While the United States had been correct to threaten the *credible* use of force, the Bush administration left no face saving way to back off once it had committed close to 200,000 troops in the region. Franco-German proposals for more muscular weapons inspections fell upon deaf ears, as did direct appeals by Iraqi officials in a last ditch effort to avert war. Saddam Hussein purportedly proposed that 2000 American weapons inspectors could participate, including scientists and the FBI, as part of a failed back channel effort to avert war. The proposal included oil concessions to the US, cooperation in fighting terrorism, and "full support for any US plan" in the Arab-Israeli peace process, as well free elections in two years. The fact that the proposal did not envision the exile of Hussein may, at least ostensibly, have been one factor that doomed the offer.[41]

The US could thus have attempted to engage in more muscular weapons inspections, along with a more vigilant containment policy coupled with "smart sanctions." Or, only if all options failed, *then military intervention could possibly have taken place with the greater support of the European and Arab states*. If all options had truly been attempted, then France would have more been willing to use force under a UN mandate (at least more so than Germany). As it stands presently, however, the failure to bring in the UN at the outset has made it more difficult to share the burden of reconstructing the country and engage in peacekeeping (and counter-insurgency). Having "demonized" the regime of Saddam Hussein, US policy boxed itself in a corner, where compromise with that regime and its leadership simply was not possible: War became a self-fulfilling prophecy.

The Israeli-Palestinian question has furthermore raised profound questions as to whether there will ultimately be a *quid pro quo*, in accord with theories of "sequencing," i.e., the elimination of Saddam Hussein in exchange for a general regional settlement. Here it seems highly ironic that the US was willing to put its credibility at stake by intervening in Iraq through the use of massive force (with all its potential moral, financial and political costs and responsibilities) and has not been able persuade its democratic Israeli ally to halt its illegal settlements and seek peace with its neighbors. The apparent inability to persuade democratic Israel to change its behavior raises profound questions as to how much and what kind of "democracy" that the US can affect in Iraq and in the region as a whole.

It proved difficult for Kuwait to open itself to greater "democratic" processes after the first Gulf War. A number of Arab states have begun to "open;" yet one can hardly transform single party leaderships or traditional monarchical societies into "democracies" or even "constitutional monarchies" overnight. These states must realize the need for reforms on their own volition. At the same time, there is no guarantee that the turn to democracy will necessarily bring with it pro-US policy; there is also no guarantee that efforts to achieve greater openness and transparency to the political and economic decision-making process will not bring with it greater instability or demagoguery.

Future Alliance Formations?

Given the clash of perspectives in regard to which groups or states pose the greatest common threats, NATO, the EU and Russia may find it increasingly difficult to proceed in a concerted fashion. This problem has been augmented by the fact that each of these "powers" has conflicting political and economic interests in supporting one group or state versus another, as well as conflicting principles and values. This situation has been exacerbated by the fact that a number of states have been attempting to use the "war on terrorism" to pursue their own agenda and interests against their political enemies—rather than seeking political compromise involving either power-sharing, the formation of confederal arrangements, or else permitting political autonomy or independence. The Bush administration's unilateral approach consequently opens up the doors for other states to either engage in unilateral intervention—or else form countervailing alliances with *parvenu* states themselves.

The Iraq question has substantially weakened the effectiveness of the UN, as well as NATO, and has raised questions about the EU's ability to forge a CEFSP. France, Germany and Russia, in particular, do not want to give US-UK intervention a *post-facto* legitimacy, at the same time, they may want to participate in the post-war reconstruction contracts, if the situation stabilizes. The US, however, would have preferred that the UN legitimize its actions; at the same time it has attempted to engage in the reconstruction of Iraq largely on its own resources and the promise of future Iraqi oil proceeds. Tensions over reconstruction of Iraq (combined with burgeoning trade disputes, protectionism and deficit spending on the part of both the US and EU) add additional cleavages to the US-EU-Russian relationship that makes security cooperation even more difficult.

The unexpected consequences of selective US actions and "unilateralism" could lead states to consider the formation of new alliances. Such alliances may not only include those directed against the US, but also those formed against the rise of other perceived threats. A Russian-Indian-Chinese alliance is not altogether unfeasible (despite mutual suspicions between the parties). Russia could seek to strengthen its Eurasian ties with Belarus, China (in support of the latter's claims to Taiwan) and to India (in support of the latter's claims against Pakistan). The possible nuclearization of North Korea could in turn militarize Japan, most likely pushing Russia and China closer together. In the not-so-long term, if the US and new Europe cannot develop a more complementary policy, and if the US does back off from supporting European security, or only selectively support European security interests, France and Germany may seek to counterbalance the US. Too assertive an American approach has already begun to press the UK into the Franco-German camp—in that the traditional US-UK "special relationship" appears to be breaking down.

Here, the Europeans may increasingly look to Russia in the effort to forge a "multipolar" world. Another possibility is that of a French-German-Chinese entente that is designed to counter-balance an instable and possibly threatening Russia as the US, EU, Japan and Russia all compete for China's allegiance (as opposed to working toward "multilateral" cooperation). This could come about if the EU fails to forge a new form of "membership" with Russia, coupled with the perception that the United States might not come to the assistance of Europe. Such a Sino-European formation (much like the Franco-Russian alliance against Imperial Germany and Austria-Hungary before WWI) could raise Russian fears of "encirclement" and result in its further militarization. Another scenario envisions the break-up of an isolated Russia—with Japan and China struggling for control and influence over the remnants.

In order to prevent the isolation and alienation of any of the major powers, and to prevent any of the major powers from fully aligning with any militant *parvenu* state, it will prove necessary to begin to thoroughly address as many of the primary regional conflicts as possible through interlocking multilateral approaches to security and dissuasion. It seems here that only a fundamental reassessment of American foreign policy itself will be able to heal the rift between the US and its Allies. Will US policy seek to stabilize its relations with its allies, and engage in truly multilateral policies, albeit led diplomatically by the US as "first among equals"? Will Washington consider the formation of a *Transatlantic Political-Economic and Strategic Council*, perhaps made up of advisors from the US, UK, France, Germany (or an EU Foreign Policy representative), as well as Russia, as a means to more closely coordinate transatlantic policy? Could it engage in a number of "Contact Groups," similar to that formed to help end the war in Bosnia, in order to help resolve regional conflicts, and make the UN, EU, US and Russian "Quartet" grouping even more effective?

Or will the US move toward a new phase of imperial overseas expansion following its intervention in Iraq, in the attempt to resolve conflicts unilaterally, after the UN Security Council officially dubbed the US and UK as "occupying" countries in July 2003? The upsurge in domestic Iraqi and international pan-Islamic insurgence (combined with domestic US opposition to a long term "occupation") has begun to pressure the US to withdraw, and turn the "occupation" over to either the UN, or to permit the Iraqi's to run the country themselves. Bush administration recalcitrance to deal with the UN, combined with violent attacks on the UN administration in Iraq, will, however, make it even more difficult to phase in the UN. At the same time, the effort to put controls in hands of a provisional Iraqi government may prove a very difficult task in that it will require a leadership with perceived *legitimacy* (that can ultimately be established through the formation of a new Constitution), and that is capable of making effective decisions that transcend ethnic and religious divisions. Any new Iraqi government will also need highly qualified national security forces not only capable of dealing with the domestic insurgency, but also capable of defending against potential threats from neighboring countries, where borders remain largely unsealed.[42] The option of a NATO-EU-Russian force, under a general UN mandate, that would provide greater domestic Iraqi support and international legitimacy for a new Iraqi government, may provide one option.

US intervention in Iraq has been compared with American actions after World War II, but analogies to the US occupation of Germany and Japan after World War II are not particularly accurate, in part as no "Marshall Plan" is available for reconstruction.[43] A better analogy may well be that of the British empire in the late 19th and early 20th century. Yet are the Americans really ready to play *Pax Britannica* following Britain's second war in Afghanistan in the 1870s-80s and its occupation of Egypt and the Suez in 1882, perhaps most comparable to US intervention in Afghanistan and its subsequent occupation of Iraq? Britain promised to leave Egypt twenty-two times between 1882 and 1922. Will the US likewise remain mired in the region?[44] In this sense, through its *preclusive* military intervention in Iraq, the US has leapt into a quagmire, and may be sinking deeper into quicksand.

Following World War I, and the break up of the Ottoman empire, Britain then established its mandate over Iraq in 1919, and was confronted with major uprisings until the establishment of Sunni authority under Emir Faysal in 1921. (One wonders whether Tony Blair had discussed with George Bush the nature of British colonial history in Iraq, and how Britain dealt with Iraqi insurrection in 1920, before the decision to intervene in Iraq was taken?) How long will it take for the US to form a viable "democratic-federal" government in Iraq? Or will it prove to be "confessional" or "theocratic" regime? Or will Iraq remain a form of protectorate?

Will *Pax Americana* essentially suffer the same fate as *Pax Britannica*, despite the fact that US military capabilities, even comparably speaking, far exceed those of Great Britain, which was at the peak of its imperial geopolitical and economic power and influence in the late 19th century, as numerous military powers increasingly challenged the latter in the early 19th and 20th centuries? Or will the American empire disintegrate more slowly, perhaps drawn and quartered by wars of attrition, as it is challenged more and more by the new threats of chaos, black market libertarianism, and raw terror, in addition to WMD? Will the terror of the Middle East, Persian Gulf and Central Asia, and Africa essentially replace that of the pre-World War I and pre-World War II Balkans (in regard to acts of pre-World War I pan-Serbian and then pre-World War II Croatian terrorism, not to overlook the late 19th century actions of the Anarchist international in assassinating world leaders)? Or will the US find itself totally overextended as it seeks to combat a mix of asymmetrical threats, combined with WMD of new countervailing alliances of powers, in effect creating a largely self-fulfilling prophecy of an "infinite" number of "circumstances that endanger the safety of the nation"—to paraphrase Alexander Hamilton, as cited in the Introduction to this book.

Notes

1 See "Declaration of War against the Americans Occupying the land of the Two Holy Place" and interviews with Bin Laden in Yonah Alexander and Michael S. Swetnam *Usama bin Laden's Al Qaida: Profile of a Terrorist Network* (Ardsley, NY: Transnational Publishers, 2001.

2 According to PEW opinion polls, Bin Laden (dead or alive) has strong popular following within the Palestinian Authority, Jordan, Morocco, Pakistan and Indonesia. See *Views of a Changing World 2003: War With Iraq Further Divides Global Publics*

The PEW Research Center for the People and the Press (June 3, 2003). http://people-press.org/reports/display.php3?ReportID=185.
3   See, for example, Baker Institute Working Papers "Guiding Principles for US Post-Conflict Policy in Iraq" December 2002 http://www.rice.edu/projects/baker. While the US had planned the war for a number of years; the peace was planned only 4 or 5 weeks prior to the intervention in an *ad hoc* manner, according to the first administrator General Jay Garner, who was replaced by State Department official Michael Bremer. "Humanitarian Assistance Following Military Operations in Iraq" Hearing of the National Security, Emerging Threats and International Relations Subcommittee of the House Government Reform Committee, Federal News Service. May 13, 2003.
4   On US intervention and problems of "nation-building," see Minxin Pei, "Lessons of the Past" *Foreign Policy,* July/August 2003. Paul Wolfowitz noted that efforts to democratize Haiti was an "expensive failure" and that Vietnam should have taught against the idea that the US military could bring democracy to a country. See Paul Wolfowitz, "Statesmanship in the New Century" in *Present Dangers,* ed by Robert Kagan and William Kristol (San Francisco: Encounter Books: 2000), 314.
5   Robert D. Kaplan, "A Post-Saddam Scenario," *The Atlantic Online* http://www.theatlantic.com/issues/2002/11/kaplan.htm.
6   See Robert Baer, *See No Evil* (New York: Crown Publishers, 2002).
7   US air attacks were timed, incidentally, to prevent strikes from hitting Chinese workers who have been helping to install underground fiber optics cables so as to improve Iraq's air defenses. (Having struck the Chinese embassy in Belgrade during the war "over" Kosovo, Washington did not want to make the same mistake in Baghdad.)
8   Between 1985 and 1990, Saudi Arabia purportedly paid up to five billion dollars for Saddam Hussein to build a nuclear weapon on condition that some of the bombs be transferred to the Saudi arsenal. A senior White House official, asked about the Saudi government's involvement and American complicity, stated: "They did spend billions on the Iraqis. It was a different world. We were ready to overlook a lot of things the Saudis were doing for the Iraqis. It's consistent with all the other terrible things we did at the time"—to shore up Saddam. Leslie and Andrew Cockburn, "Royal Mess," *The New Yorker,* November 28, 1994.
9   US Vice-President Richard Cheney, who, I had been told by an oil company lobbyist in December 2001, had initially slowed steps to war; had by August 2002, however, shifted sides: "I am familiar with the arguments against taking action in the case of Saddam Hussein. Some concede that Saddam is evil, power hungry and a menace, but that until he crosses the threshold of actually possessing nuclear weapons we should rule out any preemptive action. That logic seems to me to be deeply flawed. The argument comes down to this: Yes, Saddam is as dangerous as we say he is, we just need to let him get stronger before we do anything about it. Yet if we did wait until that moment, Saddam would simply be emboldened and it would become even harder for us to gather friends and allies to oppose him. As one of those who worked to assemble the Gulf War coalition, I can tell you that our job then would have been infinitely more difficult in the face of a nuclear-armed Saddam Hussein. And many of those who now argue that we should act only if he gets a nuclear weapon would then turn around and say that, "We cannot because he has a nuclear weapon. At bottom, that argument counsels a course of inaction that itself could have devastating consequences for many countries, including our own... Regime change in Iraq would bring about a number of benefits to the region. When the gravest of threats are eliminated, the freedom-loving peoples of the region will have a chance to promote the values that can bring lasting peace." Washingtonpost.com. August 26, 2002. http://www.rider.edu/phanc/courses/350-web/mideast/iraq/cheney/020826speech.htm.

In 1991 Cheney, as Secretary of Defense, had made the following statement: "I think that the proposition of going to Baghdad is ... fallacious. I think if we were going to remove Saddam Hussein we would have had to go all the way to Baghdad, we would have to commit a lot of force ... I think we'd have had to hunt him down. And once we'd done that and we'd gotten rid of Saddam Hussein and his government, then we'd have had to put another government in its place. What kind of government? Should it be a Sunni government or Shi'i government or a Kurdish government or Ba'athist regime? Or maybe we want to bring in some of the Islamic fundamentalists? How long would we have had to stay in Baghdad to keep that government in place? What would happen to the government once US forces withdrew? How many casualties should the United States accept in that effort to try to create clarity and stability in a situation that is inherently unstable? I think it is vitally important for a President to know when to use military force. I think it is also very important for him to know when not to commit US military force. And it's my view that the President got it right both times, that it would have been a mistake for us to get bogged down in the quagmire inside Iraq." "The Gulf War: A First Assessment" *Soref Symposium* April 29, 1991. http://www.washingtoninstitute.org/pubs/soref/cheney.htm.

10 Tony Blair: "It is important to demonstrate... that our approach to people in the Middle East ... is indeed evenhanded," Azores Summit, March 17, 2003.

11 It was estimated that Reconstruction costs could range from $25-30 billion to $100-105 billion per year. Iraqi foreign debt was estimated to be between $62 to $130 billion; Kuwaiti reparation claims, plus other unsettled business claims after 1991, may be as much as $172 billion. The total financial burden, including foreign debt, compensation claims and pending contracts of $57.2bn was estimated at about $383bn. It was furthermore dubious that Iraqi oil production *by itself* will support reconstruction: Current annual Iraqi oil revenues were at $10 billion, with existing production rates dropping at 100,000 bpd annually; it could take 3-5 years and up to $6bn in investments to get Iraqi oil up to its 1990 production rates. At the same time, much of the oil revenue is already being used for humanitarian purposes under the oil-for-food program. Costs of peacekeeping (plus counter-insurgency, the effort to search for Weapons of Mass Destruction and to find and secure conventional arms and explosives as well) could reach between $84bn to $100bn for over five years, assuming at least 75,000 troops at $1.4bn a month—which indicates such costs will need to be spread out among as many countries as possible. See Baker Institute Working Papers "Guiding Principles for US Post-Conflict Policy in Iraq" December 2002 http://www.rice.edu/projects/baker. See also Frederick D. Barton and Bathsheba Crocker, "Winning the Peace in Iraq" *The Washington Quarterly*, Spring 2003.
On October 25, 2003, the Madrid Conference on Iraq pledged some $9 billion in loans (adding to the $380 billion in bad debt and war reparations claims) and $4 billion in grants, which could be added to the $18 billion in grants that Congress approved for Iraq's reconstruction and security needs. The combined total of this estimated $31 billion still falls substantially short of the $55 billion that the World Bank and the United States assessed as Iraq's needs in the next four years. Whether the funds really materialize will depend to a large extent upon the nature of security situation in the country in the coming months (at the price of $66 billion for the US taxpayer), and which may entail long term counter-insurgence and peacekeeping, Pentagon denials to the contrary, and whether an Iraqi government with *perceived domestic and international legitimacy* can ultimately begin to function as soon as possible. See critical comments by Senator Robert C. Byrd "A High Price for a Hollow Victory," http://www.tompaine.com/feature2.cfm/ID/9301.

12 John Mearsheimer and Stephen Walt, "An Unnecessary War," *Foreign Policy* January-February 2003.
13 On 16 September 2002 Iraq agreed to allow the unconditional return of U.N. weapons inspectors. The White House dismissed the offer as "a tactical step by Iraq" and argued that "This is not a matter of inspections. It is about disarmament of Iraq's weapons of mass destruction and the Iraqi regime's compliance with all other Security Council resolutions." The United States demanded a "new, effective U.N. Security Council resolution that will actually deal with the threat Saddam Hussein poses to the Iraqi people, to the region and to the world." Associated Press, September 16, 2002.
14 James Risen, "Iraq offered US a Deal as the War Loomed" *International Herald Tribune*, November 7, 2003, 1. See also, ISN Information Services: www.isn.ethz.ch/infoservice/secwatch.
15 US Assistant secretary of Defense, Paul Wolfowitz cited in http://www.amacad.org/publications/monographs/War_with_Iraq.pdf.
16 Marwan Bishara, *Peace or Apartheid* (New York: Zed Books, 2002).
17 In regard to the latter point, Fouad Ajami has argued that "George H. Bush had resisted "linkage" between the Persian Gulf and the Israeli-Palestinian conflict, but he was to make it the cornerstone of US strategy after the guns had fallen silent." His son, George W. Bush, likewise resisted linkage between the Persian Gulf and the Israeli-Palestinian conflict almost immediately upon assuming office. See Fouad Ajami, "Iraq and the Arabs' Future," *Foreign Affairs*, January/February 2003.
18 See Muriel Asseburg, in "From Declaration to Implementation? The three Dimensions of European Policy towards the Conflict" in Martin Ortega, ed. *The European Union and the Crisis in the Middle East* Institute for Security Studies No. 62, July 2003.
19 Marwan Bishara "After Arafat, wishful thinking" *International Herald Tribune*, 17 March 2003; The October 2003 "The Geneva Accord" Haaretz.com http://www.haaretz.com/ hasen/ pages/ ShArt. Jhtml? Item No=351461.
20 Michael R. Gordon, "NATO: The Inside Story" *New York Times* 25 February 2003.
21 *Financial Times* March 24, 2003.
22 Henry Kissinger, "The End of NATO as We Know it?" MSNBC News February 10, 2003. http://www.msnbc.com/news/871141.asp.
23 In the case of Kosovo, the United States undercut EU brokered negotiations and did not obtain a clear UNSC mandate for its intervention; proposals for a NATO-Russian interpositionary peacekeeping force between Serbs and Kosovar Albanians were discarded. Yet the war was settled diplomatically in such a way as to give NATO a *post facto* legitimacy for its unilateral actions. See Hall Gardner, "The Genesis of NATO Enlargement and of War "over" Kosovo" in *Central and Southeastern Europe in Transition*, ed. Hall Gardner (Westport, CT: Praeger, 2000). In the case of Afghanistan, the US argued its attack was defensive, following September 11.
24 See Hall Gardner, "NATO and the UN: The Contemporary Relevance of the 1949 North Atlantic Treaty" in *A History of NATO*, ed, Gustav Schmidt (New York: Palgrave, 2001).
25 Taras Kuzio, AL-QAEDA Regroups. State Misuse of the Anti-Terrorism Campaign RFE/RL Volume 3, Number 5, 13 February 2003.
26 See Agence France Press, "Russia continues to push for peaceful solution to Iraq" September 13, 2002; Reuters, "China to take Active role on Iraq 13" September, 2002.
27 David Shambaugh "China and the Korean Peninsula: Playing for the Long Term" The Washington Quarterly 2003 Spring Vol. 26, no. 2, p. 43.
28 Most analysts pointed to an Al-Qaida-Iranian connection prior to September 11. See Robert Baer, *See No Evil* (New York: Crown Publishers 2002). It was only following

September 11 did the Bush administration try to establish an Iraqi connection with Al-Qaida. Following the Iraq war, it appears that Al-Qaida has, in fact, entered Iraq.
29 Douglas Frantz and James Risen, "A Secret Iran-Arafat Connection Is Seen Fueling the Mideast Fire" *New York Times*, Mar 23, 2002.
30 The March 2002 Arab Plan proposed: We reaffirm that peace in the Middle East cannot succeed unless it is just and comprehensive ... and based on the land for peace principle. Expectations from Israel: A. Complete withdrawal from the occupied Arab territories, including the Syrian Golan Heights, to the 4 June 1967 line and the territories still occupied in southern Lebanon. B. Attain a just solution to the problem of Palestinian refugees to be agreed upon in accordance with the UN General Assembly Resolution No 194. C. Accept the establishment of an independent and sovereign Palestinian state on the Palestinian territories occupied since 4 June 1967 in the West Bank and Gaza Strip with East Jerusalem as its capital. In return the Arab states will do the following: Consider the Arab-Israeli conflict over, sign a peace agreement with Israel, and achieve peace for all states in the region; Establish normal relations with Israel within the framework of this comprehensive peace ..." The Council also welcomed "the assurances by the Republic of Iraq that it will respect the independence, sovereignty, and security of the state of Kuwait and safeguard its territorial integrity."
31 See for example, Peyman Pejman "Iraq: Officials Say US Was Wrong To Dissolve Army, Intelligence Apparatus" Radio Free Europe/Radio Liberty, November 13, 2003. http://www.rferl.org/nca/features/ 2003/11/ 1311 2003 184246.asp.
32 For a critique of the democratic-federal thesis, see Marina Ottoway and Judith Yaphe, "Political Reconstruction in Iraq: A Reality Check" Carnegie Endowment, March 27, 2003, http://www.ceip.org/.
33 Robert Dreyfuss, "Tinker, Banker, neo-Con, Spy; Ahmed Chalabi's long and winding road from (and to?) Baghdad," *The American Prospect* November 18, 2002.
34 Taras Kuzio, AL-QAEDA Regroups, op. cit.
35 *Washington Post*, April 19, 3003.
36 See Centre for South Asian Studies, *Pakistan: General Elections 2002* (29, Rue de Neuchatel, Geneva).
37 Jean-Luc Racine, *Cachemire. Au péril de la guerre*, (Paris: Collection Ceri-Autrement, Editions Autrement, Octobre 2002).
38 I proposed a NATO-PfP peacekeeping mission to Palestine (under a UN mandate) at the 2–7 October 2001 Atlantic Council conference in Bled, Slovenia. Annex X of the Geneva Accords, thus far unpublished, proposes some form of multinational peacekeeping.
39 Martin Indyk, "A Trusteeship for Palestine?" *Foreign Affairs* May-June 2003.
40 Marwan Bishara, *Palestine/Israel: Peace or Apartheid* (London: Zed Books, 2001).
41 James Risen, "Iraq offered US a Deal as the War Loomed" *International Herald Tribune*, November 7, 2003, 1.
42 "We will have the US forces here, but they will change from occupiers to a force that is here at the invitation of the Iraqi government." Ahmed Chalabi, *International Herald Tribune*, November 15-16, 2003, 1. At least one member of the Iraqi governing council is engaging in George Orwell's "newspeak"!
43 See Kaplan, op.cit. The analogy to Germany and Japan is considered a false one by Paul Wolfowitz, "Statesmanship in the New Century" in *Present Dangers*, ed. Robert Kagan and William Kristol (San Francisco: Encounter Books: 2000), 314.
44 I first drew the analogy to British occupation of the Suez in a panel discussion "Crisis in the Gulf" with Ghassan Saleme and Richard Scott held at the American University of Paris on, ironically enough, on 11 September 1990. *See Scripta Politica*, American University of Paris Vol. VII, No. IV March 1991.

Index

ABM (Anti-Ballistic Missile) treaty
    (1967) 157, 158
Afghanistan
    asymmetrical conflicts 36-7
    EU 5
    Northern Alliance 3, 238
    opium 267-8
    Taliban 234, 237
    war 2, 3, 150, 172, 201, 237
Al-Qaeda 1, 11, 12, 58, 109, 167, 265
    deterrence 201-2
    network 266
    objectives 59, 278-9
    training camps 52
    war against 2, 3
    see also September 11 (2001) events
American Civil War 14, 15
American Revolution in Military Affairs
    see RMA
anthrax 1-2
Anti-Ballistic Missile treaty see ABM
Arab-Israeli conflict (1973) 55
arms reduction
    Russia 158
    treaties 157
    US 158
assured security, US 51, 61-2, 72
asymmetrical conflicts 31-2
    Afghanistan 36-7
    geo-economics 42-3
    and globalization 33-4, 36, 40-1
    meaning 39
    success 35-6
    US 34, 37-8
    weapons 40
"axis of evil" states 37
Azerbaijan, US forces 298

Ballistic Missile Defense see BMD
Baltic States
    NATO membership 100, 119, 152,
        157
    and Russia 156-7, 158, 165-6
Beirut Summit (2002) 305

Berlin Wall, fall 189
bin Laden, Osama 1, 3, 237
    Declaration of War 16
    network 266
    threat 59
    see also Al-Qaeda
Biological Weapons Convention 157
    Iran 263
Blair, Tony 285
BMD (Ballistic Missile Defense) 61, 72,
    73, 74
Bosnia, NATO 5
Bush administration 2
Bush, George W., President 79

carbon dioxide emissions 254
casualties, terrorism 265-6
CEE (Central and East European)
    countries 115, 116, 117
    NATO 152-3
CEFSP (Common European Foreign and
    Security Policy) 5, 8, 151
Central Asia
    economic development 239
    Islamic fundamentalism 233, 234
    post-Cold War 223-4, 225-7
    Russia 156, 232-3, 239-40
    security concerns 233-6
    scales of analysis 219-20
    September 11 (2001) events 223, 228
    stability, and Uzbekistan 228-9
    US 236, 237-8
    see also SCO
Central and East European Countries see
    CEE
CFE (Conventional Force in Europe)
    treaty (1999) 157, 158
CFSDP (Common Foreign Security and
    Defence Policy) 118
Chechnya conflict 117, 234, 294
chemical and biological weapons, Iran
    262-3
China
    economic growth 254

India, relations 244-6
Iraq war 295, 296
Russia 10, 159
   arms from 222
   strategic weapons 222
   terrorism, war on 294
CIS (Commonwealth of Independent States) 161
civilian populations, and war 15, 16
CJTF (Combined Joint Task Force) 164
Cold War 125-6
   deterrence 57, 62
   NATO 4, 91, 93
   US, strategy 50-1
   see also post-Cold War
Combined Joint Task Force *see* CJTF
Common European Foreign and Security Policy *see* CEFSP
Common Foreign Security and Defence Policy *see* CFSDP
Commonwealth of Independent States *see* CIS
Comprehensive Test Ban Treaty *see* CTBT
Conventional Force in Europe treaty *see* CFE
Creveld, Martin van
   on the Intifadah 46-7
   Transformation of War 35
CTBT (Comprehensive Test Ban Treaty) (1966) 157
Cuban Missile crisis (1962) 55
cultural conflicts 43-7

democratization, Iraq 210
deterrence
   Al-Qaeda 201-2
   Albert Wohlstetter on 57, 62
   Cold War 57
   criticism of 70-1
   extended 71
   immediate 54-5
   and MAD 50, 62
   meaning 49
   post-Cold War 57-9
   purpose 49
   rationality 63, 65-6, 68
   theory 62-4
   uncertainty 63, 64-6
   US 52
   WMD 49, 52, 53
   see also dissuasion
diplomacy, and terrorism 21-3
dissuasion 52
   concept 55-6
   see also deterrence; multilateral dissuasion
double standards, WMD 17-18, 60, 71, 264
drug addicts, Iran 267
drug smuggling, and terrorism 45, 160, 268
drug trade 43
dual containment strategy, Gulf 255-7, 268-70, 297

Eagleburger, Lawrence 117
Eastern Turkestan Islamic Movement *see* ETIM
ESDA (European Security and Defence Agency) 111
ESDI (European Security and Defence Identity) 204
ESDP (European Security and Defence Policy) 204, 211
ESDU (European Security and Defense Union) 177
ETIM (Eastern Turkestan Islamic Movement) 294
EU (European Union)
   Afghanistan 5
   enlargement 81, 153
      Russian view 115, 118
   Macedonia, peacekeeping 22, 161
   Rapid Reaction Force 9, 155
   regime change 208-9
   Russia, co-operation 116
   US
      attitude gap 212
      capabilities gap 211-12
      cultural differences 204-5
      relations 81-3, 175-80, 198-213
      religious differences 205-7, 213
European Security and Defence Agency *see* ESDA
European Security and Defence Identity *see* ESDI
European Security and Defence Policy *see* ESDP
European Security and Defense Union *see* ESDU

force, threat of 20
France, Iraq war 284
Friedman, Thomas L. 44, 82
Fukuyama, Francis 204-5
  The End of History... 42

Geneva Accords 290, 307
geo-economics, asymmetrical conflicts 42-3
Germany
  Berlin Wall, fall 189
  Iraq 190-1
  Iraq war 172-5, 182
  isolationism 183-4
  Kosovo 182, 183, 184, 189-90
  military operations 182-3
  multilateralism 189
  peace movement 188
  peacekeeping operations 175
  September 11 (2001) events 181-2
  terrorism 185-7
    war on 182-94, 283
  US, relations 190-4
  US forces in 155, 159-60
globalization
  and asymmetrical conflicts 33-4, 36, 40-1
  consequences 32-3
  and identity 33
  and terror 16-17, 307
  and the US 31
Gulf, The
  dual containment strategy 255-7, 268-70, 297
  Iran 254-5
  Iraq 256
  oil supplies 253-4
  strategic importance 252-3
  terrorism 265-7
Gulf War (1991) 8, 15, 34, 208, 252, 255, 285, 298, 299
  Israel 45
  see also Iraq war (2003)

Hamilton, Alexander 312
  The Federalist No. 23 2
hegemony, US 6, 11-13, 37-8, 58, 108, 171, 200, 202-3, 311-12
HIV/AIDS, Iran 267
Homeland Security Act 2
Huntington, Samuel 82

The Clash of Civilizations 44
Hussein, Saddam 2, 7, 173, 213, 255, 256, 268

ICC (International Criminal Court) 153-4, 175, 178
identity, and globalization 33
IGC (Intergovernmental Conference) 81, 82
IMU (Islamic Movement of Uzbekistan) 220, 228
India
  China, relations 244-6
  defence spending 243
  economic development 246
  nuclear weapons 243, 245, 301, 302
  Pakistan, conflicts 242-4, 246-50, 279, 301-4
  Prithvi missile 243
  Russia 159
  US
    entente 247
    trade 246
INF (Intermediate Range Nuclear Forces) treaty (1987) 157
informal economies 43
intelligence
  and power 112-13
  and September 11 (2001) events 109
Intergovernmental Conference *see* IGC
Intermediate Range Nuclear Forces treaty *see* INF
International Criminal Court *see* ICC
International Energy Agency, *World Energy Outlook* 254
interoperability, NATO/US 113-14
Intifadah 287
  Martin van Creveld on 46-7
Iran
  armed forces 257-9
  Biological Weapons Convention 263
  chemical & biological weapons 262-3
  drug addicts 267
  economic development 271-2
  GDP 270
  and the Gulf 254-5
  HIV/AIDS 267
  missiles 258-9
  and NPT 261
  nuclear weapons 261-2, 263, 264-5
  political change 272-4

revolution 254
terrorism, support for 256, 266-7, 297, 298
US
  military options 259-61
  relations 255, 270, 272-4, 296-7
  WMD 256-7, 298
Iraq
  democratization 210
  GDP 270-1
  Germany 190-1
  and the Gulf 256
  Kuwait, invasion 255
  preclusive intervention 280-6, 312
  rebuilding 151, 280-1, 298, 299-301
  regime change 19, 200, 208, 256, 281-2, 299
  US-UK bombing 282-3
  weapons inspections 7, 8, 286
  WMD 58, 63, 159, 263, 280, 285
Iraq war (2003) xiii, 3-4, 34, 121, 150-1
  China 295, 296
  EU/US differences 8, 92, 154, 172-5, 283-6, 291-6, 308
  France 284
  Germany 172-5, 182
  legitimacy 6-7
  Turkey 290-3
  UK 285
IRGC (Iran Revolutionary Guard Corps) 257
Islamic fundamentalism, Central Asia 233, 234
Islamic Movement of Uzbekistan *see* IMU
Israel
  Gulf War (1991) 45
  nuclear weapons 263-4
  terrorism, war on 286-7
  and US 45
Israel-Palestine
  conflict 46, 209, 279, 284, 287-9, 306-7, 308-9
  Road Map for Peace 8, 281, 289-90, 304, 305-6

Joxe, Alain 33

Kagan, Robert 204
Kashmir conflict 242-3, 244, 248, 301, 302, 303-4

Kazakhstan, US, entente 220
Keegan, John, *A History of Warfare* 35
Kosovo
  Germany 182, 183, 184, 189-90
  NATO 5, 21
  US 23, 110
Kurdistan, Iraqi
  organizations 299
  Turkey 163, 290
Kuwait, Iraq, invasion 255
Kyoto Protocol (1997) 157, 175

Lake, Anthony 42

Macedonia, conflict
  EU, peacekeeping 22, 161
  NATO 22
  US 161
MAD (Mutual Assured Destruction), and deterrence 50, 62
MAP (Membership Action Plan)
  NATO enlargement 95, 96
  Russia 122-43
Massoud, Ahmed Shah, General 3, 65
Membership Action Plan *see* MAP
Morgenthau, Hans, *Politics Among Nations* 64
multilateral dissuasion 60-1, 68-74
  and terrorism 70, 73-4
  WMD 69
multilateralism, Germany 189
Mutual Assured Destruction *see* MAD

NAM (Non-Aligned Movement) 244
nation, state, difference 33
National Ballistic Missile Defense *see* NBD
National Missile Defenses *see* NMD
NATO
  Article V 3, 80, 92, 120, 152, 160, 162, 178-9
  Baltic States 100, 119, 152, 157
  Bosnia 5
  CEE countries 152-3
  changing role 9, 119
  Cold War 4, 91, 93
  enlargement 84-6, 91-2, 93, 94-105, 116-21, 149, 152-3
    implications 161-8
    MAP 95, 96
    EU, Russia, coalition 164-6

as Intelligence Service Provider 112-13
Kosovo 5, 21
Macedonian conflict 22
multilateral security 110
"out of area" operations 4, 92-3, 95, 149-50, 304
Partnership for Peace 95, 117, 226
Response Force 9, 113, 155
Russia 10, 74, 84, 116-21, 160, 162
  Council 129-30, 131, 150, 151-2, 161, 178
  MAP 122-43
September 11 (2001) events 86-9, 104
Strategic Concept 88
terrorism, war on 152
Turkey, Iraq war 291-3
UN, relations 292-3
US, interoperability 113-14
NATO Response Force *see* NRF
NBD (National Ballistic Missile Defense), US 53
neo-conservatism, and terrorism 66-8
New Transatlantic Agenda *see* NTA
NMD (National Missile Defenses) 72
Non-Aligned Movement *see* NAM
North Korea, nuclear weapons 56, 295-6
Northern Alliance
  Afghanistan 238
  Russia 238
NPT (Nuclear Non-Proliferation Treaty) (1967) 60, 157
  Iran 261
NRF (NATO Response Force) 9, 113, 155
NTA (New Transatlantic Agenda) 180
Nuclear Non-Proliferation Treaty *see* NPT
nuclear weapons
  abandonment 56
  India 243, 245, 301, 302
  Iran 261-2, 263, 264-5
  Israel 263-4
  North Korea 56, 295-6
  Pakistan 243, 245-6, 263, 301, 302
  spread 13-14
  UN Security Council 59-60
  see also arms reduction
Nye, Joseph 82

opium, Afghanistan 267-8
organizations, terrorism 266
Osama bin Laden *see* bin Laden, Osama
Oslo Accords 287
Outer Space Treaty (1967) 157

PA (Palestinian Authority) 288-9
Pakistan
  defence spending 243
  Ghauri missile 243
  India, conflicts 242-4, 246-50, 279, 301-4
  nuclear weapons 243, 245-6, 263, 301, 302
  US, relations 237
Palestinian Authority *see* PA
Panama, US 41
Partnership for Peace, NATO 95, 117, 226
Pax Americana 311-12
PCC (Prague Capabilities Commitment) 113
Persian Gulf *see* Gulf, The
Petersberg tasks 9, 111, 155
post-Cold War 126-8
  Central Asia 223-4, 225-7
  deterrence 57-9
power, and intelligence 112-13
Prague Capabilities Commitment *see* PCC
pre-emption
  US 36, 52-3, 53-4, 202
  and WMD 15
preclusion, US 53-4
preclusive intervention, Iraq 280-6, 312
Putin, Vladimir, strategic thinking 124, 125

Rapid Reaction Force *see* EU, Rapid Reaction Force
rationality, deterrence 63, 65-6, 68
regime change
  EU policy 208-9
  Iraq 19, 200, 208, 256, 281-2, 299
  US policy 207-8
Rifkin, Jeremy, *The Age of Access* 112
RMA (American Revolution in Military Affairs) 34, 35, 38, 45, 51

Road Map for Peace, Israel-Palestine 8, 281, 289-90, 304, 305-6
Rome Treaty (1957) 79
Russia
  arms reduction 158
  Baltic States 156-7, 158, 165-6
  Central Asia 156, 232-3
    security 233-6
  China 10, 159
    arms sales 222
  EU
    co-operation 116
    enlargement 115, 118
  India 159
  NATO 10, 74, 84, 116-21, 160, 162
    MAP 122-43
  NATO-Russia Council 129-30, 131, 150, 151-2, 161, 178
  Northern Alliance 238
  security concerns 156-7
  September 11 (2001) events 120
  US, entente 11
  Uzbekistan entente 220-1

Saddam Hussein *see* Hussein, Saddam
Saudi Arabia
  GDP 270-1
  US
    presence 297-9
    relations 236-7
Schelling, Thomas, *Arms and Influence* 63
SCO (Shanghai Cooperation Organization) 221, 222, 223, 238
  formation 235-6, 293
September 11 (2001) events x, xii, 1, 3, 125
  and Central Asia 223, 228
  consequences 9-11, 18, 41, 58, 109, 171, 177, 200, 201, 224, 265
  Germany 181-2
  and intelligence 109
  NATO 86-9, 104
  purpose 49-50
  Russia 120, 123
  security measures 2
  see also Al-Qaeda
Sevres, Treaty of (1920) 290
Shanghai Cooperation Organization *see* SCO
Shi'ite Islam 236

Simla Agreement (1972) 303
Sino-Indian war (1962) 55, 245
Somalia, US 41
Spanish Civil War 14
Star Wars, US 50-1
state, nation, difference 33
Suez Crisis (1956) 209

Taba Accords 287
Tajikistan 234
Taliban 58, 125, 149
  Afghanistan 234, 237
  US support 238
  war against 2, 3
Tenet, George 39
terror xi-xii
  and globalization 16-17, 307
terrorism
  casualties 265-6
  containment 269
  and diplomacy 21-3
  and drug smuggling 45, 160, 268
  EU/US differences 5, 80-1
  events 149
  Germany 185-7
  Gulf 265-7
  Iran 256, 266-7, 297, 298
  meaning x-xi, 25 n.1, 185-6
  and multilateral dissuasion 70, 73-4
  and neo-conservatism 66-8
  objectives 187, 265
  organizations 266
  and Shanghai-5 221
  war on 166-7, 168
    China 294
    Germany, perceptions 182-94, 283
    Israel 286-7
    meaning xii, 18-19
    NATO 152
    and political reforms 17
    risks 209-10
    US 171-2, 200-1, 283, 308-9
    Uzbekistan 293-4
  see also September 11 (2001) events
Theatre Missile Defense *see* TMD
Tibet conflict 245
TMD (Theatre Missile Defense) 72, 73
Toffler, Alvin, *War and Anti-War* 35
Turkey
  Iraq war 290-3
  Iraqi Kurdistan 163, 290

Index

NATO, Iraq war 291-3

UK
  Iraq war 285
  Tower of Excellence program 111
Ukraine, multilateral security assurances 61
UN
  NATO, relations 292-3
  NATO/US perceptions 6
UN Security Council
  nuclear weapons 59-60
  resolutions
    No. 1144 183
    No. 1368 2, 3
    No. 1441 3, 8, 154, 173, 208
  and WMD 17-18
unilateralism, US 200, 269
urban warfare, success 36
US
  alliances, need for 23-4
  arms reduction 158
  assured security 51, 61-2, 72
  asymmetrical conflicts 34, 37-8
  "axis of evil" states 37
  Central Asia 236, 237-8
  Cold War, strategy 50-1
  defense spending 155, 211
  deterrence 52
  economic growth 254
  EU
    attitude gap 212
    capabilities gap 211-12
    cultural differences 204-5
    relations 81-3, 175-80
      dimensions 198-213
    religious differences 205-7, 213
  forces
    Azerbaijan 298
    Germany 155, 159-60
  Germany, relations 190-4
  and globalization 31
  Gulf, strategy 255-7
  hegemony 6, 11-13, 37-8, 58, 108, 171, 200, 202-3, 311-12
  Homeland Defense 51
  India
    entente 247
    trade 246
  Iran
    military options 259-61

  relations 255, 270, 272-4, 296-7
  and Israel 45
  Kazakhstan, entente 220
  Kosovo 23, 110
  Macedonian conflict 161
  NATO, interoperability 113-14
  NBD 53
  oil imports 253
  Pakistan, relations 237
  Panama 41
  Pax Americana 311-12
  pre-emption 36, 52-3, 202
  preclusion 53-4
  regime change, policy 207-8
  rogue states 41
  Russia, entente 11
  Saudi Arabia
    presence 297-8
    relations 236-7
  Somalia 41
  Star Wars 50-1
  Taliban, support for 238
  terrorism, war on 171-2, 200-1, 308-9
  threats to 23, 39-40
  unilateralism 200, 269
  Uzbekistan entente 220
USA Patriot Act 2
USSR
  dissolution 117, 126
  see also Russia
Uzbekistan
  and Central Asian stability 228-9
  Russia, entente 220-1
  terrorism, war on 293-4
  US, entente 220

Vilnius Ten group 152, 154, 162

war
  and civilian populations 15, 16
  Clausewitzian model 34-5
  cultural conflicts 43-7
  just war theory 54
  strategic thinkers 35
  see also asymmetrical conflicts; urban warfare
Washington Treaty (1949) 79
weapons inspections, Iraq 7, 8, 286
Weapons of Mass Destruction *see* WMD
WMD (Weapons of Mass Destruction) xi
  containment 269

deterrence 49, 52, 53
double standards 17-18, 60, 71, 264
Iran 256-7, 298
Iraq 58, 63, 159, 263, 280, 285
multilateral dissuasion 69
and pre-emption 15
states developing 5, 7, 12, 279
and UN Security Council 17-18
see also nuclear weapons
Wohlstetter, Albert
  on deterrence 57, 62
  The Delicate Balance of Terror 62
WTO (World Trade Organization) 161, 294